From La Strada to T

Vivian Pramataroff-Hamburger
Andreas Hamburger
Editors

From La Strada to The Hours

Suffering and Sovereign Women in the Movies

Editors
Vivian Pramataroff-Hamburger
Psychotherpeutic Practice
Munich, Germany

Andreas Hamburger
International Psychoanalytic University Berlin
Berlin, Germany

ISBN 978-3-662-68788-8 ISBN 978-3-662-68789-5 (eBook)
https://doi.org/10.1007/978-3-662-68789-5

Translation from the German language edition: "Von La Strada bis The Hours - Leidende und souveräne Frauen im Spielfilm" by Vivian Pramataroff-Hamburger and Andreas Hamburger, © Der/die Herausgeber bzw. der/die Autor(en), exklusiv lizenziert durch Springer-Verlag GmbH, DE, ein Teil von Springer Nature 2021. Published by Springer Berlin Heidelberg. All Rights Reserved.

This Springer imprint is published by the registered company Springer-Verlag GmbH, DE, part of Springer Nature.
The registered company address is: Heidelberger Platz 3, 14197 Berlin, Germany

Contents

Part I

"We Are All of Us Stars, and We Deserve to Twinkle." Self-presentations as Objects of Desire

Sunset Boulevard: Diva as Demon

1

Matthias Baumgart

Introduction

Today, a demon is considered to be an evil spirit which possesses someone. For Socrates, however, a demon was a warning inner voice. In *Sunset Boulevard,* as will be shown in this chapter, both aspects come together in the character of Norma Desmond and in the gaze on her. The unconscious fantasies associated with this constellation explain the allure this film has, even to this day.

Film Plot

Sunset Boulevard, at dawn: A dead man is lying in a pool, the police arrive. From off-screen, a voice narrates how it happened—it is the voice of the dead man, Joe Gillis (William Holden). The entire subsequent film plot is a flashback: Gillis, a broke screenwriter, struggles in vain to find new work. At a film producer's house, a young assistant, Betty Schaefer (Nancy Olson), criticises his latest draft of a screenplay. Debt collectors want to dispossess him of his car. With a flat tyre, he takes refuge in the garage of Norma Desmond's (Gloria Swanson) huge mansion. The ageing diva and her servant Max von Mayerling (Erich von Stroheim) live there in complete seclusion and mistake him for an undertaker: Norma's chimpanzee has died. When Joe reveals that he is a writer, Norma decides to hire him on the spot: she wants him to rewrite her draft screenplay on the Salome theme. He agrees, hoping to make a quick buck. But instead of paying him,

M. Baumgart (✉)
Grünwald, Germany

V. Pramataroff-Hamburger, A. Hamburger (eds.), *From La Strada to The Hours*,
https://doi.org/10.1007/978-3-662-68789-5_1

Norma entangles him in her dull life of luxury, the exclusive purpose of which is to revel in the past and yearn for new stardom, punctuated only by visits from other silent film stars. On New Year's Eve, Norma tries to seduce Joe. He rejects her and flees to a party thrown by his friend Artie (Jack Webb), where he tries to hide. There, he meets Betty, who is Artie's fiancée. She suggests that he write a screenplay with her. A playful flirtation develops between them. He quickly decides to have his things picked up from Norma's villa, but when he calls there, he learns that she has tried to slit her wrists. He rushes to Norma's house. Remorsefully, he enters into a relationship with her, albeit reluctantly. After a call from Paramount Pictures, Norma believes that Cecil B. DeMille wants to make her screenplay into a film. She goes to the Paramount studios in person. There she is recognised and feted, but Max learns that the studio only called Norma because they were interested in her car, an imposing old Isotta-Fraschini,[1] which they wanted to rent as a prop. Max keeps this a secret from Norma, telling only Joe. Cecil B. DeMille (in a cameo role) also considerately withholds the truth from her. Norma, in the mistaken belief that filming is about to start, undergoes cosmetic ordeals and manipulations to restore her former good looks. Joe, however, has met Betty Schaefer on the studio lot, who again—at first in vain—invites him to collaborate on his script together. He does eventually begin working with her—always sneaking out of the house at night. Max warns him not to upset Norma's fragile mental state. He reveals that he is her former director and ex-husband and devotes his life entirely to keeping her on an even keel. Finally, Norma discovers Joe and Betty's half-finished manuscript. At that moment, Betty confesses her love to Joe. Joe now wants to break up with Norma, but she in turn has called Betty and denounced Joe as a gigolo. On arriving home, Joe wrests the phone from her and asks Betty to come. He immediately explains the truth to her but says there is no hope of a relationship in view of the whole situation. He advises her to return to Artie. He also wants to leave Norma and confronts her with her illusions. Whereupon she shoots him. Joe falls into the swimming pool, and thus the circle to the beginning is closed. Norma is taken away by the police, but in her delirium she thinks the press hype is a crowd scene for a new film shoot. Max, holding the camera, supports her delusion. The film ends with the legendary words:

> All right, Mr. De Mille, I'm ready for my close-up.

Background

"A relationship between a silent-day queen and a young man"—according to Billy Wilder this was the basic idea he and co-writer Charles Brackett had 5 years before the actual shooting began (Staggs 2002, ch. 3). A real star was to play the leading role

[1] This is not a fanciful name, the company really existed and even the specific vehicle used in the movie survived. It is now in a museum in Turin (Cremoni 2015).

because only such a star could credibly embody the ageing Norma Desmond for the audience. Billy Wilder was immediately fascinated by the virtuoso old-school silent film acting of Gloria Swanson, who was finally chosen: "You can't learn that, you have to have grown up with it" he enthused to Volker Schlöndorff in the famous television documentary *Billy, how did you do it?* (Schlöndorff and Grischoff 1988). Swanson was ideal for the role, embodying like no other the luxury of the 1920s that was almost unimaginable, at least in the early 1950s (cf. Basinger 2000): married five times, with an annual salary of up to $1 million. The films often took place in a luxurious ambience, which the stars also publicly displayed in the exhibitionism of their *everyday lives*. It was not so much the talkies as the collapse of the former economic prosperity in 1929 that made the glamorous stars seem outmoded. At the time of release, only 20 years had passed since this era, which nevertheless also seemed infinitely distant: after the economic crisis, the New Deal and the World War, and immediately before dawning new crises, the *roaring twenties* must have seemed like a distant golden age to contemporaries. Swanson was not reclusive and forgotten in real life as Norma Desmond was, but actively present—albeit to a lesser extent—in television shows and series. She was also quite enterprising: she had already left Paramount at the height of her fame to produce her own films and market them through United Artists (ibid.). This, however, also led to her greatest defeat, namely her film *Queen Kelly*, directed by the endlessly detail-obsessed Erich von Stroheim, which was never finished. He mutates into Max in *Sunset Boulevard*, we see fragments of the real film ruin and in Norma Desmond's nostalgic private screenings. Other silent film stars appear in small supporting roles, as speechless and lifeless guests (Buster Keaton, Anna Q. Nilsson, H.B. Warner). The film is thus not only a monument to a waning figure, but also to a bygone era.

The first choice for the role of Joe Gillis was Montgomery Clift, who backed out at short notice on the grounds that he doubted his ability to play an erotic relationship with a much older woman. According to Wilder, he feared the role would ruin his Hollywood career. William Holden, on the other hand, was immediately enthusiastic and eager to take on the role. It is unclear what he was able to read from it, because the script was constantly changed, among other things to mislead the controllers of the infamous *Production Code*, who threatened to water down the script on moral grounds. The censors were concerned that the affair between a young man and an older woman might not receive enough moral counterweight: Staggs (2002) considers Joe Gillis' attempt to send Betty Schaefer back to Artie, whom she very clearly no longer loves, as a concession to the *Production Code*.

The film did not cause a scandal, it was immediately successful. But his criticism of the *Hollywood dream factory* resonated at least with the studio bosses: Louis Mayer of MGM berated Wilder savagely: "You've dragged the industry that made and fed you into the mud. You will never work in this town again". Wilder's response was a terse "Fuck you!" (Karasek 1994, p. 358). In any case, the film had a great emotional impact on contemporaries—and it still has today.

How Is the Feminine Staged in this Film?

Psychological Character Analysis: Narcissism vs. Successful Adaptation

We see two diametrically opposed women in the film. At the centre is Norma Desmond, who dominantly, even domina-like, pursues only one goal: her return to the screen and her rehabilitation as a star. Norma does not want a *comeback*—she hates that word—but rather a "re-turn" (00:19:14), a *turning back* of time, a homecoming to the era of her great successes, to her youth. The film imagery shows this very clearly: movie star portraits and other devotional objects are scattered all over Norma's huge house, idealised images which she wants to resemble again. Because only by being identical with such images does she feel alive, important, and valuable.

All the relationships we see the character Norma enter into serve the purpose of supporting or re-establishing her identity with this ideal image. To this end, she hires writer Joe Gillis to make her muddled screenplay filmable. The goal of creating a glamorous self-image also fuels her "love" for Gillis, the beginning of which she stages in the style of the fashionable twenties: as a New Year's Eve party all alone for the film-analogous lovers Joe and Norma, who wallow in luxury (00:43:29). Norma is extremely slow to react to Joe's discomfort, becoming emotionally derailed only when he rudely rejects her, at which point she slaps him. Her subsequent—ultimately manipulative—suicide attempt then forces a relationship, in a manner of speaking.

The end of the film is a heightening of this constellation: Joe leaves her, confronting her with her ageing process and misplaced hopes. Norma fends off these realities, becoming increasingly delusional:

> Nobody leaves a star *(01:42:19)*

– indeed: Joe is shot before he can do so. Shortly afterwards, she says:

> Stars are ageless—aren't they? *(01:43:20)*

Thus, when the illusion comes up against reality, in analysing the psychology of Norma's character we could say that she collapses and retreats into illusion: the delusional perception of a film set subjectively covers up her arrest. We can thus summarise: Norma is portrayed as a character who is narcissistic in the sense that, like the mythical figure, she can only feel she is herself in her reflection, as a star, and can ultimately only love this reflection. From the perspective of clinical psychoanalysis this is not implausible, except that no such patient exists. From this perspective, the question also remains unanswered as to why such an unsympathetic character and her portrayal, which could then *only be* repulsive and not *also* attractive, should still be so fascinating to this day. We shall return to this point later on.

First, however, to the counter-figure: Betty Schaefer is portrayed as a pointedly down to earth and pragmatic person, critical but also appreciative, both of Joe Gillis and of herself. She does criticise one of the drafts of his screenplay as "flat and trite" (00:6:52) when they first meet, but at the same time emphasises that she is only disappointed because she knows how talented he is from earlier writing samples. In a key scene, she also tells Joe that she, for her part, had to give up the illusion of a career as an actress because neither her looks nor her acting had reached the required level of perfection. She rates this as a good experience: "It taught me a little sense" (01:22:46). Betty Schaefer is thus introduced as a psychologically healthy person in the conventional sense: she has left immature ideals behind her and turned towards reality. Yet, on a present-day viewing, she seems clichéd and the attraction she exerts on Joe at times unintentionally comical, as for example in the following excerpt (01:23:11ff.):

Joe *May I say you smell really special?*
Betty *It must be my new shampoo.*
Joe *That's no shampoo. It's more like a pile of freshly laundered handkerchiefs, like a brand-new automobile. How old are you anyway?*
Betty *Twenty-two.*

This triggers laughter in modern cinema audiences, but the string music that accompanies the dialogue shows that Billy Wilder was quite serious about it. However, the health- and relationship model which this character impersonates is clearly outdated, and viewers no longer go along with it. The film nevertheless seems to lead us to such interpretive patterns: narcissism vs. maturity. But why? Further thought needs to be given to this. Clearly, psychological character analysis can only be the starting point of our considerations because the characters are products and not persons.

Staging of the Feminine in Relation to the Soft Male: Regressive Fear and Desire vs. Progression

We can only get further, then, if we, in the sense of Hamburger (2018, p. 65), "understand how and why the film wants to turn us into psychologists in such a way". That is, if we analyse its mechanisms of action and at the same time ourselves as viewers, who more or less respond to them at the same time. We are, after all, examining the staging of femininity in a work of art from 1950 that portrays notions of what a woman of that time should—and should not—be, and how men should or should not deal with this. In this sense, *Sunset Boulevard* confronts us with a variant of the "male gaze" in classic Hollywood film (Mulvey 1975).

What is special about it is that the entire story is indeed told from a male perspective, but from the point of view of a dead man, who addresses the audience through a narrator's voice, who wants to tell them "the facts, the whole truth" (00:02:10). In a Hollywood film, however, there are really only two reasons for the demise of the male lead: an heroic death, or else he has done something that is punishable by death according to the rules of cinema at that time. I think the latter is true in the case of Joe Gillis. After all, the whole film is a confession. In harmony with the camera, Joe makes it clear that he really was not the active hero of the classic American narrative cinema described by Mulvey (1975)—whose "trophy" could then be an attractive woman assigned to him through a happy ending. On the contrary, his "crime" was passivity and softness and surrender to a dominating woman. *The feminine is thus staged throughout the film in relation to a soft man. The feminine exists in the film only in relation to this man.*

So, if we want to ascribe a "male gaze" to the film, it cannot be found *in the* anti-hero Joe Gillis and his world view. Instead, the camera constellates a view *on him* and his relationships with women, and the narrative voice also positions him as a counterpart to whom we are listening. Joe Gillis also presents himself to the *female* viewer as such a counterpart; however since the technique of voiceover was often used in distinctly "male-oriented films" at the time, such as Tourneur's *Out of the Past* or also Wilder's *Double Indemnity,* I actually think that these elements are mainly tailored to male viewers.

The softness of Joe Gillis is illustrated right from the beginning of the film, when we viewers watch him at work in broad daylight wearing a fluffy bathrobe (00:03:19). We see him in the studios, first begging for work, eventually begging for support. We hear him say off-camera (00:08:47) that he was waiting for the *gravy train* at the time—an idiom for high-yield, low-effort work. Fleeing the debt collectors, he then contemplates a return to provincial roots, with a self-pitying expression on his face (00:10:40). We look with the sober camera gaze *at* someone who outed himself as a *loser*. We are not identified with him. Immediately afterwards, Joe arrives at Norma Desmond's garage with a flat tyre. All this suggests in terse sketches that when someone fails in this way, a dependent relationship with a woman ensues, and in this sense the film portrays regressive, primarily male, anxieties. We viewers accept the extreme portrayal of the relationship to this day. This is striking in view of the—on sober reflection—astonishing absurdity of the plot and its imagery.

I think this is because Norma Desmond's relationship with Joe, in which she alone exists cinematically, is charged with numerous aspects of an *omnipotent, preverbal, in large parts bad mother figure,* which are familiar to us as *inner* images.[2] Therefore, despite the lack of (external) realism, we still accept her as (internally) realistic enough. Strictly speaking, even everything that seems absurd at first glance makes sense if we consider it to be part of the cinematic staging of a *bad mother world.*

The only apparent incongruencies begin with the ambience: the interior of Norma Desmond's villa is sumptuous and well-kept, but the exteriors are totally neglected, precisely because the *outside world* becomes *completely meaningless in the face of maternal*

[2]The genesis and persistence of such images is a broad field (Cf. e.g. Fonagy and Target 2003). Within psychoanalytic discourse, it has also been suggested that the theoretical interest in them ultimately serves to support patriarchal structures (Rohde-Dachser 1991).

omnipotence. Norma Desmond presents herself as fabulously wealthy at several points, which the film never questions, although given her exclusive preoccupation with her appearance, it remains unclear how this wealth is organised. The *maternal power* is thus almost *magically* enacted. It requires no explanation.

When Norma hints at her wealth, Joe demands a wage of $500 a week (00:23:23), which is accepted—but he does not pay off his car, the next instalment of which would require only $290. A realistic scenario would be to demand an advance, pay off his debts, then work at Norma's villa during the day (she doesn't want to let the script leave the house). He doesn't do any of these things. Instead, all of his belongings end up in Norma's villa the next morning without his intervention. We also learn that his room was set up that afternoon, before any invitation to stay. Thus, *fairy-tale elements* creep into the narrative.

We later see Joe's car being towed away by debt collectors while Norma is sitting at the gambling table and does not give Joe the money he needs. As we have learned immediately before, she has never paid him except for his share of the game stakes, which are 1/20th of a cent per point played. He endures the humiliation. Instead, Norma's Isotta-Fraschini is restored—*so all the power remains with the mother figure*.

This is also the case in relation to Max, the only man in the house, who is a factotum in the service of "Madame" and has given up his career as a director in favour of this job. As Norma's ex-husband, ex-director, and servant, he is, so to speak, *emasculated* in every respect. The fact that Max nevertheless pulls the strings in many respects and also controls Norma does not diminish this absurdity, for all his activities are directed solely at supporting Norma's grandiosity, that is at maintaining an illusory world to which he is apparently as bound as Norma herself. *The character Max, the man of the house, exists only as an extension of the illusions of the all-powerful mother figure.*

In this *maternal world*, figures become lifeless: first, the chimpanzee which, according to Gillis voiceover, is buried like an "only child" (00:26:33). Gillis seems to be following in his footsteps. Later, there are the visiting ageing silent film stars who barely move, don't speak, and whom Joe calls "the waxworks" (00:33:34). Max von Mayerling is also mimically frozen, and Joe Gillis also loses himself: he does not pursue the "plot of my own" (00:22.10), namely, making money, and the resistance towards Norma's tendency to prevent changes to her amateurish script disappears: "You don't yell at a sleepwalker" (00:30:29). This utterance makes sense only if it is seen as an expression of *a fusion aimed at supporting the illusory maternal omnipotence*.

One can *explain* such aspects of a plot as one likes with ideas about the psychology of the characters: Gillis is just neurotic, *mother-fixated*, as is Max.[3] But if we follow the line of thought introduced before and take into account that the film exerts an effect *on us,* it makes more sense to locate the illusionary in the viewers, in us, in our unconscious fantasy world. A film like *Sunset Boulevard* creates conditions that allow this world to surface—in

[3] Stroheim indeed wanted to clarify this by having Max wash Norma's panties in fetishistic devotion. Wilder refused in order to avoid trouble with the censorship authorities (Karasek 1994, p. 359).

the form of tacit consent to a film plot that is far removed from reality and intuitively set up precisely to introduce an illusionary element.

Thus, what I want to show is that Billy Wilder succeeded in constructing a cinematic world that touches us because it creates an archaic constellation of relationships in expressively sketched characters that inwardly still come close to us. In this sense, the film is a great product of the Hollywood *illusion factory*. To create this illusion, Wilder uses the cinematic and—through Gloria Swanson—acting techniques of the silent film era.

Large parts of the film are shot in dark or dimly lit interiors that are confusing from the viewer's perspective. As a glaring contrast and often with harsh side lighting, Gloria Swanson's overdriven mimic displays emerge out of and fade into this twilight, very often showing extremely negative affects such as *rage and hatred in their purest form*. Through the camera, we the viewers are thus exposed to an at least slightly surreal situation that cannot be clearly assessed because Swanson often allows Norma to very suddenly escalate affectively. At such times, she is not acting like a usual Hollywood actress of the 1950s, but in the completely exaggerated manner of silent film. If we analyse the psychology of these aspects of the character, this is entirely implausible; the result is not a virtual person, but a caricature, which is immediately recognisable from a distance. But Norma is not supposed to be a person *like one in real life*. According to my hypothesis, Swanson's portrayal of affective extremes is so virtuosic that creates a surprising, slightly assault-like affective situation in the dark of the cinema to this day, which allows us to temporarily, but concretely experience Norma Desmond in the way a child perceives its mother when it or she or both are terribly angry, which is by no means uncommon.

When enacted in this way, the female figure therefore becomes witch-like (Fig. 1.1): We see Gloria Swanson widening her eyes as if to hypnotise Joe like the snake Kaa from The Jungle Book, her jaws often thrust forward as if to eat him or suck the life out of him. Her hands are talon-like tense claws, like those of a praying mantis. We can thus well

Fig. 1.1 Norma Desmond (Gloria Swanson) as a witch (00:45:30)

understand Joe when he says, "I felt caught, like a cigarette in the prongs of that contraption on her finger" (00:43:59).

The position Joe takes on this *mother figure* is immediately *childlike*: When he first enters her world, he is immediately rebuked by Norma's extension Max (00:14:08) and must first wipe his shoes, and he is *reprimanded* for his inappropriate dress (00:14:23, "You're not properly dressed for the occasion"). Later, his remaining resistance towards Norma also has childlike connotations, such as when he is sitting in the backseat of Norma's swanky car chewing gum, which he then reluctantly throws away (00:36:46 ff.). He buys his clothes with Norma; she decides and pays (00:36:55)—and he has to endure the disparaging looks and remarks of the salesman (00:37:30 ff.: "As long as the lady is paying for it—why not take the vicuna"). He nevertheless takes this expensive, *cosy* coat—and is again shown to be soft and lazy.

Here, the salesman directs the (male) viewer into a vicarious shame effect: what a humiliation! Again, we recognise how the *male gaze* is distanced from the main character and the powerful-feminine is always presented in relation to the ultimately despised weak-masculine. Archaic relationship foils create the film's partly ideological-normative *message*, which is developed with intuitive help of regressive fear fantasies: Don't get involved with a seemingly providing dominant woman, or you'll end up in the position of a small, unseparated, dependent boy, sucked dry by an egocentric mother figure and despised by other men.[4]

Betty, who also appears only in relation to the male main character, is the *counter-offer*: a clearly younger woman who emphasises that she needs the man because she alone is "not good enough" for screenwriting (1:13:25): When they are working together on their joint screenplay, he dictates, she types. He only goes to the typewriter when she is fetching coffee (1:19:16). Immediately after this, the aforementioned scene develops in which Betty explains to him how life has taught her common sense. From today's perspective, as previously noted, this seems old-fashioned and comical, but there is no doubt that the sections of the screenplay in which Betty appears are more *realistic* according to the social standards of the 1950s. Her relationship offering is more *progressive*: she tries to show the way to an active life.

She is also photographed differently: often in medium contrasts and steady spotlighting. Her affect is mostly moderately cheerful or only slightly ironic-mischievous. Only once do we see her really angry, when in the showdown Joe tells her about his gigolo life (01:36:19 ff.):

Joe *(…)A very simple set-up: An older woman who is well-to-do. A younger man who is not doing too well… Can you figure it out yourself?*

Betty *No.*

Joe *All right. I'll give you a few more clues.*

---

[4] Separation from the mother is more important for boys because they have to work out their gender identity, which is not that of the mother (cf. Mertens 1997), and this makes such images work quickly. However, this constellation is culturally charged and intensified, as evidenced by the film.

Betty *No, no! I haven't heard any of this. I never got those telephone calls. I've never been in this house ...Get your things together. Let's get out of here!*

But Joe does not go along with her, he continues to play the cynical gigolo to manoeuvre Betty back into the relationship with Artie—and towards his own demise. What is crucial here is the gaze on Betty: unlike the basic idea formulated by Mulvey (1975), where the woman is only a passive trophy serving to confirm active male potency, here a 1950s female figure fills an active normative position: she does not want to hear anything about the regressive, passive aspects of the man: they have to be made to disappear somehow.

Mulvey (1975, 1981) would probably see Norma's dominance as a masculine trait and, by contrast, Betty as a latently passive figure who is only seemingly active while demanding male decisiveness. But might it not make more sense to assume that in precisely this way the film illuminates a problematic situation in the gender relations of its time, in which men's regressive tendencies and wishes were associated with catastrophic fears and contempt? Of times in which, therefore, images of femininity had to be split up by men and women and could only appear in movies exactly thus? The film very clearly does not portray "integration". On the verbal, explicit level, which is represented by Betty, the denial of regressive tendencies is normatively demanded. None of this, she says, should be either heard or seen—after we as viewers have already done exactly that for a good 1½ h with a pleasant shiver. So, the film here is clearly in contradiction with itself, which makes it all the more attractive.

Of course, the film does not follow the defensive verdict represented by the character of Betty, otherwise it would not exist. And of course, it shows not only the repulsive sides of regression, but also the *longing for* it, and the *pleasure it creates*. For example, we see Joe rushing headlong from the New Year's Eve party back to the villa when he hears about Norma's suicide attempt. There he stammers: (00:54:35): "You've been good to me. You're the only person in this stinking town that has been good to me".

Other, purely visual aspects are at least as important: the rides in the Isotta-Fraschini, with Norma in a turban, cape, and sunglasses sitting on leopard skin padded seats in the rear, Max in black chauffeur's livery diagonally in front. The cinematography of this scene is so overwhelming that while watching one can hardly help wondering what it would be like to partake of this luxury and to be driven around like a child. *Here, the seductive aspects of regression are effectively illustrated*—even when Joe Gillis sits by, credibly glum. The staging of the visit to Paramount is also great: Norma is wearing a light net veil, with chauffeur Max gently but firmly giving makeup instructions via the rear-view mirror. The audience's inner reaction to the appearance of Norma Desmond/Gloria Swanson is likely to run parallel to the studio employees' enthusiastic deference shown in the film immediately afterwards.

For a strong lustful regressive reaction is also induced by the sheer presence of Norma Desmond/Gloria Swanson on the screen. Her ability to portray every affect archetypically, always effectively taking advantage of the lighting provided, leaves the viewer in childlike admiration even on repeated viewings—especially when she also improvises a perfect Chaplin parody for Gillis. Joe is bored, we are not: there is a certain regret that this kind of filming is over, never to come again. This may have been even more powerful for contemporary viewers than it is today. For many of them, Gloria Swanson was a celebrity from their distant but still remembered childhood. Such reactions of admiration and nostalgia probably make Joe's portrayed impulses to save the character of Norma understandable: because the stylistic means of this work also revive in us tendencies to preserve and relive the irretrievable past. We always carry them around within us in the form of childhood traces. The film explicitly opposes such aspirations. Implicitly, in its powerful visual world, it sets up a fabulously ambivalent monument to them.

In summary, Sunset Boulevard stages split images of women, and thus reveals problematic aspects of the gender relations in the 1950s: *The main character, Norma, portrays a mother figure who is rejected, but also secretly longed for by the man. She is experienced as demonic and the film impressively warns against her frowned-upon lures.* Betty, on the other hand, points the man in a socially adapted direction, away from passive aspirations, which thus remain unsatisfied and cannot find a place. The film does not offer a solution to this dilemma. It presents it and arouses corresponding affects in the viewer.

Further Considerations: Self-Referentiality of the Film and its Effect on Today's Viewers

One aspect of the film staging has not yet been addressed: It impressively shows the disciplined, latently self-destructive because ultimately futile grooming of the physicality of a woman, the ageing Norma, with the goal of restoring her youthfulness and her exploitability. It thus shows not only a woman's fate, but also the alienating nature of the film industry of which it is a part. The central eight-part series of shots showing this (01:15:55 ff.), underscored with dramatic music, with trembling, fast solo violin themes, lasts just under a minute: we see electric shocks, masks, sweat baths, magnifying glasses showing every wrinkle, and other impositions. We see the effort involved. In two later scenes, we see Norma a little longer wearing a bandage around her chin and band-aids on her forehead. This does not add up to much screen time, but these shots are aimed at evoking a deep sympathy with the fate of the character Norma, and they succeed in doing so to this day.

However, especially among the *female viewers*, the discussion about the film, which forms an integral part of the work of the Munich psychoanalytic film group—both among ourselves[5] and in the cinema—understandably led to movements of distancing from the impositions to which this female figure is subjected: women show that they are glad and relieved not to be living in this era and wish for other—more emancipatory—elements in

[5] Members of the film group are Eva Friedrich, Andreas Hamburger, Salek Kutschinski, Mahias Lohmer, Katharina Leube-Sonnleitner, Irmgard Nagel, Vivian Pramataroff-Hamburger, Corinna Wernz, and myself. I owe a great deal to the discussions and the resulting film presentations. My theses here are of course exclusively my responsibility.

the plot or especially in Norma's way of handling things. That makes clear: *at these points, today's women check out inwardly*. They can empathise with the suffering of the character Norma, but they remain at a distance.

Are today's women reacting to a devaluation of women? Could it not be said that the constellation hypostasised by Mulvey (1975), "woman as man's fetish", although not prominently shown in the film, is nevertheless ultimately cemented by this movie, too? After all, the ageing woman, who does not succeed in keeping the young "hero" other than through regressive, clinging pampering, is portrayed as "castrated", at least in the sense that she is ultimately left powerless, empty, and despairing.

Indeed, there are elements that suggest this: Norma boasts (00:44:41) about the apartment buildings, the oil wells she owns. "What's it for but to buy us anything we want?"—But Joe disappears for the New Year's Eve party, whereupon she attempts suicide. Economic wealth, then, cannot fulfil the woman, she ultimately cannot do anything with it, she *remains worthless in this sense because she is not attractive to a young man*. In contrast, the ageing Cecil B. DeMille is portrayed as someone who commands an empire with the power to act. He is not portrayed unsympathetically; he does not actually want to brush Norma off (01:06:58 ff. "Thirty million fans have given her the brush—isn't that enough?"). His pity, however, is above all for the former Norma, the "lovely little girl of seventeen" that she no longer is. The ageing female figure remains discarded nonetheless: she is worthless, no longer suitable as a *trophy* that confirms the virility of the man. In DeMille, one might say, the dilemma of 1950s film and perhaps also of 1950s gender relations is personified. One can regret the devaluation of females, but one cannot change it. DeMille's sentimentality, understood in this way, represents merely superficial crocodile tears of an otherwise deeply misogynistic society.

But is this really coherent? I doubt it, because the film is clearly self-referential in these parts: *never before had a Hollywood film in such a way thematised the misery caused by identification with the illusions produced there.* Louis Mayer had good reason to be enraged. This misery is certainly not displayed as a caricature, but rather—albeit in a rapid sequence of cuts—in a quite naturalistic way. As is the reaction of Norma Desmond who suspects that Joe will leave her after her scheming phone call to Betty. She speaks about it like this: (01:33:00 ff.)

> *Don't hate me, Joe. I did it because I need you. I need you like I never needed you. Look at me. Look at my hands, look at my face, look under my eyes. How can I go back to work if I'm wasting away under this torment? You don't know what I've been through these last weeks. I got myself a revolver. You don't believe me, but I did, I did! I stood in front of that mirror, only I couldn't make myself. Don't just stand there hating me! Shout at me, strike me! But don't hate me, Joe! Don't you hear me, Joe?*

Gloria Swanson plays this scene speaking in a hasty but realistic rhythm, tearful but not overly distorted, softly lit: For a moment, her performance is stripped of all caricature. The string-dominated music comments on this with moving lines focusing cello and viola parts. The film thus draws all viewers—men and women—into a compassionate stance.

We identify with the abandoned woman, the film does not affirm social reality here, but rather puts a problematic constellation up for discussion, representing it visually: here is a woman who has ruined herself, whose entire life and desire is geared towards being seen by men. A cinematically exaggerated, but nevertheless typical fate of the time: we see the destructive effect of gender norms conveyed by the media. This is shown *unvarnished* in the literal sense. The film has at least latent emancipatory aspects here. Today's viewers probably pick these up inwardly, developing ideas for alternative courses of action and trying to bring them into a constructive form.

Today, we can hardly experience the character of Betty Schaefer as offering an emancipatory option: up to date and *reality-oriented* according to the rules of the 1950s, she seems outmoded today. Hardly concealed, she conveys a superego pedagogical approach. It can probably only be understood historically: In the collective psyche of the fifties, the *roaring twenties* were perhaps still present like a buried paradise, in the form of a longing for an easy life, yes, for a kind of *gravy train* for which one latently longed would return after years of crash, crisis and war. But in 1950, something else was needed: The task was getting the country going again after the war and—as we now know—preparing it for the next wars: for the hot Korean War, and for the longer cold one with the Eastern Bloc. Betty Schaefer embodies a type of woman who was "useful" and necessary for this: efficient and filled with *a little sense*. Such a woman, according to somewhat obtrusive moral of the film by today's standards, is deserved only by someone who actively embraces life and stays away from regressive horrors. Hopefully, this will no longer attract us.

The film's appeal, however, is much more based on Gloria Swanson's irresistible portrayal of the glamorous, devouring, spoiling *mother figure*, of whom, if we are honest, we can never get enough—if only there is enough distance between us and the screen. The film plays with this ambivalence right up to the last shot: when Gloria Swanson/Norma Desmond comes towards us, "those wonderful people out there in the dark" and is "ready for the close-up" (01:49:22 ff.), greedily reaching for us, then this is eerily beautiful—but also because immediately after this shot the film ends and we can regain our distance (Fig. 1.2).

Translated by Annette Caroline Christmas.

Fig. 1.2 Ready for the close-up (01:49:34)

Film Details

Original title	Sunset Boulevard
Release year	1950
Country	USA
Book	Charles Brackett, Billy Wilder, D.M. Marshman
Direction	Billy Wilder
Music	Franz Waxman
Camera	John F. Seitz
Main actors	Glora Swanson, William Holden, Erich von Stroheim, Nancy Olson, Cecil B. de Mille Buster Keaton, Anna Q. Nielsson, H.B. Warner, Ray Evans, Jay Livingston, Hedda Hopper
Availability	Blu-ray, EAN 4 010884 254617

References

Basinger J (2000) Silent stars. Wesleyan University Press, Middletown. https://www.amazon.de/dp/B009FKVUFK/ref=dp-kindle-redirect?_encoding=UTF8&btkr=1

Cremoni, Lucilla (2015). "We Have a Car": l'Isotta Fraschini del Museo dell'Automobile di Torino. Piemonte Mese, Heft 7/8 2015. http://www.piemontemese.it/2015/07/01/we-have-a-car/

Fonagy P, Target M (2003) Psychoanalytic theories: perspectives from developmental psychopathology. Whurr Publishers

Hamburger A (2018) Filmpsychoanalyse. Psychosozial-Verlag, Gießen

Karasek H (1994) Billy Wilder. Eine Nahaufnahme. Hoffmann und Campe, Hamburg

Mertens W (1997) Entwicklung der Psychosexualität und der Geschlechtsidentität, Band 1: Geburt bis 4. Lebensjahr. Stuttgart, Kohlhammer

Mulvey, L. (1975) Visual pleasure and narrative cinema. In: dies., Visual and other pleasures. New York: Palgrave, S. 14–26

Mulvey, L. (1981) Afterthoughts on 'Visual Pleasure and Narrative Cinema' inspired by King Vidor's duel in the Sun (1946). In: dies., Visual and other pleasures. New York: Palgrave, S. 29–38

Rohde-Dachser C (1991) Expeditionen in den dunklen Kontinent. In: Weiblichkeit im Diskurs der Psychoanalyse. Pschosozial-Verlag, Gießen, p 2003

Schlöndorff, Volker, Grischoff, Gisela (1988) Billy, wie haben Sie's gemacht. TV series, part 2 of 6, quoted after https://www.youtube.com/watch?v=LIubBHvBe24

Staggs S (2002) Close-up on Sunset Boulevard: Billy Wilder, Norma Desmond and the dark Hollywood dream. St. Martin's Press, New York. https://play.google.com/store/books/details?id=iEpdlKas2d4C

2 Breakfast at Tiffany's, Style Icon as a Lifelong Lie

Mechthild Neises-Rudolf

Introduction

The topic "Women in Film" and especially the role of Holly Golightly in "Breakfast at Tiffany's" invite us to reflect on the image and role of women in the 1960s and today and to let ourselves be inspired to clarify our own perspective. The charming elegance of the protagonists seduces us, as viewers, to get caught up in the glittering façade without looking or listening. The 1961 film "Breakfast at Tiffany's" shows us the life of Holly Golightly as a light-footed party girl, charming, witty, and light-hearted. "A romantic comedy," says an advertisement. The following film scenes trace her search for prince charming, for whom she initially has only one requirement: he must be rich.

Film Plot

It is dawn. A taxi pulls up on a deserted street, Fifth Avenue in New York, and the film music "Moon River" begins to softly play. A woman steps out of the taxi, dressed in an evening gown, sophisticated and glamorous in long-sleeved gloves and sunglasses and her upper arms bare (Holly Golightly, played by Audrey Hepburn). In her hand is a cup of coffee to go and a croissant bag. Holding these incongruous accoutrements, she looks at her reflection in a shop window, absorbed, impassively contemplating herself and the luxury displays of Tiffany (Fig. 2.1).

Back home, her neighbor, called Sweetheart (Mr Yunioshi played by Mickey Rooney), is rung out again in the middle of the night. Meanwhile, a lover who had been waiting for

M. Neises-Rudolf (✉)
Private Practice, Heidelberg, Germany

V. Pramataroff-Hamburger, A. Hamburger (eds.), *From La Strada to The Hours*, https://doi.org/10.1007/978-3-662-68789-5_2

Fig. 2.1 Holly in front of Tiffany's window (00:00:53)

her now wants his bills paid and $50 for "the toilet." A commotion ensues in the hallway, the neighbor threatens to call the police, and the lover angrily leaves. The photographer neighbor is happy to put off taking his long-awaited photo of Holly until another day. Holly remains charming and cool and wishes them a good night.

Holly's doorbell rings and it is her cat that wakes her up. At the door is her new neighbor (Paul Varjak played by George Peppard). He has mislaid his house key and asks to use her phone. This is the ticket into Holly's flat, improvised and sparsely furnished—as if she had just moved in. We learn that she has been living there for a year.

Suddenly, time is pressing; Holly has to catch the 10.45 train to Sing Sing, as she does every Thursday. There in prison, she visits the mafia boss Sally Tomato (played by Alan Reed); the job was arranged for her by his lawyer. Holly receives $100 for each visit; she calls it her pension, for delivering "the weather report." Paul expresses concern, but Holly deflects, saying "I've been taking care of myself for a long time," but expresses some initial doubt as to whether the agent is really a lawyer: "he only has a phone and arranges to meet in a dive bar." Holly dresses up for the Sing Sing visit in a little black dress and a big hat. Paul is enraptured by this transformation, helping her look for and find the croc pumps. In thanks, she says, "They were cute, I wouldn't be ready without them."

Paul accompanies her out onto the street and tries to hail a taxi, which Holly summons immediately with a sharp whistle. Paul says, resigned: "I never could [do that]."

Mrs. Failenson (played by Patricia Neal) gets out of the arriving taxi; Paul introduces her and Holly as "my decorator" and "my neighbor." Holly takes off her oversized sunglasses for a millisecond and the audience sees wide eyes with a questioning look at her surroundings, one could almost say fearful. This gives us an idea of the wounded child behind the dazzling façade. At the same time, in the words of C. G. Carus (1789–1869 gynecologist and obstetrician, full quote, see page 8), she very quickly grasps the closer circumstances. With her sunglasses on, she quickly regains her impudent humor and turns away (Fig. 2.2).

Fig. 2.2 Holly with her big sunglass (00:13:20)

We learn more of Paul, who is supported by this older girlfriend and patron and constrained by her taste and lifestyle, as her furnishing of his flat makes clear, with the generous offer that everything can be changed too. This relationship is also overshadowed by the worry that she might be uncovered by her husband, to whom they are thus both financially tied. We know this since Mrs. Failenson had to cancel a dinner with Paul because the husband returned early. She pretends to be talking to a friend and superimposed on this scene is an old man's hand with a signet ring and cocktail glass.

In the evening, there is a ruckus in Holly's flat; a locked-out lover demands the return of his generous invitation and "toilet money." By the time he forces his way in, Holly has already fled down the fire escape, first changing her black evening gown for a white bathrobe. At the window to Paul's flat, Holly sees his girlfriend leaving money on her way out of the bathroom before leaving.

Now, Holly enters through the window and explains to the worried Paul, who wakes up, that his decorator has left. For the first time, Holly Golightly introduces herself to Paul by name.

They have a drink and piece both their life stories together, and the lies they live. Holly counts the money on the desk and is surprised to find it is 300 dollars. This is embarrassing for both of them, Holly apologizes, and they will both bear up. She catches Paul out. He introduces himself as an active writer, but she points out that his typewriter does not have a ribbon. At least he can show off a 5-year-old book that was introduced as promising. It is obviously a big slight to him.

Holly is touched, thinking he reminds her of her brother Fred and from then on always calls him Fred. Holly tells him her daydreams; these revolve around running a stud farm with her brother in Mexico. She looks for a resting place next to Paul's in bed, saying, "we're friends, just like that, we're friends, aren't we?" and going to sleep. In her anxiety dreams, she talks, looks for Fred, and is afraid and cold, and snow startles her. Paul is worried and asks questions, but Holly brusquely rejects him: "I won't be questioned" and goes down through the window into her flat, where it has long since become quiet again.

Holly invited him to a party that evening and the morning before also her new neighbor. With the invitation, she gave him a ribbon for his typewriter. Paul is touched and goes to the party.

It is in full swing with plenty of booze and loud music and reveals a world full of attractive women, wealthy men, and illustrious names. O. J. Berman, Holly's old friend, lets him in and calls him "Fredymouse," is corrected by Paul to "Pauly mouse." Now, we learn more about Holly, namely, that this old friend saw her potential as an actress and financed a French course for a year so that she would drop her Southern dialect. When the first screen test was due in Hollywood, she left the day before and called in from New York. When he asked her to come back immediately, she replied: "Yes, when I know what I want."

In the meantime, Holly has changed out of the Greek-looking lure robe, or perhaps bath towel, and appears in a little black dress holding a meter-long cigarette holder. She is charming, attentive to everyone, and generous.

Among the many women there is one friend, Mag Wildwood (played by Dorothy Whitney), who is treated snidely, and Holly watches as she drunkenly falls down. Unmoved, she asks the guests to clear the way; after all, her friend Mag has fallen on a blanket. This friend has brought two companions, Rusty Trawler, the richest bachelor in New York, and José da Silva Pereira, distinguished and interested in American customs, or so he introduces himself to Holly.

At this point, the angry neighbor, Mr. Yunioshi, appears again. He has called the police because of the noise. Paul and Silva Pereira manage to flee down the fire escape in different directions in time to hear the sound of the police sirens. Silva Pereira explains that he has a reputation to lose. Holly had already decided to let her guests continue partying alone and begins a stroll through the city at night with the richest bachelor under 50. On the street, she is still able to alert the policemen to the source of the noise; perplexed, Paul watches this scene.

The next scene shows Holly and Paul in Sing Sing. They are visiting Sally Tomato together, who is also called Uncle Sally. They chat about Holly's income and expenses and her inability to keep track of money. For the first time, Holly is embarrassed to talk about "toilet money, cat food," and so on. Paul is astonished to learn that Uncle Sally is also Holly's financial advisor, with a warning not to trust any bank. Uncle Sally even has a tip for Paul, the writer, that he already has all the material for his novel in her notes, which just needs embellishing. Holly, who with some pride introduces Paul to Uncle Sam, wants to know if he thinks he's nice and Uncle Sam challenges Paul to be nice to her. Just in time before leaving the visiting room, Holly asks for the weather report and hears—almost forgot—"snow flurries expected this weekend in New Orleans."

Paul is back at work on a novel about an anxious girl who lives alone with a cat.

Holly is sitting in the open window of her flat, singing Moon River to a guitar accompaniment. Paul looks out of his window; a tender greeting is exchanged and Paul's doorbell rings. Mrs. Failenson enters Paul's flat, upset and worried, and tells him that a strange man has been standing outside the house for two days. Paul wants to know what is going on, goes out, and allows the stranger to follow him through the streets until he sits down on a park bench and speaks to him: "What do you want?" And the surprising answer is

"Boy, I need a friend." Doc Golightly introduces himself as the husband of Lula Mae Barnes, who has taken the name Holly. Doc takes a seat on the park bench, nibbling nuts, and tells the story:

He met Holly and her brother Fred at a young age. Holly was 14 and she and her brother lived with a drunken farmer. "They were like two feral kittens - she had it good with me." He was a widower with four younger children and he and Holly got married—they thought it was a good solution for everyone, especially as brother Fred became part of the vet's family in Texas until he became a soldier. He points out that Lula Mae had it good with him, his daughters did all the housework, and Lula Mae got fatter and fatter; Doc tells us with a big grin.

But Holly was not satisfied, had big plans, and already had a promoter O. J. who wanted to bring her to Hollywood. But before that happened, she disappeared and reappeared in New York.

Doc wants to bring back his Lula Mae, with the news that her brother Fred is coming home soon, and asks Paul to support him. Later, it is Holly who asks Paul for support, telling Doc Golightly that she will not be coming back with him. She explains to Paul that the marriage has been annulled. Saying goodbye to Doc, she asks him not to "hold on to something you can't hold on to, not to hang your heart on something you can't tame—I haven't been Lula Mae for a long time."

Doc says goodbye to Paul, saying, "make sure she eats enough, she's so thin."

Paul lets her see her tears and self-doubt: "The bad thing is I'm still Lula Mae, buy me a drink." Holly seeks comfort and distraction, and they arrive at a strip joint, watch the show, go home drunk, and make love.

The next morning Paul arrives with the newspaper headline that Rusty Trawler has got married. Holly already knows about it and can tell him the details: Rusty Trawler is in debt; his family's money is not available to him, which is reason enough to marry a rich woman. Holly completely understands this.

Holly and Paul enjoy a day together, "doing everything we've never done before": champagne before breakfast, a new experience for Paul, and a visit to the library, which Paul introduces her to, a new experience for Holly. Then, they plan and do steal two comic masks from a department store, another new experience for Paul. So, they have fun together. Finally, they come to their scheduled visit to Tiffany's. Holly reassured by the beautiful displays and deflecting what she can't buy, "Diamonds are hideous before you're 40. I wonder if we can find anything for $10?" They meet an affable, almost fatherly salesman who supports this childish endeavor and commissions initials to be engraved on a metal ring that was in Doc's bag of nuts. Holly and Paul are united and exhilarated.

A debate ensues between Paul and Mrs. Failenson, who mocks him for his infatuation and wants to pay for a holiday for him and his girlfriend. He refuses her money and ends the relationship.

Paul looks for Holly and finds her in the library. She is dismissive; she is busy finding out about South America. Paul declares his love to her, and she rejects him. Paul is offended and gives her his publisher's check for 50 dollars, which he has now received for his article writing—of course with the offensive comment, "for the toilet."

In the evening, Holly comes home from a party with Silva Pereira and finds a telegram informing her of the death of Fred, who has been killed in a car accident. Holly is beside herself and demolishes her flat screaming. Silva Pereira stresses for the second time that he cannot afford a scandal. Nevertheless, Paul encourages Silva Pereira to comfort her and altruistically thinks his farm is the right place for Holly.

Holly is hardly recognizable; it is the night before she departs for Brazil. The décor of her flat has become homely, with Spanish-style furniture, and she is learning Portuguese. She even knits. Only with the same old sense of humor: she is not sure whether she is following a knitting scheme or Silva Pereira's remodeling plans. Holly even cooks, the table is set, and everything is arranged for a Paul's final visit. But the pressure cooker explodes and they both leave her flat for one last stroll around town. They arrive at a fountain and talk about what is important in life and love.

Back home, the narcotics squad goes into action. She and Paul are arrested and handcuffed and taken to a police station. The messenger service for the gangster boss has been busted and her client has also been arrested and is at the station. When she sees him and is asked which lawyer should represent her, she names him—apparently unable to be wrested from her consistent and cunning naivety. Again, a friend rescues her: the producer O. J., who wanted to get her to Hollywood, pays the 10,000-dollar bail. As it happens, the station is full of journalists and Holly naïve poses in front of the cameras and makes the headlines as a glamour girl. Paul, also hired by O. J., is supposed to take her to a hotel where the reporters can't find her. So, there is a taxi ride to the Clayton Hotel. Paul has already cleared out Holly's flat.

He then hands her a letter from Silva Pereira telling her that he loved her because she was different from the others, but he had to be considerate of the family name and reputation and he was a coward. Thus, the engagement is broken off and once again the dream of a rich husband. The Brazilian landowner has turned his back on her because his political career could not withstand this damage to his image.

On the surface, Holly is disappointed that this letter was slipped under the door. Nevertheless, she wants to take her flight to Brazil, despite a lot of persuasive arguments from Paul. Outside, it has started raining and there is lightning and thunder. Holly abruptly abandons her ca, saying: "We belong to no one and no one belongs to us." Paul is outraged and tell her in no uncertain terms what he thinks, that she is still running away. "You only meet yourself everywhere," he says, handing her the ring monogrammed with Tiffany's as his parting gift. He gets out of the taxi to look for the cat. Finally, after much hesitation, Holly also leaves the taxi. They both call out for "Puss" and find him and each other, rain soaked an intimate kiss and Puss between them.

"...and they lived happily ever after," as Grimms' fairy tales and Hollywood films ending assert.

Background to the Film

The film plot is based on a novella by Truman Capote and was published in 1958 under the original title "Breakfast at Tiffany's." As early as 1962, the film was released in the German dubbed version and had its cinema premiere in Germany with the same title. In 1972, it was broadcast for the first time on German television, on ZDF, in prime time. Unlike Capote's novel, however, the film has a happy ending; Hollywood knows what it owes its viewers.

Capote, the author of the novella, is said to have been very angry about this. He radically rejected the end result, stating: "It made me want to throw up." In an interview, he said that the film bears as much resemblance to his book as the Rockettes do to Galina Ulanova (Pritzke 2011). By totally toning down the book, it becomes possible to create a comedic and light-footed film, according to the name of the protagonist Golightly. Audrey Hepburn is charming; everything is stylish, light right up to the happy ending. Hollywood of the 1960s turns Capote's story of a social catastrophe into a fairy tale.

Audrey Hepburn, who was second choice in the casting for the lead role, became a style icon with her portrayal of Holly and Breakfast at Tiffany's is often discussed as an iconic film, icon as a symbol, legend, cult figure, or generally speaking a "person or thing as an embodiment of certain values, ideas, a certain attitude to life". Her "Little Black number" at the beginning of the film rather a big black designed by Hubert de Givenchy, Paris, became famous. In 2006, it was auctioned at Christie's for 692,000 euros and is considered the most expensive textile in film history.

The filming in New York lasted only one week; the rest of the film was subsequently produced in the studio in Hollywood. A look behind the scenes reveals the time pressure and the strain caused by the many spectators during filming in New York. For the leading actress, this was one of the difficulties among many others. For example, her husband Mel Ferrer—an actor himself—constantly interfered in scenes, and director Blake Edwards had the scenes repeated regularly. Added to this was her screen partner George Peppard, in the role of Paul, who annoyed everyone with his arrogance. Nonetheless, alongside Holly, he portrays a more down-to-earth film character and embodies a strong presence himself. Not infrequently, he shares with the audience a view of the protagonist: who is enchanted by Holly, marvels at her way of life and tries to find out what her hidden secret is. What probably constitutes this fragile person behind the elegant appearance.

All in all, director Blake Edwards presents us with a clapped-out, comedic, yet seemingly unified mood throughout. The fans of the first hour were themselves still so naïve that they had to see the film two and three times to see through the break and the drama.

Parallel Stories

Truman Capote actually wanted to see Marilyn Monroe in the role of Holly Golightly, but her manager advised against it because playing a prostitute was bad for her image.

The choice of Marilyn Monroe as an embodied sex symbol, her own biography and playing herself, so to speak, would have made this film something different. Perhaps, it would have attracted more interest from men, been more honest, and everyone would have understood straight away what it was about: sex sells and is sold.

Our film character, Holly, is married off, or marries off, at the age of 14 to a country vet about 30 years older than her and thus becomes stepmother to four children. For her, this is the end of a nightmarish life. Holly is rescued from the streets and from having to rely on theft, which we learn late in the film when the husband from Texas who still loves her shows up in New York, at first like a stalker, and as she progresses, Paul reveals her life story.

Holly in the novella boards a plane after the broken engagement and floats away to South America; a last trace is found in Africa and further end open. Holly in the film finds a sincere friend and love. The question whether she would be able to keep this relationship may be doubted.

Last but not least, Capote himself was born in the southern states; at the time of his parents' divorce, he was 4 years old and grew up with his grandmother. At the age of 8, his mother brought him to New York with her second husband. His adult life was marked by addiction, crises, and successes.

How Is the Feminine Portrayed in Film?

Social Images of Women

We meet Holly as a young woman in an extended phase of adolescence and self-discovery. This opportunity also involves risks; developmental tasks can be postponed and fail, or desired goals are not achieved. As is so often the case, expectations are exaggerated, and reality cannot live up to the idealization that is maintained. In his book *Singlefrau und Märchenprinz* (Single Woman and Prince Charming), sociologist Jean-Claude Kaufmann (2002) explores the question of why so many people live as singles in the postmodern era. He sees the dazzling dream image of prince charming located in an ambivalent everyday world, characterized by exuberance and sadness, hope and despair, security, and loneliness.

The question leads over to the understanding of psychological and psychosomatic symptom formation; this applies to both women and men. These symptoms manifest themselves according to the prevailing medical paradigms and social conditions, i.e., they are each embedded in a historical context (Shorter 1992). In a careful reading of Capote's novella, we come across two recommendations that Holly received to undergo psychotherapy. One came from a friend and the second from a friend with marriage plans. Holly declined with thanks, but perhaps, she will remember at 50 when beauty combined with charm no longer catches so easily.

Paul learns about Holly's moods in the first few minutes of meeting her. They both talk about what it's like "when you're sick of everything." Paul speaks of world-weariness. What Holly dismisses is that you have it because you're getting too fat, because it's raining and then you're sad. For herself, she describes something much worse, being afraid and not knowing what of. She also names the antidote "Tiffany's." It is only after Doc's visit that Paul knows about her precarious and vulnerable existence as a child and teenager. The relationship with her brother Fred, which has almost incestuous features, now becomes even more complex against the background that for a long time only these two had each other. All the more tragic that Doc Golightly not only wants to bring back his wife, whom he still loves, with the news that Fred will also be coming home in a few months.

In his gynecological textbook of 1839, Carl Gustav Carus writes as a recommendation or warning to gynecologists on how to deal with women, their patients "In the female, the purely receptive, the physically formative predominates, while in the male, the fertilising, spiritual principle prevails ... ." On the other hand, the spirit of the female more quickly recognizes the closer relationships of human life, has a certain acumen and inclination to cunning" (quoted from Seidler 1990). At least in the latter, the Holly of the 1960s can be recognized.

Call Girl and Woman

Holly's boyfriend asks Paul in the course of the conversation, "How long have you known her, what do you think: is she one or not ...?" The bell rings again and we viewers are left to our own thoughts. When the two resume the conversation, Paul asks what he means and the answer is "A crazy one." The unspoken answer was prostitute, raunchy, revealing, and starring Audrey Hepburn as call girl Holly. Holly's sly game with her admirers, in which she first flares up unmistakable hopes before locking herself in and fleeing down the fire escape to avoid the act that has already been paid for (about $300 today). It is a difficult balancing act to create this mixture of bittersweet, melancholic, thoughtful, and yet entertaining with both naive and wicked means. The audience accompanies Holly through a debauched party life in a world full of rich men, illustrious names, and beautiful women.

We become observers of her cat and her relationship with it, ultimately of relationshiplessness. This cat has no name and is simply "Puss." As Holly goes on to explain, she has no right to be named. She doesn't want a possession, not until she knows where she properly belongs. Holly already knows what it should look like there: like her place of longing at Tiffany's.

The slapstick scenes continue at a bizarre party where there are all kinds of absurd details. One small scene shows Holly setting fire to a tulle hat with her cigarette holder and then tipping over a glass to extinguish it. Holly, as the lucky child, doesn't notice any of this; only Paul is attentive in the background, dismayed, and relieved. But it is to him that she emphasizes again and again that she is only interested in marrying a rich man. Thus, the dream of luxury and light-heartedness is spun on. If prostitution is going to happen, then it should really pay off.

In numerous wickedly playful sequences that characterize Holly's everyday goings-on, it is noticeable that all the roles that revolve around Holly are male roles, including that of the cat. Only one girlfriend makes an appearance, and she doesn't come off well; she's eccentric and stupid and drinks herself into a stupor. Old women don't come off well either; they stand alone in front of the mirror and cry when they realize their distorted image. A warning to all, only Holly is not looking.

Other scenes touchingly and profoundly show Holly's mood swings and her attempt to talk to Paul about them. The life lies and life breaks are only revealed very late in the film and only through Doc's appearance. So, we learn that Holly grew up as a motherless child, neglected and neglected. How was she supposed to find her own motherhood and build up a good inner image of femininity? What do such breaks and caesurae in the biography mean for the personality development and adult life of a woman—Holly demonstrates it to us. We as viewers experience a fascination with many facets. When we identify with Holly, it is not her fragile side, but the refined, light-footed charm of the actress Audrey Hepburn.

When "Breakfast at Tiffany's" was released in 1961, it revolutionized the image of women in the USA. The American film historian Sam Wasson (2011) tells about it in a book that is as knowledgeable as it is entertaining.

If we think back to the 1960s, women did not yet have the right to vote everywhere and a profession, and an own bank account required the husband's consent. Against this backdrop, Holly is bold, free-spirited, and autonomous—but at what price, she sells her body and her youthfulness, as if she has changed her identity—again.

Reading Capote's short novel, it becomes even clearer that the casting of the role was a Hollywood-typical contemporary solution: the call girl Holly Golightly from Truman Capote's book and the girlish Audrey Hepburn. In the film, an alloy of charm, lightness, and composure is created right down to the tip of the cigarette. So, the protagonist lets everything roll off her back, but the noble, charming façade gets cracks in the course of the story, and the break becomes clear when the narrating husband closes the biographical gap and finally the death of the brother breaks into Holly's life.

It is impossible to write adequately about Breakfast at Tiffany's without waxing lyrical about Audrey Hepburn. Because in retrospect, Audrey Hepburn and Holly Golightly merge into one in film history. Yet, the introverted Hepburn was nothing like the eccentric Holly. Perhaps, it is precisely this difference between the actress and her screen personality that gives Holly Golightly her exciting appeal, her sly game with her admirers, in which she clearly gives rise to hope before eluding, such as escaping down the fire escape stairs to avoid the nude in prospect. Her outwardly portrayed self-absorption gives her an aura of untouchability. The matter-of-factness with which she rings her neighbor Mr. Yunioshi out at night because she doesn't bother to look for her front door key, all these and many more bad habits should make one aversive. But she exudes such a playful, childlike charm, as if you can't be angry with her. On the contrary, there is something fine and charismatic about her. Long before the haughty mask falls, the viewer of the colorful hustle and bustle finds himself on the side of the glamour girl.

It is Hepburn's unadulterated, simple grace that makes Holly seem to us like the easiest role of her career. Even her impulsive mood swings, during which her illusory house of cards threatens to collapse, seem unaffected and fit seamlessly into the overall characterization of the figure.

Further Reflections, the 1950s, and Today

When Truman Capote finished "Breakfast at Tiffany's" in 1958, he expected it to be printed in "Harper's Bazaar" magazine, but they refused. Too salacious, too revealing, too many unmentionable expressions occurred in this story about a young independent woman who earns her living through prostitution. The unnamed narrator is quite obviously homosexual, a parallel to the author.

The original drew a bitter portrait of a live-in girl who lets herself be kept by rich men. Holly Golightly was a condensate of several real society ladies as well as Capote's own mother, Lillie Mae.

"At the end of the fifties, Hollywood was still firmly in the grip of the moral guardians: sex was only allowed to be hinted at, if at all, and extramarital sex was out of the question; women had to be chaste, men gallant or macho, but in any case, straight. Prostitution was taboo and homosexuality even more so, and the scriptwriters had to avoid such provocative topics with allusions" (Pritzke 2011). Sex was only hinted at in the cinema and only for married couples. Strict censorship laws prevailed in Hollywood (Reichart 2011). This was a double border crossing in the 1960s, when strict images of women prevailed: "At one end was Doris Day, at the other Marilyn Monroe." It was not until the course of the 1960s that a change came. Cinema began to feel the competition of television and the revolt of the young generation turned old role patterns upside down.

The new motif was love. Holly became the charming flirt and her neighbor the straight man (and gigolo) who fell in love with her. Axelrod invented romantic scenes like the shopping trip to Tiffany's, and because this was Hollywood, there had to be a happy ending. The film can also be seen in this way; we experience an independent young woman who obviously doesn't want to marry, except into the millionaire class. Who gets involved with men when and how she wants, but nevertheless, she also has to make a living with these men.

In addition, it is the witty and sensitive dialogue that often has a surprising sharpness, whereas the novel is a lot more bearish, not to say gruff. Through it all, the audience is often drawn into Paul's sensitive observations alongside him.

And finally, Holly is well-dressed, even though she is not a princess and not rich. The fact is that the film's outfit is French haute couture; Hubert de Givenchy, Audrey Hepburn's personal friend, designed the clothes for all the films since "Sabrina." Conversely, Audrey Hepburn is referred to as his muse.

Despite all the fractures, Wasson (2010) believes that this cinematic initial spark gave women the courage to change roles. "Breakfast at Tiffany's" became a film of departure, shortly followed by the women's movement.

Each decade of the twentieth century after the Second World War stands for its own style—when we think of the 1950s, petticoats and the New Look come to mind, with the 1960s of course the miniskirt and the hippie revolution, with the 1970s bell-bottoms and lots of glamour, and so on. This is something that was not simply thought up in the abstract by designers but was only really brought to life by influential personalities—personalities who can be called style icons because they embody everything that a particular decade stands for. In the 1950s, for example, this is someone like Audrey Hepburn's girlish elegance, Brigitte Bardot of the 1960s hippie chic and glamour, Jane Birkin as an example of the 1970s with jeans and frilly top, and in the 1980s again Madonna with sexually charged provocative outfits. Kate Moss as an example of the 1990s with casual jeans as the "Wild Child of Fashion" (Schneider 2017).

What moves women to this day beyond fashion, they are still fighting for gender equality such as equal pay for equal work, access to all professions and all career stages, and equal distribution of unpaid housework and family work. The pill was developed for women and has brought them degrees of freedom and choice, but why is the pill still not available for men? The times of the pandemic and the lockdown have made it public; we still face development tasks for women and men in a democratic world based on equality.

If we look at women today, many who come home after a long day at work feel completely overwhelmed by the demands that their children place on them. How do mothers manage to divide their time and energy sensibly between work and leisure as well as partnership and caring for the children? In times of the pandemic, this question is currently moving women and men anew, perhaps also with new answers.

Why We Still Love This Mendacious/Whitewashing Film?

It is a declaration of love to the person Audrey Hepburn! Blake Edwards' masterpiece captivates with sensitive dialogue and one of the greatest acting performances in Hollywood history and tells an exaggerated story about a graceful, vulnerable young woman who tries to deceive herself with her appearance in a highly elegant way. The romance, like the film itself, is melancholy without slipping into sentimentality. The intelligent script prepares a logical ending that deviates massively from the rigorous ending of the novella but is consistent and consequential for Hollywood of the 1960s. In the film, the easy "taming of a wild creature" thus succeeds. Contrary to Holly's warning in the farewell conversation with Doc, "that he should not attempt what cannot succeed." Hollywood can!

Translated by Annette Caroline Christmas

Film Details

Original title	Breakfast at Tiffany's
Release year	1961
Country	USA
Book	George Axelrod based on a novel by Truman Capote
Direction	Blake Edwards
Music	Henry Mancini
Camera	Franz Planer
Main actors	Audrey Hepburn, George Peppard, Patricia Neill, Buddy Ebsen, Mickey Rooney
Availability	DVD

References

Kaufmann J-C (2002) Singlefrau und Märchenprinz. Über die Einsamkeit moderner Frauen. UVK-Verlagsgesellschaft, Konstanz

Pritzke M. (2011). https://www.spiegel.de/geschichte/fruehstueck-bei-tiffany-a-947345.html 04.10.2011, last access 27.05.2020

Reichart M. (2011). https://www.deutschlandfunkkultur.de/als-audry-hepburn-die-edelnutte-spielte.950.de.html?dram:article_id=140592, Beitrag vom 20.10.2011

Schneider H. (2017). https://www.vogue.de/mode/mode-trends/sommer-inspiration-15-retro-stilikonen-von-den-50er-bis-in-die-90er-jahre (last access 30.05.2020)

Seidler E (1990) Historische Aspekte des Frauenbildes bei Frauenärzten. In: Dmoch, W., Stauber M., Beck, L. (Hrsg.),0 Psychosomatische Gynäkologie und Geburtshilfe. Springer, Berlin, pp. 7–15

Shorter E (1992) From paralysis to fatigue: a history of psychosomatic illness in the modern era. The Free Press, New York

Wasson S. (2010) Fifth Avenue, 5 A.M. Audrey Hepburn, Breakfast at Tiffany's, and the Dawn of the Modern Woman. HarperCollins Publishers, New York

Le Mépris (Jean-Luc Godard 1963) and Its Story of Cinema: A 'Fabric of Quotations'

3

Laura Mulvey

In *Le Mépris*, the cinema has a central presence on various different levels. The making of a film has brought the central characters together, and the dramatic processes of film-making are often shown on screen, as a backdrop to the human drama. But woven into this overt presence is another story about the cinema: its histories and its contemporary crises. Only occasionally explicitly reaching the surface of the film, this story is concealed in signs, images and allusions. The unifying thread that ties these oblique references together is the world of cinéphilia, Godard's formative years as a critic for the *Cahiers du cinema*, and the films and directors he had written about and loved during the 1950s. That world had, by 1963, moved into a past tense: the Hollywood studio system that had produced the *politique des auteurs* had aged and had been overtaken by industrial changes; Godard was no longer a cinéphile critic but a successful New Wave director. But through allusions and quotations, the world of cinéphilia seeps into *Le Mépris*, mediating between past and present. As quotation necessarily refers backwards in time, Godard evokes a now ended era with an aesthetic device that always comes out of the past. Thus, in *Le Mépris*, form (quotation) is appropriate to its content (history).

But, on the other hand, quotation is a key modernist formal device, fragmenting a text's cohesion, disrupting traditional forms of reading by introducing other layers to a linear structure. As Peter Wollen puts it in his discussion of quotation in Godard's *Vent d'est*:

> One of the main characteristics of modernism . . . was the play of allusion within and between texts . . . The effect is to break up the heterogeneity of the work, to open up spaces between different texts and types of discourses . . . The space between the texts is not only semantic

L. Mulvey (✉)
Sussex, UK
e-mail: ubwc067@mail.bbk.ac.uk

V. Pramataroff-Hamburger, A. Hamburger (eds.), *From La Strada to The Hours*,
https://doi.org/10.1007/978-3-662-68789-5_3

> but historical too, the different textual strata being residues of different epochs and different cultures (Wollen 1982).

These kinds of insertions also necessarily address the reader/spectator and generate two possible directions of engagement: one remains with the text's overt meaning, while the other takes a detour into a latent and more uncertain terrain. To reflect on the passing references, especially if they are not underlined or emphasised by the film's action, involves a step aside from the main line of the film's narrative. The temptation is to pause, to attribute a reference to its source, or attempt to trace it until the trail is lost, as opposed to following the forward flow of a text. So, for instance, when I analyse, later in this essay, further associations triggered for me by the posters in Cinecittà; I will be giving priority to certain background images over the crucial narrative moment when Camille and Jerry meet, when Paul betrays Camille, and the theme of 'contempt' begins. Mikhail Iampolski describes the relationship between quotation and the spectator's detour in the following terms:

> The anomalies that emerge in a text, blocking its development, impel us towards an intertextual reading. This is because every 'normative' narrative text possesses an internal logic. This logic motivates the presence of the various fragments of which the text is made. If a fragment cannot find a weighty enough motivation for its existence from the logic of the text, it becomes an anomaly, forcing the reader to seek its motivation in some other logic or explanation outside the text. The search is then constructed in the realm of intertexuality (Iampolski 1998a).

I would like to reflect on those moments when references to the cinema within *Le Mépris* intrude and direct the spectator away from the internal logic of the text, its manifest narrative and towards 'other explanations'. To my mind, when followed up, the 'anomalies' begin to form a network, relating back to a latent, other story of the changes that had overtaken and were overtaking the cinema. The anomalies do, of course, take on multiple shapes or forms, deviating from a strict concept of 'quotation'. Iampolski sums up this multiplicity when he points out that an 'anomaly' takes the form of a fragment which means: 'what is traditionally considered a quote may end up not being one, while what is not traditionally seen as a quote might end up being one' (Iampolski 1998b).

Godard's 'taste for quotation' has often been commented on and he himself uses the phrase in a long interview in the special Nouvelle Vague issue of *Cahiers* du cinéma (168, December 1962). He says, in relation to *À bout de souffle [Breathless]*:

> Our earliest films were simply films made by cinéphiles. We could make use of whatever we had already seen in the cinema to deliberately create references. This was particularly the case for me. [...] I constructed certain shots along the lines of ones that I already knew, Preminger's, Cukor's etc. Furthermore, Jean Seberg's character follows on from *Bonjour Tristesse*. I could have taken the last shot of that film and added an inter-title Three Years Later . . . It comes from my taste for quotation that has always stayed with me. In life, people quote things that appeal to them . . . So I show people quoting: except I arrange their quotations in a way that will also appeal to me (Godard 1968).

Quotation, Godard seems to be saying, offered a point of cinematic transition in his trajectory from *cinéphile*/critic to *cinéphile*/director, from those days of the *Cahiers* to those of the *Nouvelle Vague*, from loving a particular shot to using it in his own films. About thirty years later, this lifelong partiality for quotation culminated in *Histoire(s) du cinéma*. *Le Mépris*, released in 1963 as a comparatively large budget fiction film with corresponding production values, adapted from a quite conventional novel, benefits from the retrospective shadow cast by *Histoire(s)*. Not only are both made up of a tissue of film quotation and reference, both were also made during transitional periods in film history. Looking back at *Le Mépris* from this perspective, its juxtaposition between cinema history and quotation gains in significance, the fiction dominates less, the characters give way to their emblematic casting, and the network-like structure, central to the *Histoire(s)* aesthetic, becomes more visible. Furthermore, *Histoire(s)* draws attention to the place *Le Mépris* itself occupies in film history, how close it lies, in 1963, to 1950 Hollywood, both as a time of industrial decline but also the decade in which the last great studio system films were still being made. It was these films that Godard loved in particular and that educated him as a director (as he points out in the 1962 interview). But the presence of history draws attention to an aesthetic shift. Quotation in *Le Mépris* is no longer simply 'a taste'. It enables an elegiac commentary on the decline of one kind of cinema while celebrating another, the style that Godard had himself developed within the context of the French New Wave. Summing up this situation, Michel Marie says:

> *The aesthetic project of* Le Mépris *is entirely determined by the context of the end of classical 'cinema and the emergence of new "revolutionary" forms of* narrative (Marie 1990)'.

It was Alberto Moravia's novel *Il Disprezzo* (1954) from which *Le Mépris* is adapted that gave Godard, in the first instance, the necessary film-within-a-film framework from which to develop his own themes and reflections. The novel was based on Moravia's own real-life encounter with the Italian film industry when, as a journalist, he visited the location of Mario Camerini's 1954 spectacular *Ulisse* (a Lux Film production with Kirk Douglas as Ulysses, also starring Silvana Mangano and Anthony Quinn). *Il Disprezzo* uses a film production of *The Odyssey* as the setting for a tight group of characters (producer, director, screenwriter and screenwriter's wife). The setting brings together the story of a film in production, a marriage in decay and intellectual debate about Homer's epic poem. The novel shows no interest in either the mechanics of film-making or the history of cinema. Godard, however, makes the most of the way that, unlike a novel, a film about a film in production is necessarily self-referential and thus modernist. But above all, Godard inserts his story of the cinema into the adaptation of the human story.

To reiterate, the latent story in *Le Mépris* makes visible a break in film history: on the one hand, there is the new flourishing cinema of the New Wave and Godard's own modernist, innovative style and, on the other, Hollywood cinema of the 1950s, and the flourishing *cinéphilia* it had fostered in Paris, both of which had declined by the beginning of the

1960s. Thomas Schatz sums up the radically changed conditions in the Hollywood industry that lay behind the disappearance of the films valued by the politique des auteurs critics:

> Gone was the cartel of movie factories that turned out a feature every week for a hundred million movie-goers. Gone were the studio bosses who answered to the New York office and oversaw hundreds, even thousands of contract personnel working on the lot. Gone was the industrial infrastructure, the "integrated" system whose major studio powers not only produced and distributed movies but also ran their own theatre chains (Schatz 1998).

In the first instance, these changes were set in motion by the Paramount Decree of 1948. The Federal Government wanted to break the restrictive practices inherent in Hollywood's vertically integrated system of production, distribution and exhibition. After the Decree, the studios had to sell their cinemas. The old financial mode of self-investment, through which production was supported by box-office returns, was gradually replaced by individual package deals put together by independent producers, stars and increasingly powerful agents and agencies, with the increasing participation of banks and other outside investors. Furthermore, during the 1950s, box-office receipts declined due to the rise of television (from $80 million c. 1950 to below $20 million c. 1960), and the industry struggled for survival. It was in this context that Hollywood began to invest in spectacular historical blockbusters. In *Le Mépris*, the conflict between Fritz Lang, representing old Hollywood, and Jerry Prokosh, who represents the new breed of producer associated with 'package deals', gestures to this history. And the film of *The Odyssey* does, of course, represent the new focus on the big movie that would, with luck, pull off a major box-office hit; this was very different from the returns made from 'a feature a week' that had sustained the Hollywood genre system and its auteur directors.

Several of the directors whose films Godard had reviewed on their release during the 1950s, and who had special significance for him, were caught up in the blockbuster trend. The impact can be seen, for instance, in the case of Anthony Mann. In one of his last *Cahiers* reviews of a Hollywood film (92, February 1959), Godard argued that just as Griffith had invented the cinema in each frame of *Birth of a Nation*, so Mann had reinvented it in each frame of *The Man of the West*. Ultimately, he claims, Mann had created a work of modern cinema. I dwell on this moment as exemplary of Godard's aesthetic and critical investment in his key directors. But as conditions in Hollywood changed (as evoked above), Mann would go on to direct the spectacular *El Cid* in 1961 and manage to continue to make films with overblown casts, budgets and limited cinematic possibility for at least most of the 1960s. He was more fortunate than others.

Some favourites of the *politique des auteurs* who had regularly produced movies year after year during the post-war period, such as Sam Fuller, could no longer find work in the Hollywood film industry, only occasionally managing to make a few independent productions over the coming decades. Nicholas Ray made no more movies after *King of Kings* in 1961 and *55 Days at Peking* in 1963. Joseph Mankiewicz, for whom Godard had a particular admiration and whom he had described, as early as 1950, as 'one of the most brilliant of the American directors', was in 1963, directing *Cleopatra* (ironically for a director with a particular talent for spare, witty dialogue and sophisticated direction of actors).[1] This long decline is vividly reflected in the *Cahiers du cinéma's* annual list of the 'Ten Best Films of the Year'. Dominated throughout the 1950s by their favourite Hollywood directors, by 1958, only three Hollywood films appear, Mankiewicz's *The Quiet American* stands at number one, Preminger's *Bonjour Tristesse* at number three and *The Man of the West* at number five. The following year, no Hollywood films are included in the Ten Best list.

The story of cinema in *Le Mépris* is vividly laid out through a kind of 'prestory' at the beginning of the film and is clearly marked by use of quotation. Leaving aside its subsequently inserted 'prologue', *Le Mépris* opens with three sequences set in Cinecittà, the film studios outside Rome, which were as evocative of the Italian film industry as Hollywood for the USA or Pinewood for the UK. Together, the three sequences form a triptych in which the 'old' that Godard loved, especially Hollywood, is enunciated through the 'new' he believed in. In his book on Fritz Lang, Tom Gunning uses the screening room sequence in *Le Mépris* to discuss the complex question of film authorship. He says: 'The film-maker functions less as a scriptor than as a fashioner of palimpsests, texts written over other texts creating new meanings from the superimposition of old ones' (Gunning 2000). For all three of the triptych sequences, the concept of palimpsest has special relevance, evoking the way that quotation and reference create layers of time, bringing something from the past into the present, which then inscribes the present onto the past. In a similar but different manner, ghostly rather than textual, the actors, too, have meaning layered into their present fictional roles. As Jacques Aumont puts it:

> Jack Palance, Georgia Moll and Fritz Lang are vehicles, in the flesh, of part of the past, of history. They are living quotations and, already survivors of a vanished world . . .: through them, Godard quite consciously evokes not only his own immediate past as *cinéphile– The Barefoot Contessa, The Quiet American* – but a more distant, already heroised and mythic past.... (Aumont 2000)

In the first sequence of the triptych, the studio lot stands idle and deserted. Francesca (the producer's assistant) explains to Paul (the screen writer): 'Jerry has sent everyone home. Things are hard in the Italian film industry at the moment'. Jerry, the American producer, then appears on the edge of the sound stage and proclaims, in long shot and as though addressing a vast audience, that he has sold the studios for real estate development. And Francesca's final remark: 'C'est la fin du cinéma' carries the sense of crisis beyond Cinecittà to the general decline of industrial cinema by the late 1950s and even to the question of cinema itself. The studio lot is itself, to adapt Aumont's terms, 'a vehicle, a part of the past, a history' and, as such, might be understood as mise-en-scène as quotation.

[1]Rather strangely, given his later dismissive comments about Il Disprezzo, Godard says of Mankiewicz 'I would not hesitate to accord him as important a place as that occupied by Alberto Moravia in European literature'.

Poignantly, the scene is set in the lot belonging to Titanus (the studio that had produced Roberto Rossellini's *Viaggo in Italia* in 1953) and which was, in fact, just about to be demolished. The fate of Cinecittà corresponds to that of the Hollywood studios at the time, more valuable as real estate than for film production.

The second sequence of the Cinecittà triptych brings together the central group of *Le Mépris'* characters who all, fictionally, belong to the cinema through their various roles in the production of *The Odyssey*. It is here that Godard introduces most intensely the aesthetic of quotation. Set in the studio screening room, the confined space is criss-crossed by quotation and reference of all kinds: spoken, enacted, written, personified and discussed. Francesca and Paul join Prokosh, the producer, and Fritz Lang, the director, to watch rushes from their production of *The Odyssey*, (part Italian epic, part Hollywood spectacule). The conversation between the characters enables Godard to juxtapose references to the contemporary state of cinema and classical European culture; and these two themes are reiterated, on the one hand, by literal quotations from European literature and, on the other, by the presence of figures with an emblematic association with Hollywood. And Louis Lumière's grim prediction, written in large letters under the screen, 'Le cinema est une invention sans avenir' ['the cinema is an invention with no future'] creates a link to the elegiac spirit of the first and third sequences.

Central to the screening room sequence are the rushes, shots of the statues of the gods or snippets of the story composed more in tableaux than in continuity. As bits of cinema, they are short and finite, as indeed are rushes, but they take on the aesthetic characteristics of quotation: fragmentation and repeatability. Several commentators have pointed out that the style with which the statues are filmed, accompanied by Georges Delerue's music, strikingly quotes the filming of the statues, accompanied by Renzo Rossellini's music, in Roberto Rossellini's *Viaggo in Italia.*

While the literary quotations are, by and large, overt and attributed, the conjuring up of Hollywood is more complex, here taking place through the signifying properties of the actors as living quotation. Fritz Lang, as the fictional director, obviously brings his own cinematic history with him, but so do Jack Palance (as Jerry Prokosh) and Giorgia Moll (as Francesca) who also represent, metonymically, particular Hollywood films that had significance for Godard. Michel Piccoli (as Paul Javal) brings to this collective of signifiers a particular resonance of Paris: as an actor, he evokes the French New Wave; as a character, he evokes Parisian cinéphilia.

As well as having appeared in Italian epic productions, Giorgia Moll had played the French-speaking Vietnamese heroine in Joseph Mankiewicz's *The Quiet American*, thus creating a direct link to one of Godard's favourite directors. He had reviewed the film on its release with his usual admiration but was also disappointed that Mankiewicz's intelligent, elegant script was imperfectly realised as film (Arts 679, July 1958). In *Le Mépris*, Giorgia Moll plays Francesca Vanini, a character invented by Godard (she is not in the Moravia novel) whose name refers directly to Roberto Rossellini's latest film *Vanina Vanini*, (which will represent him on the line of posters in the third sequence). As Prokosh's interpreter, she comes to stand for living quotation in a different sense, repeating the words of others, translating, often very freely, between the mono-linguistic Paul and Camille on the one hand, and Prokosh on the other. As well as her own native language, Italian, with Lang she can speak English, French or German and gains his approval for her recognition and translation into French of his quotation from the German poet Hölderlin's 'The Poet's Vocation'.

Jack Palance brings Hollywood into *Le Mépris* in several ways. As a star in his own right, he represents the Hollywood star system as such. But he also represents a link, both as a star and through his fictional character, Jeremiah Prokosh, to a cluster of Hollywood films-about-film that had been made in the 1950s, all of which include an unscrupulous and exploitative producer or studio boss. In the first instance, Palance would, for Godard, have linked back to Robert Aldrich's 1955 film *The Big Knife*, an adaptation of a Clifford Odets' play about the conflict between a star (Palance) struggling to maintain his ethical principles in the face of the power and persistent bullying of the studio boss, played by Rod Steiger. Palance thus brings with him a double quotation: he is the star who had played the role of a star, while in *Le Mépris*, in the persona of Jeremiah Prokosh, he references the character personified by Steiger. Furthermore, as Michel Marie points out, Prokosh is a direct descendant of Kirk Edwards, the megalomaniac, casually brutal and sexually predatory Hollywood producer in Joseph Mankiewicz's 1954 *The Barefoot Contessa*, a film that had been highly prized by *Cahiers du Cinéma*. Palance's chiselled, mask-like features (due to plastic surgery after being wounded in World War II) and his slow, almost Frankenstein-like movements recall Warren Stephen's stony, almost motionless performance as Kirk Edwards. To these two 'Hollywood on Hollywood' films should be added Vincente Minnelli's 1952 *The Bad and the Beautiful* in which Kirk Douglas plays the prototypically unscrupulous, if more engaging, producer Jonathan Shields.

Although Prokosh has been said to evoke Godard's real-life producers Carlo Ponti and Joe Levine, the iconographical legacy of these Hollywood movies is very strong. But, as well as inscribing these traits and characteristics, Godard uses Prokosh specifically to signal the decline in Hollywood production values in the face of cynicism, philistinism and a taste for kitsch. A throwaway remark of Fritz Lang's indicates that Prokosh is not, for him, within the true tradition of Hollywood independent production. Refusing his invitation to have a drink, Lang quotes a famous Goldwynism (Sam Goldwyn tended to mix up language): '"Include me out", as Sam Goldwyn a real producer of Hollywood once said'. And Prokosh's first appearance in Cinecittà underlines the new commercialism. While Godard's citation of the Hollywood-on-Hollywood films puts *Le Mépris* within this 'sub-genre', evoking a tradition of films of self-reference (that does, of course, predate the 1950s), he is also clearly gesturing towards the industry's uncertain future, underlined by the Lumière quotation. The decline, he seems to imply, was already there in the beginning.

Fritz Lang is first introduced to the film by the most well-known anecdote of his career. Paul tells Francesca that Goebbels offered Lang a privileged position in Universum Film AG (UFA), to which he had replied by leaving the following day for Paris and then the

United States.[2] Godard follows this up with an enacted confrontation between Fritz Lang and Goebbels in the screening room. In a moment that seems anomalous and strange, Prokosh violently interrupts the screening, claiming that the images on the screen were not in the script. Lang brings the argument to an end, saying calmly: 'Naturally, because in the script it's written and on the screen it's pictures, motion pictures it's called.' According to Tom Gunning, this is a re-enactment of a confrontation between Lang and Eddie Mannix, his first US producer.[3] Both these anecdotes show Lang confronting authority; but one is given its place in Fritz Lang and Eddie Mannix biography, while the other floats, functioning dramatically as a fragment but without explanation. Together, these two anecdotes represent two very different kinds of quotation, the attributed and the 'to-be-deciphered', both with very different aesthetic implications.

If Prokosh, in his *Le Mépris* role, is emblematic of changing Hollywood, Lang stands, in stark contrast, for a long history of the cinema, some of its most outstanding films and its more generally changing fortunes. Born in 1890, shortly, that is, before the cinema and making his first film in 1919, Lang and cinema matured, as it were, side by side. Due to the *Mabuse* films, *Metropolis*, and his prolific output during the Weimar period, as a 'living quotation' he brings to *Le Mépris* the memory of aesthetic achievements of German silent cinema, then, with *M* in 1931, early experiment with synch sound. (It might be worth remembering, in the context of the late 1950s blockbuster, that Lang had almost bankrupted UFA in 1927 with his spectacularly expensive extravaganza *Metropolis*.) In 1933, he joined the stream of exiles from Nazism who then contributed so much to Hollywood during the years of the studio system. From *Fury* in 1936 to *Beyond Reasonable Doubt* in 1956, he made a film, sometimes two, every year (except one). Although he was, by and large, successful (unlike some of his compatriots), he too found it increasingly hard to direct by the mid-1950s. In Germany, in the late 1950s, he directed his own versions of 'spectaculars': The *Tiger of Eshnapur* and *The Indian Tomb* as well as an attempt to return to the *Mabuse* cycle. By the time he appeared in *Le Mépris*, he had made no films for three years; on the other hand, as an early pantheon director of the *politique des auteurs*, his critical status had risen in France and Luc Moullet's book *Fritz Lang*, that Camille reads and quotes from in the apartment sequence, had been published in 1963. Godard treats Lang reverentially, himself acting the role of the fictional director's assistant. He frames and films Lang so that his literal presence takes on the mythical quality due to an old man, no longer employable but, more than any other director still living at the time, stretched across and emblematic of this complex cinematic history. Still wearing, as a badge of belonging and distinction, the monocle that signifies the old days of Weimar, Lang is quotation as embodiment, summoning up the past and inserting it into a present to which he no longer belonged.

[2] Tom Gunning analyses this anecdote and demonstrates that Lang elaborated it considerably over the years (Fritz Lang, p. 8–9).

[3] Ibid., 6.

In the third sequence of the triptych, these themes are realised and confirmed. Outside the screening room, the characters act out their scene in front of a wall of posters: Howard Hawks's *Hatari!* (1962), Godard's own *Vivre sa vie* (1962), Rossellini's *Vanina Vanini* (1961) and Hitchcock's *Psycho* (1960) (Fig. 3.1).

Apart from Godard, the three were great directors celebrated and defended during Godard's time as a *Cahiers du cinéma* critic, but all were, by this point in time, nearing the end of their careers. Appropriately, Godard inserts the figure of Fritz Lang into this series of 'hommages'. Framed alone, in front of the posters, Lang walks quite slowly towards the camera as he lights a cigarette and, emphasising the mythic nature of this portrait shot, music briefly appears on the soundtrack. In the next couple of shots, Paul, as a cinéphile, brings cinema directly into his conversation with Lang. The latter brushes aside Paul and Camille's admiration for *Rancho Notorious* (1952), 'the western with Marlene Dietrich', with 'I prefer *M*'. But Paul persists and mentions the scene in which Mel Ferrer (as Frenchie Fairmont) allows Marlene Dietrich (as Altar Keane) to win at chuck-a-luck. This was a favourite moment of Godard's, to which he refers specifically in his general discussion of the Western in his *Man of the West* review. The citation of *Rancho Notorious* has its own relevance to the posters that frame the conversation between Paul and Lang; the film is itself about ageing but mythic figures of the West (Frenchie Fairmont and Altar Keane) who have become part of its legend, just as these directors have become part of the legend of Hollywood as told by the *Cahiers du Cinéma*.

Fig. 3.1 The old cinema, Fritiz Lang, meets the new cinema, Brigitte Bardot

But this sequence is also the one in which Brigitte Bardot, as Paul's wife, Camille, first appears. As she stands against the backdrop of posters, she personifies new cinema, a new kind stardom, as well as a new kind of glamour, European as opposed to Hollywood. In the last resort, she stands for the personification of cinema. If Godard tends to fuse cinematic beauty with that of his female star, this is particularly so in *Le Mépris*. But the presence of the *Vivre sa vie* poster creates its own distinctive chain of female beauty reaching back across the history of cinema. Later in the film, Camille wears a black wig, bobbed in the style worn by Anna Karina in *Vivre sa vie*, which in turn cites Louise Brooks. Much admired by the director of the Cinémathèque Française, Henri Langlois, for an insouciant seductiveness in films such as Hawks's 1928 *A Girl in Every Port* to Pabst's 1929 *Pandora's Box*, Louise Brooks might be seen as a pre-figuration of Godard's fascination with feminine beauty that fused with the beauty of the cinema.

The bracketing of Hawks and Hitchcock conjures up André Bazin's ironic term 'Hitchcocko-Hawksianism' to describe the dedicated supporters of the *politique des auteurs* at the *Cahiers*. Both directors had started their supremely successful careers in the 1920s and had flourished under the studio system but with comparative independence (Hitchcock, of course, arriving from Britain in the late 30s). But both were old by the time of *Le Mépris* and would only make films occasionally until the 1970s. Although he was to make two more films (*Anima nera* in the same year and *Italia anno uno* in 1974), Rossellini's career in cinema was also just about over. From 1961 to the end of his life in 1977, apart from a few documentaries, he would work exclusively for television. *Vanina Vanini* was adapted from a novella by Stendhal. Set in Rome during the Risorgimento (Rossellini had celebrated its centenary the previous year with *Viva l'Italia*), the story bears witness to Stendhal's love of Italy and his fascination with its struggle for liberation. As if to emphasise its significance, Godard had 'Francesca Vanini' summoned by name over an intercom a few seconds before the film's poster appears on the screen.

In this concluding section, I would like to exemplify ways in which quotation can set in train further lines of thought that might be particular to the spectator. A quotation or reference might trigger associations for the spectator that go beyond the specific textual context and produce an 'extratextual reverie'. Thus, for me personally (and, very likely, others), thinking about *Le Mépris* in the light of *Hatari!* and *Psycho* unexpectedly draws attention to coincidences of narrative and theme. Like *Psycho*, *Le Mépris* is separated into two distinct parts; the first takes place over the course of one day during which the ordinariness of everyday life is overtaken by catastrophe: Marion's crime and death in one case and the loss of Camille's love in the other. Although the second part of *Psycho* is not, as in *Le Mépris*, streamlined into a single day, both films are overshadowed by fate: what might seem a minor ethical failing (on the part of Paul and Marion) is punished beyond reason by 'the gods' of narrativity. The relevance of *Hatari!* is more thematic and has less to do with narrative structure. The film repeats one of Hawks's preferred story settings: a small group of people are arbitrarily thrown together in some isolated situation, in which death and love intermingle with the group's internal dynamics. The Hawksian group has a certain resonance for *Le Mépris*: here, again a small group of people are thrown together by the chance contact of their profession creating a drama of professional and personal conflicts and loyalties.

I would like to end by reflecting on the particular importance of *Viaggio in Italia* for *Le Mépris*, due not only to the filming of the statues of the gods but also more generally to the story of a marriage in crisis. Here, the latent references to cinema history link specifically to the modernism of quotation as a formal device. Godard confirms the relevance of Rossellini's film very precisely: at the end of the 'audition' scene, the group leave the cinema and pause to talk outside, allowing a poster for *Viaggio in Italia* to be clearly seen in the background. *Viaggio* introduces another kind of palimpsest in its relation to *Le Mépris*. In the first instance, the story of Paul and Camille's marriage re-inscribes that of Emilia and Riccardo from the novel Il *Disprezzo*, creating another temporal layer, just as any adaptation must necessarily hover behind its retelling. In *Viaggio in Italia*, Alex and Katherine Joyce are an English couple staying in Naples whose marriage, quite suddenly, falls apart. During one of their embittered exchanges, Katherine turns to Alex with the words: 'I despise you'. But just as Godard uses the quarrelling couple in *Le Mépris* to quote *Viaggio*, so Rossellini inserts into his film, without acknowledging the source, the troubled marriage in James Joyce's 'The Dead'. Katherine retells Joyce's story as though transposed to her own memory. She reminds Alex that she had once been loved by a young man who had then died; his sensibility and his poetry continue to haunt her and irritate Alex, contributing to their deteriorating relationship. Although Rossellini uses the story for his own fiction, making no hint of its status as citation, it shares something of Iampolski's anomaly, inserting, due to a feeling of excess or oddity, a kind of blockage into a text. Katherine's monologue is quite long and furnished with a few details that belong to the original. Ultimately, Rossellini does provide a clue to its source through the couple's name: Joyce. The layering of references to a marriage in crisis across the Moravia's novel, Rossellini's film and Joyce's story creates an intertextual network that ends most appropriately with Godard's *Le Mépris*.

From this perspective, the presence of *Viaggio in Italia* in *Le Mépris* does considerably more than cite a director of the greatest importance to Godard. In *Viaggio*, the memory of the dead young man acts as a figure for a more general metaphor of haunting, but it also acts as a figure for the ghostly nature of quotation itself. The relationship of *Le Mépris* to *Viaggo in Italia* and its specific reference to Joyce generate a fragile link to his *Ulysses*, his retelling of *The Odyssey* into the great epic of modernist literature, itself a palimpsest of quotation and reference. These links bear witness to the significance of quotation as a modernist strategy and the way that a citation from the past works as an aesthetic device precisely for the destruction of tradition and the generation of the modern.

The blurb that accompanied the London Consortium's seminar on *Le Mépris* specifically mentioned the film as 'a fabric of quotations'. The phrase, coming from Roland Barthes's 1967 essay 'The Death of the Author', is a reminder that Godard's prolific and stylistic use of quotation and reference predates its theorisation. The origin of the phrase, however, is also a reminder that the search to trace the fragment and the anomaly to its source can never stabilise the uncertainty of meaning or pin down the intention that lies at the heart of quotation. Important and minor instances will always remain overlooked, hidden and locked. But all the same, Godard's use of allusion and reference, palimpsest and living quotation creates a layered form of film reading. The experience of watching the film, for me, a *cinéphile* formed by the *Cahiers politique des auteurs*, involves the triggering of memories and the recognition of the special significance of films and directors cited. For instance, the sudden, unmotivated and anomalous reference to Nicholas Ray's *Johnny Guitar* leads me back to the particular emotional resonance the film had for *Cahiers*-influenced *cinéphiles*. And the reference links back to Godard's earlier film *Le Petit Soldat* in which he quotes dialogue between Joan Crawford and Sterling Hayden ('tell me lies') and forward to its nearly invisible but key place in *Pierrot le Fou*. It is because Ferdinand had allowed the maid to go to *Johnny Guitar* that Marianne comes to babysit and they meet again 'after five years'.

If the latent story of cinema exists, as in a palimpsest, in another layer of time and of meaning outside that of the fiction, enabling a detour into the quite different discourse, it also doubles back on an allegorical level into the film's manifest content. Just as the spectator struggles to decipher the film's quotations, so Paul struggles to decipher Camille. Alongside, or overshadowed by, the enigma of Camille and her desirability are signs and clues suggesting that the cinema has a similar status for Godard as enigma and the elusive object of desire. And on this allegorical level, Paul and Camille's lost love and their mutual inability to understand their emotional history relates to Godard's sense of loss at the disappearance of the cinema that had formed him so completely. Just as Paul promises at the end of the film to become the writer he had always wanted to be, out of the ruins of his lost love, so Godard turned into a New Wave director, out of the ruins of his love of 1950 Hollywood cinema. As always for Godard, the beauty and inscrutability of his female star and of cinema are fused in his aesthetic and erotic sensibility. Ultimately, the use of quotation in *Le Mépris* shifts the uncertainty of emotion to the spectator. The uncertainties of attribution, the abrupt anomalies that erupt into the text, leave the spectator with a sense of yearning for understanding, always conscious of just missing a point, contented with some moments of satisfied recognition. In addition to its modernist significance, its layering of the text (as formal device and latent story), quotation puts the spectator into the situation of longing and loss that characterise the 'feeling' of the film as a whole.

Film Details

Original title	Le Mépris
Release year	1963
Country	France, Italy
Book	Jean-Luc Godard
Direction	Jean-Luc Godard
Music	George Delerue, Piero Piccioni
Camera	Raoul Cotard
Main actors	Brigitte Bardot, Michel Piccoli
Availability	DVD, Blu-ray

References

Aumont J (2000) 'Godard's Le Mépris'. In: Hayward S, Vincendeau G (eds) French film: texts and contexts. Routledge, London, p 176

Jean-Luc Godard par Jean-Luc Godard (1968) Editions Pierre Belfond, Paris, p. 28.

Gunning T (2000) Fritz Lang. The British Film Institute, London, p 6

Iampolski M (1998a) The memory of tiresias. In: Intertextuality and film. University of California Press, San Francisco and Los Angeles, p 30

Iampolski M (1998b) The memory of tiresias. In: Intertextuality and film. University of California Press, San Francisco and Los Angeles, p 31

Marie M (1990) Le Mépris. Editions Nathan, Paris, p 14

Schatz T (1998) The genius of the system. Hollywood film-making in the studio era. Faber and Faber, London, p 4

Wollen P (1982) 'The Two Avant-gardes'. In: Readings and writings: semiotic counter– strategies. Verso, London, p 102

4 Look Behind the Veil: What Is Actually 'Obscure' About Luis Buñuel's film, That Obscure Object of Desire? (Cet obscur objet du désir, F, ES 1977)

Manfred Riepe

> *La donna è mobile*
>
> *Verdi, Rigoletto*

A girl in a railway compartment asks the man sitting opposite why he had just poured a bucket of water on a woman [on the platform]. The child's impertinent curiosity embarrasses her mother. But the elderly gentleman she is addressing, who looks respectable and not the sort of person you would expect to behave so absurdly, proves to be very polite. He does not hesitate to explain himself. And as this explanation begins, shown in flashback, so does the story of this enigmatic film.

It is the tragicomic failed liaison of an elderly bon vivant, Mathieu, who falls under the spell of a significantly younger woman, Chonchita, and repeatedly makes a fool of himself. Even the title That Obscure Object of Desire indicates a probably trivial motif, namely, the often and diversely explored subject of the mystery of female attraction. The woman confronts the man with an unsolvable riddle (Fig. 4.1).

However, Luis Buñuel explores this motif in his own way. The title of the film itself mentions a key concept of psychoanalysis, namely, that of the object. The founder of psychoanalysis famously defined the object is 'the thing in regard to which or through which the instinct [drive] is able to achieve its aim', specifically: 'It is what is most variable about an instinct [drive] and is not originally connected with it, but becomes assigned to it only in consequence of being peculiarly fitted to make satisfaction possible' (1915, p.122). Freud already understood the object to be an almost incidental possibility of satisfying the

M. Riepe (✉)
Frankfurt, Germany

V. Pramataroff-Hamburger, A. Hamburger (eds.), *From La Strada to The Hours*,
https://doi.org/10.1007/978-3-662-68789-5_4

Fig. 4.1 Mathieu (Fernando Rey) falls for the seductive Conchita (Carole Bouquet) (00:28:38)

drive; he sees an irreducible gap[gulf] between the subject and the (genital) object. In contrast, later object relations theorists such as Donald Winnicott, Michael Balint or William Fairbairn conceived the object as part of a pre-established harmony. Freud's conflictual drive model was replaced by the concept of a natural maturation of the sexual drives, which establishes a relation between subject and object according to the lock-and-key principle. If the subject fails to achieve a satisfying sexual relationship, it is the task of the analyst to help the patient achieve mature object relations.

From the perspective of such an ideal, the behaviour depicted in Buñuel's film is the result of anything but a mature object relation. The question arises: Is the failure of a sexual encounter that Buñuel and his scriptwriter Jean-Claude Carrière present the cinematic equivalent of a patient whom the analyst must assist in achieving satisfying object relations? Do the protagonists fulfil 'the criteria for narcissistic personality disorder in Mathieu and histrionic personality disorder in Conchita', as the psychiatrists surmise in their interpretation of That Obscure Object of Desire according to the DSM IV diagnostic manual (Dulz and Kohlmorgen 2014, p. 311)?

Or could the opposite be said to be true? Is a failed encounter recorded on film actually not to be taken as an indication of a pathological deviation? Rather, does it show the object as Freud defines it? Does the masterful depiction of the withdrawal of the genital object in Buñuel's film even cause sexual desire in the first place?

According to Freud, pleasure is inseparable from the allure of the beautiful, but this is a paradoxical concept. Freud said, 'There is to my mind no doubt that the concept of "beautiful" has its roots in sexual excitation and that its original meaning was "sexually stimulating"'. His footnote in later editions is interesting: 'This is related to the fact that we never regard the genitals themselves, which produce the strongest sexual excitation, as really "beautiful"' (1905, p. 155). [Three Essays] Is Freud perhaps not already describing the obscurity of the object here?

Since the subject of sight as dealt with by Freud also has to do with cinema and the way femininity was portrayed in it, the view of Buñuel's film presented here expands to include both striking examples of cinema history and a key aspect of psychoanalytic theory. I would therefore like to address the question of sexual difference in the context of Freud's theory of femininity, against the background of the specifically visual aspect of fetishism, which will be discussed in connection with [voyeuristic] curiosity in cinema. Thus, in discussing sexual difference and Freud's theory of femininity, we can refer to the specifically visual aspect of the fetish, which is closely related to curiosity in cinema.

The brilliant casting of two actresses in the female leading role, which is a unique selling point of the film, will lead us to the film's enigmatic final scene, in which for the first time Mathieu stands in harmony next to Conchita, the obscure object, watching a seamstress mend a dress in the window of a shopping arcade: What exactly interests him about this bloody piece of cloth that is being sewn up? Does this motif have anything to do with the character of the obscure and of fetish?

Plot

The plot is divided into partially interlocking episodes. In the first one, Mathieu, played by Buñuel's favourite actor Fernando Rey, meets his new housekeeper Conchita for the first time. She has been hired that day by his servant. With a matter-of-factness that suggests a well-rehearsed habit, he tries to seduce the woman who is dependent on him. Annoyingly for him, she refuses and leaves his house without having given an address. Thus, the first episode ends.

Months later, he meets her again in Switzerland, apparently by chance. She is accompanied by some young men who had previously stolen some money from him, which she is now returning to him. She tells him her address in a poor Parisian neighbourhood, where she lives with her deeply devout mother, who, despite exhorting her daughter to maintain high moral standards, accepts money and food from her daughter's wealthy suitor. Mathieu is thus confirmed in his belief that he can buy Conchita. However, he waits in vain in a flat that he has prepared as a love nest. Conchita tells the admirer in writing that she cannot be bought. He finds the mother and daughter's flat abandoned.

Sometime later, Mathieu meets Conchita again (in the very restaurant where he dines with his cousin, an influential judge who later has the unruly mistress and her mother deported from France—apparently at Mathieu's instigation). Conchita works there as a dresser. When her boss reprimands her, she decides to quit her job and follows Mathieu to his country house, promising to finally succumb to him there. But when he expectantly pulls back the covers, he sees that she is wearing a tightly laced corset that cannot be opened no matter how hard he tries.

Although Conchita does not comply with him, he continues to let her stay with him. However, after he catches her with a young lover, he angrily throws them both out of the house. Without her, however, he falls into melancholia, until he learns that Conchita has found a job as a dancer in Seville. He follows her but discovers to his horror that she is posing as a stripper in a back room in front of Asian tourists. There is a commotion [scandal]. To reconcile his mistress, he buys her a house. But when he visits her there expectantly, she allows him to witness her succumbing to a young lover the other side of the barred courtyard door.

Contrary to expectations, she returns to him the next day, apparently remorseful. A scuffle ensues, during which Mathieu loses his temper and beats the young woman. Conchita makes off. The humiliated humiliator then boards the train to Paris, where Conchita follows him. At the end of the journey, which also ends Mathieu's story, Conchita returns the favour by now pouring a bucket of water over Mathieu. This reciprocity apparently leads to reconciliation. In the French capital, they are both strolling through a shopping mall when a bomb planted by terrorists goes off.

The Background

That Obscure Object of Desire, from 1977, is Luis Buñuel's last film. The director was 77 years old at the time of filming. Five years later, he died. The film is based on Pierre Louÿs' 1898 bestseller La Femme et le Pantin, which was published in English in 1908 under the title the Woman and Puppet, translated by G.F. Monkshood. The novel has often been made into a film, first in 1919 as a silent film with the title The Woman and the Puppet and then, in 1928 by Jacques de Baroncelli, followed in 1935 by Josef von Sternberg starring Marlene Dietrich (The Devil is a Woman). When Julien Duvivier's fourth film adaptation was released in 1959 under the German title Ein Weib wie Satan (A Woman Like Satan) with Brigitte Bardot, Buñuel himself had already thought of adapting the book. He dropped the project, however, only to take it up again almost 20 years later (Vincenzo Orlando mentions other film versions in the epilogue to the new translation of the novel, cf. Louÿs 1898, p. 170 f.).

According to Jean-Claude Carrière, the renowned screenwriter, who wrote the script for The Unbearable Lightness of Being (1988) and The Tin Drum (1979), among others and with whom Buñuel collaborated five times, namely, on The Specter of Freedom (1974), The Discreet Charm of the Bourgeoisie (1972), The Milky Way (1969), Belle de Jour (1967) and Diary of a Chambermaid (1964), Pierre Louÿs is one of three authors with whom the director had repeatedly had dealings. The other two are Octave Mirbeau and Joris Karl Huysmans. Buñuel filmed a novel by the former, Portrait of a Chambermaid, a story which shares several themes with That Obscure Object of Desire. Buñuel also intended to make Huysmans' book Tief unten [Downstream] from 1891 into a film, but he dropped the project because he was afraid it would overly fulfil the expectation of a Buñuel film.

All three authors, with whom Buñuel felt a spiritual affinity, were adherents of Symbolism, a movement that began in the late nineteenth century. This nineteenth-century genre of art and literature was inspired by Stéphane Mallarmé and is not concerned with the naturalistic depiction of social realities but with a radical subjectivism characterised by decadence, expressed in the creation of aesthetically exaggerated art worlds. In the spirit of such a symbolist worldview, Buñuel and Carrière create the main character of a (puppet) man, a wealthy idler who leads the life of a playboy but has the outward appearance of an aristocrat who is not affected by the banality of social reality even when he is robbed or bombs go off around him. The motifs of the story about a femme fatale hover between Prosper Mérimée's 1847 novella Carmen and Vladimir Nabokov's 1955 novel Lolita.

In contrast to Buñuel's earlier films from is surrealist phase, Mathieu's story is told in a comparatively conventional way. This return to [solid] conventionality is also reflected in the choice of subject matter, boy meets girl, which in some measure is the stock in trade of popular narrative cinema and also runs through many of Buñuel's films. However, the director transforms this supposedly banal subject by using a unique device that has gone down in cinema history. He cast two actresses in the leading female role, an astonishing move even to this day. Like many striking ideas in film history, this unusual remedy came about by pure chance, born out of necessity. Buñuel had already begun filming, but his original leading lady Maria Schneider, who had risen to fame in her role in Bertolucci's film The Last Tango in Paris (1972) five years earlier, was so ill suited to the director's ideas that he was ready to abandon the project.

Producer Serge Silbermann, Buñuel's long-time assistant, urged the directors to go out and look for alternative actresses. Before long, screen tests were held with Carole Bouquet, who was 18 years old at the time and new to the film industry, and with Ángela Molina, a flamenco dancer who was also an unknown but who had already worked in television. Since Buñuel liked both actresses equally, he was faced with the dilemma of having to choose one. The almost deaf director was dejected at the time because he was worried that his last project would fail. However, legend has it that the following day he came to the set with shining eyes and declared he would take them both.

The casting of two actors in the lead role is rare in popular cinema. This defiance of convention is immediately recognisable, for example, in Tod Solondz's Palindromes (2004) or in Ultimately, the Universe Doesn't Care About Us (2019). However, the experimental nature of these films seems top-heavy and monotonous. This is not the case in That Obscure Object of Desire, where the double casting fits seamlessly into the narrative cohesion. The swap is always unpredictable and there is no set role type assigned to each actress, making the double casting seem irritating to this day. Thanks to this artifice, the content of the film coincides amazingly well with the way it is presented. Due to the double casting, which is mentioned in the opening credits but not addressed in the film, the object of desire, in other words the desired woman, becomes utterly obscure. But what exactly does obscure mean in this context?

This problem is reflected in the cinematic narrative, which does not progress in a straight line, as the initial rendering of the plot suggests, but is framed several times. Thus, the story of the (puppet) man pursuing a younger woman who rejects him, only to lure him back, is underscored at the beginning by that martial bon mot from Friedrich Nietzsche's Thus Spoke Zarathustra, which is quoted by Mathieu's servant in colloquial form: If you go to see a woman, you must not forget the whip. In the film, however, it is rather the woman who symbolically holds the whip.

There is a further framing: during a train journey, the prevented lover himself recounts his story to fellow passengers; a psychologist of small stature, a public prosecutor and a mother with her daughter. 'Through this dissipated frame narrative', says Hans Blumenberg, 'which clearly points to the traditions of the bourgeois novel, the plot seems particularly absurd in the flashbacks. Mathieu recounts his obsession as if in a civilised society play. The surrealistic tension of the film arises from the contrast between the old-fashioned narrative style and the occasionally bizarre actions: how a bourgeois erotomaniac persists with the composure of his high rank until the double Conchita has turned him into a whimpering jumping jack ...' (Blumenberg 1978).

Obscure Femininity?

On the way to an interpretation, we are reminded that the series of terrorist attacks woven into the narrative thread is no less obscure than two background actors. One is the aforementioned servant who almost always accompanies Mathieu. In one scene, Mathieu suddenly realises that he has never spoken to him about anything personal. Aside from the master-servant theme, this casual emphasis on anonymity indirectly allows a glimpse of the fantasy of availability that is typical of a certain kind of homoerotic object choice. The homoerotic theme is echoed in the scene in which the thwarted lover suggests anal intercourse as an alternative to the reluctant Conchita, who wishes to keep her virginity intact. Thus, the nature of the obscurity of the object is, in part, that different forms of sexual orientation are at least hinted at.

Another striking secondary character is Conchita's mother. Although she talks and acts like her daughter's pimp in the scenes in which Mathieu visits them in their shabby flat, it still seems like a family home. One aspect of the varying motifs of the object's inaccessibility is obviously connected to the prohibition on incest. You're not my father, says Conchita to Mathieu at one point, which she would not need to say if he were not, at least on a fantasised level. This association is supported by the later scene in Mathieu's country estate. In this house, Conchita grandiosely promises, I shall become your mistress. However, at this point, believing himself to be so close to finally reaching his heart's desire, Mathieu presses the young woman, who in his fantasy is his daughter, to have relations under the photo of his deceased wife, of all things. And she once more rebuffs him on these grounds (Fig. 4.2).

The two symmetrical scenes, in which Mathieu first douses the maligned lover with a bucket of water, to which she later reciprocates in kind, seem to indicate that they have equal rights in the relationship, in the sense that the roles are interchangeable. But this is

Fig. 4.2 Conchita (Ángela Molina) drives Mathieu (Fernando Rey) crazy (00:31:57)

contradicted by one of the first scenes in which the pair meet. With the help of this servant, Mathieu arranges a veritable scene in which Conchita, who has yet to serve him a nightcap, is to fall into his trap. She is the object; he the subject.

The fact that the longed-for sexual act does not take place may also be related one of Mathieu's fears, which is casually illustrated when he hears a mousetrap loudly snap shut just as he is handing Conchita's mother a thick wad of notes with which he intends to buy her daughter from her. This trapped mouse, however, is not only the recalcitrant lover: through a Freudian twist, it could also represent the narcissistically engaged organ that is repeatedly wounded by rejection. One could thus interpret the scene as a castration fantasy. The banishment of this castration anxiety is related to a marginal motif that first appears in rare quiet moments, such as the beginnings of harmony arising between Mathieu and Conchita on that stroll. Conchita asks her companion the surprising and disarmingly banal question, Why do you want to sleep with me so badly?—to which he replies: All people who love each other do that.

In this scene, a 'moment of truth', for the first time Buñuel and Carrière smuggle in the surreal-seeming motif, wholly absent from the book, that seems to have nothing to do with the manifest narrative. Namely, the ominous cloth sack that Mathieu sometimes carries over his shoulder. At one point, a servant asks him for the sack, and on arrival at the station in Paris, it can incidentally be seen lying on a luggage trolley.

During the final scene in the Paris shopping arcade, we finally learn something about the contents of this sack. After Conchita served food in the first scene (thus appearing in an oral context) and later returned stolen money to Mathieu (an anal motif), according to the usual interpretation of the fairy tale The Wishing Table, there should be a cudgel symbolising the phallus in this sack. This idea is not entirely wrong, but it is also not quite right, either: We do not know why, but the sack is in a shop window, where a woman sitting there takes a bloodstained dress from it, among other things (in this scene, for the second time Buñuel and Carrière deviate from the book, which they otherwise follow to the letter). A close-up shows how the dress has been inserted into an embroidery frame, on which the seamstress is repairing the fabric: Mathieu, it has already been noted, pays a lot of attention to this scene. What does he want to see here? Does this dress being sewn have anything to do with the obscurity of the object? And if so, what?

Laura Mulvey and the Visual Pleasure of Narrative Cinema

In her famous essay of 1975, Laura Mulvey uses the concept of the object, but she tries to turn it critically against Freud's understanding. She characterises classical Hollywood cinema as seeking to visualise femininity in that repressive form as a reified object, which is also the theme of Buñuel's film. Thus, quite a few theorists declared this short text to be the feminist bible. On the one hand, according to Mulvey, the film illusion creates a familiar perspectival space similar to that of Renaissance painting, which seems to resemble reality. On the other hand, the representation of the female body in close-ups breaks this illusion by triggering desire and fear in the (male) viewer. In this constructed world, the male protagonist, with whom Mulvey believes men and women in the auditorium identify equally, exercises his authority by respectively having the female protagonist put on display. While the man controlled the film's fantasy, the woman was visualised as a sexual object according to an active-passive heterosexual division of labour. Mulvey uses a wealth of examples, essentially from Hitchcock and von Sternberg, to plausibly argue that traditional Hollywood films do indeed repeatedly proffer variations on such a narrative.

When the female star on screen descends from Olympus like a goddess, this reflects the ruling ideology with its paternal phallocentrism. Women's image on the screen has 'continually been stolen and used for this end' (Mulvey 1975, p. 65). This theft, the author continues, is based on 'the beauty of the woman as [an obscure] object', which is 'immediately associated with castration'. Mulvey's central criticism is that woman 'can exist only in relation to castration and cannot transcend it' (ibid.), because both castration and the lack of a penis 'are posited on nature (or on anatomy in Freud's famous phrase)'. She goes on to say that psychoanalysis is in the service of this oppression since, according to Freud's paradigm of anatomy as destiny, it objectifies women and has the psychical structures to back this up and thus exclude women from the symbolic order.

However, the corollary of her own argument is that the mere objectification of women is by no means enough to explain the fascination exerted by classical Hollywood cinema which Mulvey so convincingly summarises—and which Buñuel also reflects in his film. If, as Mulvey points out, '[t]he presence of woman [on screen] is an indispensable element of spectacle in normal narrative film, yet her visual presence tends to work against the development of a story line, to freeze the flow of action in moments of erotic contemplation' (ibid.). In which case, then surely the phenomenon of female sexuality, which Hollywood film repeatedly portrays, must be more complex than Mulvey's reduction of femininity to mere 'physical beauty of the object' (Mulvey, ibid.)? After all, as Mulvey indirectly suggests, that special something which portrays 'the magic of the Hollywood style at its best' (ibid.) must surely be a moment that is always sought anew: a moment with a complex structure that does not interrupt the plot but, as Buñuel's film also demonstrates, artfully induces it, time and again.

This extraordinary moment is connected in each case to the fact that the supposedly stolen beauty of women is not an objective state of nature. Female attractiveness on screen is based on staging and masquerade, which also represent Conchita's obscurity. Lacan remarks that masquerade and/or clothing, not only in film but in general, does not merely serve to 'hide the pudenda' (Lacan 1994 [1956-57], p. 166). 'In all clothing', he says, 'there is something that participates in the function of transvestitism' (ibid.). Therefore, the pith of Lacan's interpretation of Freud states that 'clothes are not only there to hide what one has—in the sense of having or not having—but also precisely what one does not have' (ibid., p. 195). But why does 'what you don't have' have to be hidden at all? Or rather: What is it that 'you don't have'?

This question ties in with the above-mentioned paradox, according to which 'we never regard the genitals themselves, which produce the strongest sexual excitation, as really "beautiful"' (1905, p. 155). Hitchcock's Vertigo is also about precisely this paradox: The film's famous denouement, which has gone down in the history of cinema, is that Judy, the vulgar brunette, almost entirely transforms herself into the policeman's ideal image under his meticulous direction. However, something is still missing: Madeleine was wearing a necklace with a striking gemstone. When Judy finally puts on this necklace—which can only be owned by the woman who, in the policeman's view, is dead, the latter suddenly and painfully realises that Judy and Madeleine are one and the same person and that she has deceived him. But that is only the manifest level of the narrative. The decisive point is that the moment the object has been reconstructed to perfection, it abruptly loses all its erotic appeal or its aura of obscurity.

On the latent level, the necklace thus represents something that was hidden beyond the veil and was surprisingly mirrored into 'this world'. The dialectic outlined by Lacan, according to which clothes hide not only what one has but also what one does not have, comes down to the fact that what is hidden behind the 'veil' or under the skirt or behind the cinema screen is something which cannot be represented in the usual sense. For this reason, the veil itself participates in that lack which it conceals. The moment when the policeman in Vertigo sees the necklace that completes the mosaic is also the moment when the function of the veil collapses—and thus, the reason for the object instantly losing all attraction; it is no longer obscure. It is the moment which popular German singer Udo Lindenberg croons about in his song 'Leider nur ein Vakuum', when Lady Horror is lying next to him after a night of heavy drinking. Buñuel's film also revolves around this special moment.

The Fetish

In Buñue''s film, as in Vertigo, the logic of the film narrative culminates in the fact that a certain something, which is connected with the woman in that it makes her desirable in the first place, is to be detached from her and isolated as an objectified something. As I have argued in my essay on Peeping Tom (Riepe 2019), the associated collapse of the eroticising effect of the object would be the imaginary endpoint of a specific exploratory movement familiar to psychoanalytic thought. It is the exploration in which the boy's curious eyes, which, as Freud states in his essay on fetishism, gradually wanders up his mother's legs until his inquiring gaze would finally get to see that impossible something which is his focus of interest but which frightens him at the same time: the mother's penis. With reference to Lacan, and the equally worthwhile reading of Elke Rövekamp's remarks on seeing the uncanny (in Das unheimliche Sehen), I have tried to show that a fetish is an imaginary object. For this reason, visual curiosity is structured like a permanent exploratory movement. This consists in the effort to appropriate the imagined object—the fetish. But this appropriation fails time and again. This permanent back and forth supports the repetitive movement of the search itself.

In their variation on Pierre Louÿs' novel ending, which relates how Conchita masochistically enjoys the man's beatings, Buñuel and Carrière introduce the motif of the dress sewn in the embroidery frame, which is not present in the original. They change the structure of the narrative and focus on the exploratory movement, the repeated postponement of the sexual encounter between Mathieu and his obscure object. This postponement coincides with a visual motif that, as I will now show, is related to the logic of the fetish; the fetish that Buñuel invokes with his last film image.

Before I return to that enigmatic piece of bloody fabric that is being repaired in the last frame of the film, notably by a woman's hand, I would like to recall two scenes in which the display of a specific moment of the obscure object's visualisation also concerns the fetish. In the Parisian flat, for example, Conchita poses provocatively in front of the mirror while Mathieu looks into it over her shoulder—a scene that does not appear in the book. She later also poses in the country house, this time completely naked, in front of the mirror into which Mathieu and she are looking together: This scene is also missing from the novel. The pleasure Conchita obviously feels as she gleefully looks at herself in the mirror surely results from the fact that she also sees Mathieu pining for her (Fig. 4.3)

In this sense, especially in the scene in the back room of the flamenco bar, where Conchita strips professionally, Mathieu is incensed with rage. He needs to see—in a double sense. He needs to see that others want to see the same thing as he does. And he has to accept that to Conchita he is no different from one of those faceless Asian tourists who gawk at the object of his desire in the same way.

This scene is described in greater detail than in the film in Pierre Louÿs' original literary version: The narrator Don Mateo says, 'never had I seen her so beautiful. Dress creases always disfigure a dancer's expression and do not allow her true grace to shine. But here, like a revelation, I saw gestures, tremors, movements of her arms, her legs, her supple

Fig. 4.3 Mathieu (Fernando Rey) is repeatedly led up the garden path by Conchita (Carole Bouquet) (00:52:11)

body and the muscular loins that seemed to be constantly renewing themselves before my eyes: from the centre of the dance itself, her little black-brown belly' (Louÿs 1898, p. 97, emphasis: M.R.).

This obscure something that seemed to be 'constantly renewing itself before my eyes'—does it not mirror the classic Hollywood film that, in the course of presenting femininity, keeps heading for that magic moment that, as Mulvey wrote, tends to 'freeze the flow of action in moments of erotic contemplation' (Mulvey 1975, p. 55)? And this repeating structure: Does it not coincide with the searching gaze for the maternal penis that pauses just before the traumatic moment and begins again?

As Elke Rövekamp elaborates in her differentiated psychoanalysis of the gaze, the perception of the fetish is not an isolatable quantity (Rövekamp 2013, p. 327) in the sense of a still image (which is why Mark's project fails in Peeping Tom). Instead, it is 'integrated into temporal sequences and cognitive processes' (ibid., p. 327). The boy's gaze Freud described as wandering up a woman's legs is therefore not conceived spatially so much as temporally. Consequently, the expectation of seeing the woman's penis is not linked to the idea of immediately and simultaneously being able to grasp the object in a field of vision. This is already implied in Freud's formulation: 'It seems rather that when the fetish is instituted some process occurs which reminds one of the stopping of memory in traumatic amnesia. As in this latter case, the subject's interest comes to a halt half-way, as it were; it is as though the last impression before the uncanny and traumatic one is retained as a fetish'. (1928 [1927e]: 154) Freud clearly wishes to express that in the fetishistic structure the obscure, in the truest sense of the word, object of interest becomes such by way of a gradual approach to the visualisation of female castration. As Lacan specified, the dimension of time is crucial for the formation of the fetish because, according to Rövekamp, 'it does not arise directly from perception, but afterwards, from the memory of a visual impression of an object' (ibid.).

One suspects that this staging of a fictitious memory of the logically impossible 'perception of something absent' (ibid.) has something in common with the cinema-specific phenomenon that, since Hitchcock, has become known as suspense. One senses that the masquerade which hides what one does not have, the something, the fetish, is actually created by the logic of the staging. When Mulvey and along with her the feminist critique of Freud and Lacan object that the concept of female castration naturally objectifies woman, this critique omits the fact that, like the cinema screen, the masquerade hides an imaginary 'obscure' thing that only comes into existence through this masquerade.

The bloody piece of cloth that is repaired by a woman's hand sewing in the closing scene of That Obscure Object of Desire exists in a subtly woven focus between narrative and motif, form and content. Thus, we must recall, the plot is cyclical in structure. Mathieu boards the train at the very beginning of the film. However, the story he goes on to tell has already happened at this point. This ambiguity indirectly points to a detail that is easy to overlook: Mathieu, who kids himself that he is quite a gentleman, sends his accompanying servant into the second-class train compartment, where he is met by a heavily pregnant woman. The girl with the big belly is not Conchita but has something to do with her in terms of motif, because her name, Conchita, is short for concepción, the conception that cannot be separated thematically from Mathieu's desire.

The incidental portrayal which implies the goal of his efforts goes hand in hand with a pregnancy (which he does not want on a conscious level) is again related to the argument Mathieu had with Conchita before leaving Madrid. We recall: She came back towards Mathieu. A scuffle ensued; Mathieu hit her. The stick came 'out of the bag'. Conchita's nose bled—her dress was also stained with it. What is not shown in this scene is Mathieu deflowering Conchita. In the film, this interpretation remains problematic because it is unclear whether she had in fact already given herself to her young lover in the 'primal scene' staged for Mathieu. In the novel, however, Conchita enlightens her admirer: 'I am still a virgin. What happened yesterday was only a comedy ...' (Louÿs 1898, p. 117).

The bloody dress, the repair of which Mathieu contemplates at the end as if hypnotised—while the love duet from Wagner's Valkyrie drowns out his words—is thus not only associated with defloration but also with its consequences for the one who performs it. In his essay on The Taboo of Virginity, Freud explains that defloration has become for the man 'has become the subject of a taboo—of a prohibition which may be described as religious. Instead of reserving it for the girl's bridegroom and future partner in marriage, custom demands that he shall shun the performance of it' (1918, p. 193). According to Freud, it was a matter of 'denying or sparing precisely the future husband something which cannot be dissociated from the first sexual act' (ibid. p. 199).

This ominous something, which cannot be detached from the first sexual act, is also the subject of the enigmatic final scene, which is marked by Mathieu's hypnotised gaze. This final image, which, according to co-screenwriter Carrière, was so important to Buñuel that he rearranged it two weeks after filming had finished, has been linked to another emblematic image found at the very beginning of Buñuel's oevre: the cut eye in Un chien andalou from 1929, a scene that contributes to the birth of his work and left its mark on cinema history. After the surrealist and poetic gesture of destruction that gives rise to the act of creation, says film historian Arnaud Duprat, the next necessary stage is that of repair, without which no other work would have been created.

This repair of the fabric, the interpretation suggests, is a motivic counterpart to what the policeman sees in Vertigo when Judy puts on the necklace that completes the constructed ideal image of the desired woman and thus destroys the erotic desire of the object. It is the gradual approach of the fetish that, respectively, structures the film narrative. Like the policeman in Vertigo, Mathieu gets too close to the fetish[istic object]. It is no coincidence that shortly after he has seen this piece of cloth, the explosion occurs which tears him and Conchita apart in the final scene.

Conclusion

According to the basic paradigm of the object-relations theory which is anchored in the minds of quite a few post-Freudian analysts, generally speaking right and a wrong exist; to be precise, a fulfilled sexual encounter and its pathogenic disorder. According to this view, Buñuel's film clearly illustrates something that is wrong, a pathological deviation from an illusorily assumed harmony. Psychoanalyst Peter Canzler describes the struggle between Mathieu and Conchita as not a relationship between equals (Canzler 2005, p. 67). For Mathieu, 'the mistress is not a substitute for his deceased wife' (ibid.). Therefore, he remains 'an invasive father to the end' (ibid., p. 67). According to this interpretation, Conchita is 'depriving herself of her own femininity' (ibid.). She 'does not become a woman, but pretends to be' (ibid.). This raises the question: If she were not just pretending, would Conchita then be a bona fide replacement for his late wife? Would there then be a harmonious coming together? What kind of film would that be?

Against the background of the argumentation touched upon here, things look rather different. Buñuel's film relates a sexual encounter that fails. At the same time, however, it seems that something about this failure is working. There is a method to the failure—a method that is often varied, especially in traditional Hollywood melodrama. Buñuel distorts this narrative beyond recognition. He not only tells the story of a (puppet) man whom the object constantly attracts, only to refuse him again afterwards. At the same time, he depicts the characteristic that makes the object as such. Buñuel's film is a meditation on that moment of obscurity that is inherent in the object and without which there would be no object. When Freud, in his essay 'On the Universal Tendency to Debasement of the Sphere of Love"(1912), puts forward the thesis according to which, "however strange it may sound, we must reckon with the possibility that something in the nature of the sexual instinct [drive] itself is unfavourable to the realization of complete satisfaction' (1912,

p. 89). Lacan reads from this non-realisation of full satisfaction the structural logic of the object in itself. In this concept, that which appears to be wrong or pathological in object relations theory becomes the essence of the object itself. Lacan explains it thus in his late 1970 seminar: 'The going wrong, that is the object' (Lacan 1975, p. 55). To add: 'The essence of the object, that is going wrong'.

Translated by Annette Caroline Christmas

Film Details

Original title	Cet obscur objet du désir
Release year	1977
Country	France/Spain
Book/Idea	Luis Buñuel, Jean-Claude Carrière, based on a novel by Pierre Louÿs
Direction	Luis Buñuel
Music	Richard Wagner et al.
Camera	Edmond Richard
Main actor	Fernando Rey, Carole Bouquet, Ángela Molina, André Weber, Julien Bertheau
Availability	DVD, Blu-ray, Streaming (Amazon Video)

References

Blumenberg H (1978) Frau und Hampelmann. Die Zeit 17(11):1978

Canzler P (2005) Luis Buñuel: that obscure object of desire. In: Schneider G, Bär P (eds) Luis Buñuel, In Dialogue. Psychoanalyse und Filmtheorie [Psychoanalysis and Film Theory], vol 3. Cinema Quadrat, Institute for Psychoanalysis and Psychotherapy, Mannheim, pp 64–69

Dulz B, Kohlmorgen J (2014) Die Last mit der Lust. Oder: Über Liebe und Triebe. [The burden of lust. Or: About love and instincts]. In: Doering S, Möller H (eds) Mon Amour trifft pretty woman. Liebespaare im film. Springer, Heidelberg

Freud S (1905) Three essays on the theory of sexuality. The Standard Edition of the complete psychological works of Sigmund Freud, vol. VII, p. 126

Freud S (1912) On the universal tendency to debasement of the sphere of love. In: Three essays on the theory of sexuality

Freud S (1915) Instincts and their vicissitudes. Standard Edition, vol. XIV p. 117–140.

Freud S (1918 [1917]) The Taboo of virginity (contributions to the psychology of love III). SW 11:193–208

Lacan J (1975 [1972–73]) The Seminar of Jacques Lacan, book XX. Encore. Seuil

Lacan J (1994 [1956–57]) The Seminar of Jacques Lacan, book IV. La ralation d'objet. Seuil

Louÿs P (1898 [1993]) That obscure object of desire. DTV, Munich

Mulvey L (1975) Visual pleasure and narrative cinema. In: Screen, vol. 16, (Autumn 1975), pp 6–18 http://www.screen.arts.gla.ac.uk/ in http://screen.oxfordjournals.org AND: OUP (1992) Film: psychology, society and ideology, in film theory & criticism: introductory readings. edited by Gerald Mast, Marshall Cohen, and Leo Baudry, pp 803–816

Riepe M (2019) Medusas Blicke [Medusa's glance]. Notes on Michael Powell's Peeping Tom. Psyche Z Psychoanal 73:442–462

Rövekamp E (2013) Das unheimliche Sehen—Das Unheimliche sehen des unheimlichen. Zur Psychoanalyse des Blicks [On the psychoanalysis of the Gaze]. Psychosocial, Giessen

Part II

Strong Feelings. Women as Persistent Subjects

Poetry and Reality. Devastated Landscapes of the Soul: *La Strada* (*The Road,* I 1954)

5

Katharina Leube-Sonnleitner

Introduction

There are not many films that, like *La Strada*, evoke intense emotion, even deep sadness, in most viewers to this day. The simple story of a mismatched couple on their ill-fated journey through impoverished, rural post-war Italy, a road movie made before the term existed, marks the beginning of the global career of Fellini, who was born and raised in the provincial coastal town of Rimini in 1920. Fellini, formerly a gifted cartoonist, journalist and screenwriter, had already received much acclaim from audiences, juries and critics for his third feature film—*I Vitelloni* (*The Idlers*, 1953). However, *La Strada* entered the canon of most film critics and scholars as a masterpiece after winning countless international awards. The name of the brutish showman portrayed by Anthony Quinn, Zampanò even became a common word for a braggart and would-be leader in German, although not in Italian.

Fellini developed the film's script together with his co-author Tullio Pinelli, with whom he was to have a decade-long close collaboration and friendship. They started out with differing ideas, with Pinelli contributing a memory from his travels across the Apennines: 'And on one of the mountain passes I saw Zampanò and Gelsomina, that is, a colossal man pulling a covered cart with a mermaid painted on it and a little woman pushing it from behind. This stirred my memories of [...] all the markets and fairs, of people moving from one village to another, and of the unpunished crimes committed along the way' [own translation] (Kezich 2005, p. 227). The musical score, a work by the composer Nino Rota, with whom Fellini had an inspiring collaboration until his death, became world famous. For anyone who has seen the film, it is affectively inseparable from the fate of a simple girl from the lumpenproletariat.

K. Leube-Sonnleitner (✉)
Munich, Germany

V. Pramataroff-Hamburger, A. Hamburger (eds.), *From La Strada to The Hours*,
https://doi.org/10.1007/978-3-662-68789-5_5

Before shooting began, extremely laborious negotiations were held with a succession of producers; Ponti/de Laurentiis also did not want Giulietta Masina in the leading role, but finally acquiesced in the face of Fellini's resolve, also with regard to the rest of the cast. Fellini and Masina had married in Rome at the age of 23 and 22, respectively, shortly after the fall of Mussolini in 1943 during the Second World War. They remained married for half a century until his death in 1993. However, this was not the reason he insisted on her participation. He simply could not imagine any other actress in the meticulously planned role, which he himself had captured in drawings, having studied her everyday body language in detail. Anyone who has seen Giulietta Masina as Gelsomina knows he was absolutely right to cast her. As a director and writer, Fellini anticipated the later French *politique des auteurs*, the auteur film. He worked closely with his co-writers, actors, technology, music, etc. The atmosphere on his sets was often described as creative improvisation and adventure; even so, none of his collaborators would deny that every Fellini film wholly bears its author's signature. Fellini found his two male leads somewhat by chance during other shoots in Rome, and his unerring instinct for faces and personalities for his films was also already evident in these cases. The filming was arduous and full of privations, the budget low, the fees sometimes symbolic. Nevertheless, Anthony Quinn, who was later to become an international star, wrote the following to Fellini and Masina in 1990: 'You two are still the highlight of my life. Antonio' (after Kezich 2005, p. 233).

A film beyond time and space. A single *Esso* sign shows that we are in the post-war period; after the indication that we are in Rome, near *San Paolo fuori le Mura*, the church is only briefly glimpsed in the background.

Likenesses have often been drawn between film and dream, a comparison that is essentially inaccurate. Nevertheless, Fellini is possibly the director who borrowed most from his own dreams for his phantasmagorical film worlds and did so long before he became aware of psychoanalysis, particularly the work of C.G. Jung. Soon, dream, memory, fantasy and so-called reality were to be merged into formally and visually indistinguishable sequences in his masterpiece *Otto e Mezzo* (8 1/2, 1963). Something of this is already evident in *La Strada*.

Film Plot

A ragged, barefoot girl (Giulietta Masina) appears between the dunes and the seashore. Her numerous siblings are excitedly calling her, *Gelsomina, Gelsomina*, to come back to fatherless family's humble shack. The man with the motorbike cart, who had already taken her sister Rosa, had come. Now, Rosa is dead and the mother sells Gelsomina for ten thousand lire to the sinister stranger Zampanò (Anthony Quinn); apologetically, she describes her daughter as somewhat whimsical. Gelsomina's face openly expresses very contradictory feelings: Sadness because of Rosa, fear, curiosity, hope. As they drive away, the camera shows the titular road as it grows long and longer between the young girl and her family, everything she has known so far.

Their new life begins with the first of a total of five of the simple shows that the travelling showman Zampanò has to offer: He uses his pectoral muscles to burst open the hook of an iron chain placed around his chest. There is some sparse applause in a poor village square, and Gelsomina joins in. They later eat their meagre minestrone by a little campfire. She ladles hers down in secret, already showing us her comedic talent. He kits her out with clown shoes and an oversized military coat and teaches her with unwavering pride how to announce his performances with drum rolls and a chorus of praise. She later acts as a clown in *comedic*, rather simple numbers, for example, playing the role of a duck.

On the first evening, she sheepishly suggests sleeping outside, but Zampanò roughly coerces her to camp together inside his three-wheeled, motorcycle-powered cart. When she looks at the still sleeping Zampanò the next morning, her face reflects a mixture of confusion, fear and also tenderness.

The two enter a simple trattoria and Gelsomina orders abundant food for herself; her gestures show that she feels she is his wife. Zampanò knows the people there, and, after drinking copious red wine, he grandiosely invites a coarse woman who is obviously a prostitute to continue drinking. The friendly Gelsomina meets her guilelessly. After leaving the restaurant, he manoeuvres the woman onto the cart and orders Gelsomina to wait. She waits all night and, the following day, desperately squatting by the roadside and spurning the food of the compassionate villagers. A riderless horse like a ghostly apparition had walked past her in the lonely night. When she is told that the cart is in a meadow outside the village, she runs to it, joyfully finds Zampanò sleeping in the open and then, childlike and almost rapturous, walks back and forth in the barren nature. She expresses her disappointment during the journey: 'So you go with other women?' and asks him in vain about her sister Rosa.

A peasant wedding party. The two give a meagre performance on the fringes of the party, after which the children draw Gelsomina into the eerie old house, where she is supposed to cheer up the little disabled boy Osvaldo, a virtual prisoner in a gloomy room; but they are all chased away by a cantankerous old nun. In the meantime, Zampanò has become involved with the widowed peasant woman, who dresses him up in a pinstripe suit and hat in gratitude. When Gelsomina sings her unforgettable melody to him for the first time at this point, he is only interested in his new conquest. During the following night in the hayloft, Gelsomina, disappointed by his second infidelity, decides to leave him. She leaves her shoes and coat behind and is shown walking along a road in the morning, attentively looking at the creepy-crawlies along the way. Like another apparition, three musicians process past her in single file and she follows them into a small town where this little procession turns into a large, religious one. In the midst of the festival, a tightrope walker performs at a great height. Gelsomina is fascinated and excited, and then she catches a glimpse of the artist, called *Il Matto, The Madman* (Richard Basehart). At night, the familiar motorbike rattles into the square and Zampanò drags his reluctant slave back inside.

She finds herself in the midst of a small group of circus caravans one morning and hears her melody being played by nimble, mocking Matto on a tiny violin. The circus people allow the couple to perform at their shows, payment being the money collected by passing the hat round. Zampanò is deeply irked by Matto's mockery of his paltry arts. A physical confrontation ensues, foreshadowing disaster. The tightrope walker, who is only seemingly funny, comforts the increasingly desperate Gelsomina, who has lost her sense of purpose in life, even though the circus people have offered to let her move on with them. She is plunged into deep confusion by the profound conversation with Matto. He convinces her that she has a purpose after all, inviting her to come with him, and at the same time telling her that Zampanò is lost without her. Her decision becomes apparent when Matto drops her and the vehicle off in front of the police station the next day. The sullen Zampanò, who had been forced to spend the night there, is somewhat incredulous. He cloaks himself in his coarseness as he does in his leather jacket, which she hurriedly helps him into.

They take a trip to the seaside on the way. Gelsomina runs towards it like a child seeing its home, saying: 'Now I feel like I'm at home with you'. In his limited faculty for comprehension, which is reduced to biological functions, he interprets this to mean she won't have to go hungry anymore. Following this, she only attempts one more time to make human contact with him. Having run out of petrol, they spend the night in the barn of a monastery. For the first time, she plays the by now familiar melody that Matto had taught her on the trumpet. She had proudly shown her small, mobile home to a young nun, who in the ensuing conversation compared her devotion to the man with her own vocation. This strengthens Gelsomina's affection for Zampanò. That night, she once more attempts to establish a connection between them, asking if he is a little fond of her and even offering to marry him. She is unsettled when he later tries to steal the church treasury but still follows him. At the side of the road, they come across Matto, who needs to change a tyre. She is delighted; however, Zampanò avenges his mockery by brutally bludgeoning Matto; he staggers to the grass and, to Gelsomina's horror, dies right in front of her. Zampanò throws the body and the car into a nearby river.

On her last journey, the trees are bare; she is still distraught and incessantly repeating: 'He's in a bad way, he's dying'. Zampanò, who sees nothing wrong in what he has done other than that he might be found out, thinks she has taken leave of her senses and gets rid of her on a wintry hill one icy day, leaving her sleeping like a bundle of rags with a few lire and the trumpet.

We encounter him again years later. Visibly aged, he gives his tired old performance with a new partner in a small seaside town. He hears a young woman hanging laundry singing Gelsomina's melody, inquires about her and finds out she has died in a state of mental derangement. In the evening, he gets drunk, starts a fight and staggers to the beach, where he collapses and cries desperately while looking up at the stars.

Background

Fellini had begun his film career as a screenwriter on Roberto Rossellini's *Roma città aperta* (*Rome, Open City*, 1945), which has gone down in film history as one of the first and most important films in the genre of Italian neorealism. In little more than a decade, this new style took the film industry by storm, other important examples being *Ladri di biciclette* (*Bicycle Thieves*, 1948) by Vittorio de Sica, *Riso amaro* (*Bitter Rice,* 1949) by Guiseppe de Santis and, as early as 1942, Luchino Visconti's *Ossessione (Obsession)*. Shot in black and white on original locations, on a low budget and with amateur actors, rather than the American dream factory, these films aimed to show real life in the war-ravaged streets, squares and landscapes of Italy, for which they were internationally celebrated. This fresh look at the reality of Italian life was linked to the hope that cinema or art could contribute to an improvement in the miserable living conditions of the proletariat and the rural population and was thus eminently political and naturally—after the calamity that Mussolini's rule from 1922 to 1943 had brought upon the country—first and foremost anti-fascist. Seen from today's perspective, the documentary film style of these productions does not seem to totally break visually from film productions of the fascist era. After all, Mussolini had always supported the film industry and preferred a popular style in competition with glamorous Hollywood productions. The dictator had built the still world-famous film studio Cinecittà in Rome and even founded a *Centro sperimentale della cinematografia*. Unlike Goebbels or Stalin, he had not promoted pure propaganda films (cf. Bondanellea and Carney 2002, p. 44). After the fall of fascism, people naturally wanted to distance themselves from it; Marxism and other social utopias became popular ideas among artists and intellectuals. At the same time, the disreputable role played by the Catholic Church and Pope Pius XII during the war attracted public criticism.

Only against this background can the uproar caused by *La Strada* after it was shown at the Mostra cinematografica in Venice in 1954 be understood and the fact that its author was accused of betraying neorealism. While the film was enthusiastically celebrated by a large proportion of the audience and by French critics, led by André Bazin, it was vehemently opposed in Italy, especially by the Marxist-oriented, influential critic and film historian Aristarco, who edited the journal *Cinema nuovo*. Although the film gives a visual experience of poverty and physical and spiritual misery by depicting impoverished characters, shabby masonry, rubbish and debris strewn along the roadside and inhospitable natural surroundings, Aristarco criticised it for a lack of apparent social reality. Fellini seemed to have been won over by the Catholic camp with his portrayal of Gelsomina's angelic innocence and unshakeable virtue and the cracking of Zampanò's mental shell, which can be interpreted as a conversion (the Church, however, turned its back on Fellini in 1960 after *La Dolce Vita*). Fellini emphatically claimed for himself that he did not want to be taken in by either side. He famously said that in Italy there were more Zampanòs than bicycle thieves, namely, people at the bottom of the social pyramid who had so little chance of changing their situation that they could not even participate in the class struggle (quoted from Thomas Koebner 2008, p. 231). His view of (Italian) man also resonates, which he will later lovingly develop beyond the social question, especially with his friend Marcello Mastroianni.

The harsh criticism came mainly from intellectuals, less so from the other important neorealist directors. In the 1950s, both Roberto Rossellini and Michelangelo Antonioni in particular turned away from the direct depiction of social ills and towards a look at the individual and his or her conflicts, with a special focus on female protagonists, such as Fellini in *La Strada*.

La Strada is a melodrama and also a circus film, a genre in which the circus world and the travelling folk are often depicted as a parable for human life with all its conflicts, suffering and joys: in short, a world in miniature. There is probably no other director in the history of cinematography besides Fellini for whom the circus and the marginalised people who dwell in it have played such an eminent role, as memory, fantasy, dream and metaphor. He hardly made any films that did not feature a circus show in one form or another. The three protagonists of *La Strada* each represent a version of the clown, that classic figure whom we laugh at so we can bear their sadness and our own. Zampanò and Gelsomina are poor-man's versions of the authoritarian whiteface clown and the doltish auguste figure, while the happy-go-lucky Matto, with his artistry and musicality, has a premonition that he will die young.

In any case, to avoid embarrassment, the Venice jury compromised by awarding the Golden Lion to another film. *La Strada* received a Silver Lion; but *Senso*, the film by the avowed communist Visconti, received no awards at all. This outraged the communist fraction and resulted in a division of the film-going public into Fellinians and Viscontians that lasted for years.

The film then went on its triumphal march around the world, bringing its director the first of a total of five Oscars for Best Foreign Language Film, a new category at the time, and still moves viewers to tears today, 66 years after it was made.

La Strada is pure poetry. The road which these two unfortunates travel leads through misery, guilt and loneliness, makes us forget time and ends in an incarnation: becoming human.

Image of Femininity

Fellini said that 'cinema, with its irresistible art of seducing, has in its essence something feminine'. And he admits unapologetically that he always found it much more exciting to invent the female characters in his films and that he liked to cast female roles with women who are attractive and sexy. He believed that strong and sensual female characters could be just as appealing to female audiences as they were to male audiences.

Indeed

Years before, the Felliniesque cosmos, with its grotesquely plump breasts, garishly made-up faces and buttocks filmed from below, was created and fed by Federico Fellini's memories, dreams and fantasies, he conceptualised the character of a child-woman as a seemingly innocent and helpless victim who is sexually, emotionally and physically exploited, not only in *La Strada* but also in *Le Notti di Cabiria* (also with Giulietta Masina). Cabiria is surely the most chaste strumpet in film history, and Gelsomina appears to be a sexual being only very indirectly; for her, sexuality, which seems more like rape in the viewer's imagination when Zampanò takes possession of her in the showman's cart, leads to tenderness and in the course of time to understanding and something like love. It is reflected in her face after that first night.

Why don't we disapprove of this image of feminity? One could attempt to justify this by saying that such images were typical of the times or deliberately showed an exaggerated version of grievances in order to arouse pity and provoke indignation. However, such justifications have no place here. Although the film creates a strong emotional reaction, as a viewer, one does not feel manipulated. Feelings are not prescribed, hammered in (despite Nino Rota's inimitably sad music) or forced: The compassionate description of the circumstances is enough. Yes, this character is exploited and eventually discarded, but in some mysterious way, she is nevertheless not a victim, for she shows indomitable strength, poetic purity, unflinching kindness. She is by no means drawn as a saint in the Christian sense. Although it is difficult to describe exactly how, Gelsomina gives the enigmatic impression of not being a mere victim. This effect can only be seen as an expression of the director's art.

In the very first shots, she is sacrificed by her mother while still a half-child, subjected to the same fate as her sister. Child sacrifice as myth, incantation, expression of patriarchal power has existed in religions and archaic cultures since time immemorial. Every day in our consulting rooms today, we see the consequences of violence against children, especially girls, the victimisation of children in the service of maintaining family structures.

Many authors think that the animalistic Zampanò has no interest in Gelsomina as a woman; otherwise, why would he 'go whoring' at every opportunity? We are not shown any sexuality or even implied nudity. The scene with the peasant woman is only a hint at anything of the kind. You wonder if it is just you who is fantasising the exhausted woman getting down to business with the sinister but somehow attractive man at some point between the antipasto and the main course. Only Gelsomina's face confirms the suspicion when she belatedly realises what is going on. In a way, it is him who becomes a whore in this situation, rewarded with a suit and hat.

The fact that Gelsomina serves her companion not only as a slave, water bearer, drummer, provider of sympathy and the brunt of his aggression but also as a kind of sexual service provider is not mentioned or is contested in most reviews. To me, it seems obvious and contributes greatly to the enormous impact of the portrayal of this naïve, somewhat simple-minded, not very pretty and not at all sexy girl whose facial expressions and body language openly express her emotions. To my amazement, I only notice on watching the film again that she actually loves her tormentor, is jealous, shows a whole range of clichéd female behaviours that revolve around him, such as wanting to save him. On the other hand, she is also portrayed as too stubborn, a gifted comedienne, and stoically insisting on her own values. Ultimately, she eludes all clichés (Fig. 5.1).

Based on the observation that women are both absent and present in culture, art, film and society and that they do not find themselves reflected there although they are relent-

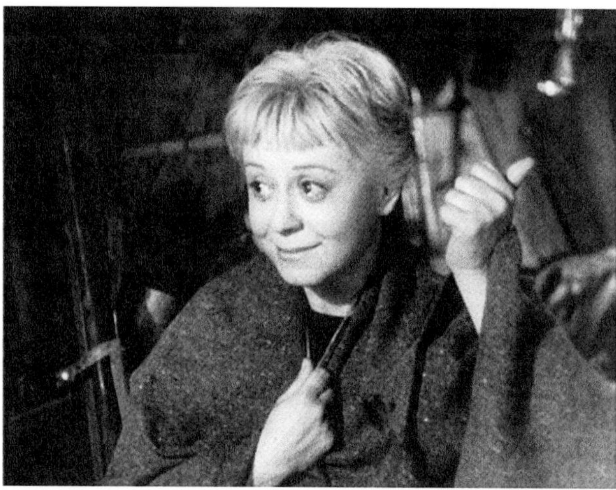

Fig. 5.1 Gelsomina says goodbye to Matto after deciding one last time to stay with Zampanò (01:07:28)

lessly made objects of artistic representations and social processes, film scholar Teresa de Lauretis distinguishes between the terms *woman* for a social and historical individual and *Woman* for the sum of social images of femininity that individuals energetically try to pursue in one form or another. She is thereby referring to a fictional construct, the essence of femininity ascribed to all women in countless Western cultural discourses (cf. de Lauretis in Chaudhuri 2006, p. 62 ff.).

In this sense, Gelsomina would clearly have to be seen as a *woman*, as a female being who absolutely does not correspond to all general, cultural and cinematic images of femininity. Nevertheless, most female viewers will probably only be able to identify with partial aspects of the character, whose uniqueness stems entirely from the imagination of her creator. On the one hand, they see themselves reflected in the film as fairly normal women and on the other hand not at all because they hope to gain a little more control over their fate than Gelsomina does. Analogous to Fellini's remark about *more Zampanòs than bicycle thieves*, one could say that Gelsomina likewise eludes the general role expectations of women at that time, as she is forced to live below the radar of propriety. Remaining a virgin until marriage was an absolute dogma in post-war Catholic Italy (this a major theme of Fellini's previous film *I vitelloni*). The cinematic and societal stereotypes of the 1950s completely passed Gelsomina by restraint, dressing according to masculine taste but not too provocatively, compliance, taking on the role of housewife and mother purely out of love, and so on. What she can do is provide for her husband, whom she is not allowed to choose herself, and she tries to do so in all aspects of life. She is sold like a slave. But was the far-reaching economic dependence of many women on their husbands really so fundamentally different from this? In the 1950s, a wife needed her husband's permission to be gainfully employed; breaching her *marital duties* could make a woman the guilty party in a divorce and thus lead to destitution. Thus, on the one hand, the figure of Gelsomina could be seen as a metaphor for these conditions. On the other hand, she is specifically forced to act against all the above-mentioned categories and stereotypes of culturally expected female behaviour. She manages to remain herself under the most adverse circumstances, which is why she touches us. She is a symbol and at the same time a suffering woman with feelings. She is a victim but always remains the subject of her decisions: She runs away from her master when she wants to; however, when she stays with him, contrary to the wishes of the audience, this is also her own choice (Fig. 5.1). She thus follows her momentary state of mind, which she clearly feels, as is commensurate with the natural being she is portrayed as. For in all her poverty she has found a task and wants to fulfil it, as the young nun approvingly confirms to her.

Details about time and space are left vague, and there are correspondingly also no psychological explanations or a back story that could make the characters' actions more plausible. We do not learn what has led to Zampanò becoming so hardened, nor why he is looking for a new partner in Rosa's family, of all places, when he seems to be responsible for her death. Nor what the old conflict with Matto is or any confirmation of the implicit connection between the two. Gelsomina's decisions are not made plausible and the characters' actions usually lack expected consequences. The film does not attempt to describe the character of the protagonists, rather portraying them through their appearance; accordingly, they always figuratively stay in costume. The characters seem symbolic and individualised at the same time.

In psychoanalytical discourse, we are familiar with the role of the depressive victim, for example, women who deny a depressive conflict by being altruistic and always doing good, however, regularly expect something in return, are constantly disappointed and thus perpetuate their depression. Therapeutic goals are to achieve more self-responsibility and autonomy and to let go of the victim role.

This is nothing like Gelsomina.

The victim role is avoided by her often still childlike appearance. She plays with children and animals and is part of nature. In this respect, she is a real victim without playing a victim role and yet, contrastingly, also remains an active and decisive subject. The factors together contribute to the viewer being able to feel genuine pain and compassion instead of anger at the woman's self-sacrifice.

In the film, Gelsomina finds herself in the company of plenty of women who presumably did not freely decide to make a living as a nun, whore, hard-working peasant woman or beggar (slave trader). It is significant how even the consolations of a traditional family life, depicted at the wedding in the countryside, cannot apply to Gelsomina: Marginalised, she dances a lonely dance on the fringes of the festival and Zampanò shows her once again that she does not really belong to him. Instead, in an uncanny scene, she meets a kind of alter ego in the little sick prisoner, Osvaldo. We dread to think how Gelsomina will be reassigned her lonely place in the world.

Gelsomina's development from a docile child to a sensitive subject, aware of more than her immediate surroundings, is always visually and thematically at odds with Zampanò's stasis, while they nevertheless take the same symbolic road. The repetition of his performance five times makes this clear: The first time she is quite an admiring pupil, the second time she already plays the leading role and provides sympathy, the third time marks the turn to disaster due to Matto's mockery, which she anticipates, the fourth time she is broken by the consequences of Zampanò's brutality, and she does not participate in the last time, with a finally destroyed Zampanò.

Further Thoughts

Gelsomina as Creature of Nature, Zampanò in the Circle, Matto Aloft

Beyond the film's concept of femininity embodied by the character of Gelsomina and her relationships with the two male protagonists, the film offers a wealth of philosophical references concerning nature and religion. Gelsomina is developed entirely from herself, for instance, by being shown as an almost animistic part of nature with a special relationship to the sea, animals and plants. We see the world through her eyes when she is not at all surprised by the stray horse trotting by or finds a donkey seemingly growing out of the ground next to her cart, mimics a tree, is interested in beetles and tomato seeds, remaining completely childlike in all of this. The mocking Matto compares her head to an artichoke. Her loving and empathetic relationship to animals, which have even less rights, is countered by Zampanò being compared to animals several times as a metaphor for his misanthropy. Matto tells her that Zampanò is like a dog and that he seems to want to say something but can only bark; and his joke that the circus also needs animals, with Zampanò in mind, forms the core of the fatal enmity. Later at the seaside, Gelsomina, with a newly developed capacity for abstraction, realises he is an animal when, in his usual manner, he can only relate her shy declaration of love to the satisfaction of hunger and thirst.

The image of the child-woman Gelsomina that the film portrays cannot be described in isolation from the cinematic development of the other two protagonists and how they relate to each other.

Zampanò remains trapped in his burly, unconnected gravity until almost the end (Fig. 5.2). His only perceptible needs are eating, drinking, sex and sleeping, his extreme touchiness the only affect that cannot be attributed to carnal satisfactions. He tries to symbolically escape the restraints of the physical by repeatedly breaking the chain around his chest, however does not succeed in doing so. This helps us as viewers not to hate him, as one might otherwise be expected to, given the repeated evidence that he is out of touch with himself and others, his brutality and his lack of values. Rather, we feel pity, which also has to do with the view of him adopted by Gelsomina, i.e. the identification with her.

In contrast, Matto, the tightrope walker, is an aerial being, the link to the firmament, seemingly light and airy. When he first appears, he is wearing angel wings (in the first shot of Gelsomina by the sea, she is carrying a bundle of gathered twigs across her back that look like wings). In the central philosophical conversation, from which Gelsomina will emerge comforted, with the help of a pebble, he relates her existence to the whole of creation, again with a look heavenwards. The conversation gains a psychotherapeutic quality when he makes it clear to her in one sentence that Zampanò must have had a motive to recapture her: Zampanò needs her; he loves her.

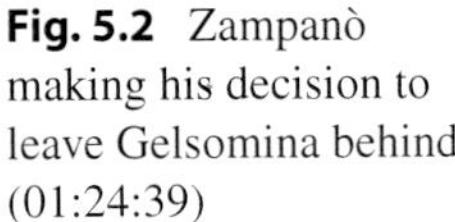

Fig. 5.2 Zampanò making his decision to leave Gelsomina behind (01:24:39)

In terms of the elements, Zampanò could be compared to earth, Matto to air and Gelsomina to water, because of its ability to penetrate softly and smoothly everywhere, but also to burst rock.

But things are never quite that simple with Fellini. Matto, the angel, eats a plate of spaghetti on the high wire in a very earthly way, and in the face of Zampanò's collapse, the camera ultimately turns upwards towards the stars.

Zampanò has traced a circular arc until that moment. He places the chain in a circle around his chest, he circles the audience with his pacing, he performs a cyclical rhythm of performance, eating, sex (only with altered objects of desire) and sleeping. Gelsomina is the second girl from the same family after Rosa who does not survive her encounter with him. Last but not least, the circus ring could symbolise the cycle of life; as a spectator, you have several viewing options there, unlike in the cinema.

In contrast, Zampanò's antagonist Matto opens up a second, vertical narrative plane, starting with his dizzying performance with a view to higher spheres in the church square and moving on to spiritually higher things such as his musicality and philosophical discourse.

The Sacred

The religious implications of the film can hardly be overlooked. It is, after all, the story of Gelsomina's martyrdom and Zampanò's purification.

However, the end of the film only superficially and parabolically allows for this definition: like everything else, it happens without the voice of providence. Rather, we find ourselves in an indefinable milieu of coincidences that change the fate of the protagonists without any immediately recognisable meaning. The events fall as if from the sky or grow out of the earth, according to the vertical construction of the film, in contrast to a logical, horizontal narrative development. Each episode is subject to perfect economy and stands on its own, but each also participates in an order that in retrospect proves to be a necessity; here, too, one could see higher powers at work.

More specific references for sacred symbolism: Gelsomina and Matto as winged beings, the latter interpreting creation from a pantheistic viewpoint. Zampanò drags the dead Matto away with outstretched arms—a crucified man. During the procession, the ecstatic crowd drives Gelsomina right past a Madonna figure, and so on.

Not only is this depiction far removed from any official church doctrine, but it reaches us through the visual memory instilled in us by European cultural history and religion. It is all the easier for us to imagine the iconographic, inner worlds of a Catholic boy who grew up in Italy's fascist-clerical province in the 1920s. And even in his subsequent films, which, like *La dolce vita* (1960), were very displeasing to the Church, 'what counts in Fellini is that which endures eternally and absolutely in his broadly Catholic ideology is his loving and sympathetic optimism' (Pasolini 1993, p. 107). Gelsomina definitely does not want to stay in the convent either, having already turned down a life in the circus along with Matto.

It is no coincidence that I could not accommodate these observations in the chapter on the image of women. Although this film makes a victim of its lovingly drawn, female main character and raises her almost to the level of religiosity, while portraying her sacrificial affection for her tormentor, I for one do not find it upsetting, but instead a deeply moving parable of the human condition. Tackling the question of why this should be prevents the religious aspect from becoming overpowering. When a film is repeatedly experienced in such a positive, moving, artful, humane, even enlightening way over some 40 years of occasional viewing, when one loves Italian cinema of that era in general and also has a great affection for Masina and Fellini, one can somehow integrate the disagreeable parts. In this case, it turns out that it is actually this paradox between the character's inexplicable power and her victim status that makes the film so timelessly interesting.

Translated by Annette Caroline Christmas.

Film Details

Original title	La Strada
Release year	1954
Country	Italy
Screenplay/idea	Federico Fellini, Tullio Pinelli, Collaboration: Ennio Flaiano
Direction	Federico Fellini
Music	Nino Rota
Camera	Roberto Girardi
Principal actors	Giulietta Masina, Anthony Quinn, Richard Basehart
Availability	DVD: Arthaus, special films, Kinowelt Home Entertainment GmbH: Federico Fellini: La Strada. The Song of the Road

References

Bondanellea P, Carney R (2002) The films of Federico Fellini. Cambridge University Press, Cambridge/New York

Chaudhuri S (2006) Feminist film theorists. Routledge, London/New York

Kezich T (2005) Federico Fellini. Eine Biographie. Diogenes, Zurich

Koebner T (ed) (2008) Film directors. Reclam, Stuttgart

Pasolini PP (1993) The Catholic irrationalism of Fellini. In: Bondanella P, Degli-Esposti C (eds) . Perspectives on Federico Fellini. Hall & Co, New York

Woman as a Black Bird: The Presentation of Femininity in Alfred Hitchcock's *The Birds* (US 1963)

6

Gerhard Schneider

Approach

The images of birds attacking a town and its inhabitants in Alfred Hitchcock's 1963 eponymous film form part of the collective visual (film) memory of the twentieth century. The destructive bird attacks constitute one level of the film. The other is that of the two protagonists Mitch Brenner and Melanie Daniels getting to know each other and becoming closer, which is complicated by the jealous and defensive attitude of Mitch's mother Lydia Brenner towards Melanie.

How are the two levels linked? One possibility is to regard the attacks as independent from the narrative, their experienced apocalyptic intensity being heightened by the spectators' identification with the protagonists. This is in line with the *cosmological* and *ecological* explanatory approach expressed by Robin Wood (1989) in answer to the question of what do the birds mean/why do they attack?

In the first case, the 'bird attack [is the] embodiment of the Hitchcockian vision of the universe […] as a system—peaceful on the surface, normal in its course—that can be upset at any time and thrown into chaos by sheer chance'; interpreted theologically, this is the 'vision of a cruel, tyrannical and inscrutable God who can bring about disasters at any time' (Žižek 1998, p. 184). Not too distant from this approach is the second one, which proposes that the action is to be understood as nature's revenge: The birds 'function as a condensation of an exploited nature that finally rises up against the ruthless exploitation by man' (ibid.).

The opposing view is to assume there is an internal connection between the two levels, such that the bird attacks are understood to be a visual realisation of the drama of the

G. Schneider (✉)
PIHD, Mannheim, Germany

V. Pramataroff-Hamburger, A. Hamburger (eds.), *From La Strada to The Hours*,
https://doi.org/10.1007/978-3-662-68789-5_6

developing relationship. For Wood, this is the 'familial approach', according to which 'the intersubjective relationships of the main characters (Melanie, Mitch and his mother) [are] anything but an insignificant by-line of the "real" plot, the attack of the birds' (Žižek 1998, p. 184 f.). My previous works on *The Birds* (Schneider 2007, 2017) have been written from this perspective and I maintain it in the present context of the *staging of femininity*.

As I see it, *The Birds*—like its three predecessors *Vertigo* (1958), *North by Northwest* (1959) and *Psycho* (1960)—is about the following: What happens when a system that seeks to avoid dependence on its environment, and which I therefore call a *(self-sufficient) narcissistic universe*, is invaded by something alien to it, that is to say something that cannot be integrated into the system's mental logic? The 'narcissistic universe' in this case is the Brenner family dominated by the mother; the 'invading stranger' is Melanie as a woman. The increasingly violent attacks of the birds can be understood from this perspective as a double expression of a threat: On the one hand, they show how threatening the intruder appears to the family system and, on the other hand, how much she herself is threatened in return. In this respect, there is a threat of mutual annihilation, on the part of the family system and on the part of Melanie, who becomes an *endangered-endangering woman* by getting closer to Mitch. The central question will thus be what the film associates with Melanie *as a woman* that makes her so (apocalyptically) dangerous.

The Plot

San Francisco. In a bird shop, lawyer Mitch Brenner (Rod Taylor) wants to buy a pair of love birds for his sister Cathy (Veronica Cartwright), who is turning 11. He talks to an attractive young woman, Melanie Daniels (Tippi Hedren), as if she were a shop assistant, knowing full well who she actually is, and she playfully and flirtatiously accepts the role. He eventually calls her by her name and ends the flirtation rather brusquely.

Melanie obtains his address and at the weekend takes a couple of love birds with her to Bodega Bay, where Mitch is staying for the weekend with his mother Lydia Brenner (Jessica Tandy) and his sister. The father died a few years ago, and during a subsequent conversation his former lover, the teacher Annie Hayworth (Suzanne Pleshette) tells Melanie that Mitch has been forced into the role of a substitute husband by his jealous mother: In her eyes, there is no room for another woman. As Melanie becomes increasingly involved with the Brenner family over the course of the weekend, a natural threat develops that eventually takes on apocalyptic proportions: Birds are attacking the people and the town of Bodega Bay. At first, it is only a single seagull that injures Melanie, and then, it is flocks of crows and seagulls that chase the schoolchildren. In the end, birds attack the Brenners' house and seriously injure Melanie in the attic room. During the period of nondescript calm in the early morning of the day after, Mitch, his mother, Cathy and the traumatised Melanie, who is paralysed with fear, leave the house as it were besieged by flocks of birds. They want to try to drive to San Francisco and get to safety.

Background

Literary Model and Special Features

The film is based on the short story of the same name (1952) by Daphne du Maurier, which is set in Cornwall, although only the bird attack theme has been taken from it. It is remarkable that the usual film music cannot be heard. Rather, Hitchcock uses a collage of artificial bird calls and other sounds composed on a trautonium, a precursor of the synthesiser. Also noteworthy are the extensive animation technology and special effects, some of which were novel solutions.

Visual Reminiscences of the Two Previous Films

One of the most striking (film) images of the last century is a scene from *North by Northwest* (US 1959): On a completely straight country road in the barren boundlessness of the Great Plains, Cary Grant (aka Roger Thornhill) is running, being chased by a plane that swoops down on him several times—a steel bird in 1959 as the forerunner of the live birds in 1963. Furthermore, the movement of the birds repeatedly stabbing Melanie (in a phone box, the attic) echoes the murder scene in *Psycho* (USA 1960) in which Norman Bates (Anthony Perkins) repeatedly stabs and kills Marion Crane (Janet Leigh) in the shower—also a memorable image in the visual archive of the last century.

Hitchcock's Staging of Femininity in The Birds

Opening Credits

In the opening credits of *The Birds* (Design: James S. Pollak), crows initially fly restlessly back and forth through the picture against a grey background. Then, the name Alfred Hitchcock emerges from light green fragments and crumbles again. The other names all appear in the same light green, at first complete, before breaking apart into fragments and crumbling as if they were being chopped up. Beating wings and bird cries can be heard. At the end of the opening credits, Hitchcock's name appears again. At this point, 'the bird cries reach their climax. His name also crumbles to pieces, the fragments swept away by fluttering wings. Then the screen goes pitch black' (Paglia 2000, p. 30 f.). Black is thus the colour of destruction. It is the colour of the crows and the suit in which Melanie is first seen in the film.

The opening credits contain the essence of the film in condensed form. In a seething, unstructured dynamic, the name of the director, the '(film) creator', develops as the representative of a symbolic order. This happens again for each of the following names, all in the colour green, the colour of Melanie's suit, which she wears throughout the film except for the opening scene. The names crumble, just as the man-made world in Bodega Bay is threatened with destruction—the final image of the film thus matches the final image of the opening credits.

From a psychoanalytical point of view, the opening credits are already the visualisation of a trauma:

> The symbolic order breaks down under the onslaught of violence from outside that can no longer be contained. It ends in deep black, the extinguishing of visibility. This symbolises both violence and a dissociative absence: closing the eyes against the intolerable.

The *woman* Melanie is thus related to the emergence, (self-)preservation and destruction of a symbolic order through the two colours green and black—which are those of her suits. She is thus characterised as a 'endangered-endangering woman', according to the Brenners family's 'narcissistic universe'.

Melanie in the Mirror of Her Encounters

The easiest way to get an idea of how Hitchcock films Melanie as a woman is through her encounters with other characters in the film, especially, of course, Mitch. I'll pick out the ones that are most important to me, starting with the opening scenes in the pet shop. Mitch recognised her straight away because he once represented a client against her in a case about a smashed window. He wants to teach her a lesson, playing a 'trick' on her by addressing and presenting her as a shop assistant. At the end of the scene, he tells her that she 'tricked' his client and was to blame for the damage done, but because of her father's influence, i.e. because of her name, she unjustly got off without any punishment. He succeeds in his plan because she is obviously incompetent, so much so that one of her birds escapes, which he then recaptures. However, Melanie does not show any offence, accepts the challenge and returns the favour with a 'counter-blow', the pair of love birds.

What image of Melanie does Hitchcock create in this scene? The carefully chosen clothes and her appearance suggest that she stems from the upper class, which is confirmed by the reference to her father as an influential newspaper publisher. She is clearly self-confident and has a mind of her own and is quick and decisive in her decisions, as her 'revenge plan' shows, probably also at least a little extravagant (suit, high-heeled shoes), perhaps also a little anarchic, protected by her background (the 'escapade'), in any case not bound by a tight corset of bourgeois norm(ative ideas). Overall, in this scene, Hitchcock shows us that Melanie is a self-confident, outgoing and non-self-limiting, attractive young woman with a mind of her own, who seems free and independent, not normatively constrained.

The next personal encounter between Mitch and Melanie takes place after dinner at his mother's house. She is sitting in her sports car ready to drive back to Annie's, where she is staying the night. He is standing next to the car facing her, filmed from a characteristically top-down angle, which appears again and again in the film. A brief argument ensues during which he reproaches her for something his mother had told him: that she had jumped (naked) into a fountain at night that last summer, which is reminiscent of a scene in Federico Fellini's *La dolce vita* (I 1960). In doing so, he adopts a super-ego approach, which could already be heard in the pet shop. She responds with a palpable pang of bad conscience and regret at her behaviour, however also defends herself before finally driving off, clearly angry at his insistent interrogation style. Beyond what has just been said, in this scene, we experience her as a woman who allows herself to be critically questioned and who critically questions herself, but who is also capable of distancing herself in self-preservation.

Her self-reflexive, self-critical side is deepened in the third and longer conversation with Mitch at Cathy's birthday party. Melanie has inwardly turned away from the way of life she had in Rome and has found her way (at the level of her origins) into working life. We also hear about the loss of her mother, who left the family for another man when she was 11. She does not have a positive, maternally loving image of her mother, but above all is angry at having been abandoned.

Melanie's image needs to be supplemented by several aspects that become clear in her relationship with Lydia. Lydia is initially very hostile towards her, and Mitch has to insist on the various invitations to dinner, to Cathy's birthday and finally to a sleepover after the birthday, because Lydia almost tries to force Melanie to stay away from her house, transmitting a message of 'stay away, you're not wanted!' During her sleepover at Annie's, Melanie learns about the back story to this rejection: Lydia's husband died 2 years ago, and she has substituted him with her son, whom she wants to bind to her and keep with her at all costs. Melanie naturally senses this rejection but, because of Mitch's clear signals to come, does not allow Lydia to prevent her from coming to dinner and the birthday party.

After the attack of the seagulls outside and then that of the sparrows through the chimney inside the house itself, there is a touching scene: Broken dishes lie scattered, Lydia absent-mindedly and resignedly picks up the pieces. Melanie notices her in what I experience to be a compassionate way, without any words being said.

The next morning, after discovering the dead neighbour and fleeing home in panic, Lydia lies in her bed, deeply affected by the shocking events. For the first time, she can now admit Melanie's presence and inwardly affirm it by allowing Melanie to care for her: She tells her about her husband's death and her loneliness and then asks her to pick up Cathy, whom she is worried about, from school.

Thus, beyond the opening scene, Hitchcock deepens Melanie's image in the other encounter scenes. She is not only the attractive, self-confident, independent young woman who is not constrained by norms but is also self-reflective, self-critical and empathetic. All of this is set against the backdrop of a drastic experience of loss in her late childhood (her mother), which has left recognisable affective traces.

Melanie as a Black Bird

The image of Melanie as a woman, which has been developed so far in her relationship with the other two protagonists Mitch and Lydia, matches the light green that is representative of the symbolic order in the opening credits. At the very beginning of the film, Hitchcock does not hesitate for a second to establish a connection with the destructive black of the opening credits through Melanie's connection with the black birds. First, we see a cable car moving out of the picture to the left—the film curtain has opened. We are in Union Square in the centre of San Francisco; our eyes fall on an attractive young woman on the opposite pavement in an elegant black suit with a tight skirt. It is the only scene in which Melanie is not wearing the light green suit. She is wearing high-heeled stilettos and can only cross the street in short steps because of the tight skirt. She has to get from the roadway to the pavement with a hint of a 'hop step'. There can be no doubt: Hitchcock films her as a metaphorical *black bird*, which is subliminally associated with the menacing quality of the opening credits (Fig. 6.1). Camilla Paglia writes:

> The … woman is the crow, her high stiletto heels are the claws of rapacious nature (Paglia 2000, p. 33).

The reference to the dark is already contained in the first name 'Melanie', which is derived from the ancient Greek *mélas*, meaning black/dark, or dressed in black. Moreover, Hitchcock establishes another Melanie/bird connection in this opening scene. She hears the admiring whistle, presumably of a man, turns around in surprise, lips pursed in indignation and then looks up as if attracted by something. Through her gaze, we see a flock of large black birds distantly circling in the sky. Melanie is looking questioningly and slightly

Fig. 6.1 Melanie as a black bird (00:01:52)

worried at a disconcerting event. From a psychoanalytic point of view, it could be understood to be her becoming aware of something external that could in some way be connected with her but about which she has absolutely no idea. Seen in this way, it could be said that Hitchcock is enacting Melanie's unconscious connection to a dark, threatening bird-like quality.

This is an attempt at interpreting Melanie's reaction to seeing the flock of birds psychoanalytically. Of course, another interpretation is also possible: Melanie ponders for a moment about a natural phenomenon that she cannot yet grasp, which has nothing to do with her as a person. I prefer the psychoanalytical interpretation at this point because it allows us to understand Melanie as a lady in a green suit, as I have observed she is portrayed in her encounters, and the visible picture of Melanie as a black bird, as a whole person with two quite different sides.

The Unfolding of the Relationship Dynamic Between Mitch and Melanie

In order to present Hitchcock's enactment of femininity in the character of Melanie in more detail, I shall now go into the development of the relationship between Mitch and Melanie in more detail. I have already formulated my *first premise*: In the familial perspective, I take the attacks of the birds to be a cinematic expression of this dynamic, not a representation of an independent event confronting them both. My *second premise* is that I see the process as Mitch's confrontation with Melanie's femininity, as the penetration of the woman 'Melanie' into his inner world. In this perspective, I see the family system and especially his mother Lydia as an external representation of his inner world. It is characterised by a strong attachment to the mother who made him a substitute for her deceased husband. Psychoanalytically formulated: The film suggests that there is an inner 'mother' object in Mitch's inner world who has a jealous claim of ownership over him and seeks to assert it.

Two things have become clear from the account given so far in relation to Mitch. On the one hand, to Melanie he has clearly superego-like features (criticism of the 'escapade', of her loose lifestyle in Rome). It is as if he wants to control her, to make her a ward of norms and conventions, so to speak. On the other hand, he definitely has a mind of his own (towards the inner object) of the mother, so he is not simply subjected to her (cf. the invitations to Melanie's house), which is what allows the (inner) conflict to unfold in the first place. The psycho-logic of the event is such that the further Melanie penetrates into his inner world or he allows and encourages such penetration, one would expect the dynamics of the conflict to intensify, and consequently the intensity of the bird attacks, as their cinematic expression increases.

And the film does show such an increase. First, a single seagull flies into and injures Melanie's forehead while Mitch is waiting for her after the boat crossing. When she drives back to Annie's in the evening, he has told her that he wants to see her again, the telephone lines and the roof of the house are full of menacing-looking black crows, and at the end of the evening, a seagull flies into Annie's closed door. Both events seem to be ominous.

The first major bird attack (by seagulls) takes place on Cathy's birthday. It begins as soon as Mitch and Melanie return from their conversation to the group as a couple and are perceived as such by Lydia. Later in the house, Mitch and Lydia clash over whether Melanie should stay, and his wishes prevail. It is as if this argument is calling the birds: Melanie sees a sparrow in the chimney, and then hundreds and hundreds of them invade it, wreaking havoc. Mitch then stands up to his mother again, so Melanie stays the night—symbolically taking the mother's place for the first time when she puts Cathy to bed.

The next morning, escaping back to her home, Lydia's fight with Melanie can be seen directly. Melanie, wearing her fur coat over her night clothes, is standing with Mitch, engrossed in conversation. They see Lydia staggering out of the car and want to come to her aid. But Lydia pushes them apart—an expression of her desire *not* to let them get together.[1] This is followed by the birds' most violent attack yet on Bodega Bay and its inhabitants (during which Annie dies). Melanie, locked in a phone box, becomes the direct target of a major attack for the first time, visually anticipating the attic room scene at night.

The ever-deepening closeness between Melanie and Mitch becomes clear once again before the final attack scene, when Mitch, with Melanie's help, barricades the house from the outside. Afterwards, they go back into the house; he has his arm around her shoulders; she is walking close by his side. A little later in the house, in her fear Lydia accuses him of failing and not protecting her: *If only your father were here!* Melanie now seems to belong there. She sits on the sofa with Cathy, her arm protectively around her, and helps her when she vomits in the toilet out of fear. Mitch sits diagonally under the large portrait of his father above the piano, which is against the wall, Lydia in the free space between the piano and a short transverse wall. When Melanie and Cathy return from the toilet, they sit down on the sofa again. Melanie leans back somewhat relaxed and crosses her legs, her skirt sliding up a bit over her knees—certainly not a lascivious position in any way, but it does seem a bit more revealing than before. Immediately afterwards, a soft chirping of birds is heard, which then turns into a terrifying crescendo of bird cries and pecking against the doors and walls. It is the prelude to the major bird attack on the house, which only holds out because the attack ends as suddenly as it came.

Formulated in my perspective above, a point of extreme actualisation of the conflict dynamic has been reached that calls into question and threatens Mitch's entire inner system, whereby this intensification is first shown indirectly in the attack on Bodega Bay, and then directly with reference to the inner system (family) itself in the attack on the house. Consequently, in both cases, Melanie, who as an intruder is taking up more and more space inside Mitch, is also a victim of this attack. The telephone booth scene already indicates that she, *as the intruder* who has set the inner events in motion, is also the target

[1] For the sake of readability, I have expressed this in film images; the translation into an event in Mitch's inner world according to my second premise is self-evident.

of attack separately from the others. This happens in the Brenner's house in the attic room scene in a final climax that traumatises her.

Psychoanalytically speaking, something is being enacted here that goes beyond what has been said so far: a fantasy about the connection between sexuality and violence. What happens? In the middle of the night, the three Brenners are sleeping; Melanie is awake; she hears a barely audible, rather gentle flapping of wings. She speaks quietly to Mitch, who does not wake up, and then, hesitantly but also purposefully—we know her to be bold and determined—makes her way cautiously up the stairs to the attic room, past the two love birds in the cage, who are behaving normally. The attack on Melanie (Fig. 6.2, 01:43:58) remains quiet. Halfway into the room, she sees the gaping hole in the roof—the protective shield of the house has been breached. Frightened, she takes a step into the room. The light falls on the four-poster bed opposite her: It is full of black and white birds that pounce on her, tormenting her with their pecking in repeated waves of attack.

The attacks are so forceful that Melanie cannot manage to get out of the room again. Her green suit is torn to shreds; the blows inflict wounds on her head, arms and legs. She slowly sinks to the floor against the wall, her defensive movements becoming weaker, until she remains lying halfway to the door, the fierce bird attacks continuing unabated. At the last minute, Mitch manages to pull her out of the room, carry her into the living room and together with his mother give her first aid. When he tries to pour her a cognac and she sees his face above her, to her he seems to become a bird. She uses her hands as protection and to fend it off.

Similarly to the opening credits, the attic room scene can be seen as a visual representation of a traumatic event: The gaping hole in the roof directly demonstrates that the walls of the house can no longer protect its interior, i.e. also Melanie, from the closing in of a violently destructive outside; the (stimulus) protection (Freud 1955 [1920], p. 26 ff.) has been breached, as the birds' pecking at Melanie shows. The essential point is that the violence breaking in is not simply pure violence, as the film has shown so far, but is linked

Fig. 6.2 The attack against Melanie (01:43.58)

to sexuality. I have already mentioned a perceptible brief moment of erotic charge in connection with the bird attack on the house. There is a sexual innuendo associated with the two love birds Melanie passes: At the pet shop, Mitch comments on his 11-year-old sister to Melanie, the 'shop assistant', saying that a child of her age should not spend all day watching the birds rub their bills together. Another word for 'bill', of course, is 'pecker'—and the birds force themselves on Melanie with their peckers. There is thus the linguistic coding of a linking of (sexual) tenderness with aggression (tool function of the beak) up to (potentially lethal) violence. There is also a white four-poster bed in the room, the low canopy of which probably indicates a girl's bed, as do the children's books scattered on the floor (Paglia 2000, p. 118). Childhood, that is (in a positive, normal case) on the one hand security and an orderly-safe world, but on the other hand also curiosity about the unknown-attractive beyond, and this includes sexuality and the parents' sexual intercourse. In the underlying fantasy, the *fantasy of the primal scene*, arousal *and* violence are connected, because the sexual event still cannot be classed (positive normal case) loving togetherness. This fantasy can be understood as a latent dimension in the relationship between Mitch and Melanie, if one adds the subsequent living room scene in which the caring, helpful Mitch briefly internally becomes an attacking bird for Melanie.

The (potential) violence that the film thus inscribes in the horizon of a sexual relationship between the two of them is murderous in its final intensification. As already mentioned, the birds closing in on the phone box where Melanie is trapped and is visually comparable to Norman Bates stabbing Marion in the shower scene in *Psycho*. The attic room scene is a heightening of the violence in the phone box, the (barely) protective casing of which has disappeared, just as Bates ripped away the shower curtain in front of Marion. To be precise: In the final analysis, the idea of sexuality/sexual intercourse being equated with the killing of a woman appears on the horizon (cf. Schneider 2017).

Once Again the Black Bird Melanie: The Abyss of Desire

All in all, the mounting uproar of the birds appears to be an actualisation, building to a climax in the attic room scene, of the violence latent in the erotic encounter between Mitch and Melanie, a latency that is initially 'far removed' from Melanie in the image of the flock of birds over San Francisco, then closer to her in the crowd of black birds around Brenner's house after her initial conversation with Mitch, and which finally becomes a direct mortal danger in the form of a large flock of crows ready to attack that had been silently gathering at the school building behind her back. By entering into the encounter with Mitch and penetrating his inner world, Melanie thus actualises a danger associated in the film with the coming together of the pair: As an attractive, independent and autonomous woman, she triggers an *erotic desire* in Mitch. Unlike Annie the teacher, she is not subject to regulations or a strict moral code.

By allowing his desire—or put in Melanie's perspective: By allowing herself to become a black bird for him—Mitch enters into a double conflict. As his superego-control-oriented behaviour towards her shows, he wants to 'have' her, but 'in a cage', so to speak, as a *tamed* bird, which implicitly represents a threat to her. A fundamental problem appears on the horizon; however, the film does not show it directly: *jealousy*. Structurally, jealousy means that the gaze of the desired object should be turned solely towards the desirer; any gaze of the object towards a third party threatens the claim the desirer has towards *his* object.[2] In the film, this is the motif of the inner object of the 'mother', since Lydia wants Mitch *exclusively* for herself. Mitch's other conflict is the threat to his relationship with the inner object 'mother' through his desire and, in connection with this, the threat to his inner balance.

How does the theme of the primal scene fantasy relate to this? One possibility would be to see the attic room scene as a representation of an event within Melanie, as an activation of the unconscious fantasy in her. However, I think this idea is a little forced. It seems more appropriate to me to understand the scene as an expression of the potential violence inherent in the relationship dynamic. It would thus involve a radicalisation of Mitch's already mentioned striving for control and power in relation to the independent Melanie.[3] As a woman who is desired and perhaps also has desires of her own, which is only passively hinted at in the film through her involvement with Mitch, Melanie thus becomes a dangerous object due to the inner logic of the desiring man Mitch. She *becomes* the dangerous black bird she *potentially* was. 'Potentially' has two aspects here: On the one hand, without her own active intervention, she may become dangerous to the man due to his gaze on her, which triggers his desire; on the other hand, she can herself attract such a gaze through her own behaviour: The film shows both (Mitch approaches her in the pet shop of his own accord; she drives to Bodega Bay of her own accord). At the same time, as shown, Melanie's independence in Mitch's eyes has a particular potential for conflict.

Positivity and Scepticism: The Openness of the Final Scene

In contrast to what has been said so far, it could be objected that I am presenting the relationship dynamics too negatively and that, due to the self-preservation forces of Mitch's inner structure, I ascribe too low a probability of there being a positive development in the relationship. On the other hand, Mitch's inner space for Melanie is steadily growing—as expressed in film images: She is increasingly becoming part of the family, showing her own openness in her reactions (empathy), and she has also integrated herself into the 'bourgeois normal world' (working week). Mitch is not under the dictates of his mother, is obviously prepared to engage in conflict with her and is not a 'mummy's boy'. Moreover, his character could in no way be compared to that of Norman Bates. Thus, overall, despite all the conflict intensity expressed by the increasing bird attacks, there would be a *positive*

[2] In *Psycho*, jealousy is a central theme (cf. Schneider 2017).

[3] In the follow-up film *Marnie* (USA 1964), Marnie (Tippi Hedren) is immediately locked in the cage of marriage by Mark Rudland (Sean Connery).

development that offered space for the development of the couple relationship, whereas my reflections would suggest, if not assert, a negative, failing relationship. To put it in clinical terms: Events are not heading for a catastrophe but, in Bion's sense, for an ultimately positive 'catastrophic change'.

Tippi Hedren expressed a positive view thus: Lydia "accepts the daughter and that they will live happily together afterwards! […]. The character of Melanie Daniels is a strong and independent woman who refuses to be a victim, even in the face of extreme danger" (cit. after Paglia 2000).—A closer look, however, reveals that the outcome of the film is to be considered open-ended.

In the positive view, the final scene, in which all four leave the house to head for San Francisco through the giant army of birds that have gathered, in Melanie's sports car, Mitch at the wheel, Cathy next to him with the love birds, the badly injured Melanie in her fur coat in Lydia's arms in the back seat, can also be regarded to be positive: 'The birds […] represent the arbitrary, the inexplicable and the unforeseen, which breaks into the supposedly perfect world of Bodega Bay and causes the relationship between the characters to become reordered. The attacks thus have a catalytic function in that they reorganise familial allocations, allow the lovers to find themselves and define priorities in the way humans live together' (Schmidt 1998, p. 526).

For me, the final scene does not convey such positivity. Rather, it makes me doubt. This is condensed in the final image: As the car drives away, an increasingly loud birdcall begins. The film thus ends with the pervasive presence of the birds. How is it possible to believe that everything is all right, after we have just seen that the world has fallen apart, even though everything seemed to be in perfect order at the beginning! It was apparently also Hitchcock's wish that there were to be no final words 'The End', as if he wanted to avoid the impression that the horror is now over, that the film's end is at the same time a happy ending for the actors.

And what of Melanie? Three days hence, she arrived in Bodega Bay at the wheel of her car. Now, overwhelmed by the trauma of the bird attack, she sits in Lydia's arms in the back seat of her own car, Mitch having taken the wheel. Once in the shelter of the car, Melanie's hand closes around Lydia's arm and she looks at her. Lydia looks back with a warm gaze and wraps her in her arms, into which, it is minimally implied, she has sunk—this is emotionally coherent and comprehensible at that moment, for the confidently explorative young woman has become a creature in need of protection.

On the positive side, the scene can be understood as Melanie inwardly regaining her mother, whom she had lost when she was 11, the same age as Cathy. But is the content of the scene really reducible to the increasing emotional closeness of the two women? It seems to me that Melanie's vulnerability to Lydia brings to life the shadow of Annie Hayworth, whom Lydia accepted when Mitch no longer desired her as a woman. Unlike before, Lydia is now in a position of strength and power over Melanie. It could even be said that the embrace expresses her triumph over the defeated bird intruder Melanie. In other words: In Mitch, the inner object 'mother' has brought the intruder under his control.

Melanie would thus, psychologically speaking, become Lydia's daughter and consequently Mitch's sister, who would thus lose her *as a woman*—and it is the girl Cathy who sits beside him with the two tame love birds in the final image.

The film thus leaves the outcome open between the success and failure of the relationship, because of course Mitch could also continue to detach himself inwardly from his mother and have Melanie by his side *as a wife*, once recovered. This open-endedness is addressed by the aforementioned Robin Wood (1989) when he asks whether Melanie 'develops into true womanhood or eventually relapses into childlike dependency' (quoted in Paglia 2000).

The ambiguity of the ending of *The Birds* is thus not resolvable *either* in terms of the positive *or* the negative or rather sceptical view. As stated in my account of the final scene, I myself tend towards the sceptical view of the failure of the relationship, even though I do not deny the positive development of the relationship between Mitch and Melanie as such: I believe it shows the widening of Mitch's inner distance from his mother as an inner object. However, under his inner conditions is he capable of developing a truly equal relationship with the actively independent, attractive and sexually desirable Melanie? With the image of the severely traumatised Melanie as a victim of the violence triggered in the relationship dynamic in mind, the film seems to me to imply an image of the man-woman relationship in which this is *not* possible. *As a desirable woman*, Melanie turns into a black bird for him, which *as such* would throw his world into chaos. She would therefore have to become a tamed and, so to speak, literally devoted 'inseparable' for a relationship to become possible. It seems to me that the film, perhaps sadly, opens up a view of an inner world in which a free relationship as equals based on mutual desire and mutual recognition is not possible.

Further Considerations

Hitchcock and Tippi Hedren

The #MeToo movement has made it obvious that the boundary between private person and artist (in the sense of a role) as well as personal and artistic obsession is quite precarious, threatened and not a self-evident given which is adhered to. In this respect, reference should be made to Hitchcock's well-known (cf. Spoto 1983) decidedly negative ways of dealing with his leading lady, which have once more been publicised through Tippi Hedren's autobiography (2016).

Tippi Hedren was a model until Hitchcock discovered her as a film actress and signed her exclusively for several years, apparently wishing to substitute her for his favourite actress Grace Kelly, who was no longer available after her marriage to the Prince of Monaco—the Pygmalion motif in *Vertigo* (USA 1958) transferred from the film world to the real world. In connection with this, there was a kind of exclusive claim to her private life, which escalated to sexual advances during the filming of *Marnie* (USA 1964), in which she also had the lead female role. These advances were, one could say, the libidinous counterpart to the sadistic behaviour towards her that he displayed during the filming of *The Birds*, when he spent 5 days shooting repeated birds attacks in the attic, thus psychologically torturing and physically endangering her (Spoto 1983, pp. 523–562).

Overall, Tippi Hedren comes across as very confident in her response to the Hitchcock experience. Volker Kreitling (2016) writes on the occasion of the publication of her autobiography:

> Hedren spoke regularly about the difficult time with Hitchcock. But she publicly praised him for his work, she attended his funeral in 1979. There had been two Hitchcocks for her, she said, and she had admired the artist.

Hitchcock's Image of Women

The 'woman' theme is present in Hitchcock's entire oeuvre. Over time, the image of the fascinating, frightening, dangerous woman developed in his films, the type of the blonde, beautiful, mysterious, on the one hand cool, but under this surface possessing an intense eroticism.

At the dark centre seems to be the connection between sexuality and violence or more precisely killing. In his penultimate film, *Frenzy* (1972), the main character is an impotent killer of women who strangles his victims. Murder, then, at the point of sexual intercourse. Here '[the curtain] will be wide open. The *Hitchcockian primal scene* is *femicide,* and the murderers are among us. They are quite simply the men. And they act as their *trauma* enjoins them to. In Hitchcock's favourite film, *Shadow of a Doubt* (USA 1943), the murderer's motive is detailed in passing over a family dinner. The motif is the fear of women and their boundless qualities, which appear to be a subversion of the male symbolic system and male ideas of identity and order, or are experienced as something repulsive, dirty' (Feldvoß 2018 [2003], p. 25).

Translated by Annette Caroline Christmas.

Film Details

Original title	The Birds
Release year	1963
Country	USA
Book/Idea	Evan Hunter
Director	Alfred Hitchcock
Principal actors	Tippi Hedren, Rod Taylor, Jessica Tandy, Suzanne Pleshette
Availability	DVD: Hitchcock Collection *The Birds/Marnie.* 2 Movie Set Universal

References

Feldvoß M (2018 [2003]) Alfred Hitchcock. Im Dialog: Psychoanalyse und Filmtheorie, vol. 1. Psychosozial, Giessen, pp 18-28

Freud S (1955 [1920]) Beyond the pleasure principle. Standard Edition Vol. XVIII Hogarth Press

Hedren T (2016) Tippi: a memoir. Williams Morrow, New York

Kreitling V (2016) „Es war sexuell, es war pervers und es war hässlich." ["It was sexual, it was perverted and it was ugly.] DIE WELT. 01.11.2016

Paglia C (2000) Die Vögel.. Der Filmklassiker von Alfred Hitchcock. Europa Verlag, Hamburg/Wien

Schmidt JN (1998) Die Vögel. In: Koebner T (ed) Filmklassiker, vol. 2: 1947–1964. Reclam, Stuttgart, S 525–528

Schneider G (2007) Alfred Hitchcocks, *Die Vögel*'—Der Einbruch in ein narzißtisches Universum als Apokalypse. ['*The Birds*'—Breaking into a narcissistic universe as apocalypse] Psyche—Z Psychoanal 61:1226–1240

Schneider G (2017) Tetralogie mit Vorabend. Hitchcocks visu-psychoanalytische Untersuchung des narzisstischen Universums [Tetralogy with eve. Hitchcock's visu-psychoanalytic investigation of the narcissistic universe]. In: Gehrig G, Pfarr U (eds) Die Ästhetik affektiver Grenzerfahrungen [The aesthetics of affective borderline experiences]. Psychoanalytische, kunst- und medienwissenschaftliche Zugänge [Psychoanalytical, art and media studies approaches]. Psychosozial, Giessen, pp 117–146

Spoto D (1983) The dark side of genius. The life of Alfred Hitchcock. Little, Brown & Co, Boston

Wood R (1989) Hitchcock's Film Revisited. New York, Faber & Faber

Žižek S (1998) Warum greifen die Vögel an? [Why do the birds attack?] In: Žižek S et al (eds) Ein Triumph des Blicks über das Auge. Psychoanalyse bei Hitchcock. [Big Brother, or the triumph of the gaze over the eye. Psychoanalysis in Hitchcock]. Turia & Kant, Vienna, pp. 184–190

Trauma, Depression and Transgenerational Suicidal Tendency: Psychoanalytical Notes on the Film *Die Wand [The Wall]* (A, D 2012)

7

Marianne Leuzinger-Bohleber

Introduction

The film adaptation of *The Wall* (2012) by Austrian director Julian Pölsner, starring Martina Gedeck, is based on the 1963 novel by Marlen Haushofer. For a long time, the Upper Austrian author remained largely overlooked, overshadowed by big names such as Elfriede Jelinek, Thomas Bernhard, Peter Handke, Ingeborg Bachmann, Ilse Aichinger or even Ödön von Horváth, who had already been admitted to the pantheon of twentieth-century Austrian literature. Her simple, non-experimental language of 'magical realism' (cf. Antes) and the subtleties of her texts may have contributed to this underestimation of her work, however perhaps also the prevailing prejudices against a writer who was also a housewife and mother. One thing Marlen Haushofer has in common with the 'great' Austrian writers is that she described the latent brutality, exclusion and murderous.

impulses towards anyone who was different, foreign or a woman in bourgeois Austrian society—using motifs, metaphors and wording reminiscent of the quiet psychoanalytical 'voice of reason'. Marlen Haushofer finds radical, unsparing images and words for the desperate attempt of women to free themselves from the shackles of their social environment, role constraints, and latent and manifest expectations, but also from the determining influence of these in their own unconscious. Although Julian Pölsler strictly adheres to the original novel, he nevertheless adds his own reading to it.

M. Leuzinger-Bohleber (✉)
University Medicine, Mainz, Germany
e-mail: mleuzing@uni-mainz.de

V. Pramataroff-Hamburger, A. Hamburger (eds.), *From La Strada to The Hours*,
https://doi.org/10.1007/978-3-662-68789-5_7

Film Plot

In a remote hunting lodge, an unnamed woman with short hair, dirty fingernails, cloaked in a shabby woollen jacket, begins her written report by the light of a paraffin lamp: 'Today, the fifth of November, I shall begin my report. … I'm not writing for the sheer joy of writing So many things have happened to me that I must write if I am not to lose my mind. There's no one to think and care for me. I am totally alone, and I must try to survive the long, dark winter months'. The protagonist, who is clearly living a Robinson Crusoe life, is writing to stave off the fear that creeps up on her from all sides. 'I don't want to wait until it gets to me and overpowers me'.

Throughout the film, we see the narrator, interspersed by flashbacks of the central scenes of her narrative, which are initially very brief, ghostly incursions, becoming longer and more haunting towards the end of the film. The protagonist remembers the day she drove through the idyllic alpine landscape in a Mercedes sports car with her cousin and her wealthy husband: Nobody was speaking, the ageing couple in the front seats were swaying to the rhythm of a pop song about freedom. The woman in the back, who is also no longer in the first flush of youth, slipped on her headscarf to protect herself against the mountain wind. A dog gazed into the landscape. Once they had arrived at the idyllic hunting lodge, the couple decided to go down to the village for a short while: They would not be long. They wanted to be back soon, because the next day they were going hunting bright and early. At nine o'clock, the woman goes to bed and locks the door, taking the key to bed with her. She is woken by the dog and discovers that the couple have not returned home. She worries that something could have actually happened to the hypochondriacal Hugo. She runs downhill in her white city dress and high heels, through the ravine, until the dog suddenly jumps back at her, yelping. He has hurt himself, which seems strange. A little later, the woman comes up against an invisible wall. She hears a loud noise: It is her own heart beating loudly. 'My heart was afraid before I knew it'. Only then does she notice that the streets are completely empty, devoid of life. She checks what she is seeing three times, thinking it must be a sensory illusion. The same wall is there between them and a small farmhouse. She cannot believe her eyes: An old man is standing by the well in front of his house, frozen in the middle of his evening wash. His wife is sitting on the bench in front of the house, likewise frozen. 'I simply couldn't believe it, these things simply didn't happen, and if they did, not in a small village in the mountains, not in Austria and not in Europe …'. But the next day the same thing happens: The wall is impenetrable; the two old people are still frozen in their last actions. It then dawns on the woman: If these two experienced sudden death, then the same must have happened to everyone in the valley. 'If this was death, it had come quickly and gently, in an almost loving way. Perhaps it would have been wiser to go to the village with Hugo and Luise'. Lux finds a cow that has apparently survived on the woman's side of the wall and runs towards her. She cannot leave her behind, so builds her a stable at the hunting lodge. 'I was the owner of a cow and the prisoner of a cow'. She christens her Bella. The woman checks all the other paths leading out of the valley. She tries to drive the car through the invisible wall but crashes full force into it. The woman uses a map to mark out the boundaries set by the invisible wall. Only many days later does she realise that how bad the situation is. 'But we were not completely lost because there were two of us …'. She throws herself into work and clings to the hope that someone will come looking for her, although she actually knows that this will never happen.

The townswoman becomes a farmer's wife: She plants potatoes and beans, cuts hay for the cow, collects mushrooms and fruit in the forest and reluctantly learns to hunt. She finds killing difficult. It makes her ill one time. She is haunted by the dead heart of the deer she shot, which 'froze into a lump of ice' in the storehouse. She cannot understand why some people love killing. 'I pity the animals and I pity people because they are thrown into this life unasked'. She tries to find her way in her new life, takes in a cat one rainy night, which becomes the fourth member of the survival community. The woman learns men's heavy work, such as mowing and haymaking. Exhausted, she falls into a severe bout of despondency. She barely manages to get out of bed for a fortnight. But Lux resolutely insists, pulling her out of her depressive breakdown: She does not like to look back on those 2 weeks. In winter, she experiences two births: Pearl, the newborn kitten, has a touch of Angora about her. This genetic predisposition will make survival in the forest impossible for her. Bella gives birth to a little bull in February. The woman helps her give birth.

She writes that the first year was mostly about caring for the animals, less about her own survival. In summer, she moves to the alpine pasture, experiencing rapture in the new surroundings, which, like everything unknown, lures her. The mountain world, the elements of nature, the scents of the meadows and the violence of thunderstorms and storms comfort and calm her. She does not continue writing her report but notes afterwards: 'For the first time in my life I was soothed, not satisfied or happy, but soothed. It was as if a big hand had stopped the clock in my head'.

She discovers a new self that becomes increasingly differentiated from her old self. In the face of the overwhelming mountain world, her former urban self, which had been so important to her, seems ridiculous: an 'inflated nothing'. Instead, she develops a 'we-feeling', having become one with nature and animals, her newer self 'being absorbed into a greater whole'. Lux is more than just her dog: He has become her friend, her alter ego. Both have changed: Lux has also 'become calm'. He seems to have lost his canine fear of being abandoned at any moment. The woman befriends a white crow who is less afraid of humans than her fellow crows, who will expel her from their community for being different. She loses Pearl on a windy night before the onset of the second winter. She had been killed by a fox. The woman later discovers the fox by the stream and is in a position to shoot it. She does not do so, recognising that only man knows right from wrong. Animals unsuspiciously follow the laws of nature.

The second summer she does not feel the same rapture: The alpine pasture has become a stranger to her and has closed itself off from her. Does she foresee the catastrophe that is brewing? In autumn, she cut off her long hair, distancing herself from one of the last feminine features of her life in the city. She repeatedly writes about her deep sadness at losing Lux, whom she misses not only because he ensures her survival and helps her when out hunting but because she *is truly alone* without him.

How did it happen? A flashback in the film with a dramatic soundtrack shows Lux and the woman returning from a day's work at the hunting lodge, when they discover a strange man in front of the alpine hut brutally beating the little bull. Lux races off, jumping at the man's throat. He cannot be called back. We see her storming into the hut in slow motion to get her rifle. Instead of her desperate cries, we hear a solo Bach partita and, repeatedly interposed, the face of the remembering writer turning away.

In great anguish, she buries her dog and takes care of the roaring Bella. Only then does she look after the man. She drags him to the precipice and lets him roll into the valley. 'I was glad he was dead; it would have been difficult for me to have to kill an injured person. And I couldn't have left him alive after all. Or could I, I don't know'. The woman spends the night on the bench in front of the hut in the cold mountain wind. 'But I was colder than the wind and didn't freeze'.

The next day she leaves the mountain pasture, taking Bella with her. She throws herself into work. Only after a week does she 'give up the pointless escape and face my thoughts … I want to know why the strange man killed my animals. I'll never know, and maybe it's better that way'.

Writing the report made her feel calm. 'I see a little bit further. I can see that this isn't the end. Everything goes on … Memories, mourning and fear will remain, and hard work, as long as I live …'. The report ends on 25th February because there isn't any paper left. 'When [the crows] are out of sight, I shall go to the clearing and feed the white crow.

It will already be waiting for me'.

Background

Marlen Haushofer's Novel. *The Wall* was considered unfilmable. Various directors acquired the film rights but failed to realise them. In an interview, Julian Roman Pölsler said he had dreamed of making a screen adaptation of *Die Wand* ever since the book had been published in 1963. And in 2016, [4 years after the first film adaptation of a Haushofer novel], Pölsler also made a film of *Wir töten Stella [Killing Stella, 2017]*, also starring Martina Gedeck. He found her ideal for the role of the nameless woman. Her minimalist, unpretentious acting style makes the film a true work of art.

The result is an extraordinary, one might say unique, grandiose film that condenses the long novel in a masterly way without losing any of the essential elements. The major creative achievement that this condensation represents only becomes apparent when, like me, you read the novel after you have seen the film. Essential themes, such as the relationship with the woman's children and husband, her health crises and her involvement with religion (e.g. at Christmas and on All Saints' Day) are systematically omitted, as are the sexuality of animals and the phenomenon of time. Perhaps, this is why the film manages to be a unique combination of calm, at times almost to the point of stagnation, and suspense.

Roman Pölsler worked on the script for 7 years. He avoided all the pitfalls of a sentimental regional film. It is unwieldy, horrific, paralysing: the full force of nature and existential dangers for the people inhabiting it. The mountains are overwhelmingly beautiful and at the same time threatening: They surround the hut of the nameless frozen people like an eternally constant backdrop, reflecting the cruel truth that nature will always survive whatever catastrophes humans are guilty of. They don't seem to care. For an entire year, eight cameramen captured the most extreme natural phenomena, including thunderstorms, snowstorms, but also blossoming spring meadows and dreamlike snowy landscapes, which are used to poetically underlay the text and create unforgettable effects (such as the woman's face as she lies in bed lit up by lightning, full of horror, fear and loneliness).

The quiet shots, the slow pans, the flashbacks and the long, precisely composed silences, at times filled with powerful spherical sounds, alternating with solo partitas by Johann Sebastian Bach (played by violinist Julia Fischer), serve as a background to Maren Haushofer's text and Martina Gedeck's voice. Her voice is brittle, melancholic, quiet and introverted. There is no escaping it. Her voice resonates for a long time.

The text is sober, concise and cool but always accurate, coherent. The woman comments, reflects on what she sees and experiences or philosophises about the relationship between humans and animals, about grief, pain and the need to survive, about love and the 'banality of evil' (Hannah Arendt), to which only a human being can fall prey. People are the only ones who do not belong in the forest, because they can destroy it, wantonly, consciously and reflectively. Only a person can decide to kill or else show mercy.

The Wall as an Opportunity for Self-Determined Female Identity?

With its haunting portrayal of trauma, depression and transgenerational suicidal tendencies, *The Wall* addresses the (self-)destruction of female creativity. This subliminal theme is addressed in the storyline of a female finding her identity in the wilderness.

After the gruesome discovery of the wall, the woman is in a state of shock and denies her circumstances for a long time. She then faces reality, without self-pity or sentimentality, out of responsibility towards the animals. She is a townie who masks her feelings in the opening scene and is eyed suspiciously by Lux but decides to continue living in the forest. She becomes a farmer's wife, a huntress, a hard manual labourer who is solely, entirely responsible for her own survival. The whole film focuses on her inner and outer transformation process.

Marlen Haushofer writes: ['... once built, a barrier does not always have to be seen as negative ...']. The wall (surreally) offers the nameless woman a life beyond all social expectations or roles and conventions: an opportunity, albeit a cruel one. Amidst the elemental forces in the daily struggle for survival with a dog, a cat and a cow, the first-person narrator develops a new self, a new identity; this is an old philosophical theme, as the Zurich philosopher Michael Hampe (2020) writes in his new book *Die Wildnis, Die Seele, Das Nichts*:

> Civilised man exists in himself only through social mediation. Those who want to get to know themselves supposedly directly (if there is anything to get to know at all) must therefore go into the wilderness, albeit alone. The only question is whether he can really find himself there, whether there can actually be an immediate relationship derived from one's self. (p. 64)

On the one hand, the first-person narrator answers this question clearly and without any illusions: 'That's the way I am, and the forest hasn't changed matters'. Or later, in the report: 'The wall forced me to make an entirely new life, but the things that really move me are still the same as before: Birth, death, the seasons, growth and decay'. And yet she changed, had to change. She had no other choice. In her report, the woman states several times that she has become an Other. Dagmar C.G. Lorenz (1979) postulates in her doctoral thesis that loneliness should not be seen as a self-chosen, pleasant solution or a desirable asceticism but as the only means to preserve individuality and integrity as a woman (cf. Brandtner and Kaukoreit 2012, p. 96).

Transformations of Self and Identity in the Shadow of Traumatic Experiences

The formation of self and identity are described in modern psychoanalysis as complex developmental processes on the border between inside and outside, self and other, individual and society. They require mental integration processes akin to the early differentiations of self and object representations towards the end of the first year of life in the intermediate space according to Winnicott (1969). Identity is never fixed; it is always a creative endeavour on the part of the individual: 'Identity is found at the intersection of the social expectations addressed to the individual and his psychological uniqueness. It is the product of a mediation between both these parts as well as a dynamic balance between them' (Bohleber 1992, p. 107). However, it is also always partly conflictual, as it is enforced by an antagonistic society. Moreover, it is determined by the 'non-identical', the unconscious. The first-person narrator's account can illustrate these processes: The common thread is that the woman compares her own perceptions of her inner self with social expectations imposed on her from the outside, internally balancing her new experiences back and forth by writing (in the intermediate space).

Mirroring and affective resonance processes between the infant and its primary objects (the significant other) are described as the second precursor of identity formation. As infant researchers such as Daniel Stern (1985/2018), among others, have convincingly conceptualised, the self can only develop in the empathic, holding and containing relationship with the primary object. Throughout life, the formation and consolidation of identity involves a mirroring process in the ego that bears many similarities with these earliest relational experiences. In the intermediate space, one inwardly mirrors new experiences to oneself and considers whether or not they should be integrated into the sense of self and identity. Particularly in adolescence, but also later, during life crises or, as in the case of the first-person narrator, after traumatic experiences, self and identity become destabilised and require new psychic integration processes that subjects earlier aspects of identity to scrutiny, modifies them, mentally rejects them or otherwise integrates them into current events and new identity experiences.

Therefore, separation and mourning processes always play a major role (as a third dimension) in forming an identity, because unconscious decision-making processes are constantly taking place: What forms part of one's own self, and what is experienced as coming from outside, as not or no longer forming part of the self and as such banished into the unconscious, the non-identical (cf. Leuzinger-Bohleber 2009, p. 102 ff., among others, on the development of identity cf.)

The first-person narrator is thrown through the *wall into* the wilderness. She is all alone, lacking in any human counterpart. Only the animals, particularly Lux, form a mirror, a sounding board. The woman projects her own longings, fears, emotions and fantasies onto them and subsequently recognises herself in a process of projective identification. The report she writes before the third, long winter in the forest to prevent herself from losing her mind is one of mirroring in the intermediate space, of tentative self-assurance, without which she would succumb to a gradual loss of self and identity in madness. However, her mental transformation does not take place under usual circumstances in any sense but during an extreme struggle for survival. She is existentially compelled to undergo the process by the trauma of a catastrophe and of being locked behind the barrier. Therefore, identity transformation cannot be considered separately from the process of trauma processing.

> There is no impulse more rational than love. It makes life more bearable for the lover and the loved one. We should have recognised in time that this was our only chance, our only hope for a better life. For an endless army of the dead, mankind's only chance has vanished forever … I can't understand why we had to take the wrong path. I only know it's too late ….

Too late for creative identity development as a woman? Too late for a couple's love and their shared transgenerational creativity behind the barrier? Also, too late for the survival of humanity in the face of the nuclear threat and climate catastrophe?

The entire film is underpinned by the melody of depression, not only the scenes in which the first-person narrator writes explicitly about it, about her 'great despondency' of 'autumn sickness' or the longing for the 'snow light', which she recognises to be dangerous for lonely people. Pölsler masterfully succeeds in capturing this melody in the soundtrack which accompanies the film.

Does the film depict the first-person narrator's process, after the initial shock, of struggling not to allow the self to be overwhelmed by traumatic losses and, after a painful mourning process, of achieving an initial self-healing? Does the psychological transformation eventually fail due to a new severe traumatisation, ultimately leading to a severe depression (cf. Leuzinger-Bohleber et al. 2019)?

Trauma Processing, Self and Identity: An Attempt at Self-Healing?

Traumatic Loss and Shock

The surreal catastrophe—the annihilation of all life—had a traumatic quality; it was 'too much'. The self was overwhelmed by the fear of death and panic, a trauma. Perhaps, it not only froze the movements of the two old people in the farmhouse but also the movements inside the woman, like a shock which was her initial reaction to the traumatic loss of everything she had ever known. Her gaze reflects terror and horror in the face of death. She can only turn away abruptly from the unbearable reality. As many psychoanalysts have described, traumatic experience irredeemably destroys the inner structure of the subject: A sense of basic trust in a helping other and one's own self-agency are lost. Psychological shock is known to be a first survival reaction to extreme trauma:

The unbearable emotions, thoughts and fantasies are made to disappear. All efforts are directed towards clear action and immediate survival. 'I was amazed that I didn't feel sad and desperate'.

The Decision to Continue Living and the Function of the Inner Glass Wall

The woman decides against suicide, in favour of a life in the forest and taking care of her animals. The mental mechanism of dissociation helps her to banish her unbearable perceptions, feelings and fantasies into an inner capsule, a crypt. This enables her harsh survival in the forest during the first year, centred around caring for the animals and only secondarily for herself. However, before the third long winter, she feels that she cannot continue with this robot-like mental functioning. In order not to lose her mind, she starts writing the report. In the traumatic capsule, she struggles to establish a dialogue with herself and the lost good object, an inner mirror, in the latent longing to be heard and understood by another, a good object, one day. She captures the images in words—the shrouded trees, the white, endless snow, the phobic, buried alive feeling of the cold *wall*. Is it a desperate struggle to breathe life into the capsule, to regain contact with one's self and the lost, good objects? The *woman* has retained a spark of hope in her autistic-seeming capsule, which allows her to project fantasies, longings and emotions onto Lux and to hope (at least in the novel), against all her better judgement, to one day be released from her forest prison, to be rescued: 'But it's just a dream. Evidently people never stop daydreaming', the author writes in the novel [p.87]. This inner good object world is threatened when she has to kill. After shooting a deer, she falls ill. Does the woman only survive because, on the one hand, she can fall back on the good inner object relations just outlined and, on the other hand, she had developed a kind of resilience for dealing with traumatisation, e.g. by retreating into a cocoon, an autistic capsule, and has recourse to this extreme form of a 'psychic retreat' (John Steiner)? The inner wall as a survival strategy? 'It wasn't the first day of my life that I had to survive like this … I had to simply stay quite calm and simply get through it'. And does this resilience break down when she experiences another trauma?

Approaching Mourning for What Is Lost

This is how the first-person narrator discovers the Royal Road to the unconscious, her dreams. 'My dreams had been empty up until then; from that winter onwards they had been cluttered. I only dreamed about dead people, for even in my dreams I knew there were no more living people. The dreams always started out quite safely and deceitfully, but I knew from the first that something bad was going to happen, and the plot slipped inexorably along to the moment when the familiar faces took shape, and I awoke with a groan ...'. (novel, p. 111/112). In the film, too, the clinically familiar processing of traumatic experiences is precisely portrayed. Traumatised people can often barely remember dreams in their initial state of shock, and if they do, they are often invaded by an endless emptiness and vague fear. Traumatised people are later plagued by nightmares. Like the woman, dreamers do not want to give in to their nightmares but turn away from them and deny them. However, the first-person narrator gradually recognises the need to pay attention to her dreams and reflect on the traumatic experiences of loss in the 'inner life of the sleeping state', of accepting them as communications to herself.

'I realised that the composure with which I had adapted to my situation from the first day had only been a kind of anaesthetic. Now the anaesthetic was wearing off, and I was reacting quite normally to my loss'. She faces the memories of earlier Christmases, grieving for the time with her young children, but also for the death of her adult children and everyone who shared her former life with her.

In this, the woman is vividly describing a painful but healing self-analysis. She sees the unconscious effects of traumatic losses in her dreams and tries to fully appreciate their full significance, to rediscover her inner connection to the lost objects and to psychologically accept and mourn losses and destruction. She describes how this grieving process brought her inner peace.

In her writing, she encompasses her almost imperceptible transformations and puts them into words. The recovered good inner objects allow her to experience grief, loss, despair and loneliness and thereby her frozen self and to rekindle a sense of self-agency. Unlike Captain Ahab in Moby Dick (Melville), for example, she does not fly off into a blind frenzy of revenge for her ruined life, merging in a violent death with the depths of the sea. Nor does she direct her rage and despair against those entrusted to her, the animals, the symbolic children, as does the protagonist in Elfriede Jelinek's story *Lust*, in which humiliation, abuse, violence and depression end in infanticide (cf. von Hoff and Leuzinger-Bohleber 1997). After introspectively regaining her good objects, the first-person narrator seeks to become absorbed into something larger, nature. She discovers the 'we'. A new self has developed that has become increasingly clearly differentiated from her old self. In the face of the overwhelming world in the mountains, her former, urban self, which had once been so important to her, now seemed 'something pathetic and absurd, an overinflated nothing'.

Looking back on the first summer on the Alm, she notes: 'For the first time in my life I was calm, not content or happy, but calm. ... It was as if a big hand had stopped the clock in my head'.

But then she experiences another severe trauma: Her still fragile self-healing process collapses. The whole film inexorably moves towards this trauma, in which she herself plays a decisive, active role: the murder of the intruder. After this, the woman is no longer just a victim of fate, of the cold *wall* that has come between her and the rest of the world and of the catastrophe that has extinguished all life: She has become a perpetrator herself.

The Collapse of the Ego Ideal (The Revenge of the Superego) and Depressive Breakdown

In psychoanalytical terms, the fact that she is capable of murdering another human being erodes her basic self-esteem and destroys her self-idealisation of being a peaceful, caring person who was born to love and not to kill (Fig. 7.1). From a psychoanalytical point of view, self-idealisation is a relatively primitive defence mechanism which, it can be assumed, blocks the first-person narrator's psychic access to her own aggressive-destructive impulses and makes it impossible for her to integrate them into a stable self-image characterised by mature ambivalence. This increases the danger of extremely destructive fantasies or actions erupting against the self and/or the object.

On the same mountain pasture where she first found some inner peace a year earlier, she senselessly throws herself into the fray and, without a moment's hesitation, shoots the intruder who has killed her bull and beloved dog. The nameless woman has become a person who, identifying with her hunting dog, instinctively defends her territory, unsuspiciously following the laws of nature. She does not need a man to do the killing for her: She does it herself. She, a woman, shoots a man who is standing in her way, threatening her utopia and survival philosophy. The inhibition on killing is lifted. The only man still alive within the confines of the wall along with her dies. The law of civilisation, 'Thou shalt not kill', is impulsively overridden. The woman's revenge for the death of her beloved animals wipes out human life, for good.

After burying Lux and rolling the dead man down the scree, the woman retreats further into herself, perhaps for good. Presumably, by experiencing herself as a murderer, her connection to the inner world of good objects has been broken and with it her basal positive self-cathexis. By committing murder, she can no longer sustain her inner self-ideal of being the sort of person who, through her capacity to love, could prevent destruction and devastation, war and catastrophe.

Fig. 7.1 A new self, a new identity? (01:13:23)

Her inner warmth, the empathy for the life that inhabits her, is extinguished: She cools down.

Perhaps, the senseless impulse to kill is also connected to the protagonist's unconscious hatred of men? The love for a dog or other animals can be fed by such mentally split-off sources: You can control a dog, adapt it to your needs, even train it; this is hardly possible with a love object. World literature bears witness to the resulting tragedies (cf., e.g. von Matt 1989). In psychoanalytical terms, extreme depressive withdrawal is always also a powerless and grandiose vendetta against the lost object, lost ideals, values and self-ideal images. After unbearable loss, the aggression is relentlessly directed against one's own self: The depressive inflicts on himself the pain he has suffered from the object and its loss. Anger and hatred are now aimed at one's own self. The severely depressed person identifies, Old Testament style, with a cruel superego, destroying self-esteem, and the libidinal cathexis of the self and object. He inwardly brings about the traumatic catastrophe himself in order to never again be passively and helplessly at its mercy.

The psychoanalytical assumption is that the stoic-sounding phrase with which the film ends does not so much betray a mature, existentialist attitude to life as a plunging of the self into the shadow of Saturn, a severe depression.

'Everything goes on … I shall [go to the clearing and] feed the white crow. It will already be waiting for me', thus ends both the film and the book. These sentences recall the words of Marlen Haushofer shortly before her death: 'Don't worry—it will all have been in vain—like everyone before you. A completely normal story' (quoted from Antes 2000, p. 284., own translation).

Who should not worry? The dying one? The people who lose them and mourn them because they loved them and therefore rebel against the depressive truth that 'it will all have been in vain—like everyone before you?' Even an existentialist being 'thrown' into the world (Martin Heidegger) is not obliged to capitulate to depressive certainty and its destruction of literary, cultural and familial transgenerational effects. This destruction is not a 'completely normal' but a depressively darkened story, hiding trauma and its inner and outer destructive power under the cloak of the 'normality of the human condition'.

Further Considerations

Rediscovered by Researchers of Women's Literature, the Second Women's Movement and Feminism

The film adaptation *The Wall* contributed significantly to the rediscovery of the novel and its author in 2012. The novel was first published in 1963, in a social climate that was still patriarchal to an extent that would be difficult to imagine today. Women were responsible for childcare. Marital rape was considered a 'marital duty'. In divorce law, the principle of fault applied. If a housewife was cited as 'at fault' in a divorce settlement, she did not receive any financial support. Against this background, the surrealistically exaggerated struggle for survival of the 'nameless woman', who does not shy away from murdering a man, hits the mark.

Her process of self-discovery and identity, the 'mixture of the demonic and the idyllic' (Haushofer, quoted in Stigl 2000/2009, p. 179), has fascinated feminists and researchers of women's literature and made the novel a great success. *The Wall* has become a parable of female rebellion and self-assertion (ibid., p. 271). The excluded one, the stranger to the male-patriarchal world, now excludes herself. Lorenz (1979) compares Marlen Haushofer with Simone de Beauvoir, who envisioned equality among men and women in future societies. For Haushofer, on the other hand, such equality is inconceivable; the male and female worlds cannot coexist. Therefore, for women, the only solution is separation, the solitude of a separate female sphere. Only thus can she maintain individuality and integrity as a woman.

Marlen Haushofer was convinced that women actually have no way out once they have allowed themselves to be locked in the golden cage of the nuclear family and have taken on the role of wife and mother—an inescapable fate that they also pass on to their daughters. *The Wall* thus may reflect the aforementioned fascination with strong women who violently free themselves from the shackles of role expectations and degrading gender relations. The first-person narrator loses her female self in the second year in the forest, as Martina Gedeck describes and masterfully portrays in the film (Brandtner and Kaukoreit 2012, p. 87). She can also barely be physically distinguished from a man (cf. Fig. 7.2).

Whether shaped by an omnipotent defence of the existential dependence on one's own body, one's own gender, the successive generations and trans-generativity, but also by the life-giving, identity-forming other? As is well-known, we all carry the fantasy of being whole and omnipotent in our unconscious, like the spherical people once described by Aristophanes in Plato's Banquet: to be able to provide for ourselves, to fertilise ourselves and to make ourselves happy, without having to depend on the opposite sex, the anchoring

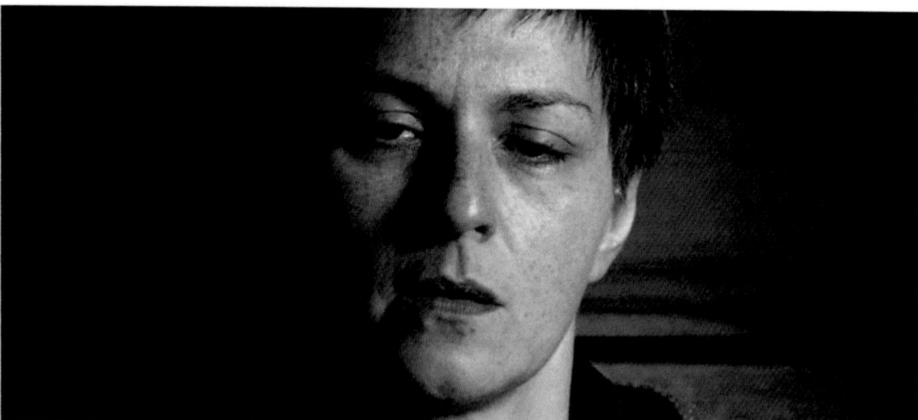

Fig. 7.2 The woman is hardly distinguishable from a man any more (01:37:15)

in the generations and the existential and psychological provision by another (cf. on this, among others, Leuzinger-Bohleber 2009). '... In the novel *The Wall,* autonomy of the female personality is demanded at any price, even that of the whole of human coexistence, of the human future' (Lorenz 1979, quoted in Brandtner and Kaukoreit 2012, p. 96). Not only Simone de Beauvoir but many others, such as Judith Butler, Juliet Mitchell and Jessica Benjamin, have since then sketched out an intersubjective vision of gender relations that thrives on a mature object relationship between man and woman, in the constant struggle for mutual recognition in interdependence, of ambivalence towards one's self and the object of love. Jessica Benjamin takes, among other things, Hegel's struggle for recognition, which she links to psychoanalytical thoughts. The three figures on the famous cover of the 1988 Pantheon edition of Benjamin's *Bonds of Love are* only apparently bound together: Their faces are reflected within the confines of a mirroring well.

The Wall can therefore be considered a *roman à clef* about the second wave of the women's movement, which contributed greatly to the emancipation of women. However, *The Wall* could also just as well be justifiably considered a *pioneering novel of ecofeminism* and be assigned to the third wave of feminism. 'At any rate, this is the interpretation Pölsler's screen adaptation follows, by strongly emphasising the protagonist's gradual embedding in the natural scenery that dominates the film. This is shown in detail and is virtually enveloped by the spherical sounds that symbolise the invisible wall. In contrast, the film often refuses the narrative use of the camera. For example, we only see a front view of the man who kills the animals for a few fractions of a second and later only sections of his head and body as she shoots and gets rid of him. The plot between the woman and man is unimportant. The camera gaze lingers on the dead Lux for a long time. The film thus connects the woman, in the position she has now reached, with the untamed animal kingdom. Admittedly, she uses the gun to protect this bond, thus enlisting the power of human civilisation' (Comment: Andreas Hamburger).

Film Adaptation of a Cult Book for Civilisation Sceptics and Prophets of Doom (Nuclear Apocalypse)

The Wall appeared a year after the Cuban Missile Crisis (1962), which had brought the world to the brink of nuclear catastrophe. 'Back then, there was always talk of nuclear wars and their consequences ...'. The surreal scenario created in *The Wall* was not only present in nightmares and the apocalyptic gloom of the time. In Austria and Switzerland, many built nuclear bunkers and fantasised about what life would be like for survivors after a nuclear catastrophe. *The Wall* conjures up a similar nightmare or social vision, so it became a cult book for many in the anti-nuclear movement. 'I assumed [the wall] was a new weapon that one of the major powers had managed to keep secret; an ideal weapon, it left the earth untouched and killed only humans and animals .... Once the poison, at least I imagined a kind of poison, had ceased to be effective, it would be possible to seize the country .... Judging by the peaceful appearance of the victims, they hadn't suffered; it all seemed like the most humane piece of devilry to have ever occurred to a human brain'. Is this an early vision of the neutron bomb? Marlen Haushofer knew nothing about the neutron bomb but accurately guessed the development of potential technology of weapons of destruction. In any case, she captures the mood of an entire generation in her novel. Against this background, the murder of the intruder to the survival utopia, the harmony of man, animals and nature, takes on a profound meaning: The brutal killing of the bull becomes a symbol of a male-dominated destruction of life and nature and thus the eradication of the transgenerational perspective on our planet.

Through his film adaptation of *The Wall*, Julian Pölsler has brought the novel out of obscurity and shone a light on its relevance in the face of the climate crisis. 'I only know it's too late …', says the film protagonist, anticipating one of Greta Thunberg's catchphrases.

Translated by Annette Caroline Christmas.

Film Details

Original title	Die Wand [The Wall]
Release year	2012
Country	Austria, Germany
Script/idea	Julian Pölsler
Direction	Julian Pölsler
Camera	J.R.P. Altmann, Christian Berger, Markus Fraunholz, Martin Gschlacht, Bernhard Keller, Helmut Pirnat, Hans Selikovsky, Thomas Tröger, Richi Wagner
Music	Bernd Jungmair
Main actors	Martina Gedeck, Karlheinz Hackl, Ulrike Beimpold, Wolfgang Maria Bauer
Availability	DVD, Blu-ray

References

Antes K (2000) Nachwort zu Marlen Haushofer, Die Wand, [Afterword to Marlen Haushofer, The Wall], 20th edn. Ullstein Paperback, Hamburg

Bohleber W (1992) Identity and the self. Interactional and intrapsychic paradigm. Significance of infant research for psychoanalytic theory. Butterflies in my head. Springer-Verlag, Berlin-Heidelberg

Brandtner A, Kaukoreit V (2012) Marlen Haushofer. Die Wand [The Wall]. Erläuterungen und Dokumente. Reclam, Stuttgart

Hampe M (2020) Die Wildnis, Die Seele, Das Nichts [The Wilderness, The Soul, The Nothingness]. Über das wirkliche Leben [About real life]. Hanser, Munich Haushofer M (1990 [1963]) *Die Wand*: Originally published by Classen-Verlag GmbH, Düsseldorf. Translation by Shaun Whiteside, Quartet Books, 1990/Cleis Press Inc., Pittsburg Edition, 2020. Ullstein, Hamburg

von Hoff D, Leuzinger-Bohleber M (1997) Versuch einer Begegnung [Attempt at an encounter]. Psychoanalytische und textanalytische Verständigungen zur Elfriede Jelineks Buch "Lust" [Psychoanalytical and text-analytical understandings of Elfriede Jelinek's book "Lust"]. Psyche Z Psychoanal 51:763–804

Leuzinger-Bohleber M (2009) Frühe Kindheit als Schicksal? [Early childhood as fate?] Trauma, embodiment, social disintegration. Psychoanalytical perspectives. With child-analytical case reports by Angelika Wolff and Rose Ahlheim. Kohlhammer, Stuttgart

Leuzinger-Bohleber M, Hautzinger M, Keller W, Fiedler G, Bahrke U, Kallenbach L, Kaufhold J, Negele A, Küchenhoff H, Günther F, Rüger B, Ernst M, Rachel P, Beutel M (2019) Psychoanalytic and cognitive-behavioural long-term treatment of chronically depressed patients in randomised or preferential allocation. Results of the LAC study. Psyche-Z Psychoanal 73:77–105

Lorenz DGC (1979) Marlen Haushofer—eine Feministin aus Österreich [an Austrian feminist]. Modern Austrian Literature 12(3/4):171–191

Stern DN (1985/2018) The interpersonal world of the infant: a view from psychoanalysis and developmental psychology. Routledge, London

Stigl D (2000/2009) "Wahrscheinlich bin ich verrückt ... [I'm probably crazy]" Marlen Haushofer—the biography. Ullstein, Berlin

Von Matt P (1989) Liebesverrat: die Treulosen in der Literatur [Betrayal of love: the faithless in literature]. Hanser, Munich

Winnicott D (1969) Child, family and environment. Ernst Reinhardt Publishing House, Munich

Resilient Femininity in *Three Billboards Outside Ebbing, Missouri*

8

Svetlozar Vassilev

Whoever fights monsters should see to it that in the process he does not become a monster—F. Nietzsche

Introduction

Sarcasm, protest and rebellion against the system are distinguishing characteristics of Martin McDonagh's dramaturgy. His biography describes him as an ex-punk, but his work is proof that a true punk-rocker remains one for life. Only the means of expression change. It is then no surprise that rebellion against war; against class, race or gender-based exploitation; and against falsity and demagoguery features heavily in his plays *A Beheading in Spokane* (1997), *The Lonesome West* (1997), *The Pillowman* (2003) and *Hangmen* (2015), and the films *In Bruges* (2008), *Seven Psychopaths* (2012) and *The Banshees of Inisherin* (2022). The theme of grass-root resistance typical of punk is at the centre of *Three Billboards Outside Ebbing, Missouri* (2017), which garnered numerous awards and, more importantly, left no viewer unmoved.

The film owes its success to the storyline, the acting performances and the compelling dialogue. A viewer versed in psychoanalysis will immediately realise that the choice of actors is closely linked to the film's themes of violence and social justice: Frances McDormand, adopted at 18 months by a nurse and evangelical pastor, had to move around frequently and face the hostility of neighbours and peers; Woody Harrelson's father was a hitman sentenced to life in prison for the murder of a judge; and Sam Rockwell, the son of divorced parents, had a difficult childhood. Unsurprisingly, the cast brilliantly fit into the scenes of fury, guilt, grief and love.

S. Vassilev (✉)
New Bulgarian University, Sofia, Bulgaria

Bulgarian Psychoanalytic Society, Sofia, Bulgaria

V. Pramataroff-Hamburger, A. Hamburger (eds.), *From La Strada to The Hours*,
https://doi.org/10.1007/978-3-662-68789-5_8

Martin McDonagh, director and screenwriter of *Three Billboards Outside Ebbing, Missouri*, has said that the film is based on the true story of the rape and murder of a young girl in a small American town in 1991. The crime was ignored by the police because the perpetrator was from a wealthy and influential family. The billboards rented by the girl's mother can still be seen just outside Vidor, Texas. The film's impact is created by the alternating episodes in which we are repulsed by the arrogance and distance between the characters and then drawn in by their newly found closeness.

The story unfolds in the fictional town of Ebbing, Missouri. The film opens with shots of three enormous, abandoned billboards by an empty country road. Mildred pulls over and starts thinking. She is a single mother whose daughter was raped and murdered seven months before. Spurred by the lack of arrests following the investigation, she provokes the town's sheriff with the following messages on the billboards:

'Raped While Dying'

'And Still No Arrests'

'How Come, Chief Willoughby?'

Over the course of the film, Mildred manages to turn everyone against her—the townspeople, her son, her ex-husband, the church, the police and the media. Although she becomes the target of a series of threats and violence, she doesn't back down and gradually wins over the hearts of her opponents: first, the terminally ill Sheriff, Willoughby, then James, the town's dwarf, and then her fiercest opponent, Officer Dixon. In the closing scene, former enemies Mildred and Dixon travel to Idaho, brought together by the idea of killing the alleged perpetrator. While driving, they realise their desire for vengeance has lost some of its fervour. Mildred's tragedy makes us ask ourselves what we would do in her position. Would we be able to retain our humanity or would we give in to the impulse for revenge?

This chapter attempts to answer the above questions. The first part will analyse the film through the viewer's experience, while the second will explore the metamorphoses of the female characters in the film.

Part I. Analysis of the Spectatorship[1]

The first shots reveal Mildred and the billboards as the most important characters in the film. These billboards, looming like cathedrals of contemporary marketing, exude despair and decadence. Thomas Moore's[2] melancholic 'The Last Rose of Summer' (1813), performed in Renee Fleming's soprano, is playing in the background:

---

[1] The analysis of the spectatorship is a method from the field of psychoanalytic film criticism. For details see A. Hamburger (2018) Filmpsychoanalyse: Das Unbewusste im Kino - das Kino im Unbewussten. Psychosozial Verlag GbR and S. Vassilev (2019). Mirror of the Imagination. Colibri Publishing house, Sofia.

Vassilev *Mirror of the Imagination* (Colibri Publishing House, 2019) and A. Hamburger *Film Psychoanalysis* (New Bulgarian University, 2020).

[2] Thomas Moore was an Irish poet, composer and songwriter, and 'The Last Rose of Summer' is his best known poem.

Tis the last rose of summer,
Left blooming alone;
All her lovely companions,
Are faded and gone;
No flower of her kindred,
No rose-bud is nigh,
To reflect back her blushes
To give sigh for sigh!

The story can now unfold. The contrast between Mildred's unglamorous appearance and the slick, professionally produced red-and-black posters confuses us, and we find ourselves puzzling over the coexistence of beauty and ugliness in the same woman. Her contradictory nature is the first sign that ambivalence is both the theme and the main vehicle for creating an impact on the audience. Dressed in her plain work overalls, Mildred is 'as tough as an old boot', constantly swearing, cursing, and with nothing good to say about anyone. Her first encounter with Willoughby draws us emotionally into the conflict between them and confronts us with the moral dilemma of whose side to be on. We sympathise with the Chief, who has done everything in his power to track down the killer, but our hearts go out to Mildred, who is the main expression of emotional suffering throughout the film. This dilemma is complicated by our feelings for Willoughby, who has terminal cancer. McDonagh complicates matters by showing Mildred's unscrupulousness in the following dialogue:

Willoughby: I got cancer. I am dying.
Mildred: I know it. Most everybody in town knows it.
Willoughby: And you still put those billboards?
Mildred: Well, they wouldn't be as effective after you croak, right?

We wonder why Mildred in all her suffering cannot feel empathy for a fellow sufferer. Is she heartless, or is there another explanation for her behaviour? A few scenes later, she calls a local priest a paedophile and then puts a hole in a dentist's thumb with his own drill. The screen is splattered with blood, and we are shocked once again. This same feeling is evoked in a later scene when Mildred throws a Molotov cocktail at the police station while an unsuspecting Dixon is reading Willoughby's heartfelt letter. *The Last Rose of Summer* is playing once more, the shots are gloomy, and the red flames against the dark backdrop intensify the feelings of grief and the anger inside us. Her deed leads to the disfigurement of Dixon, who escapes death only because he is rescued by his recent enemy, James.

We cannot accept but we can justify Mildred's behaviour when we realise that she was the victim of systematic domestic abuse by her husband. We realise that she has found the strength to divorce him and no longer allows anyone to mistreat her. We feel respect for her when we find out that her ex-husband is trying to deal with their daughter's death by having an affair with a shallow nineteen year old, leaving Mildred to fight for justice on her own.

As the story unfolds, our disoriented perceptions are soothed by Mildred's increasingly softer image. A key scene in this respect is when, while interrogating her, the Chief coughs up blood in her face. For the first time, she shows genuine concern for someone else and calls for help. The viscerality of the moment when the blood connects them in a conspiratorial bond is meant to suggest this as the turning point in the story. From here on, they both begin to change. The Chief's machismo mellows: as paramedics are wheeling him out on a stretcher, he orders his subordinates to release Mildred from custody. In the next scenes, we witness his infinite love for his wife and daughters, and our compassion for him deepens as he reads his farewell letters. In his letter addressed to Mildred, he expresses genuine regret that he failed to arrest the killer and says that to atone for his negligence he has paid the next month's rent for the billboards.

The film gradually draws us deeper into Mildred's world where, surprisingly, love, tenderness and cruelty coexist side by side. We are charmed when she is blunt, when she defends Denise, her black friend, and when she is talking to a deer. One of the most touching moments is when she is sitting by the billboards and imagines that the deer is a reincarnation of her daughter. A little later, we see her cry for the first and last time.[3]

Willoughby's suicide propels the dynamic of the story and changes our experience of the film. Enraged by the Chief's death, Dixon beats the advertising agency owner, Welby, to a pulp; the billboards are set on fire by an unknown perpetrator, and then, the police station is set on fire. From this moment onwards, our experience of desperation is mitigated. We are immersed in the scenes of forgiveness, solidarity and support: Mildred's ex-husband confesses to setting the billboards on fire, and James and Welby help Dixon despite having been bullied and publicly humiliated by him until recently.

Willoughby's farewell letter changes not only Dixon but the entire film. It is also an important source of information for us, the audience. As we observe his reactions, we realise that for the first time in his life he is experiencing the feeling of being liked by someone other than his mother. We experience the same joy that he feels on receiving Willoughby's advice that he can achieve his dreams, as long as he does not let hate drive his behaviour. Yet another act of forgiveness from Willoughby[4] allows Dixon to search for answers on the road to redemption. Up until this moment, Officer Dixon has been a blundering man, sexually repressed and dominated by his mother, reminiscent of Norman Bates in *Psycho* (Alfred Hitchcock 1960). For the third time, after Mildred and Willoughby, the portrayal of one of the characters gains depth and complexity, after those of Mildred and Willoughby. Only after we find out from the letter that Dixon is an orphan do we understand his hatred is rooted in his anger at his father, while his subconscious guilt forces him to be inseparable from his mother. Willoughby's death is a loss but also a discovery: Dixon finally finds the father figure he has always yearned for, one who loves him and believes in him. Thanks to this, Dixon is able to understand his guilt towards Mildred and helps the investigation actively—by letting himself get beaten up in order to secure DNA evidence from Angela Hayes's suspected killer. The sinner becomes a saint.

[3] McDonagh uses the conversation with the deer to express Mildred's tenderness and femininity. This moment is a counterpoint to the aggressive masculinity and a reference to the film *The Deer Hunter* (dir. Michael Cimino, 1978), in which the main characters kill deer for pleasure.

[4] We know that in the past Willoughby did not fire Dixon, despite an accusation of racially motivated violence against a detainee.

And just when we start to believe once again that good can triumph over evil comes the news that the DNA samples don't match. Nevertheless, Dixon suggests that he and Mildred take justice into their own hands.

Are they capable of murdering the perpetrator? Even if he is not guilty of this particular crime? Just then, Mildred asks, 'Are you sure about this?' Dixon replies, 'Bout killing this guy? Not really. You?' The last line in the film is again Mildred's: 'Not really. I guess we can decide along the way'. The final shots are of a man and a woman driving down a quiet country road. She, the older of the two, is driving and talking about the purpose of their journey.

Our identification with Mildred is inevitable. Each and every one of us has experienced loss and has faced injustice and violence. Her dilemma takes us back to moments in which we have responded to aggression with aggression, felt guilt or managed to come out of the situation with dignity. The film finale is where the real challenge comes. We are made to question whether we should justify the premeditated murder or believe that goodness will prevail and we will once again side with the victors.

Part II. Metamorphoses of the Feminine

The Female Images in the Film

Mildred is a heroine who has erased everything feminine from herself. She is a female warrior with an androgynous appearance, hair and clothing. If we examine her from a psychoanalytic perspective, however, we will find that her approach to everyday situations is feminine: unlike the dentist, she does not use unwarranted violence against her opponents, nor does she throw them out of windows, like Officer Dixon. Her weapon is completely legitimate—advertising is the most powerful modern tool for exerting influence, and Mildred turns it against the most influential man in town. She uses her weapon so skilfully that first she disarms Chief Willoughby and then wins him over to her side. The interaction between the two of them sets off a series of acts of solidarity and caring that transform their community.

To get to that point, however, there is a long way to go. Mildred is extremely consistent in defending her cause. She opposes her son who is terrified of losing his friends because of her; and she opposes her husband, who strikes at the heart of her efforts by setting the billboards on fire. She also withstands the threats of the psychopath who visits her shop. Perhaps, the toughest battle of all is the one with Chief Willoughby, who is dying of pancreatic cancer. McDonagh forces us to think about how tough Mildred can be with a dying and well-respected man. The answer is very tough! It is precisely thanks to her confrontational character that she wins this conflict with the Chief—after the initial shock, Willoughby returns to his duties, reopening the Angela Hayes's case, restoring the discipline in his team and supporting Mildred at a critical time by paying the rent for the billboards.

Fig. 8.1 Femininity in contrast to masculinity (0:43:04)

Ambivalence is a key theme in the film and McDonagh's success is owed to the fact that it pulls the viewer into the conflict between love and hate experienced by the characters. The moment when a coughing Sheriff Willoughby spits out some of his lungs, literally garnished with blood, onto Mildred's face is the first situation in the film when an ugly and repulsive relationship is replaced by mutual understanding and support. Thanks to his support, Mildred abandons her arrogant attitude and increasingly begins to rely on the femininity within her. It is through her sensitivity and receptivity that she is able to win Willoughby and Dixon over to her side and overcome the indifference of the townspeople (Fig. 8.1).

Her conflicted nature is the most important expressive device in the film. McDonagh keeps us on our toes and only at the end does he allow us to realise that even though Mildred has erased femininity from her exterior, she has preserved it in her inner world. The conflict is both internal and external as she wages battle against male rapists, racist policemen and paedophile priests. She has divorced her husband because he abused her and withstands his attacks when he grabs her by the throat, but at the same time, she is prepared to kill to avenge her daughter's death.

McDonagh uses the image of Mildred to bring to light our most primitive, unconscious fears of the phallic homicidal mother.[5] From the very first shots, we sense that she is aggressive and dangerous, and when she evades prosecution for setting fire to the police station, we are alarmed by her untouchability. Dressed in denim overalls and with a bandanna[6] tied on her head, Mildred is the female counterpart to Sylvester Stallone in *Rambo*

[5]According to Freud, the phallic stage of psychosexual development is common to both sexes. This phase culminates in a transition from a psychic organisation dominated by the idealisation of the phallus to a psychic organisation based on identification with the symbolic function of the penis as a link. This allows for the emergence of mature sexuality and the perception of sexuality as the highest form of emotional intimacy.

[6]The bandanna is a reference to and expression of McDonagh's admiration for the film *The Deer Hunter*, in which Robert De Niro and Christopher Walken wear bandannas while fighting in Vietnam and playing Russian roulette.

(Ted Kotcheff 1982) and the Vietnam veterans in *The Deer Hunter* (Michael Cimino 1978). We breathe a sigh of relief later on when she increasingly starts acting through receptivity and containment.[7] This expression of her femininity allows the men around her and the community to rediscover their dignity. And just when we are feeling calmer, the open-ended finale makes us wonder once again if Mildred is not a murderer after all.

Images of Mothers in the Film

Three Billboards can also be seen as a film about the contradictory nature of motherhood. McDonagh draws us into the juxtaposition of two simultaneously loving and repulsive images of mothers – those of Mildred and Mama Dixon. Mildred is presented as a mother experiencing unimaginable loss yet retaining her dignity and love. McDonagh tells the story in a way that inevitably makes us sympathise with her lonely struggle and admire the resilience with which she faces the attacks following her rebellion against the system.

Despite the similarities between them, both are single mothers with an edgy personality who have experienced a string of losses and dedicated their lives to their children—Mildred is a counterpoint to Mama Dixon. On the surface, she is the more aggressive of the two: in almost all exchanges between her and her children, she quarrels with them, while Mama Dixon lives in complete harmony with her son. However, Mildred's perceived aggression is based on values and a cause that she openly declares and which she finds important enough to willingly fight for. In contrast, Mama Dixon's mothering is based on blurring differences and channelling hatred and tension outside the mother-son pair. Anyone could end up on the long list of objects of her projections—Mildred, black people, homosexuals and anyone with a different worldview than hers.

McDonagh juxtaposes Mildred and Mama Dixon in order to draw us in emotionally. He makes us sympathise with one and loathe the other, only to confuse us by reversing their roles a moment later, and further to remind us that ambivalence is the emotional state we regress to at critical moments.

Psychoanalysis, Femininity and Resilience

Femininity

Contemporary psychoanalytic views on femininity are dominated by the differences and contradictions between the various schools. One of the areas which most authors agree on is that the mature version of gender identity results from a favourable combination of the successful processing of intrapsychic conflicts and the presence of support from signifi-

[7] Wilfred Bion coined the term containment to refer to the mother's ability to understand and soothe the unconscious anxieties of the infant. Thanks to identification with the mother, the child gradually internalises her receptive ability and applies it to relationships with all subsequent figures in its life.

cant figures in life (Birksted-Breen 1993). This is a significant development from Freud's original views (Freud 1905), which dominated the debate in the first half of the twentieth century. A leading figure over the next few decades was Robert Stoller, who described and differentiated core, gender and sexual identities (Stoller 1968, 1975). Specialist interest in the late twentieth and early twenty-first centuries largely focused on linking masculinity and femininity to the functions of activity and receptivity (Birksted-Breen 1996).

The analysis of the three central characters through the prism of these ideas is particularly worthwhile. Sheriff Willoughby embodies mature masculine identity and fatherhood. Almost until the end of the film, he is the only man capable of harnessing his potency for the purposes of development. In contrast, Dixon's behaviour is phallocentric, and the transition to mature masculinity is realised through the internalisation of Willoughby as a symbolic father. Mildred's image is the most complex. Her maternal role is solid, but her gender and sexual identity deserve further comment. For most of the film, she acts like a man, and her sexuality is absent. The topics of sexuality in her relationships are defined by references to violence and abuse. Let us recall the last exchange between her and her daughter:

Angela: I hope I get raped on the way!

Mildred: Yeah, well, I hope you get raped on the way too!

Another moment that presents us with conflicting emotions is when Mildred uses paedophilia as a reason to drive the priest out of her home. The counterpoint to this is sexuality as the supreme expression of love and intimacy, as exemplified in Willoughby's relationship with his wife and James's attitude to Mildred. Viewed through the prism of gender roles, Mildred shows both feminine and masculine behaviours. Psychoanalysis takes it as axiomatic that psychic bisexuality is part of human nature and associates masculinity with the desire to penetrate (the active function), and femininity with the desire to be penetrated (the passive function). Contemporary developments and research into gender identity have led to the understanding that receptivity, not passivity, is the central feature of femininity. Mature masculinity is in turn seen as a role and a function, an essential part of which is to protect women from the malignant projections of the baby and real threats in reality (Steiner 2017). It is therefore not surprising that Mildred is both receptive, i.e. feminine, and militant, i.e. masculine. The second type of behaviour is characteristic of the first two-thirds of the film when she is alone and has no male support (Fig. 8.2).

Through his suicide and the way he parts with his loved ones, Willoughby sets an example of powerfully masculine behaviour to the men around him. The support that Mildred receives from them allows for the emergence of a triadic space which makes self-reflection and the containment of pain possible. Therefore, from this point on, she begins to control her aggression and starts to behave receptively, that is, to display behaviour characteristic of the woman's role. This evidence is in support of the thesis that femininity is defined not only in relation to itself but also to masculinity. Maturity for both genders implies integration and identification with the maternal and paternal object in a way that frees up personal resources for symbolisation and creativity. The ending of the film suggests that the protagonists have come a long way and have reached this level of development.

Fig. 8.2 Alone Against the World, Including Her Own Family (00:39:10)

The Resilient Ego: Traumatism Versus Activism

At the centre of the story are recurring relationships of violence, pain, sadness, anger and more violence. Everyone is looking for confrontation and is ready for a fight with Mildred, but instead of being traumatised, she withstands every attack. Today, we believe that the first condition for successfully overcoming psychological trauma is to acknowledge to those who have experienced it that they are victims. Recognising trauma certainly enables it to be treated but has an associated adverse effect—the label 'victim' deprives people of a dignified way of surviving. McDonagh's contribution is to show that traumatisation can be overcome not only through humility but also through taking an active social stance. We derive satisfaction precisely because of Mildred's 'Protest and Survive'[8] position in the film. The only scene where she loses her resilience is when she discovers the burning billboards. The destroyed billboards symbolise the destroyed hope that her daughter's death will be avenged, and in one brief moment, she is prepared to burn with them. Just then, however, she is helped by her son, who brings a second fire extinguisher. It's a double victory—he finally takes her side, and she saves the billboards.

By identifying with Mildred's willingness to use any means to further her cause, McDonagh allows us to feel relief and to believe that fighting against the injustice of the system is a higher value. Mildred succeeds precisely because she manages to unite her masculine and feminine sides. Over the course of the story, she overcomes the aggressive part of herself through her feminine qualities. Thanks to this metamorphosis from being an outsider into the emotional leader of the community, Mildred transforms the primitive atmosphere of the town.

Such a position requires mental resilience, which can be defined as the ability to overcome stressful situations with as little damage as possible. Freud demonstrated that resil-

[8] 'Protest and Survive' is one of the slogans of the punk-rock movement.

ience depends on the ego's capacity to process loss and mediate between internal and external reality (Freud 1917, 1923). His view suggests that ego-resilience is not only expressed in damage limitation but also in the ability to be open to new possibilities. Later writers, a key figure among whom is Melanie Klein, link resilience to overcoming ambivalence during the transition from a paranoid-schizoid to a depressive position.[9] Unfortunately, publications on the topic rarely focus on the gender differences between men and women and even less on the role of motherhood. Maternal resilience depends on mothers' ability to tolerate ambivalent feelings towards their children, a characteristic that is closely related to personal maturity and the presence of a supportive environment provided by the father and the wider environment (Luthar 2006, Baraitser and Noack 2007).

Three Billboards Outside Ebbing, Missouri is particularly interesting in this respect because the Hayes's family confronts extreme loss and violence. In cases such as theirs, not only are the lives of those affected marked by psychological trauma, but the traumatic effects are passed down the generations. The film illustrates the fact that long-term damage can be avoided not only through therapy but also by taking an active social stance (Salberg and Grand 2017).

Conclusion: Love Begets Love

The film is about the relationship between ambivalence and the great moral issue of our time, violence and the abuse of power in patriarchal societies. The central character is a woman, and we know all too well that women are much less likely than men to have a chance of justice when their rights are violated. The story told by Martin McDonagh is aligned with the psychoanalytic view that redemption and forgiveness are impossible without first overcoming one's own anger and arrogance. McDonagh continually draws us into ambivalent experiences, and these always unlock memories of early childhood relationships with the mother.

Through the audience's impassioned identification, the film unlocks the conflict in our unconscious and forces us to feel and to think about what we would do if we were in Mildred's place. Since she does terrible things for a good cause and the film's ending is left open, it suggests that the path is neither easy nor black and white. Mostly, it depends on our ability to turn enemies into allies.

Translated by Lora Ward and Tim Ward.

[9] The transition from the paranoid-schizoid to the depressive position is crucial for psychosexual development. Melanie Klein postulated that this transition first occurs in infancy, resulting in the infant becoming able to tolerate feelings of hatred and love for the mother and to adequately appraise internal and external reality (Klein 1957). The fluctuation between the two positions is characteristic of later life stages, but as experience is gained, the ability to enter into lasting relationships of affection and trust increases.

Film Details

Original title	Three Billboards Outside Ebbing, Missoury
Release year	2017
Country	USA
Book	Martin McDonagh
Direction	Martin McDonagh
Music	Cartel Burwell
Camera	Ben Davis
Main actors	Frances McDormand, Woody Harrelson, Sam Rockwell, John Hawkes
Availability	DVD, Blu-ray

References

Baraitser L, Noack A (2007) Mother courage: reflections on maternal resilience. Br J Psychother 23:171–188

Birksted-Breen (1993) The gender conundrum. Contemporary psychoanalytic perspectives on femininity and masculinity. Taylor & Francis, Routledge

Birksted-Breen D (1996) Phallus, penis and mental space. Int J Psychoanal 77(4):649–657

Freud S (1905) Three essays on the theory of sexuality, SE vol 7, pp 1–246

Freud S (1917) Mourning and Melancholia, SE vol 14, pp 8

Freud S (1923) The ego and the Id, SE vol 19

Hamburger A (2018) Filmpsychoanalyse: Das Unbewusste im Kino - das Kino im Unbewussten. Psychosozial Verlag GbR

Klein M (1957) Envy and gratitude. The writings of Melanie Klein, Vol. 3: envy and gratitude and other works, 1946–1963. Hogarth Press and the Institute of Psycho-Analysis, London

Luthar SS (2006) Resilience in development: a synthesis of research across five decades. In: Cicchetti D, Cohen DJ (eds) Developmental psychopathology: risk, disorder, and adaptation. John Wiley & Sons Inc, pp 739–795

Moore T (1813) The last rose of summer. In A selection of Irish melodies: volume V. Gill & Son, Dublin, Ireland 1963

Salberg J, Grand S (2017) Wounds of history: repair and resilience in the trans-generational transmission of trauma edited by Jill Salberg and Sue Grand. Routledge, London & New York, p 2017

Steiner J (2017) Lectures on technique by Melanie Klein. Taylor & Francis, Routledge

Stoller R (1968) Sex and gender: on the development of masculinity and femininity. Science House, New York City

Stoller R (1975) Perversion: the erotic form of hatred. Pantheon, New York

Vassilev S (2019) A mirror of imagination. A psychoanalysis of film experience. Colibri Publishing House

Part III

Mothers and Daughters

Why Mothers Are Immortal (All About My Mother)

9

Christa Rohde Dachser

All About My Mother—a film that allows us to participate in the devastating grief associated with losing a child and takes us down unexpected avenues in the process.

Plot

Argentinian Manuela (Cecilia Roth), a former actress, is a nurse in the transplant department of a hospital in Madrid. On her son Sebastian's 17th birthday, after a performance of *A Streetcar Named Desire*, the boy chases after leading actress Huma Rojo to get her autograph, is hit by a car and killed. After his death, Manuela is asked to agree to an organ donation: his heart could save the life of another young man.

Manuela falls into a deep crisis. Esteban had left a manuscript entitled 'Todo sobre mi madre', in which he bemoans the fact that he has never met his father, whose identity Manuela has kept secret from him. Her reasons in doing so are because Esteban's father no longer has the same name as his son but has undergone gender reassignment and is now called Lola. Lola has no idea he has a son. Now, Manuela goes looking for him on her son's behalf.

This article is based on a film review published on 12th June 2006 in the context of the 'Psychoanalysis and Film' series by the DPG Frankfurt/Main Institute for Psychoanalysis. It has been slightly revised and its structure adjusted for the present book edition.

C. R. Dachser (✉)
Hannover, Germany
e-mail: crd@crdh.de

V. Pramataroff-Hamburger, A. Hamburger (eds.), *From La Strada to The Hours*,
https://doi.org/10.1007/978-3-662-68789-5_9

While searching for Lola in Barcelona, Manuela meets her old transsexual friend Agrado, the actress Huma Rojo and the nun Maria Rosa, who works in a shelter for prostitutes. She has slept with Lola, who has infected her with HIV, and is now expecting his baby. Manuela becomes entangled in these events and abandons her search for Lola. She starts working as an assistant for Huma Rojo; one night, she becomes an impromptu stand-in for Huma's drug addicted lover Nina at a performance of *A Streetcar Named Desire*, thus returning to the stage once more.

However, she then bumps into Lola at Maria Rosa's funeral (the nun has died in childbirth) and tells him about Esteban. She adopts Rosa's son, who is christened Esteban, and moves into Rosa's parents' house with him. Rosa's father suffers from severe dementia, so she is introduced to him as 'the new cook and her child'. When the truth about the child's father being Lola (who infected Rosa) comes out, she has to leave this precarious home and return to Madrid with her child.

Years later, Manuela, Huma and Agrado meet again and Manuela says that little Esteban has miraculously not been infected with his father's HIV.

Background

Pedro Almodóvar's 14th film won the Academy Award for *Best Foreign Film* and numerous other major awards. He had already presented a number of highly acclaimed films which had garnered international interest: *La ley del deseo* (*The Law of Desire*, 1987), *Mujeres al borde de un ataque de nervios (Women on the Verge of a Nervous Breakdown*, 1988), *Átame! (Tie Me Up! Tie Me Down!* 1990) and *Tacones Lejanos (High Heels*, 1991).

All About My Mother contains countless allusions and references to other films, literature and theatre. The title itself recalls the classic film *All About Eve* by Joseph Mankiewicz (USA 1950), which is about a dangerous stalker. The dead boy, Esteban, is strongly linked to Tennessee Williams' *A Streetcar Named Desire* (1947)—the play he saw just before his accidental death (his mother will later make a stage come-back in this same play)—and Truman Capote's *Music for Chameleons*, which his mother gave him as a birthday present on the same day.

Capote had been ostracised after his book of revelatory stories was published and sank into drugs and depression, however made a triumphant return to the literary stage with this same book in 1980. These two references can be seen as a commentary on the cultural environment of the film: since Franco's death in 1975, Spanish cinema had been concerned with cultural upheaval and the question of how to shape a new, modern society after the collapse of fascism. Through his playful portrayal of this search for identity, Almodóvar sets a completely new tone and develops his own visual style. In this respect, the literary references also emphasise a contrast and indicate that 'This is a whole new movie'. Another literary reference is Federico García Lorca's play *Yerma* (1934), in which a woman kills her husband because he denies her a child. Huma Rojo plays the role of the Yerma, desperate because she cannot become a mother, in the last evening performance at the end of the film. This is also a direct allusion to Spain: the birth rate declined drastically in the post-Franco era. Women were refusing to bear children due to the sudden opportunity to express themselves in other ways than the imposed traditional role of having large families. *Yerma* was rediscovered as a key drama; as well as appearing in *All About My Mother*, Pilar Távora released a remake of the pre-war play in 1999. This shows how closely the social upheaval after Franco was intertwined with the topos of femininity and especially motherhood in the cultural discourse of Spain.

The intertextual references mentioned all have something to say about femininity. *All About Eve* concerns a young woman who uses unfair means to take the place of a diva. In *A Streetcar Named Desire*, Blanche, lost, an outcast and childless, is seeking an identity—and a haven with her conventionally married and pregnant sister. And finally, Capote's book above all represents his comeback, however also refers to the women whom he had previously publicly exposed in his masterly essay writing, even driving one of them to suicide, which ultimately also led to his own downfall. Characteristically, Almodóvar visualises the social rupture and the onset of the compulsion to rebuild society from the standpoint of women, and he does so in gaudy burlesque. Femininity and motherliness run through Almodóvar's entire oeuvre, which always revolves around the dissolution of traditional patriarchal family constellations; he consistently presents his arguments through parody. *All About My Mother* is also a particularly fine example of this.

Femininity

We experience the way Manuela—it is presumably no coincidence that her name shares the same initial letter as Maria, the Pietà in the Christian gospel—collapses over Esteban, who has been hit by a car, wailing, 'My son, my son'. We feel drawn into the psychological liminal space that Manuela traverses before she can agree to give her son's heart to an anonymous recipient, a young married man who will then carry on living with it and owe his life to it. Manuela follows her son's heart to find the recipient. She watches him leaving the transplant hospital with his wife and his new heart, breathing 'like before'. His life goes on, but Manuela will no longer be part of it. She lets him go, and then, instead of her son, who died without finding out who his father was, she goes in search of this father whom she left long ago, as if in hindsight she wanted to complete her family, half of which had been missing up to that point.

We take the train with the grieving Manuela, whom we know only as a nurse, through a long tunnel back to her past, to Barcelona, where to our surprise we find ourselves in a milieu of prostitution, gender reassignment, violence and drugs. We meet people who are at home there, and finally Lola, the father of the deceased Esteban and a new son, whom Manuela holds in her arms at the end of the film, almost as if her son were born again inside this baby. I myself took a long time to understand this unexpected course of events and to extract any psychoanalytic meaning from it.

Opposites

In general, the film is considered a homage to motherhood. But it is difficult to reconcile the red-light district with motherhood. On the contrary, our ideas of motherhood and sexuality are usually mutually exclusive. In psychoanalysis, there are two separate ideas of motherhood: firstly, that of the early or pre-oedipal mother, whose entire attention is on the child—Mary holding baby Jesus is the most striking example—and secondly, an oedipal or sexual mother who maintains a sexual relationship with the father from which the child is excluded. Here, the child has lost its unique place in the mother's eyes or heart and instead has to compete with the father for her. The child therefore always finds the Oedipal mother a treacherous one, whom the child does not easily forgive for focusing her desires on someone else. This defence is very deeply rooted in each of us, as is evidenced by our reaction to an image of a child accompanied by a woman wearing makeup as if she were actually expecting her lover to arrive. 'That kind of woman can't be a good mother', we immediately think on seeing her, indirectly confirming how strongly we separate motherhood and sexuality from one another. Almodóvar's film takes a different approach in this respect.

With few exceptions, there are no 'real' men in the film. The film protagonists are either transsexual or senile or, like the first suitor La Agrado, embody a form of male sexuality that is associated with extreme violence and does not baulk at committing murder. La Agrado is a transsexual with a penis and breasts, and sometimes when one of her co-workers is feeling desperate like a child, she even lets him suck on one of them. Actress Huma Rojo, who is playing Blanche in *A Streetcar Named Desire*, is a lesbian with a drug addict lover who makes her life miserable. Lola, the father of both Manuela's and Rosa's sons, is transgender and appears in the guise of a woman, beautiful, a drug addict, HIV infected, macho and unfaithful. In other words, someone who, according to Manuela, unites all the bad qualities of men and women and still somehow manages to look majestic. Even zanier, there is also a nun, Maria Rosa, who is held to be the maternal guardian angel of prostitutes and is about to go to El Salvador for a nun who was murdered in the civil war. However, because she slept with Lola, she herself is now infected with HIV and pregnant. This nun figure is pretty much a unified vision of everything which, according to our cultural ideas, should be mutually exclusive: virgin, nun, guardian angel of prostitutes, lover of a transsexual drug addict, infected with HIV and carrying a child. Manuela herself, Esteban's mother, does not easily fit into this milieu. We first get to know her as a nurse who works in a hospital where she is responsible for transferring organs for transplants. In concrete terms, this means that in the moment the EEG of a dying (usually adolescent) patient flatlines, she will step away from his bed to inform the transplant centre of a possible donor organ. The maternal, caring qualities that are associated with nursing thus seem strangely fractured, despite all her superficial persuasiveness. At the start of the film, she is standing by the bedside of a patient whose death does not cause us any grief at all. Rather, Manuela is waiting for his death in order to inform a colleague at a transplant centre who is responsible for organ procurement that an organ has become available. We are only confronted with her *own*, genuine grief when her son's heart is concerned, which she inwardly follows wherever it takes her from that moment on. But perhaps, transforming the death of your dearest loved one back into life is also a supreme expression of maternal love, even if it is somebody else's life. It would be no different if Manuela used to be a prostitute herself. When her son asks her if she would also walk the streets for him, she says, 'I've already done just about everything for you'. And we wouldn't be surprised if Manuela had said, 'I've already done that for you, too'. According to Agrado, Manuela used to be the famous Barceloneta, whatever that may mean in concrete terms[1] and during that time got to know the brothel milieu of Barcelona, in which she still feels at home today. But this also raises the question of how motherhood and prostitution relate to one other: as irreconcilable opposites, which according to Freud is also expressed in the split between Madonna and whore, or whether motherhood is a difficult to understand, fundamental female form of existence that also puts its specific stamp on female sexuality in all its manifestations, including prostitution and transvestitism.

The question is all the more difficult to answer due to long sections of the film seeming to be a play. In an epilogue, Almodóvar himself dedicates the film to all those who like to act as men or women and all the men who would like to be mothers. Some of the film's protagonists are also actresses. This also applies to Manuela, who used to be an amateur actress herself and who plays the same role again in the film and still knows her lines by heart: Stella in Tennessee Williams' play *A Streetcar Named Desire*. The same work recurs in the well-known American feature film *All About Eve*, which the mother and son watch together on television over dinner. And, during a training course for doctors in the hospital, Manuela also repeatedly plays the theatrical role of a woman whose husband has just died. Two doctors then negotiate with her whether or not she agrees to release her husband's heart for transplantation. All three plays force their meaning on the film from the outset, in that they gruesomely come true or, conversely, end in absurdity, as in the film *All about Eve* in which Eva in the character of Manuela, who is only out for her own interests, is juxtaposed against a mother who ostensibly seems to be primarily concerned with other people's wellbeing and who understandingly steps back when she is no longer needed to play the role. A closer look at the plot of *All About Eve* and *A Streetcar Named Desire* will help us to better understand this interconnectedness. The film *All about Eve* concerns a young woman, Eve, who seems superficially friendly but nevertheless does everything she can behind the scenes to wrest the leading role and lover away from an ageing actress who has been very kind and maternally loving towards her, in order to become a famous Hollywood star *like her*. The role that Eva wants to appropriate from the diva is that of Blanche from Tennessee Williams' drama *A Streetcar Named Desire*, which also plays a prominent role in our film.

[1] Barceloneta is actually a district of Barcelona that, after Franco, was still quite like a fishing village but had a very lively subculture, until it was 'rehabilitated' in a capitalist makeover after the 1992 Olympics.

Tennessee Williams' famous play is about *Blanche*, a young woman from a respected family who is spoiled by success and faces financial and social ruin after the foreclosure of her mansion. Her sister Stella is happily married to Kowalski, who in Blanche's view is rather primitive, and Blanche seeks refuge at their home in New Orleans. Stella embraces Blanche lovingly, and she continues to act out her lie as a highly respected, desired and spoiled woman from the southern states, even in the new milieu that she basically despises. When the truth finally comes out and she is raped by Kowalski while his wife is giving birth to their first child in hospital, she breaks down and is taken away to a psychiatric institution. When Stella hears what has happened, she leaves the house with her newborn child, never to set foot in it again.

We know from Manuela's stories that, as a young woman, she played the role of Stella in an amateur production of *A Streetcar Named Desire.* Her lover to be and Esteban's father played the role of Kowalski in the same play, as if her later fate had already been somehow planned in advance in this play. Her son Esteban is particularly interested in the same play, although mainly on account of the actress Huma Rojo, who plays the role of Blanche.

Sham Existence

For his 17th birthday, he asks to go to the play with Manuela. We see both of them sitting in the auditorium while the last scene of the play is being acted out on stage, in which the psychiatrist also appears. Blanche vehemently resists her role as a psychiatric patient with all her might and only calms down when the psychiatrist addresses her as 'madam' and politely asks her to come with him, thereby colluding in her sham existence. Stella reacts differently, drawing a line and leaving home with her son, who will henceforth grow up without a father. Esteban sees his mother crying next to him.

After the show, Esteban and his mother wait for Huma Rojo because Esteban absolutely has to have her autograph. While they are waiting, Esteban asks his mother to tell him about his father, which she has never done. She has only told him his father had died before he was born. Manuela now promises to break her silence and, since today is his birthday, to tell him about his father as soon as they get home. When Huma Rojo leaves the theatre with her companion and they both get into a taxi, Esteban knocks on the taxi window to get Huma's autograph. Huma looks at him intently through the closed window for a moment, as if she has known him for a long time, and then, the taxi drives on. Esteban tears himself away from his mother and runs after the car. He is knocked down by another vehicle and later dies of his injuries in hospital. We see Manuela throwing herself on him, crying out in the deepest despair, 'my son, my son', as if the pain of his death would never end.

We first have to extract ourselves from the emotionality of this scene in order to ask, from a psychoanalytic point of view, what psychodynamic explanations there are for Esteban's death and his mother's despair. One such psychoanalytic interpretation could be that Esteban had to die at this point because his knock on Huma Rojo's window, the actress who played Blanche in the play, and wanting her autograph can be understood as an unconscious attempt to unmask his mother's lie about his father's death. In this case, Huma Rojo, or Blanche, would then represent a mother who lives in a relationship with her son from which the father is excluded, through a lie that would have been uncovered by that evening at the latest—the evening of his 17th birthday. The close and superficially very harmonious mother-son relationship would have suffered a rift that could never have been reconciled. It is surely no coincidence that while Esteban is running after the car, Manuela is standing alone in the rain with her umbrella, literally 'out in the rain'. But one could also assume that Esteban's death prevented Manuela, who played the role of Stella in *A Streetcar Named Desire*, from suddenly becoming Blanche, whose sham existence would have been exposed by Kowalski. Her son Esteban would thus inadvertently end up in the role of Kowalski. This perspective also allows us to decipher the reasons Almodóvar chose an oversized screen as a poster for the film *All About My Mother*, on which the face of Huma Rojo is depicted as Blanche and in front of which Manuela is standing, small and inconspicuous, waiting for her son with an umbrella under her arm. Huma Rojo's face seems both imposing and enigmatic; it exudes promise, seduction, sadness and longing all at once, which is how some people describe the Mona Lisa, while at the same time its visionary look into the future contains almost intolerable pain. Because even Manuela cannot permanently banish the father from the relationship between herself and her son. Esteban would have been 17 years old the day he died. He has outgrown his mother in terms of his age. His desperate search for an autograph from Huma in the role of Blanche can therefore also be understood as an attempt to escape from this mother-son relationship that has become too intimate. This perspective allows us to understand Esteban's reaction to his mother's birthday present, which she brings to his bed at night while he is writing his diary, which he quickly hides under the pillow when his mother comes in. His mother gives him a book for his birthday, and he asks her to read it to him as she used to when he was little. It begins with the author's foreword, in which the writer's skill is described not only as a gift but also as a scourge. When she notices his reaction, she wants to put the book away, but Esteban sees himself as a writer and his own fate described in the foreword: the fate of a boy who was everything to his mother, not just a child but also a partner and father, in a relationship that is incestuous, not because it is a sexual relationship but because in its uniqueness and inseparability it cannot tolerate any rivals and is established in perpetuity, and which must therefore also rupture as soon as the third party, the father, claims the position to which he is entitled. This does not mean that incestuous fantasies hadn't also been latently present in mother and son. Otherwise, the mother-son conversation about which of them would walk the streets for the other could not have taken place. I rather suspect that it is precisely this constellation that gives motherhood, to which this film pays homage in many ways, its irresistible tragedy. In the reading proposed here, Manuela's role-playing at the hospital and the transplant scene negotiated there also take on a completely different meaning. Esteban's great wish, after all, was to watch his mother act in the role expected of her at the hospital. He watches her with an intensity as if his own fate were also at stake there, and shortly thereafter, it is actually his own heart that is up for negotiation. **In the role of the grieving woman, Manuela says that she doesn't have any family, so nothing to hold onto other than her late husband. And later, when the focus was on her son's heart, she had nothing left to do other than go after it.** In this respect, the role-playing scene is a reflection from Manuela's point of view of what the hunt for Huma Rojo's autograph meant for Esteban, namely, the severing of a symbiotic mother-son relationship which permeates every fibre of their being, which the son is unable to survive and to which the mother responds with endless, ineradicable grief. So, Manuela cannot help but follow her son's heart.

Creating a World in Which There Are Only Mothers

I would also like to do this in the following and look at a world consisting entirely of mothers to try and understand it through the eyes of the son, to see how it works. What form do the childish fantasies that try to explain this world take? How are conception and birth rooted in it, and what understanding is there of separation and death? The first hint of this is to be found in the opening scene of the film.

Transplantation and Primal Scene

In it, we are confronted with liquid dripping from a large IV bag—which immediately reminded me of a large mother's breast hanging over everything that holds this world together, nourishing and caring for it. We then travel through the hospital, passing by countless technical devices and buttons with indecipherable functions, until we arrive at a patient whose EEG is flatlining. Manuela receives this signal and carries out the duties it requires of her. She goes into an adjoining room and calls the transplant centre to say that an organ is available, specifically a heart, and the woman in the office there consults her files to find a suitable recipient. There are posters on the office wall of a boy and a girl, both looking happily and contentedly out at the world, with the caption 'transplantation', as if both were born due to a transplant or were kept alive by one (Fig. 9.1).

The film plot continues by showing the transplant of Esteban's own heart. Here, we also see the recipient of the heart, a man in bed next to his wife, who answers a call from the hospital in the middle of the night telling him the expected heart is ready and that he should get to the hospital as quickly as possible. Parallels between expecting a heart and expecting a baby come to mind, except that the recipient of the heart (in our analogy, the baby) is clearly a man and not a woman. This may be the expression of a childish wish that not only women but also men could be capable of this. We can also follow the heart's destiny. The heart is transported in a freezer through several hospital wards, being carried by a series of different hurrying people dressed in white, and occasionally also transported by plane, until it reaches the recipient, who is already lying on the operating table. We do

Fig. 9.1 Born by transplantation

not learn anything about the transplant itself. However, we see the patient leaving the clinic 3 weeks later, accompanied by his wife, with a transplanted heart, saying he can breathe, 'like before'. There are a number of indications that an infantile birth fantasy lies behind this: life is passed on through an organ transplant and someone has to die so that a new person can be born who will carry on the dead person's life. The fantasy feeds on the mother's statement that Esteban's father died before childbirth. Manuela's role-playing game is also interesting in this context. The woman desperately hopes that her dying husband can be given something to keep him alive, until the doctors make it clear to her that it would be better if he gave up something (his heart and thus his life) in order to save someone else's life. **Esteban's childish fantasy could then be: 'My father died before childbirth, but I carry his heart inside me, just as my heart will live on in another man later on. My father's life continues in me'.** In this fantasy, Manuela is someone who can interpret the signals when the time has come—an *archaic mother* who decides over life and death. Young children are known to wonder what mummy and daddy are doing if they shut the child out of the bedroom and do not want to be disturbed. They also gradually become familiar with the function of sex organs, which play a role in this. A psychoanalytic concept in the same context is the *primal scene,* the fantasised archetype of the sexual encounter between a man and woman. In the film *All About My Mother,* these fantasies are somewhat different. There is no mention of the penis as a genital organ, except in the brief scene in which mother and son are talking about who may have to walk the streets for whom and the son says you need a 'big dick' for that. The mother is astonished and asks where he learned to talk like that, as if it were out of place to do so in the maternal world in which they both live. But where there is no penis, there is no coitus and therefore no incest. Only once do we see Esteban as a budding writer in close-up, pointing the tip of his pencil between his fingers at viewers as a reminder that he is actually about to grow into a man and that the transplanted organ might also be a penis. **In this maternal world, right from the start, this is juxtaposed by the breast symbolised by the infusion**

bag—one might say a mother's heart. The IV bag has two ports, one of which is disabled, as if indicating that half of the subsequent movie is missing.

Inner Objects

Against this background, if we also take the brothel milieu in which the further film takes place to be a product of Esteban's fantasies about the maternal world in which the two of them live together, the presence of both breasts and a penis in most of the characters becomes understandable. The gender difference and along with it the sexual relationship between men and women and thus also between mother and son are omitted. Instead, Esteban unconsciously fantasises about mothers-fathers who are self-sufficient and who, as well as providing nourishment and comfort with their breasts, can also always do so with their penises if someone asks, as Mario does in the film. So, sexuality is manifested in a maternal guise. Male violence is also left out or, as in the scene in which Agrado is almost murdered by a suitor, is averted by a stone that Manuela uses to knock the suitor down. Then, both maternally help the injured man to get back on his feet and to seek shelter somewhere. For Esteban, all of these figures are internal objects that not only reflect his fantasies about the maternal world in which he lives but can also be understood as a reflection of the early maternal relationship in which the maternal body still contained everything the infant needed to live. This also includes the fantasy of an idealised mother who, despite her intense grief for her son, seems in the film to be a woman who can master anything. She is a nurse, cook, bar owner and actress, comforting, helpful, assertive and considerate and—unlike her namesake Eve in the film *All About Eve*—steps back when she is no longer needed. But there is also another mother figure, namely, Rosa's mother, who paints Chagall forgeries (a false mother?) and who unsuccessfully tries to reach her daughter Rosa. Her own interests and expectations interfere too much in the mother-daughter relationship, in which the main focus is on the needs of the child. The mother also suffers from this lack of contact and keeps asking herself where she has gone wrong. So, she is also a mother suffering from *maternal guilt*. A mother like that apparently also played a role in Esteban's childhood and was internally adopted by him in a process of introjection. The man who is Maria Rosa's father and this mother's husband is now apparently so senile that he can't find his way home without the family dog and, unlike it, does not even recognise his own daughter, only managing to ask her stereotypically: 'How old are you?' and 'How tall are you?' This means, however, that his questions are not really to be taken seriously. The associated latent message is that 'fathers are senile and useless'. And then, there is *Maria Rosa*, the new Esteban's mother, who, as a nun, is as virginal in appearance as any boy could wish for his mother and in her generosity and love is the image of the Virgin Mary. It is hardly credible that she actually slept with Esteban's father, a transgender drug addict, and conceived a child by him. Her wish for the child she was carrying under her heart to only belong to her and Manuela also stems from Maria Rosa. Before she undergoes the caesarean section, which will cause her death, she makes

Manuela swear that if anything should happen to her, she will take the child with her and that she should not hide anything from him when he asks her questions, especially not about who his father was, in stark contrast to the experience his namesake, Manuela's son, had with his own mother.

A Redemption Fantasy

However, this birth fantasy, from which the new Esteban will eventually arise, differs in one crucial aspect from the first, in which the death of the father was the prerequisite for Esteban's birth. In this instance, it is the *mother*, Maria Rosa, who dies for her son and thus makes room for the father, as if both could not exist simultaneously. While Maria Rosa's funeral is still taking place, we see Lola, Esteban's father, majestically walking down the path to meet Manuela. Manuela tells him that he has a son and Lola is deeply touched, as if his deepest wish in life had been fulfilled. Both he and Manuela weep for their dead son, and Manuela gives him a photo of Esteban to remind him of him always (Fig. 9.2).

But Lola also feels guilty about the HIV legacy he passed on to his newborn son and kisses newborn Esteban deeply one more time as he feels his own death approaching. A more wonderful father-son meeting as depicted in this fantasy is hardly imaginable—nor a more sentimental one. In my opinion, the dead Esteban could have dreamed of his father thus.

At the same time, the *second birth fantasy* seems to be a fantasy of salvation, in which nothing comes to an end: what has been lost returns at some point and everything begins again. Esteban did not know anything about his biological father and presumably filled the gap with a divine father, who, although invisible, steers his son's destiny according to his providence. When at the end of the film Esteban imagines seeing his biological father, now called *Lola*, majestically walking down the path to finally see his newborn son, then in

Fig. 9.2 Both weep for the dead son (01:27:08)

Esteban's imagination this divine father becomes visible for a moment before he disappears into oblivion again and Esteban finds himself in the maternal world, which from now on is filled with the sacred aura that also surrounded Lola.

Perhaps, it is thus no coincidence that among the many things that Lola stole from Maria Rosa while he was staying with her (attending her?) was a statue of the Virgin Mary, which she particularly venerated. And just as the names Manuela and Maria have the same initials, the name 'Rosa' is also reminiscent of the 'Mater Dolorosa', who holds her crucified son across her lap and mourns his death. But it is also the same mother who, like Maria in the nativity story, brings the divine child back into the world anew, as is the case in *All About My Mother* with the newborn Esteban, whom Manuela calls *her* son in the final scene (i.e. no longer Rosa's).

The new Esteban is also no longer infected with HIV—the deadly virus has miraculously disappeared. If one espouses a deep hermeneutic understanding of this as the fulfilment of an unconscious fantasy of salvation, then there will henceforth be no more original sin and no death; if the disappearance of the HIV virus is to be understood on the level of the mother-son relationship, then the fathers, as carriers of the virus, who brought sexuality and death into the world, have also disappeared with the virus. What persists is the image of the grieving mother, embodied again at the end of the film by Huma, who in a drama by Lorca plays a mother who mourns her son with lacerating words. In her grief, she even licks up the son's blood—like an animal or (it occurs to me) a blood-licking Erinys—thus reabsorbing him in a final, never-ending (re)union. Agrado had said that the changes you make to your body make you more authentically resemble what you have dreamed of being. If that were the case, then this would be the resurrected image of a happy mother with a happy child in the voice-off, into which they both disappeared during the film, and again without a father, just like in the photos that the Esteban who died in the accident had found at home, with one half missing. The last image we see is that of Huma Rojo looking into the camera before the play in which she is starring begins again, the last stop of which is called Desire.

Translated by Annette Caroline Christmas.

Film Details

Original title	Todo sobre mi madre
Release year	1999
Country	Spain, France
Screenplay/idea	Pedro Almodóvar
Director	Pedro Almodóvar
Musical score	Alberto Iglesias
Camera	Affonso Beato
Principle actors	Cecilia Roth, Marisa Paredes, Antonia San Juan, Penélope Cruz
Availability	DVD

Understanding Bridget Jones. The Staging of Post-Feminist Female Identity in *Bridget Jones's Diary* (GB, IRL, F 2001)

10

Sabine Metzger

> It is said that analysing pleasure, or beauty, destroys it. That is the intention of this article—Laura Mulvey (1975)

Introduction

The intention of this article is to analyse a comedy which people still often say should not be discussed to death, in order to reveal a far less humorous layer beneath the amusing surface.

The film *Bridget Jones's Diary* (2001) was an enormous success with the public. The novel it was based on was chosen by *Guardian* readers in 2007 as one of the 10 books that best defined the twentieth century, along with *The Great Gatsby*, *The Diary of Anne Frank* and *Catcher in the Rye*—and as *the* book that best represents the 1990s. The protagonist was hailed as the mother of chick lit[1] and an icon of post-feminism, triggering a 'Bridgetmania' that went far beyond the media figure: The terms 'Bridget Jones', meaning a single woman, 'emotional fuckwit' and 'singleton' have entered into the lexicon of the English language. This wide-reaching commercial and cultural success is an indication of this film being a cultural symptom.

[1] Chick lit is literature for, by and about women. Compound word from chick(en) and lit(erature) (Barklamb 2019). The seemingly disparaging abbreviation of the term is a nod to the insignificance that chick lit devotees ironically appropriated for the genre.

S. Metzger (✉)
Institute for Psychoanalysis and Psychotherapy Heidelberg-Mannheim, Heidelberg, Germany
e-mail: praxis.s.metzger@gmx.de

V. Pramataroff-Hamburger, A. Hamburger (eds.), *From La Strada to The Hours*,
https://doi.org/10.1007/978-3-662-68789-5_10

Bridget Jones's Diary came on the crest of a wave of British romantic comedies in the 1990s that evoked a fairy-tale idyll of England and shared many similarities in set design, personnel and cast (*Four Weddings and a Funeral*, GB 1994, Dir.: Mike Newell; *Notting Hill*, GB, USA 1999; Dir.: R. Mitchell). However, it also differs in crucial aspects. It is the first time that women are portrayed in this way. With the advent of *Bridget Jones*, the contemporary female attitude to life found its way into mainstream cinema as a film subject and struck a chord with many women.

I spontaneously chose this film because I know it well. It has always made me laugh out loud, and I quite unthinkingly enjoyed the wit of the dialogue and the actors' comedic talent. Bridget Jones' irony made it a delight for me, although I usually find romantic comedies too saccharine: It allowed me to 'knowingly' dream. In later viewings, I also enjoyed going back to something familiar and comforting.

Film Plot

The protagonist of the film is Bridget Jones (Renée Zellweger), a London publishing clerk in her early 30s, and single. The plot centres around the love triangle between Bridget, her boss Daniel Cleaver (Hugh Grant) and the lawyer Mark Darcy (Colin Firth).

It starts with the annual New Year's dinner at the Jones family's home. The family is presented as a collection of grotesque characters: a tipsy uncle who unabashedly gropes Bridget, a resigned father, an aunt who pesters her with questions about her biological clock and, above all, a mother who greets her daughter with a critical eye as a 'dumpling'. Mrs. Jones wants to set Bridget up with a man, as she does every year, and so introduces her to the newly divorced Mark Darcy—adding that Bridget played with him naked in the paddling pool as a child. Bridget tries to bridge the awkward silence with small talk; Darcy brusquely turns away from her and makes disparaging remarks about her to his mother.

After this setback, we see Bridget singing, smoking and drinking wine in her untidy flat. Off-camera, we hear her worrying about dying old and lonely. She seems desperate but also revels in emotions, as if celebrating her downfall by throwing herself into song and dance.

She decides to change her life and starts a diary containing 'the whole truth about Bridget Jones', meticulously recording her weight, how many cigarettes and alcohol units she consumes, as well as her resolution to:

> … find [a] nice sensitive boyfriend to go out with … and not continue to form romantic attachments to […] alcoholics, workaholics, commitment-phobics, peeping toms, megalomaniacs, emotional fuckwits, or perverts. And especially will not fantasise about a particular person who embodies all these things…

—namely her boss Daniel Cleaver, whom we see in the next shot.

Cleaver begins an email flirtation with Bridget, making a lewd remark about her miniskirt. While in the off-commentary she tells herself not to flirt with the office lothario, against her better judgement, she walks past his office in a see-through blouse.

Bridget's launch of the current new release, *Kafka's Motorbike,* turns into a disaster. She meets Mark Darcy at the event. He is accompanied by the striking Natasha, who introduces Darcy as a 'first-class lawyer', while he introduces Bridget with the paddling pool anecdote, thus embarrassing her. Cleaver comforts Bridget by saying she looks sexy and takes her out to dinner. We learn from Cleaver that he and Darcy had been best friends until Darcy stole Cleaver's fiancée. Cleaver seduces Bridget.

Bridget's frustrated mother leaves her husband for a TV jewellery salesman who has discovered her as a sales talent and who satisfies her sexually.

Bridget thinks she has reached the goal of her dreams when Cleaver invites her on a weekend trip to the country. There, they meet Darcy and Natasha. Cleaver tells Bridget that he has to go back to London for work and cannot go with her to her aunt's fancy dress party. Bridget confronts Cleaver with her doubts about his feelings but allows herself to be twisted around his little finger. Frustrated, Bridget goes to Cleaver's flat after the party and discovers that he is having an affair with the perfect American Laura.

When Bridget finds out that Cleaver is engaged to Laura, a collapse involving spoiled food leads to a flight forward: She replaces her self-help books on understanding men with ones for autonomous women, looks for a new job in television and triumphantly quits her job at the publishing house. However, her new boss is also only interested in her body and wants to watch her slide down a fireman's pole during her TV debut. Her skirt rides up and the close-up of her bottom makes her famous.

After a couples' dinner, at which Bridget is the only single person to be insulted with innuendos, Darcy declares his love to her: He likes her the way she is—despite all her ridiculousness.

Darcy 'saves' Bridget from two more disasters: He enables her to get an exclusive interview and helps her with her failed birthday dinner. Cleaver comes along and Darcy challenges him to a duel. Cleaver loses but seems to have conquered Bridget's heart and proposes to her and her miniskirt again. Bridget is thoughtful and replies that that is not enough for her.

She spends a tragic Christmas with her father. Surprisingly, Mrs. Jones returns. The parents have a discussion, which rekindles their love. Bridget learns from her mother that it was not Darcy who cheated with Cleaver's fiancée, but the other way around. This vindicates Darcy in Bridget's eyes. At a party in the Darcys' home, she declares her love to him and gives a crazy speech to try and stop him from moving to New York.

Bridget resigns herself to being single. However, Darcy returns to her. When nothing seems to stand between them, Bridget interrupts their kiss to put on some erotic underwear. In her absence, Darcy reads her diary: 'Mark Darcy acts like he's got a giant gherkin thrust up his backside [...] is rude [and] dull. [...] I hate him!' He leaves the flat. Bridget runs after him half-dressed. She plays down her feelings towards him: 'Everyone knows diaries are just full of crap'. Darcy agrees and gives her a new diary. They kiss.

Background

The character of Bridget Jones originated in an *Independent* newspaper column by the author Helen Fielding in 1995. The novel on which the film is based, and which has been translated into more than 33 languages, was published in England in 1996, in the USA in 1998 and the sequel *Bridget Jones—The Edge of Reason* in 1999. The film adaptations were released in 2001, 2004 and *Bridget Jones's Baby* in 2016. Each was directed by Sharon Maguire, a friend of Helen Fielding and the archetype of Bridget's friend Shazzer. Fielding, an Austen enthusiast, crafted the plot along the lines of Jane Austen's *Pride and Prejudice* (1813). The film cites the 1995 BBC adaptation of the Austen novel as sources for the character of Mark Darcy and the casting of Colin Firth in the role.

The film appeared at the height of the third wave of feminism (post-feminism). While the second wave of feminism in the 1960s and 1970s featured collective political activism and was aimed at ending the oppression of women, post-feminism was more concerned with the individual: Its goals were empowerment through freedom of choice and the hedonistic-playful re-appropriation of femininity in language and aesthetics (make-up, high heels, girl power), accompanied by a depoliticisation of the feminist movement. The dynamics of post-feminism were shaped by a generational conflict. The rebellion and aspirations for autonomy of the second-wave feminist mothers, who had challenged traditional notions of femininity, implicitly lead to a backlash, as summed up in Susan Faludi's 1991 bestseller *Backlash—The Undeclared War on Women*.

The Staging of the Feminine or: De(con)struction of Beauty and Comedy

Bridget Jones is praised by critics and fans for her authenticity, her heartfelt, humorous nature and her intense feelings, all traits with traditionally feminine connotations. Thus, Bridget's acting out of her own inhibitions and wishful fantasies is idealised by viewers. It is also meant to keep envy of her spontaneity at bay. And idealisation is supposed to ward off criticism: Bridget should not be openly criticised, because her deep vulnerability and insecurity, her almost childlike innocence, can be sensed. Bridget is not respected because she doesn't fight back, nor is she portrayed as an ethereal, exquisite beauty of the silver screen. This is also what makes her so likeable. She is a 'one-woman disaster', despite her education and professional status. Her (mis)use of her resources is deplorable. Her professional potential remains largely unfulfilled: The workplace serves as a place for romance rather than performance.

Bridget has no self-awareness: She does not talk about her feelings and does not reflect on them. The split between what she thinks and feels and what she does is repeatedly shown in the contrast between the cinematography and the soundtrack. Bridget tolerates degrading, sexist treatment without fighting back. The soundtrack is replete with revenge fantasies towards her female co-worker and the disparaging name she reserves for her male colleague Fitzherbert ('Tits Herbert, more like'), while no trace of this can be seen in the cinematography. When Fitzherbert's eyes bore into her, she looks down at herself unhappily, almost in disgust. Her defencelessness is depicted as the typical female inhibition of aggression, while we also see that her sexual allure for men brings her recognition—something which her mother denies her.

The extent to which Bridget Jones fails to live up to her potential and how little she fights back were particularly annoying to the 'Big Sisters' among us in the discussion group.[2] More painful feelings of worthlessness, emptiness and shame emerged later, when I was working through the film alone. Conversations following the group discussion also expressed the inkling of sadness being kept at bay, the elusive lack of depth and the worry about destroying a tender seedling. The full extent of the horror, the tragedy behind the comedy, only becomes clear after watching the film several times. These feelings had been laughed off before. This can partially be attributed to the power of genre and staging but also to the need to protect Bridget and her awkwardness and, of course, to not allow one's enjoyment and the laughter to be spoiled.

In this paper, I intend to show this inner process of working through with the film and to deconstruct the comedy, shattering the entertaining surface in the process.

Bridget Jones: A Childlike Heroine of Everyday Life

> There you are, dumpling', Mother Jones says to Bridget in the opening scene as she looks down at her disparagingly. 'You'll never get a boyfriend, if you look like you've wandered out of Auschwitz.[3] [...] I've laid out something lovely on your bed.

Bridget sullenly submits to her fate. From her mother's gaze to the weaving of the audience into the protagonist's inner monologue, Bridget is viewed from above. The DVD cover depicts her from a bird's-eye view, dressed in something almost resembling a school uniform. It is probably no coincidence that this mise-en-scène is reminiscent of Britney Spears' outfit in the music video of *Hit me, baby, one more time* (1998), as it refers to the sexualised, sadomasochistic undercurrent of the film.

---

[2]The material for my film analysis is derived from examining my changing feelings as I worked through the film and from a discussion with my Intervision discussion group, Philine Freudenberg, Maryam Mohraz and Andrea Zimmermann—whom I thank for their contributions as well as the many other sources inspiring my article that could not explicitly named in the list of literature for reasons of space.

[3]This is just one example of the film's relentlessly jarring quality.

Watching this perfectly imperfect heroine fail is a relief for viewers. However, Bridget does not have the heroic courage to be aware of the risk. She is the type of 'secretary' who lets herself be seduced and awkwardly gets herself into difficult situations. Thus, Bridget's peculiarly waddling walk is reminiscent of Charlie Chaplin but also of the gait of ballerinas, who are never supposed to show any sign of effort. As she handles embarrassing situations with humour and unapologetically carries on, it comes across as light and lacks the tragedy and pain that would give her character depth. She is childlike in her unabashed naivety, and as is the case for children, failure seems meaningless and inconsequential (Genazino 2013; Radtke 2013). Since she hardly reflects, does not grieve or learn from her mistakes, it all seems effortless. However, she hardly goes through any development and is stuck in a protracted adolescence.

If, as Sennett (2000) asserted, failure is the great taboo of the modern age, then this childlike naivety also represents her resistance to the performance mindset demanded of the neoliberal subject. Natasha better corresponds to this type of streamlined subject. However, the film does not show her hard work, which gives her an understated air despite her doggedness and makes her seem perfect. Natasha represents discipline and control. **Bridget is desire. She is not efficient. Therein lies her subversive side. This disobedience, fed by drives and emotions, is something feminine, but in Bridget's case, it is above all defiance towards her mother**: The segue to the wishful fantasy of marrying Cleaver during her email flirtation is so deftly put together that the fade-in of the beaming mother is hardly consciously noticeable, symbolising Bridget's (unconscious) identification with her mother's dreams. She wants the same as her mother but has to fail in doing so. It is thus sugar-coating to interpret Bridget as a subject who is resistant to the cultural, neoliberal imperative (Peitz 2010). For her to be so, she would have to reflect upon it. As a 'child of *Cosmopolitan* culture', however, she conforms to this imperative with its myth of self-perfection just as unquestioningly as she does to her mother's ready-made clothes. She is not (yet) a subject; her drives make her incapable of reform. She cannot help herself. Her narrative is also comical because, although she sins and confesses, she does not want to change. On the contrary, she celebrates the dysfunctional, normal self.

Comedy is still a male domain today. One of the accomplishments of chick lit is to establish a humorous woman without ridiculing her, as, for example, in *Sex and the City* (USA 1998–2004; Dir.: M.P. King). However, the film version of *Bridget Jones's Diary* does not achieve this, as the humour is at Bridget's expense. Her comedy stems from loss of control, the direct connection to her inner stream of consciousness. She is not the author of the comedy but its object, something the British film poster depicting her confidently holding the author's pen is meant to obscure.

The film exposes Bridget almost in its entirety. The audience laughs away all the cruelty—just as Bridget herself does in the film, portraying clumsiness as heterosexually desirable forms part of cinematic mythmaking, because it triggers the masculine impulse to rescue and male desire (Maddison and Storr 2004). Or is this a regressive women's fantasy to ease the regime of self-optimisation?

To lay the protagonist bare presupposes voyeurism and the presence of a laughing third party: The spectators, identified with a male gaze that is more judgemental than empathetic and having feminist ideals, are censors to whom the spectacle of laying bare is addressed. During Bridget Jones' disastrous book launch, both the viewers in the film and those in the cinema feel a vicarious embarrassment that extends to the physical. Her nervousness makes it very difficult for her to suppress her inner monologue and look professional. This is underlined by the fact that the camera gets at her by zooming in on her.

In the episode about the weekend trip, facets of femininity and failure intertwine. Bridget cheers: Hurrah. Am no longer tragic spinster but proper girlfriend of bona-fide sex god. [The spectators know, he just wants sex; note from the author] He′s also protecting me at [the] hideous Tarts and Vicars fancy dress party. 'What *being a woman* actually means is still defined in the negative: A single woman is a tragic spinster, the alternative being 'girlfriend of'. And as if Bridget's disavowed thoughts had alighted on the viewer (engaging the audience as a knowing, critical voice in her inner monologue), she responds evocatively: 'This can't be just shagging. A mini-break means true love'. When her headscarf blows off, she feels 'like screen goddess in manner of Grace Kelly. Though perhaps ever so slightly less elegant under pressure'. She fails at being elegant because she does not fulfil the role expectations: She is clumsy under pressure. The fact that Bridget Jones embodies all these imperfect facets in a way that makes her seem fresh and funny, and yet her vulnerability remains palpable, is thanks to Renée Zellweger's performance.

Post-Feminism, Irony and Sexism

A characteristic feature of *Bridget Jones' Diary* is its ironic tone. Irony creates distance to feelings that it would be crass to reveal. For Bridget, irony is also a protection against her mother's humiliating gaze: Anticipating being made fun of by doing it to yourself takes the wind out of critics' sails.

In post-feminist discourse, irony is also a way of making sexist points while claiming that you don't mean it. In the email flirtation with Cleaver, Bridget speaks of the brazen sexual harassment but at the same time enjoys the desire in his gaze and the transgression of feminist taboos. Just as ironically, Cleaver replies that he is deeply ashamed of this. Since everything is dealt with at an ironic distance, there can be no real contact and no change in gender relations. It remains a game. Thus, the film cements the idea that an emancipated attitude as a woman is incompatible with a heterosexual relationship.

The scene on the lake shows Bridget and Cleaver playfully and exuberantly parodying English classics as if they were adolescents, specifically Colin Firth as he plays the romantic hero in a wet shirt, as he had in the 1995 BBC adaptation of *Pride and Prejudice*. Bridget seems to be relaxed, which she otherwise seldom is in the film. Why is that? Parody enables a humorous, distancing appropriation of tradition. The reference to tradition and to one's own history, in which the inferiority and devaluation of women is always invoked, is thus even turned into something pleasurable. Cleaver parodies the Darcy of

1813, but at the same time, he presents himself as a spectacle of the self-deprecating man: The 'king of the world' has toppled, standing in the water in his wet shirt, a crumpled cigarette between his lips. Bridget can identify with this laddishness, and at the same time, it frees her from the obligation of being womanly for the male gaze.

On the other hand, irony and retro décor are key instruments of the sexism of the time. Sexism is presented as something in the past, which legitimises the portrayal of scenarios that would be objectionable from a contemporary perspective. On a weekend trip in a vintage car, Bridget can indulge in regressive needs and snuggle up to Cleaver. The humorous cultural inverted commas protect against (feminist) criticism. What this stylistic device obscures is the unabashed matter-of-factness with which men have control over Bridget's body, which is dumbfounding. But Bridget is a knowing, cool player. In the bed scene during the weekend getaway, Cleaver alludes to anal sex. His joke about the pain this causes the woman can barely be heard above the romantic music, while the camera pans to a bride and groom dancing in front of the window. A pair of lovers can be heard teasing each other, along with Bridget's laughter, in a montage of the music and the set pieces of romance. What the content has to say about gender relations is almost lost. The humour masks Bridget's longing to be loved and her submission to a sadomasochistic arrangement in order to maintain the relationship. But why does Bridget allow this to be done to her? She is also a profiting player. The female role model has slightly changed in the course of post-feminism and there are now new options for sexual permissiveness, hedonism and playing with sexual power as a woman: Men can be dated as objects of lust for sexual interest. Women now have the option of taking an active part in sexual activity that was previously only allowed to men. Women are thus subjects participating in objectification. Bridget does not fight back because she is also complicit. Refraining from criticising is a condition of her permissiveness.

When Darcy makes a derogatory remark about Bridget at the New Year's dinner, the camera zooms in on Bridget, who has heard the insult but doesn't let on. A freeze frame emphasises that she smiles and bears it (Fig. 10.1). This is a decisive moment in introducing

Fig. 10.1 Bridget (over)hears Darcy's insult. Freeze frame at the New Year's dinner (00:05:22)

the character: It captures her 'false self' (Winnicott [1974] 2002), her social masking. At home, no longer subject to the gaze of others, she displays her private feelings: despair, anger and rebellion. Is this her 'true self?" Does she know it? Later, these feelings find their way into her diary. Bridget, however, seems to enjoy the dramatisation and is even self-pitying: This is the (self-)staging of the psychological crisis of the hysterical female subject as a spectacle.

It is normal practice to condense a novel for a screen adaptation. However, in a comparison between the film and the novel of *Bridget Jones' Diary,* it is striking that in the film adaptation the feminist content and other aspects relevant to the representation of women have been reduced even further (Dhrodia 2005). While Bridget still had outbursts of rather feministic rage in the novel, none of them are portrayed in the film. Shazzer is quite bland without her righteous feminist anger: She often says 'fuck' instead of making feminist remarks (i.e. feminism becomes the F-word under the male gaze). Bridget's mother is also stripped of all feminist aspects. In the book, the love scene between Cleaver and Bridget ends with her resisting him: She senses his selfish interests and leaves him. In the film, nothing stands in his way.

In the literature, this critique of Bridget Jones' unemancipated cluelessness is often treated from a cultural studies perspective as a conflict between second and third wave feminism: The spoilsports of the second wave begrudge the younger ones their romantic dreams and are jealous of the hedonistic Bridget. However, in my view, this falls short.

Bridget and Her Relationships

The Mother-Daughter Relationship

The mother is portrayed as an unfulfilled woman, true to the typical comedic figure of the self-centred, dysfunctional mother, who has to put her daughter down because she herself feels worthless as a woman:

> To be honest, darling, having children isn't all it's cracked up to be. Given my chance again, I'm not sure I'd have any. And now it's the winter of my life and I haven't actually got anything of my own. I've got no power, no real career, no sex life. I've got no life at all.

She compensates for this frustration in two ways: her work in sales almost pornographically promoting an egg peeling device and an affair with her boss.

This mother is a caricature and an anti-role model for her daughter, her self-realisation a parody of emancipation. The gap in Bridget's female identity is filled by pop culture. The film, which satisfies the longing for emotional edification and portrays the female fantasy of being loved even if imperfect as attainable, is a comfort in lonely moments for many Bridget Joneses. One non-academic reader and critic, borrowing a term from the music industry, described the escapist quality as 'poptimist' (cited in Hannah Engler 2017, p. 52).

When Bridget's parents enter into coupledom again and her mother is thus no longer a devalued loser, Bridget can leave her place at her father's side. Only when her mother is rehabilitated and recognised as a woman can her elucidation also be of use: The cheated party was Darcy, not Cleaver. Bridget can only fall in love with Darcy when she herself is somewhat detached from her parents.

Bridget and the Men

Bridget's father is a sympathetic, introverted, sometimes resigned, powerless father. The character of Darcy also has these traits, while Bridget is portrayed as more extroverted, supports her father and is thus almost the better partner for him.

Bridget and Daniel Cleaver

Cleaver is a charming narcissist with a capacity for self-mockery. Bridget's diary introduces him as a 'pervert'. He calls her 'Jones', and they sometimes seem more like a couple of lads rather than a man and a woman. The slightly homoerotic-voyeuristic nature of their relationship is evidenced by the sex scene, in which Cleaver jokes about Bridget's giant mummy pants, saying he wears something similar and that they could show each other their underwear. At the same time, however, he also relieves Bridget of her perfectionist superego. The new lad, who rebels against feminism, celebrates authentic masculinity and stars in the novels of Nick Hornby and others in the 1990s, is the male counterpart to the chick.

Cleaver lies and objectifies, he has no female aspects and devalues them (e.g. mocking Keats' poetry with a lewd limerick), but he is also a challenge and motor for Bridget's development. Unlike Darcy, Cleaver seems unafraid of Bridget's permissiveness. However, for him, contempt is neutralised in perversion: He wants a non-committed relationship with a partial object, Bridget's skirt, which he wishes to 'fatten up' (oral level), and her bottom, which the skirt covers, as illustrated by the bed scene on the weekend trip (anal level). The wish to be saved by her is the idealising flip side. Bridget's realisation that this is not enough for her is an important moment of self-reflection in her identity development.

Bridget and Mark Darcy

Mark Darcy, being prudish, reserved but respectful, is the counterpart to the chaotic Bridget and the moral counterpart to the amoral Cleaver. Bridget's diary entry refers to his anal traits: inhibition, rigidity and control. In contrast to the novel, Mark Darcy is ubiquitous in the film from start to finish (like the early childhood mother). In the book, Bridget doesn't meet him again until long after they first met and she has broken up with Cleaver. The film condenses this conflict between the two suitors into Bridget's central dilemma, culminating in the fight on her birthday.

Both Darcy and Cleaver want to bind her into a caring relationship, each in his own way. While both respond to Bridget's neediness, they also belittle it by addressing it at an oral level: Darcy demands she eat at the New Year's dinner and Cleaver wants to take her out to 'fatten up' her skirt.

When she first meets Mark Darcy, Bridget is wearing the suit her mother had picked out for her, and he is in a silly reindeer Christmas jumper, a gift from his mother. They are united by their mothers' bad taste. Their clothes symbolise the protracted adolescence which binds them to their parents.

In the kitchen scene, Bridget is presented as an incapable child, Darcy as a saviour figure with a hint of maternalism. While Bridget's mother obtains satisfaction by satisfying men (with the *have it oeuf* device), Darcy knows how to handle eggs, whipping up an omelette that saves Bridget's dinner party; he parodies her family, thereby creating distance; Bridget's mother forgets her birthday and only talks about her own sex life; Darcy congratulates Bridget, even on her professional success: Darcy is the better woman and mother. This scene associates disgusting food with erotic desire. This connection is significant in that the birthday dinner represents a turning point in Bridget's autonomous development. After Darcy has shown that he is motherly, the two recall meeting as children, naked in the paddling pool—a paradisiacal scene which appears only in the deleted scenes, and the closing credits of the US release. Bridget calls Darcy 'quite a pervert'; Darcy agrees and looks at her breasts, her femininity, the gender difference. Bridget sees perversity flaring up in Darcy as potential development: the imperfection, the lust in the anal character—a dash of Cleaver in Darcy, a dash of laddishness in the aristocratic lawyer. Closeness and eroticism arise in mutual recognition; they no longer have to be embarrassed in front of each other. The disgusted rejection of food represents the repudiation of the maternal body and is necessary in order to become a subject: Disgust is an instinctive negation (Kristeva 1982). Disgust separates the child from the parents. On the other hand, the 'abnormal' overstepping of the barrier against disgust, the triumph of libido over aversion, is necessary so that the Life Drive is not extinguished (Freud 1915). Darcy's inner movement in some way illustrates the Freudian notion of the inner recognition of one's own perversity as a precondition to the chance of sexual happiness, the connection between tender and sensual flow (Freud 1912). After the kitchen scene, Bridget's off-comments all but disappear, which is an expression of the increasing integration of the different parts of herself.

Bridget turns away from Darcy disappointed after the fight. This does not fit with her romantic wish for non-ambivalent love with an ideal partner. The female viewers, on the other hand, perceive Darcy showing his aggressive side as a developmental step. Bridget matures in her relationship with Darcy through disillusionment and the integration of hatred towards him: Only as a 'bad boy' can he kiss really well.

Bridget's separation from both men and being thrown back on her own resources is a further step in her autonomous development. This time, she is not filling the gaps in her knowledge with new self-help guides. She starts a new diary from a self-reflexive point of view but cannot yet enjoy her situation as freedom.

Fig. 10.2 Happy ending? Bridget's and Darcy's kiss (01:28:45)

Bridget wishes to be saved by a man. Thus, for the sake of her relationship with Darcy, she betrays her true feelings, which she keeps in her diary, and her perception that Darcy has not always behaved impeccably. The imagery of the final scene makes it clear where the hope of being saved by the man leads: He puts his coat around her after the camera has passed over her bottom once more. To compensate for her dysfunctional family, Bridget slips under the wing of the male hero—who is the real hero of the film and steals the show as far as Bridget's development is concerned. From a bird's-eye view, all you can see is Darcy's silhouette: like a noble man (Fig. 10.2). Bridget's bare legs and her blonde mop of hair almost disappear against the snow-white background: an apotheosis, Prince Charming as the Madonna with a sheltering cloak to protect (and smother) Bridget? A new beginning or self-denial and fusion with the ideal as a happy ending?

Female Body and Ego Ideal

It is hard to tell if Bridget is more concerned with finding a partner or struggling with her body/ego ideal. Such is the extent to which the male view of women has been internalised, with all the male fantasies to ward off fears of female permissiveness. These fears and defences against them are illustrated by Darcy's judgement of Bridget's licentiousness (verbally incontinent, drinks like a fish) along with the further associative sequence in the film (single life, alcoholism, loneliness, depression, murder, death). At dinner with the smug married couples, the question about her biological clock is meant to push Bridget, who is unattached and has a job, into the patriarchal system of being a wife and mother, and to worry her with the threat of an expiry date. Bridget counters this with her female perspective: The problem with the search for a partner is that a woman's body is parcelled into measurable units, not her career.

Bridget's self-esteem depends on shaping social norms regarding her appearance and the male gaze. She makes herself desirable for this gaze. Her 'false' self (Winnicott [1974] 2002) very much resembles a male fantasy. The biggest dilemma in preparing for the book launch is staged as choosing the appropriate underwear: a giant 'mummy-pant horror' or a sheer wisp of nothingness on the off chance of an erotic encounter that evening.

For the first time, a film looks behind the façade of female physical beauty and demystifies the supposed effortlessness but presents it as the protagonist's personal weakness rather than a social problem. It is a cold, calculating and dehumanising gaze, with which Bridget partially identifies. It is the gaze of a cultural superego, symbolised by the billboard ad, but also in the opening scene in the gaze of the mother's cold, blue eyes on her daughter. And the rage of repressed hatred of her mother is vented on her body as self-hatred: Instead of inwardly killing her mother and becoming oedipal, Bridget tortures her body with depilatory strips.

Bridget has a normal, slim build compared to the British average. She is played by a Hollywood actress who gained an extra 22 pounds for the performance, which was quickly lauded as method acting. A woman whose weaknesses are supposed to arouse our sympathy has to be portrayed as a woman with enormous self-discipline. The camera and set emphasise and exaggerate these staged weaknesses (frog's-eye view, too-tight outfits). The female body is staged as a fetish. In the relationship with Cleaver, the miniskirt is a pars pro toto for Bridget. And the camera also denies the protagonist wholeness by fetishistically presenting her buttocks (in bunny costume, control pants, a close-up on her TV debut, tiger-stripe briefs). Remarkably, the choice has not fallen on the primary and secondary female reproductive organs, the vulva and breasts. On the contrary, these are a blank space: Even in the bed scenes, Bridget's breasts are not visible. The scene in which Bridget's father says that her mother accused him of not knowing what a clitoris was can only be found among the 'deleted scenes'. Does this represent a levelling of the gender difference to defend against femininity?

The male leads are heartthrobs Grant and Firth, while Bridget, played by Zellweger, is made to look ugly to the Hollywood eye, which could be seen as a devaluation: The men are stylised into the ideal ego. Grant has an anecdote which illustrates how the system fights back on this point: He and Firth had typically feminine concerns about their appearance during filming, while Zellweger was able to enjoy pizza and beer in peace. But the handsome leading actors are also a spectacle for the Bridgets among the female audience. This is pointedly illustrated by a scene that was cut, in which Bridget interviews Colin Firth as himself, being so pushy in sexualising him that he takes fright and runs away.

Conclusion

The dramatically increased intensity of self-monitoring in the wake of post-feminism and the omnipresent monitoring focussed on the psyche and self-optimisation are reflected in the staging of the feminine in *Bridget Jones's Diary*.

Women just can't get it right. They are pressurised from both sides: by a cultural super-ego determined by the male gaze (Mulvey 1975) and also by the Big Sisters of second-wave feminism. The malign internalisation of these imperatives—also through emancipation—comes in the form of internalised monitoring. The film is about how a normal woman, which Bridget Jones also is, struggles with this. Gill has described 'post-feminist sensibility' as the knowledge of transgressing the pleasures censored by feminism (white weddings, dependency and attachment needs, domesticity, choosing not to pursue a career, enjoying clothes, aesthetics) with the explicit articulation of feminist *and* anti-feminist ideas (Gill 2007). The two possible interpretations of whether this is the return of the repressed or traditional patriarchal ideals packaged as post-feminist liberties are not mutually exclusive. The matter-of-factness, the sexism nullified in form and genre and centuries-old role models which the film brings with it while purporting to be a women's film are insidious. The post-feminist viewer is tasked with being aware of this and still being able to enjoy the film, whether for the first time or not.

Translated by Annette Caroline Christmas.

Film Details

Original title	Bridget Jones's Diary
Year of publication	2001
Country	GB, IR, F
Screenplay/Idea	Helen Fielding, Andrew Davies, Richard Curtis
Direction	Sharon Maguire
Principle actors	Renée Zellweger, Hugh Grant, Colin Firth
Availability	DVD

References

Barklamb S (2019) Written by women, for women, about women: chick lit and why we should study it. MA Thesis, Utrecht University

Dhrodia R (2005) "Have you met Miss Jones?": feminism and difference in the Bridget Jones's Diaries. MA thesis. University of Ottawa, Ottawa

Engler H (2017) Poptimist feminism: contemporary women reading Bridget Jones's Diary. BA thesis. University of Michigan, Michigan

Freud S (1912) On the universal tendency to debasement in the sphere of love. S.E. 11:177–190, Hogarth, London

Freud S (1916/17 [1915]) New introductory lectures on psycho-analysis. S. E., 22: 1–182, Hogarth, London

Genazino W (2013) Omnipotenz und Einfalt. Über das Scheitern [Omnipotence and simplicity. About failure]. In: Gaßner B, Kölle B (eds) Besser scheitern [Fail better]. Cologne, Walther König, pp 10–14

Gill R (2007) Postfeminist media culture. Elements of a sensibility. Eur J Cult Stud 10(2):147–166

Kristeva J (1982) Powers of horror. An essay on abjection. Columbia University Press, New York

Maddison S, Storr M (2004) The edge of reason: the myth of Bridget Jones. Rodopi, London

Mulvey L (1975) Visual pleasure and narrative cinema [Screen, Volume 16, Issue 3, Autumn 1975, Pages 6–18]. In: Braudy L, Cohen M (eds) Film theory and criticism: introductory readings. Oxford UP, New York, pp 833–844

Peitz A (2010) Chick Lit. Genrekonstituierende Untersuchungen unter anglo-amerikanischem Einfluss [Genre-constituting studies under Anglo-American influence]. Lang, Frankfurt am Main

Radtke M (2013) Again and again and again—Buster Keaton & Charlie Chaplin in der Endlosschleife des Scheiterns [Buster Keaton & Charlie Chaplin in the endless loop of failure.]. In: Gaßner H, Kölle B (eds) Besser scheitern. [Fail better]. Walther König, Cologne, pp 15–17

Sennett R (2000) Die Kultur des neuen Kapitalismus [The culture of the new capitalism]. Berliner Taschenbuch, Berlin

Winnicott DW ([1974] 2002) The maturational processes and the facilitating environment. Int PsychoAnal Lib 64:1–276. London: The Hogarth Press and the Institute of Psycho-Analysis, London

From La Strada to the Hours: Suffering or Sovereign Femininity in Feature Films—Ida and Her Mothers

11

Nadia Kozhouharov

A mother's job is to be there to be left (Anna Freud, quoted by Erna Furman in ***Furman, E.*** *(*1982*).)*

Introduction

A woman who has pledged her body and soul to God is a fertile cinematographic object. The on-screen presence of an unattainable woman wrapped in secrecy inevitably arouses the audience's curiosity about what is hidden beneath her habit. Cinema relies on this, and the nuns on-screen are usually presented in a way that gives us the feeling that we can gently lift the folds of their long, black robes to look for the woman underneath and uncover the secret of her perfection. Most films about 'God's brides' try to humanise this idealised, religious symbol—women able to sacrifice everything they have in the name of the perfect love, possible only with God. Cinema appears to satisfy our desire to look at what is forbidden, to expose these women, find their weakness, and bring them down to our level, that of ordinary people. It is a need born of our narcissistic vulnerability, which persuades us that we are unworthy of ideal love and that the love between two human beings is inferior to the divine. Nuns in cinema usually experience a conflict—between religious dogma and liberation, the spiritual and the sensual and the sacred and the human. Some films present caricatures of nuns (films with Louis de Funès and the 1982 *Sister Act*

English translation: Tanya Kirilova, Tim Ward

N. Kozhouharov (✉)
Sofia, Bulgaria

V. Pramataroff-Hamburger, A. Hamburger (eds.), *From La Strada to The Hours*,
https://doi.org/10.1007/978-3-662-68789-5_11

with Whoopi Goldberg), while others portray them as irresistible (*Viridiana*, 1961), as rebels (*The Nun*, 2013), as monsters (*The Nun*, 2018), as classy women (Audrey Hepburn in *A Nun's Story*, 1959, and Ingrid Bergman in *The Bells of Saint Mary's*, 1995) or as women torn between religion and their personal beliefs (*Dead Man Walking*, 1995) and between their duty to God and their duty to themselves (*The Novitiate*, 2017). The portrayals of nuns on the big screen, different as they are, even incomparable in some ways, are meant to show us that humanity, despite its imperfections, cannot be sacrificed entirely on the altar of faith. Desire and passion always find their place in life, even when condemned by the Church. This feeling brings satisfaction to the audience; the myth is debunked, and humanity is rehabilitated. What is more, it thrills us by granting us the experience of opposing one of the oldest, most powerful and influential institutions of modern civilization—the Church.

The individual opposition to the omnipotent mother represented by the Church on the part of her devoted daughters, hidden away in convents, is a truly inspiring act. In psychoanalysis, separation from the mother marks the beginning of psychological development. The helpless infant is completely dependent on the mother, and so, their first imago of her is of an omnipotent being. A person's psyche is forever marked by this initial helplessness before the mother.[1] The stories about nuns often represent a symbolic separation from the powerful, primal mother figure at the beginning of everyone's life. It brings relief to the audience as it resonates with the deepest human fears of helplessness, passivity, and submissiveness to someone essential for their survival. These stories reveal how the power of the primal mother is overcome by broadening one's horizons and investing emotional energy to something else.

Polish director Pawel Pawlikowski's black-and-white film *Ida* is probably the most delicate story of opposition, liberation and self-discovery. Viewers are captivated by the on-screen transformation of the novice Anna on the verge of coming of age. We witness what psychoanalysis would call a ' psychological birth'. The audience is relieved to notice the subtle nuances signalling Anna's change and eagerly awaits the next redeeming step towards her maturity. However, the black-and-white retro aesthetic and chamber composition are incongruous with the optimism of growing up. All the senses through which we experience the film, its images and music, evoke feelings of longing, sympathy and sadness. The beauty of the film lies in this very contradiction which cannot leave us unmoved. This is where psychoanalysis comes in, helping us not only to make sense of our perceptions but also to organise our experience with this new knowledge of human nature. In psychoanalysis, the perception of the external reality is always coloured by our inner world and our earliest experiences. And so, we realise that the short episode of Anna's life that we have seen is not just a sequence of people and events but encounters with special relevance to her story. We witness three real-life incarnations of the inner image of the mother, each of which plays a role in her formation as a person and a woman. At the end of the film, we can breathe a sigh of relief—Anna has found her own path of separation not only from the Mother Church but also from her dead biological mother and the mother who grants her the freedom to be a woman.

---

[1] Chasseguet-Smirgel J (1976).

Film Plot

Ida introduces us to the young novitiate Anna in the last few days before she takes her vow. She has no family; she was raised in the convent and knows nothing about her own past. Her mother is the Church; she is a child of God. Her daily life is monastically austere. The Mother Superior insists that Anna get to know her aunt Wanda Gruz before the ritual. Her mother's sister and only living relative has never wanted to visit her. Anna has to undertake her first independent journey into the outside world, which will lead her to her personal story and the story of her family. Wanda is known as 'Red Wanda', a former prosecutor who sentenced the 'enemies of the people' to death. Anna finds out from her who her parents were, what their fate was and who she is—a Jewish girl called Ida. By some miracle, she survived the Nazi occupation of Poland while her family was killed. She and Wanda travel back home to find where their family were buried. The man who hid the family during the war takes the two women to their burial site and confesses to their murder himself. Only Anna was spared, young enough to pass for a Christian. Wanda survived because she wasn't there at the time. She was fighting for the communist idea. She left her little boy with her sister, and he was killed with the others. The two women bury their relatives' remains in a deserted Jewish cemetery, each mourning their loss in her own way.

Wanda uses her time with Anna to provoke her to get a taste of life outside the convent. On the way to the hotel, she picks up a hitchhiker, a young saxophonist called Lis, and gives hints to her niece that he is an attractive young man. Despite her resistance, Anna is smitten by him, influenced by the beautiful saxophone music, and for the first time feels desired as a woman.

After burying their relatives' remains, the two women part in front of the convent. After everything she has been through, Anna decides to postpone her vows. Overwhelmed by depression and guilt, Wanda ends her life. At her funeral, Anna meets Lis again. She puts on her aunt's dress and high heels and is transformed into a beautiful young woman. The two dance and then spend a night of love in Wanda's apartment. Lis asks Anna to come with him and paints a disillusioned picture of their life together. In the morning, while he sleeps, Anna quietly puts on her habit and returns to the convent.

Context

For Pawlikowski, *Ida* is a deeply personal film. Of himself, he says 'I make films depending onwhere I am in life……. life is a journey and filmmaking marks where you (the audience) are in life and it marks where I am in life…'.[2] Born in Poland, Pawlikowski emigrated to Britain in his teens after his parents divorced. There, he started directing documentaries and later on feature films. After overcoming the loss of his wife between two successful feature films (*My Summer of Love,* 2004, and *The Woman in the Fifth,*

[2] Levine (2015). https://blogs.sydneysbuzz.com/interview-dir-pawel-pawlikowski-on-his-oscar-shortlisted-film-ida-62c25ad5b3d1.

2011), Pawlikowski felt a strong need to return to his motherland, which to him was a reassurance and inner stability, 'return to important things of the past'.[3] *Ida* is a self-reflection on the importance of returning to one's roots. Initially, he wanted the film to recreate life in socialist Poland as he remembered it from the 1960s through the unprejudiced eyes of the young novitiate, but that original plan changed in the course of making the film. The film lacks ideological clashes. The action treats them without undue passion or prejudice, and they become part of the grey reality of Poland in the early 1960s. Instead of frustrating black-and-white contrasts, a grey tonality of disillusionment and resignation is revealed before our eyes. We sense the transient nature of these juxtapositions and how inevitably life crushes them into the greyness of everyday existence. The director himself claims that *Ida* 'is a film about identity, family, faith, guilt, socialism and music'.[4]

The title *Ida* is a very purposeful choice. In the short time that Anna spends with her aunt, we witness the development of her personality and her getting to know herself. The film has a melancholic undertone. In Pawlikowski's distinct style, the narrative is concise, and the characters are sparingly chosen. The images are minimalist, without details. The frames are almost empty. The movements are few, and the dialogue is short. The viewer is left with a sense of physical absence—of movement, people, colours and sounds. It is a void that you want to fill. Emotionally, the film is the exact opposite. We witness the filling of what is missing—of belonging, of a mother figure, of identity, of one's own history, of life experience and of love. The audience is emotionally drawn to the hastily created bond between the two women that will fill what was taken away and missing—for Ida, being someone's daughter, and for Wanda, being someone's mother.

How Is Femininity Constructed?

The Church: The Omnipotent, Primal Mother

In Christianity, and especially in Catholicism, the Church is often referred to as 'mother' because of its function to nurture and support the faithful. In 1965, in the documents of the Second Vatican Council, Pope John XXIII called the Church 'Mother and Teacher' of all nations. Recently, in an interview for Vatican Radio, Pope Francis said: 'Church is a mother and must have that loving and tender maternal feeling and human warmth as otherwise all that remains is rigidity and discipline', an all-caring and all-forgiving mother, limitlessly generous and loving, but also an austere, principled and demanding mother, an abstract, omnipotent mother, without a face and without a feeding breast, a mother you love without seeing, trust without knowing, follow without doubting and an absolute mother from whom it is impossible to separate, because she is everywhere.

[3] Ibid.

[4] Ibid.

In the first shot of the film, we see Anna intently painting the face of a wooden figure of Jesus Christ. She puts all her effort into creating an image of something unknown to her. With this first scene, the director pinpoints the search for something missing and its embodiment into human form as the main driver of the action. By giving a human face to an abstract image, Anna is able to connect to it. Later on, she will turn to that particular image for comfort, support and advice. We see the painted face of Jesus for the first time when Anna is anxious about going to the big city alone. At night, she is like a frightened child looking for a source of security, support and encouragement. In this moment of uncertainty, she literally 'grasps' for the symbol of her faith, the cross she wears around her neck, seeking reassuring physical contact with the only mother she has, the Church.

These few shots tell us something very important about Anna. We feel that she knows what to do when she is upset. Anna has been taught to seek and receive reassurance. It is as if Anna has had the experience of being comforted. But at the same time, we have just learned that she is a full orphan, raised in a convent. How then does she have a memory of something we know she has been deprived of? Psychoanalysis is less concerned with the mother one has or does not have in reality than with one's internal image of her and the relation to it. In this sense, although orphaned, we understand that Anna has an inner object of a mother that she turns to when coping with anxiety. She has an unconscious memory of her mother, a feeling she acquired early in life. It is this exactly the feeling she finds within herself in moments of anxiety that compels her to seek out an object.

The shots in the convent with empty spaces and minimal human presence reinforce the visual deprivation of the missing image. At the outset, it is difficult to identify the protagonist among the uniformly veiled and inaccessible female figures. To maintain our connection to the narrative, the director challenges another of our senses, our hearing. The beautiful female voices chanting the prayer, the only living presence in the chapel, captivate with their soothing sound. Pawlikowski is adept at using women's singing voices in his films as a means of expression. Here, it can be seen as one of the symbols of the maternal function. Immediately afterwards, we see the nuns eating. The associations that are evoked in the spectators are of the mother's voice and the feeding breast, the two sources of comfort we had as newborns. And yet, there is a feeling of coldness, scarcity, rigidity and emotional distance. The Church is a mother who cares platonically for her daughters. She loves their souls but not their bodies. The body in all its expressions is hidden and this creates a sense of coldness. The warmth of the bodies is missing; they are not used to expressing emotions. The wooden figure of Jesus that the novitiates carry outside seems lonely in the empty snowy circle, and they communicate with Jesus stiffly and from a distance. It is snowy and cold.

The main goal of monasticism is spiritual union with God through prayer and bodily deprivation—asceticism, fasting and abstinence. To become a nun, Anna will take a vow of 'virginity, modesty and obedience'. In a symbolic sense, this means symbiotic fusion with the 'all good' symbiotic mother (Mahler, 1972), represented by the Church, the faith and God. In return, this omnipotent mother offers an existence free of pain and suffering. From a psychoanalytical perspective, this is reminiscent of a return to the earliest phase of life when one is in a symbiotic relationship with the mother who satisfies all needs 'who was at one time part of the self in a blissful state of wellbeing'.[5] This is also the time when the newborn held in the mother's arms still has no awareness of their body being separate from hers. In one of the most striking shots, the novitiates are lying face down in the temple, arms outstretched so that a larger area of their bodies can touch the floor (Fig. 11.1). But this is not a loving embrace. They are asking for forgiveness, surrendering their bodies because they belong to God and must not be defiled. By condemning the flesh and preaching spiritual union, the Mother Church breaks the possibility of separation and maintains dependence. Her faithful daughters are seduced into remaining in a blissful state of disembodied safety and contentment.

The ideal around which women's monasticism is organised is that of the Immaculate Virgin Mary. The pleasures of the flesh are in opposition to faith in God. A woman has already been assigned by the Bible the role of seductress, and hence, she is burdened with greater guilt for human sinfulness. For this reason, women's monasticism has always been stricter than men's.[6] Nuns have to prove their devotion to the ideals of their God more convincingly. The Mother Church has no body with which her daughters can identify.

Fig. 11.1 Physical contact (00:59:25)

[5] Mahler MS (1972).

[6] It was not until the late 1950s and early 1960s that the Second Vatican Council gave nuns freedoms like other believers. Until then, their vestments were extremely strict and not even high-ranking nuns, unlike male clergymen, were allowed any ornaments and decorations.

They, like her, must live as if they had no female bodies that could be loved, that could attract, excite and bring pleasure. Nuns must not provoke men's fantasies. They can be mothers, comforting and nurturing, but they cannot arouse desires. By concealing their femininity, nuns nobly take on the responsibility to keep male desires away by not arousing them. This is one example of how the need to civilise men's attraction to women has led to the creation of both religious and secular practices in which women are either idealised (mothers and saints) or demonised (whores and seductresses). The scene in which the girls bathe with their clothes on, because in the convent nudity is forbidden even in the bathroom, is perhaps the most erotic in the film because of the young women's delineated bodies, see-through gowns and loose hair. It shows us that despite the innocence of the novitiates, their sexual energy finds a way to be communicated, even when they themselves are unaware of it. It is a part of real life that cannot be denied and cannot remain veiled and hidden for long, either under the grey robes of the novitiates or under the thin veil of snow covering everything at the beginning of the film. The composition of the shot in which we see Anna leaving the monastery shows how her inner world is organised (Fig. 11.2). The frame is dominated by the convent's powerful, grey building, the Mother Church. Against it Anna, the daughter, looks small and insignificant. In the background,

Fig. 11.2 Leaving the monastery (00:04:47)

we can barely see the figure of Jesus whose face she painted—the only element of her subjective experience. Everything is white and cold, it's snowing.

Ruja, the Lost Mother

The first thing Anna learns when she meets her aunt Wanda is that she does not belong solely to the powerful Mother Church. She is Jewish—'Ida Lebenstein, daughter of Chaim Lebenstein and Ruja Herz'. From this point on, we find it difficult to call her anything else and completely forget the name given to her by the Church. Ida is a human being, just like all of us though she has a dramatic history, she belongs to the human world and we are allowed to relate her experiences to our own. From this point, the viewer is challenged to construct Ida's human image in the film's narrative.

Wanda shows Ida a photograph in which she sees the face of Ruja, her birth mother, for the first time. Remarkably, in this photo, Ida is in her mother's arms, right where every baby belongs. The camera shows the photo long enough, so we can get a good look and see the natural bond between mother and child. This photo answers the question why Ida is able to find a source of comfort within herself. The mother's embrace in the photograph is the first bodily contact we see on screen. The mother's physical holding of the child is one of her most important functions. The warmth of a mother's body and the skin-to-skin contact have an intensely calming effect. From the photograph, we see that Ida had a 'good enough mother'[7] who held her in her arms, calmed her excitement, created physical closeness and feeling of bodily integrity; she reflected her emotions, responded to her needs, contained her distress. These first experiences shaped Ida's very early and, for that matter, unconscious memory of the mother's holding function, which is activated every time she needs it. In reality, Ida was dramatically separated from her mother, but in her psychic space, the internalised mother continued to play a major role in her emotional survival.

The aunt inducts Ida into the family history and the image of the mother is fleshed out. We find out that Ruja was a creative, artistic and attractive woman. There is a generosity and playfulness about her. She has made stained glass 'to make the cows happier', random pieces of coloured glass glued together, like the words and images from which Ida is trying to piece together her mother's image. 'This is so Ruja. Beautiful stained glass next to cow shit', Wanda says to convince her niece that her mother was extraordinary. Ida gazes longingly at the stained glass as if it were an icon, a distant image, an incomprehensible and new manifestation of femininity in which she expects to find something familiar and close, something that would belong to herself.

How much of that femininity had passed into Ida in the short time she had with her mother? Primal sensations of femininity are imprinted on the girl through intimate physi-

[7] The term was coined by D. Winnicott and denotes a mother who provides a degree of care which, while not always impeccably responsive to the baby's needs, is adequate enough to protect the baby from harmful influences and to lay the foundation for subsequent healthy development.

cal closeness with the mother. The mother's affection passes through the infantile erogenous zones, the skin, the mouth and the anus and helps the little girl to establish a relationship with her own body. The mother cares for the little girl's body as a woman familiar with the female body. She sees the future woman in her daughter. Through these early physical sensations and through her body, the daughter acquires the mother's relationship to femininity. All her life she will simultaneously identify with and differentiate herself from this first model of femininity. With such implicit and intuitive knowledge that we possess as humans, we wait to see on the screen how this unconscious femininity will manifest despite the taboos imposed by the Church.

Ida now knows who she has lost and what she has lost through her. Ruja is her real, biological mother, whose loss can now be grieved. Psychoanalysis discovered that it is impossible to mourn for someone we do not know. The loss of something which has no conscious expression cannot be experienced in reality and remains smouldering as an undefined pain. It seems insurmountable, condemning the subject to a vague sense of guilt and melancholy.[8] When Ida finds out who was her mother the first thing she needs to do is to visit her parents' grave. She can finally connect the loss of her parents to real persons and events and is ready to begin the mourning process.

Wanda, the Found Mother

Many define *Ida* as a road movie. Wanda and Ida take a journey back to their family history and to each other. The meeting of two complete strangers, connected by a shared traumatic past, seems like the meeting of two incompatible worlds. One is young and inexperienced, having spent her entire life in a rural convent. The other is an experienced woman because she survived the political terror of post-war Poland. One is in a hurry to discover what she doesn't know, and the other wants to forget what she does know. These differences have the potential to burden the story with multiple contradictions—between the secular and the religious, morality and depravity, naivety and cynicism, memory and forgetting and the physical and the spiritual. But shared loss erases all these differences.

The trial in which Wanda has to deliver a verdict is ridiculous. Ideals have lost their meaning and cannot serve as justification for the sacrifices made in their name. The loss of her child is insufferable. Cynicism is her psychological defence against guilt, despair and absence of meaning. She dulls her sorrow with alcohol and men. At the same time, we see Ida kneeling in prayer to God, her way of coping with suffering. Both strategies, the aggressive and the passive, are misguided and soul-crushing, and both hinder coping with loss (Fig. 11.3). That is why the two heroines look equally lonely and unhappy; Ida and Wanda must live with their differences, complement each other and unite in the face of grief.

[8] Freud S (1917).

Fig. 11.3 Different and united in grief (00:14:21)

A remarkable change comes over Wanda when her eyes fall on Ida alone at the station. Her face lights up fondly, just like a mother seeing her own child. One single shot of precise acting reveals this transformation to us. 'There is no such thing as an infant'[9] . A baby alone doesn't exist and, respectively, there is no such thing as a mother either. What exists is the reality of their unique relationship—a 'nursing couple.' The needy child incites a caring attitude, and the unfulfilled maternal feeling finds an object. Wanda recognises her niece as her lost child. Ida finds in Ruja's sister a possible mother. Each can invest in the other and find what she lacks most. It is as if it is not just Ida and Wanda connecting, but the child in one and the mother in the other. Thus, tightly bound, more by their unconscious needs than by the task they have set themselves, Wanda and Ida set out to uncover the tragedy of their erased family.

This appears to be Ida's first opportunity to become close to a woman who can play a holistic role in her development, combining the physical and the spiritual. She addresses the nun in the convent as 'mother', but this mother is wrapped in a habit, speaking in the voice of God and keeping the relationship strictly according to protocol. Through Wanda, Ida immediately discovers that there is a different version of her than the nuns have imposed. 'You're sweet... men will go crazy,' says her aunt, seeing her youth and energy.

[9] Winnicott DW (1960).

Ida's smile reveals that these words have an effect on her. As an emancipated and free woman, Wanda knows the sexual desire in the female body and brings it out with her banter. 'Do you have sinful thoughts sometimes? …About carnal love?' she asks, to provoke her niece, but really because she understands how Ida feels under the habit. A taboo is removed with a flourish. Femininity and female sexuality come into play. Part of us will continue to be curious about their manifestations. The audience is not voyeuristic; they are looking for mature sexuality as an expression of a woman's development.

Wanda treats her niece with concern as if she has something that needs fixing or making up for. She knows what Ida doesn't yet know about herself—her young body is capable of experiencing pleasure, like Wanda at the same age or like her sister Ruja. Will Ida join the women of the Hertz family or remain faithful to the Church that saved her? Will the femininity imparted by her mother but forbidden by the Church become part of her identity? Wanda seems set on bringing her back to her family roots. 'I won't let you waste your life' she tells Ida, and it sounds like a spat between a mother and her rebellious grown daughter. So, Ida's decision to take a vow begins to look more like youthful defiance than a conscious choice. But the argument here is not about the choice of religion. It is about the choice between the woman and the nun, between the sensual, the human and the immaculate and the ascetic, between the love that needs an object and the love that seeks unity or between separation and symbiosis.

The femininity we see in Wanda evokes mixed feelings. The first thing Ida sees in her home is the love bed and an anonymous man slipping out of it. Such are Wanda's men in the film, cameos. She uses sex to dominate them and create distance instead of connection. Wanda can be rude and arrogant and satisfies her desires through force and power. She seems to be the antithesis of femininity or at least the form we traditionally observe—passive, sacrificial and masochistic.

Ida finds herself between two extreme manifestations of the feminine. On the one hand is the Church personified in the abbess—a kind, nourishing and asexual woman. And on the other side is her aunt—an aggressive, seductive and sexual woman. The good mother who nurtures versus the bad mother who frustrates. The mother whose body exists only as a source of nourishment and comfort versus the mother whose body is a source of desire. Wanda's authentic maternal pain erases those differences. Anti-femininity is a traumatic reaction, a defence against the unbearable suffering of the loving mother. We see the close embrace between the 'Madonna' and the 'whore', merging into one, just as the two extremes are inseparable from the feminine nature. As spectators, we have overcome one of the most universal dichotomies of femininity—the mother and the sensual woman have merged into one (Fig. 11.4).

How a girl's feminine identity will develop depends on how the mother will relate to her daughter's femininity and sexuality. In addition to feeding and nurturing her, the mother is tasked with imparting her femininity. She teaches the girl how to be a woman by discovering and encouraging the feminine in her, by setting her own example and introducing her to the world of women. A young girl's attitude towards men is also influenced by the mother's conscious and unconscious attitudes towards men, the objects of her affections.

Fig. 11.4 The found mother (00: 43:15)

Wanda's flirtatious conversation with the young saxophonist manages to plant in Ida the seed of the attractive power of masculinity. Wanda associates the saxophone with sensuality and masculinity, and we are able to gain insight into her fantasy world in which men have the power of attraction. The message to Ida is that as a woman she is entitled to be attracted to men. Ida's prerogative is to see the young man as an object of romantic and erotic love. Another taboo is shattered and love enters the film's narrative, and the sound of the saxophone will remind us of that feeling.

The Daughter's Separation

A child's development presupposes a gradual separation from the mother. This task is harder for girls than for boys. The daughter finds herself in the paradoxical position of simultaneously differentiating from and identifying with the same object—her mother. She can separate from her mother because she no longer needs her care, but she remains strongly connected through her femininity as a very important part of her personality. Perhaps, this is why the daughter can never completely separate from her mother. What is most important for a woman's emotional development, therefore, is not simply the relationship with her mother but the extent to which that relationship can be both overcome and preserved.

The only realm in which a girl can both retain her femininity and distance herself enough is love or when a third party intervenes. In the early years, this role is played by the father, the first love object of the little girl. Later, the young woman finds different ways to overcome her dependence on the mother and to invest feelings in other people, objects or areas. Separation from the mother is usually a long process ending when the daughter finds a partner she falls so deeply in love with that the mother is displaced as the object of attachment and love.

Ida's relationship with Lis, the saxophonist, has a different effect in the context of her relationships with the three manifestations of the maternal image—the Church, Ruja and Wanda. Initially, the feeling is of something forbidden. Ida goes down to the hotel restaurant where the musicians are wrapping up. She seems to be experimenting with the forbidden. The singer in the orchestra is feminine and seductive; the music has an incendiary message to the body. Coltrane's piece is beautiful and irresistible. The composition of the shot in which she and Lis first talk is telling. The two are static, positioned at the bottom of the screen (Fig. 11.5). We can easily guess that love and attraction are inadmissible and must remain either secret or and hidden. They are a betrayal of the omnipotent Mother Church, who can punish her daughter by withdrawing her love from her.

Fig. 11.5 Love as separation from the omnipotent mother (00:36:27)

Ida realises that Lis thinks she is beautiful. Alone in front of her mirror, she removes her hood and lets her hair down, a symbol of femininity she inherited from her mother. It is as if that inner mother intervenes again to bring calm and confidence, this time in femininity. When they are saying their goodbyes outside the convent, Wanda tells Ida 'It's a pity Ruja couldn't see you' and reminds her that she no longer belongs solely to the Church, because she is connected to the real world through her mother, a world in which love is not divine but a shared experience. Ida has just buried her mother's remains, but she revived her memory by finding the roots of her feminine nature.

In the convent, we see a different Ida. No matter how hard she tries, she is no longer like the other novitiates. Her inner world is filled with new and revived objects that she communicates with. She experiences conflict and doubt. Ida once again leans on the figure of Jesus Christ for support. But this time she doesn't seem helpless. Her conversation with Christ seems more like the inner dialogue of a person who knows herself and can make a conscious decision to postpone the vow.

At the very beginning of the film, Wanda tells Ida 'You wouldn't have been happy with me' to explain why she didn't take her from the orphanage. Her suicide also follows that pattern. Wanda's tragedy is that she sees herself as a bad and unworthy mother, damaging to her children. Another mother abandons Ida. Once again, we see that close human contact, however brief, can fill an absence. Wanda finishes what Ruja started, releasing the unconscious and primal femininity Ruja set the ground for. In the end, she literally bequeaths to her niece the attributes of femininity. We see Ida in the empty apartment after her aunt's death, 'putting on' the image of a grown woman. Ida puts on Wanda's accessories and tries to behave like a woman, according to societal norms outside the convent. She imitates Wanda and, albeit uncertainly, begins to do the things girls her age do—dance, kiss and have sex.

The culture we inhabit is dominated by Christian values, and, according to them, there is a single expression for a woman's first act of love. She 'loses' her virginity. Entering mature sexuality, the readiness of a woman's body and psyche to perform a sexual act is associated with loss and is therefore cause for sadness. But does Ida mourn her night of love with Lis and the loss of her virginity, or is this the mourning of those who prefer to see her as immaculate, innocent and passive? Defloration is an irreversible change, a milestone in female development. It is experienced as a personal achievement if done in love and mutuality. It is a symbol that the young woman no longer needs her mother because she herself can be a mother. The mother can be left behind, the daughter no longer needs her protection, and she has learned enough to start on her own path of love.

In the last shot of the film, we see Ida walking down the road to the convent. Pawlikowski's trademark is to place his characters at the bottom of the frame, so we can feel the weight of the drama, repressed emotions and lack of freedom. This time, Ida is in close-up and looking us openly in the eye. The last shot is handheld, and this creates a sense of dynamism and real presence. It is as if Ida has entered the life we are in. The world for Ida is no longer split in two. The sheltered space of the convent and the chaotic world outside are one—her life. In it, she is a woman, she has family, roots and history, the important elements of identity. Ida can choose who she loves and what she believes, she can determine her future, and she has control over her life. All these achievements of her developing personality create a sense of self-worth and autonomy. This puts a distance between Ida and the Church. She returns to the convent, probably not because she is dependent but because she feels attached, and this is her home. The Church can now be seen as that part of the image of the good mother that allows herself to be left but is always there when you want to return to her.

The best thing a mother can do for her grown daughter is to build her up as a woman and give her the freedom to love without feeling guilty. In the world she has achieved, Ida can learn to be a woman without remorse. Ruja, her mother, has passed on femininity through her genes. She has taught her body to experience happiness and pleasure from being close to another person Wanda, the living connection to the female word, has given her the freedom to explore and know her femininity without guilt. It is a new world where one can be whole and experience happiness from living shared with another. This united maternal image of the lost and found mother shows us how strong human connection can be. It can heal, restore and evolve. The film proves to us that the strongest aspect of human nature is the ability to connect with one another and to draw from that on to develop and grow. It is something we clearly do better with each other, rather than with God. It demonstrates what psychoanalysis teaches us, that the psychic and the biological birth of any human being require another. Leaving the womb is a clearly differentiated event. By contrast, emotional autonomy is an often imperceptible process that unfolds over time, but through which everyone must be guided by someone else.

Yet the film is melancholic rather than joyful. Perhaps, it is because of the anger we, the viewers, feel at the injustice of war, the Holocaust and the totalitarian regime that caused so much suffering. But have we chosen an acceptable target for our anger? Does our indignation in fact stem from the deeper layers of our vulnerability awakened by the perceived absence of the mother in the film? The mother is so palpably absent that she must constantly be created and reinvented in every aspect of the film's narrative. We cannot find a direct equivalent to our resentment on screen, and so it remains repressed and displaced in both us, the viewers, and the protagonist until the end of the film. The silent anger towards the mother who is present mainly through her absence and deprives the child of her life-affirming love is there somewhere on the screen. It is in the lack of passion, joy and genuine interest in life, in the sadness, resignation and greyness. Will Ida understand and forgive the women in her life? Will she find a balance between love and resentment towards mothers, so she can experience happiness at being a woman like them? It seems she already has much more maturity and emotional resources to do so. Perhaps, that is what is coming. The ending is open.

About the Film

Original title	Ida
Release year	2013
Country	Poland, Denmark, France, Great Britain
Book	Pawel Pawlikowski, Rebecca Lenkiewicz
Direction	Pawel Pawlikowski
Music	Kristian Eidnes Andersen
Camera	Riszard Leneczewski, Lucasz Zal
Main actors	Agata Kulesza, Agata Trzebuchowska, Dawid Ogrodnik, Joanna Kulig
Availability	DVD

References

Chasseguet-Smirgel J (1976) Freud and female sexuality—the consideration of some blind spots in the exploration of the 'Dark Continent'. Int J Psychoanal 57:275–286

Freud S (1917) Mourning and melancholia. In: The standard edition of the complete psychological works of Sigmund Freud, vol XIV (1914–1916): on the history of the psycho-analytic movement, papers on metapsychology and other works, pp 237–258

Furman E (1982) Mothers have to be there to be left. Psychoanalytic study of the child, vol 37. pp 15–28

Mahler MS (1972) On the first three subphases of the separation-individuation process. Int J Psychoanal 53:333–338

Winnicott DW (1960) The theory of the parent-infant relationship. Int J Psychoanal 41:585–595

Part IV

Women's Suffering. Illness and Mystery in the Film

Black Swan

12

Irmgard Nagel

Introduction

The ballet genre has a rich history in global cinema and relies on the rhythmic movements of the human body to convey the emotional state of the characters. Through dance, audiences can experience an embodied sensual representation that conveys more than words ever could. For example, Michael Powell and Emeric Pressburger's classic film *The Red Shoes* (1948), based on Hans Christian Andersen's eponymous fairy tale, tells the story of a girl who becomes consumed by dance after putting on her red shoes, leading to her eventual demise. In this allegory, the theme shapes the film's content, while the fairy tale-like aspect has been turned into the protagonist's psychological drama. Similarly, Herbert Ross's *The Turning Point* (1977) delves deeply into the psychological profiles of two ballet dancers whose friendship takes divergent paths, leading each dancer to make significant sacrifices. *Billy Elliot* (2000), Stephen Daldry's debut feature, is a typical coming-of-age tale that follows an 11-year-old boy from an English coal-mining family as he pursues his love of ballet against a backdrop of homophobia and opposition from his community, including his own father. This film challenges stereotypes about male ballet dancers and questions the idea that ballet is only for girls and women.

Lastly, there is *Pina* (2011), Wim Wenders' homage to the choreographer and dancer Pina Bausch, who passed away in 2009. The documentary showcases a selection of Pina Bausch's famous dance theatre works and emphasises her deviation from the typical ballet training regime. By liberating her dancers from physically demanding, painful movements and difficult postures, which can only be performed for a certain amount of years, Bausch

I. Nagel (✉)
Munich, Germany

V. Pramataroff-Hamburger, A. Hamburger (eds.), *From La Strada to The Hours*,
https://doi.org/10.1007/978-3-662-68789-5_12

allowed her ensemble to age with time and transform the aging process into an expressive advantage.

Unlike any other dance film, *Black Swan* (2010) defies the categorisation of genres, shifting between drama, psychological thriller and horror. Much like *The Red Shoes*, Aronofsky's movie intertwines the fate of its primary character with the storyline of the world's most famous ballet, *Swan Lake*. The story follows a psychologically fragile young dancer seeking redemption from both external and internal restrictions that ultimately lead to her breakdown.

Storyline

The film revolves around Nina Sayers (Natalie Portman), an ambitious ballerina at the Lincoln Ballet Company in New York. Choreographer Thomas Leroy (Vincent Cassel) plans a stunning modern production of the outdated ballet *Swan Lake*, and part of it involves having one talented young ballerina dance both the White and Black Swan roles. Nina is assigned the role of the White Swan due to her ethereal beauty and innocent appeal, but she lacks the sensuality and erotic charm of a lascivious seductress, which is required for the Black Swan role. Lily (Mila Kunis), a newly joined dancer in the ensemble, possesses these qualities, leading to a battle of rivalry and jealousy among the female dancers, especially after the former prima ballerina, Beth (Winona Ryder), is sidelined due to age and eventually attempts suicide.

Thomas, the charismatic but demanding director, fuels his students' ambition by provoking them with his thrilling bluntness. He cruelly confronts Nina, revealing her lack of sexuality and allure while attempting to physically arouse her. When Nina bites Thomas' lip in response to his kiss, he is stunned but attracted to her impulsive reaction, leading him to cast her in the starring role of the two swans. Nina's struggle to interpret the passionate, sensual Black Swan role becomes obsessive and increasingly desperate as the movie progresses.

Nina is a woman in her mid-twenties who lives with her dominant mother, Erica (Barbara Hershey), a former ballet dancer who has dedicated her life to her daughter's success. Erica controls every aspect of Nina's daily life in their small shared flat, where life seems to stand still. Nina's life is entirely devoted to ballet, with her bedroom containing remnants of her childhood, complete with stuffed animals and fluffy, pink decor. Their cocooning and claustrophobic world is disrupted when Nina's repressed dark side emerges, and she becomes aware of her own sexual desires and libido.

At first, Nina indulges in small acts of identity theft, such as stealing lipstick and earrings from the dressing room of the adored dancer Beth. But later, she surrenders to the persuasions of Lily—her admired but also feared rival—and accompanies her on a debauched night club tour. As her mental state deteriorates, Nina becomes more and more confused about her identity, resulting in a state of mental derangement.

As Nina's mental state continues to deteriorate, the boundaries between reality, dreams and imagination begin to blur. What initially appeared as minor irritations, such as a possible lookalike in the subway or a chance meeting with Lily, who momentarily seemed to have Nina's face, take on an increasingly intense and threatening quality, becoming almost persecutory. Nina cannot determine whether her sexual experience with Lily was real or a dream or if her confrontation with her mother, who intruded into her bedroom, was real.

In an ever more paranoid world, Lily ultimately appears in Nina's dressing room during the premiere, and a murderous fight ensues, with Nina driving a shard of broken mirror into her supposed rival's stomach. However, the truth gradually emerges, revealing that this dark and threatening self-image was a hallucination. Despite everything, Nina successfully dances the Black Swan role to thunderous applause. It's only during the final act, where Nina portrays the dying swan, that the tragic wound in her own stomach becomes apparent. The film ends with Nina's final words: 'I was perfect', before the screen fades to white.

Background

Darren Aronofsky is considered one of the most successful contemporary filmmakers today, having garnered critical acclaim and widespread recognition for his works. Aronofsky was born in 1969 in Brooklyn, New York City, to a Jewish family. He attended Harvard University where he pursued cultural anthropology as well as film and animation studies before eventually joining the American Film Institute after graduating from MCL.

Aronofsky achieved early success with his debut film, *Pi* (1998), winning the Director's Prize at the prestigious Sundance Film Festival. He subsequently received numerous accolades globally, including the Golden Lion at the 2008 Venice Festival for his fourth film, *The Wrestler* (2008). *Black Swan* (2010), his next film, cemented Aronofsky's place in the international film scene, garnering critical acclaim and an impressive haul of Oscar nominations, including Best Film and Best Director. Natalie Portman received the Oscar for 'Best Actress in a Leading Role' for her performance as the ballerina Nina.

Aronofsky is recognised as an accomplished auteur of the film industry, with a distinctive signature in his scripts and films. His works explore recurring themes such as love, death, vulnerability, the exploitation of the body, the tension between perfection and excess and the loss of control. Aronofsky typically collaborates with a trusted team of artists and technicians, including screenwriter Mark Heyman, cinematographer Matthew Libatique and his friend, composer Clint Mansell.

Aronofsky, along with his cameraman, developed a unique method to capture the mental states of his protagonists. They attached a portable camera, the Snorri Cam, to the performers' bodies to capture each movement from up close. In *Black Swan*, this technique showcases the dancers' exertions, creating an almost intimate connection with the audience through tight close-ups of their faces. This effect is enhanced during the fractured mirror visions and eerie duplicate images, creating a surreal, terrifying effect that blurs the boundary between reality and fiction, much like the protagonist's experience.

Another signature of Aronofsky and composer Mansell is the 'hip-hop montage', which incorporates heavy beats and electronic sound effects with time-lapse sequences, creating a tangible and sensual experience for the audience, allowing them to feel the excitement and intoxication of the film's characters. Mansell's use of Peter Tchaikovsky's late romantic music in the soundtrack for *Black Swan* is notable, but he also disassembles and reconstructs the music several times, infusing it with a powerful effect tailored to the film's plot.

Although *Black Swan* was released in 2010, Aronofsky had been considering a ballet movie for years. He was inspired after reading Dostoevsky's *The Double* and seeing a performance of Tchaikovsky's *Swan Lake*, particularly after noting the contradiction of the apparent ease of the dances with the strenuous ballet work behind the scenes. From there, Aronofsky started to develop the concept for his film, which had Natalie Portman already cast as the Swan Queen. However, he had to put off making the movie due to other projects, leading to a delay of several years.

Black Swan is considered by some to be the twin of *The Wrestler*: Both films focus on the exploitation of the body in high-performance sports, aiming to challenge the audience's threshold of discomfort, although one sport is perceived as an amusement for the masses, while the other is a refined art form. Natalie Portman, a trained ballerina since childhood, was thrilled to be offered the role of the prima ballerina but underwent an additional 10 months of intensive training before rehearsals began. She also lost 10 kg for the part of Nina. Benjamin Millepied, who is also Portman's husband, served as the film's choreographer and danced the role of Prince David.

Black Swan marks Aronofsky's first foray into horror, delving into the horror of losing control of one's life. It is the director's first movie to feature a female lead and three female antagonists, making the enactment of the feminine a central theme.

How Is the Feminine Staged Within the Film?

Fairy Tales, Myths, Archetypes

Far from being subtle in the portrayals of his characters, Aronofsky exaggerates their characteristics as if they were supposed to symbolise a specific type of woman/man. Just as the fairy tale story of *Swan Lake* touches on the primal fears of humankind, in *Black Swan* the viewer is inevitably drawn into the looming downward spiral of Nina, the protagonist. The dominant black and white colours that permeate the movie are emblematic not only of a clearly made distinction between good and evil but also of Nina's inner turmoil. The dark, forbidden, most taboo aspects that she does not allow herself to feel nevertheless haunt her like a shadow.

The film characters are reminiscent of fairy tale figures and mythical beings, which are also known to be universal symbols or archetypes. According to Carl Gustav Jung

(1935/2018), they belong to the collective unconscious. Archetypes are primal images of the soul that are instinctual and spiritual in nature, displaying a universality that transcends different cultures. One such classic archetype is the 'shadow', which symbolises the dark side of the ego. It contains repressed or denied parts of the personality, i.e. the unloved and morally rejected attributes.

The shadow is like a mirror image and follows us everywhere, representing a twin that we cannot escape. Often, the individual deals with their shadow by projecting it onto someone else, so they can fight and reject the despicable in that other person, instead of working on the repressed inner conflicts within themselves. Symbols of the shadow are, for example, dark lookalikes or evil adversaries of the hero or heroine.

Black Swan draws heavily on these threatening symbolic figures. In addition to the protagonist Nina, the perfectionistic, compulsive child-woman who gradually falls into a state of desperation due to her inner struggles, there are also three female antagonists: Erica, the overpowering, witch-like mother who cannot let go of her grown-up daughter; the competitor Lily, a 'femme fatale' who is the exact counterpart of Nina—her 'dark side'; and Beth, the once-spurned, now vengeful lover whose fate is a mirror of what awaits Nina. Encircled by these women, we find Thomas Leroy, the artistic director of the theatre, who, as his name suggests—Le Roi—is the king. He is primarily concerned with art and disregards the 'casualties' he leaves behind along the way.

Nina, the Conformist Daughter

Nina is initially portrayed as an innocent, lovable creature who has a dream that she is a princess-turned swan, reminiscent of *Swan Lake*, where the evil sorcerer Redbeard has turned Princess Odette into a White Swan. When Nina wakes up, she recounts her dream to her mother Erica—at least the viewer assumes she does, as in the scene no one can be seen but there are noises coming from the kitchen.

Nina's mother is always present. Nina and Erica seem to conform to the idea that the mother should look after her daughter as if she were still a small child. They appear to share everything with each other, even the joy of a ballet dancer's meagre breakfast consisting of an egg and half a grapefruit. Their seemingly loving mother-daughter relationship is suffocatingly close with an omnipresent and overbearing Erica controlling and shepherding her daughter's life, making the viewer feel almost physically repulsed at the lack of privacy.

This suffocating mother-daughter dynamic is highlighted when Erica helps Nina to get dressed, hugs her goodbye and then asks if she can accompany her to the theatre, which Nina amiably declines. Erica's cold look into the camera when she says goodbye to her 'sweet girl' is both disturbing and intimidating (Fig. 12.1). There is something dishonest and threatening about her look, which appears to send a contradictory message to the 24-year-old child: 'go on your way, be successful, but don't ever leave me!' Nina has barely left the house when her mobile phone rings; the display shows 'Mom'. This invis-

Fig. 12.1 Erica's cold look into the camera (15:14:33)

ible metaphorical umbilical cord represents the need for constant contact, implying that separation is impossible. And yet, there is a timid resentment on Nina's part, a reluctant attempt to detach herself when she doesn't answer her mother's call.

Erica, The Phallic Mother

Erica Sayers is portrayed as a lonely woman, who views her daughter as her sole source of affection since she has no husband or friends. She is presented as a mother who is completely enmeshed in and at the service of her daughter's life, resulting in a symbiotic relationship. However, the backstory reveals that this love is highly ambivalent as Erica lost her career and lover, who was also a choreographer, due to her pregnancy. The negative feelings towards men that Erica projects onto Thomas Leroy, the ballet's choreographer and her daughter's instructor, seem to stem from this past experience. The expectation for Nina to become the prima ballerina is both a completion of Erica's unfulfiled aspirations and a forbidden one, intended to prevent the strain on their mother-daughter relationship. Erica, too, has a dark, secluded aura about her. Aronofsky portrays Erica as a former ballerina, always dressed in black with a severe hair bun, which adds to her grim aura. Erica cannot admit to her tormenting jealousy and envy of her daughter's success; time and again, the camera catches Erica's cold stare, which doesn't seem to match her 'friendly' smile at all. Her intrusive hands seem to control her daughter's flesh and life, as if Nina were her property. Erica's love is obsessive. Indeed, her threatening 'black omnipresence' enables the viewer to sense that any possible maternal care or concern for her daughter's unstable mental health comes second to her fear of losing Nina.

Detachment entails separation and separation can lead to death when one depends on the other for survival. Nina is portrayed as a young woman who strives to be a perfect daughter for her mother, someone her mother can be proud of, while also desiring freedom and self-determination. This creates an unsolvable conflict for Nina, leading to feelings of guilt on the one hand and aggressive emotions on the other. However, as she is a 'good girl', she is not allowed to express them. Her anxiety and overwhelming rage are psychosomatically expressed through the body. According to Anzieu (1996), the skin forms a boundary both to the outside and to the inside. In Nina's case, the dysfunctional relationship with her mother is evidenced in her skin. She 'cannot get out of her skin'. The immense inner pressure finds an outlet through self-harm in the form of her violently scratching her skin open on her shoulder, serving as an allegory for the unbearable mother-daughter conflict: 'I want to fly away' versus 'I'll clip your wings'.

Nina's habit of nail-biting and tearing off bits of cuticle as well as her eating disorder are additional manifestations of her unresolved conflict of simultaneously needing her mother and having to keep her at a distance. The imperfect mother-daughter relationship is also highlighted in the 'cake scene'. Nina has obtained the long-awaited role of the Swan Queen. To celebrate, her mother buys a rich, creamy cake, which in itself already conveys an ambiguous message: Being a dedicated ballerina, Nina has to follow a strict diet, so this gift means 'let's celebrate your success', but also 'you aren't supposed to succeed!' As a result, Nina shows no enthusiasm, which highly offends her mother. Erica's fear and anger at an impending abandonment by her daughter are personified when she threatens to throw the cake into the dustbin. Erica becomes more threatening, akin to a witch, in her demeanour. She waves a large kitchen knife towards Nina, a phallic symbol (I will cut you if you disobey me) and forces Nina to lick the white cake cream off her raised index finger, a phallic symbol demonstrating power. Nina obeys with a smile, saying: 'hmmm'. The viewer experiences overwhelming disgust and profound aversion, feelings that Nina must not express yet are becoming ever more prominent in her.

Nina in Search of a Father

The model of femininity corresponding to Nina's persona is that of an adorable ballerina who dances perfectly, blissfully ignorant of the world beyond the stage. Growing up without a father and lacking experience with men, the ballet director's remark that she lacks the sensuality required to portray the Black Swan terrifies her deeply. Sensuality and sexuality have no place in her rigid, tightly scheduled high-performance life with her mother. She feels humiliated and inadequate. And yet, she is curious about a part of herself she has yet to discover, something elusive within her that remains undefined. So, who is the 'whole' Nina? What shapes her identity, her being?

After the forced kiss, Nina impulsively bites Thomas's lip, declaring her desire for more. The music echoes her shadow, her libidinous and sultry side, accompanied by the increasingly frequent and intense rustling of bird wings. Without any erotic traits of her own, just like a little girl, Nina steals some lipstick and earrings from the admired dancer Beth, slipping into the shoes of the idealised woman. In a childlike, naïve way, she aims to seduce Thomas so that he will give her the role of the Swan Queen.

As the male role model, Thomas is depicted negatively and more so as a father figure. Though he desires to develop Nina's sexual and feminine qualities, he ultimately seeks to mould her into his ideal dancer for the White and Black Swans and, possibly, his mistress or 'little princess'. His crude and degrading manner of introducing her to sexuality further humiliates the insecure Nina.

And yet he manages to awaken the young woman's sexual desires, causing her to acutely feel her internalised prohibitions and repressed inner conflicts. While masturbating lustfully—'homework' set by her teacher—she suddenly has a vision of her sleeping mother in the corner of her bedroom, shocking and embarrassing both her and the viewer, who now feels like a voyeur. As Nina begins to decompensate psychologically, brief flashes accumulate. In an outburst of violence she is getting rid of her stuffed animals to rebel against her mother's infantilisation and concurrently fuelled by her mother's snide remarks about Leroy's intentions, she is driven further into her fantasies of behaving like a whore.

Erica senses Leroy's growing influence on her daughter, and her longing for differentiation and boundary setting pushes Erica to secure 'her claim of ownership' over Nina even more. Much like Thomas, who reduces Nina to her breasts and genitals by groping her while attempting to teach her the meaning of 'seduction and letting oneself go' in a manner reminiscent of the possessive Redbeard the sorcerer, Erica similarly becomes a menacing demon as she obsessively searches Nina's body for scratch marks. She trims Nina's fingernails down to the flesh, symbolically attempting to 'declaw the cat' by constraining her libidinous attraction to the 'father-object'.

Unable to tolerate the oedipal triad due to her fear of abandonment, Erica believes that a daughter's love for both mother and father is impossible. Erica believes there can only be one. She conveys this belief to Nina, who is unable to please both her mother and Leroy, who in turn cannot fulfil the fatherly role due to his own narcissistic interests and demands that clash with those of Nina's mother. Nina wants to please them both, which is bound to fail, thereby strongly contributing to her psychic fragmentation. Nina's desire to dance both the White Swan and the Black Swan simultaneously is a metaphor for her desire to unite the opposing elements of white and black. As her distortions of reality and hallucinations intensify, they start becoming increasingly alarming.

Lily, the Much Sought-After Rival

Nina and Lily's first encounter is brief. On the underground to Lincoln Station, Nina sees a young woman in another compartment who at first seems to be her own mirror image. According to Otto Rank (1925), a student of Freud, Lily represents Nina's shadow or also her doppelganger. She embodies her dark unconscious side, while Nina is the overly slender, fair-haired dancer, focused on technical perfection and ideally suited to the role of the White Swan. In contrast, Lily has striking tattoos on her shoulder blades, which she displays in black, low-cut garments. Her dancing is sensual and spontaneous.

Nina's ascetic lifestyle is entirely devoted to the art form of ballet. The camera captures close-ups of her tense, yet beautiful face and her flexible, limber torso, but her 'lower half', where libido and sexuality are located, is either absent or shrouded in darkness. In contrast, Lily indulges in hamburgers, parties, drugs and sex, eagerly flouting rules and perfectly embodying the Black Swan, as she is Nina's opposite.

The next encounter of the two women happens in the dancers' changing room. They assess each other in the mirror without making eye contact, their rivalry palpable. The audience intuits that Lily is Nina's mirror image, showing her everything that she is not. Lily flaunts her sensuality frequently, enlisting the attention of Leroy—Nina's idealised father—and threatening to steal Nina's role as the Swan Queen. Nina simultaneously envies and fears Lily's natural spontaneity and sexual drive while being reminded of her own imperfections by Lily, who is not only her shadow but also a thorn in her flesh. Despite or perhaps because of her challenging training, Nina cannot achieve the lightness in her balletic expression that Lily embodies. Nina's psyche is torn between wanting to mimic Lily and being distinct from her.

Nina's psyche starts to rebel, and her increasing paranoia leads to hallucinations, where figures resembling Lily suddenly transform into Nina's face. Sexual fantasies flood her mind: She watches Lily and Leroy having sex backstage and then imagines herself as Lily engaging in intercourse with Thomas Leroy, who then transforms into Redbeard. Her obsessive-compulsive denial of her prohibited 'dark side' begins to break down, as previously thwarted taboo desires rise to the surface.

Lily, the Temptress

Lily, portrayed as a temptress, could derive her name from Lilith, a rebellious woman in Jewish mythology who used her sexuality as a tool to challenge patriarchal norms and refused to submit to Adam, ultimately leaving the Garden of Eden. She was punished, becoming an 'immortal creature of the night', and was later associated with female vampirism in the horror genre. During the early feminist movements, however, Lilith symbolised sexual liberation and freedom.

In *Black Swan*, Lily embodies the Lilith archetype. She is a rebel who enjoys her pleasures lustfully and is the complete opposite of the obsessively perfect Nina. While Lily intimidates Nina, she also acts as a 'tempting serpent', introducing alcohol, teaching her to seduce and spurn men. Her epicurean bite into the meaty burger hints at libidinous uses for her sensual oral region. Later, in the bar, Nina borrows a sexy black shirt from her competitor, in which she now also feels powerful and seductive. After hesitating, she even accepts drugs from Lily, which lead her into a maelstrom of unfamiliar sensations, driving her into sexual activity with an unknown man. Under the flickering lights of the dance floor, her soul seems to positively explode. As surreal figures and flashes of light appear, hinting at her shattered sense of identity, the audience can only make out the surreal figures of the kaleidoscope-like flashes in a detailed resolution. Harmless men transform into Leroy, who becomes Redbeard, then multiple Redbeards, and Nina splits into multiple selves. Lots of Lilys sway around her. Lily materialises as the Black Swan, alongside Beth as the White Swan, and a haunting voice whispers 'sweet girl, sweet girl' as demon eyes follow Nina's frenzied dancing.

These hallucinatory images strongly reflect Nina's current psychological state and her shattered sense of self. All these surrounding influences are demonised and experienced as parts of her own inner monster: inadequate, insignificant and unable to achieve perfection. She experiences murderous rage towards herself and people she depends on. Still under the influence of drugs, Nina allows herself to be sexually seduced by Lily and can finally let herself go. She obviously enjoys oral sex with Lily. With her help, she has created a separation from her mother and has been able to open up to a previously inanimate side within herself. Or perhaps not?

In the horrifying pillow scene, where Lily represents Nina's internalised nightmarish double suffocating 'mother's sweet girl', it becomes clear that Nina is severely psychotically ill and her condition is a matter of life and death. The next day, Nina realises that Lily, too, has used her to outdo her and take the role of the Swan Queen from her. But most of all, she is deeply hurt by Lily's smug remark about whether Nina was having a lesbian dream about her. For the bewildered and baffled viewer, it is now unclear whether Nina and Lily's sexual encounter was real or merely a figment of Nina's imagination.

Nina, the Black Swan

The borders between Nina and other characters progressively dissolve, exemplified in the many mirror scenes. Firstly, Lily and Nina merge into a single person in a three-part mirror, then Nina's body splinters into countless Ninas, and lastly Nina's reflection seems to take a life of its own. Nina's sense of identity disintegrates entirely, and the split can no longer be sustained. Her rejected and suppressed dark side fiercely breaks through, fuelling uncontrollable rage and fear of destroying everything that is keeping her alive: her mother and her dream of becoming a prima ballerina who may end up just like her mother.

Nina wants to break free from her mother's grasp and claim her own inner space, which her mother refuses to recognise, symbolically igniting a dramatic struggle for access to her bedroom. Erica tries to force her way into the room, but Nina braces herself against the door, painfully jamming her mother's intrusive fingers. This time, Nina 'trims the mother's claws'. The viewer is deeply unsettled by Nina's self-dissolution, as the camera transitions from showing Nina's supposed reality to crossing the line into her delusion, revealing her physical transformation with duck legs along with a black feather sprouting from a shoulder wound. The madness becomes unstoppable, leaving the audience shaken to their core.

The naive girl's metamorphosis into a menacing creature has begun, and her mother's final attempt to protect, but also infantilise her, is unsuccessful as Nina explodes with violent rage. She holds up a mirror to her mother, exclaiming 'I don't want to end up like you!' and rushes off to the theatre. It is the day of the premiere. Throughout the perfor-

Fig. 12.2 Nina's transformation into a demon swan (*Black Swan*, 01:31:13)

mance, Nina is tormented by hallucinations of Lily, dressed as the Black Swan, sexually caressing Prince David, who appears to enjoy it, while four little swans sneer at Nina. During her star role as the White Swan, Nina stumbles and falls, shattering the archetype of her honourable, virtuous character. Devastated, she returns to her dressing room, where a murderous fight between the two rivals, Nina and Lily, breaks out. Nina pushes Lily into the giant closet mirror, breaking it, before driving a phallus-shaped shard into her body. Symbolically, she destroys her mirror image, claiming her power.

On stage, Nina now dances the dance of her life and receives a standing ovation, her inner transformation embodied in eerie, beautiful imagery of her skin transforming into a swan's, growing large black wings, while she transforms into a demon swan (Fig. 12.2). Back in her dressing room, she is hit by the realisation that she has not killed Lily but has instead, in her delusional state, inflicted the fatal wound on herself.

In the final act of the performance, Nina dances as the dying swan and, despite her success in staying true to herself and exclaiming 'I was perfect', she cannot escape her inner struggle for self-determination.

Only in death does she find release, and her last searching gaze is directed at her mother in the audience, leaving the meaning open to interpretation. What does it mean? It could be a figurative metaphor representing her newfound freedom, a symbol of the unbreakable bond between mother and daughter, or an indication that she must destroy both her white and black sides to rediscover herself. The question remains open.

Black Swan: A Feminist Film?

Aronofsky's portrayal of his film characters is a clear critique of the patriarchal structures still prevalent not only in ballet but also in the film industry and in various other forms of society.

Ballet as a Representative of a Patriarchal Society

Dance and ballet, as forms of artistic expression, are associated more with femininity and females, evident in ballerinas' graceful movements and supple, slender bodies, the common ideal of femininity, especially among young women who want to radiate a certain delicacy yet resilience. The male dancers, contrastingly, are expected to lift and lead the ladies with elegance and strength.

Aronofsky's world is primarily female, yet it is defined by the presence of a male authority. When the artistic director, Leroy, or 'Le Roi', enters the rehearsal room, the atmosphere immediately changes: The dancers straighten up as they seek his approval. He's depicted as a dominating figure with the ability to select who's suitable for what role, manipulating the women's feelings. Sometimes, he is their knight in shining armour, sometimes their prince, sometimes the seducer or even the daunting Redbeard, but at heart, he is a man who ruthlessly manipulates and pursues only his own interests. Thus, Leroy represents the phallic power that rules the world of ballet. Laura Mulvey (1988 [1975]), a feminist film scholar, argued that female characters in films are in fact representations of male fantasies and reduced to objects. The 'male gaze' on the object 'woman' arouses lust. It also stirs up feelings of control and power in the viewer, whether a man or a woman, exemplifying how patriarchal structures exist in film as well as society.

One example is Nina's enthronement as the new Swan Queen. At this moment, Leroy introduces her as his creation, and the observer fantasises that she is his future 'little princess'. As expected, Nina is supposed to smile prettily and remain silent; she is Leroy's beautiful and desirable object to showcase. In contrast, Beth MacIntyre, the former prima ballerina and Leroy's lover, has been made redundant and is publicly dismissed with cold indifference. This is a severe narcissistic blow to Beth, who believed that Leroy had picked her because of her sex appeal, not because of her potential as a dancer. Her entire self-worth is rooted in this perception of her femininity as the object of male desire, which she now feels she has lost. Full of anger and resentment towards the younger Nina, she insults her with sexually explicit language: 'Did you suck his cock, you little whore?' Degraded and reduced to nothing, Beth attempts to commit suicide and as a result destroys her legs. She has no use for them anymore, neither as a dancer nor as fetishistic feminine attributes.

The Abject

This concept of the abject was introduced by the psychoanalyst and philosopher Julia Kristeva (1982). The abject stands for things that trigger violent aversion, disgust and repugnance in people, as well as profound fears, which must be eliminated and expelled. In *Black Swan*, Beth personifies the abject. Discarded by her lover and kicked out of her professional career as a prima ballerina, she becomes a loathing woman full of self-hatred, anger and jealousy, who is self-destructing because she has no other inner means of action available to her. Her mutilated legs cause both Nina and the audience to feel utter horror and disgust. Beth represents something that people fear encountering and do not want to be like, something they try to fend off. A cruel mirror, she foretells Nina's future: 'You too will be sorted out one day'. In another chilling scene, Nina tears an annoying piece of skin off her finger, imagining herself skinning half her finger, a metaphor for the abject, the unnecessary that must be eliminated.

The Ideal of Femininity in Ballet

In one sequence of the film, a pair of new dancing shoes is brutally mangled, bent, cut and shaped with scissors. Then, in a close-up, a battered, bruised female foot appears, its toes being bandaged one by one before being slipped into one of the dancing shoes. All bruises and wounds are now concealed, and everything looks graceful and ready for pointe technique. This scene is one of Aronofsky's wonderful metaphors, showing us his view of the contradictions of the ballet world: on stage, the beauty of effortless dancing, and backstage, battles of rivalry and the mercilessness of a high-performance sport.

From a feminist perspective, however, in this scene Aronofsky also reveals how women endure painful self-injuries and deprivations to please the male gaze. The female shoe/foot can be viewed as a fetish representing the extent to which women are willing to sacrifice for beauty. Similarly, the young rivals of the ballet scornfully mock Beth, for being an 'old woman', although she is only 40. In societies where youth and the beauty of youth are overinflated and permanently idealised, especially among women, aging is perceived as something threatening, worthy of concealing beyond all means. Kristeva argues that in a male-dominated world, women cannot escape this devaluation because as a matter of fact they age, making them vulnerable in their own perception of self-worth. Under patriarchal conditions, *Black Swan* replicates the fate of women who have been unable to develop their own female identity and end up becoming psychologically broken, self-destructive and perhaps suicidal.

Translated by Cordula Nagel and Katie Anne Whiddon, with revisions by Annie Christmas.

Film Details

Original title	Black Swan
Release year	2010
Country	USA
Book	Andres Heinz, Mark Heyman
Direction	Darren Aronofsky
Music	Clint Mansell
Camera	Matthew Libatique
Main actors	Natalie Portman, Vincenet Cassel, Mila Kunis, Barbara Hershey, Winona Ryder
Availability	DVD

References

Anzieu D (1996) Das Haut-Ich. Suhrkamp, Frankfurt am Main

Jung CG (1935/2018) The archetypes and the collective unconscious. Collected works. Patmos, Dusseldorf

Kristeva J (1982) Powers of horror. An essay on abjection. New York, Columbia University Press

Mulvey L (1975/1988) Visual pleasure and narrative cinema. In: Penley C (ed) Feminism and film theory. Routledge, New York

Rank O (1925/1993) *The double. A psychoanalytic study.* Internationaler Psychoanalytischer Verlag, Leipzig; reprint: Turia & Kant, Vienna

Irmgard Nagel, psychologist, psychoanalyst, and teaching analyst (BLÄK/DPG/DGPT, Academy for Psychoanalysis and Psychotherapy Munich) at her private practice in Munich, is a founder and member of the Munich working group "Film and Psychoanalysis" since 2007.

13 'You Freud, Me Jane'?—Images of Womanhood and Love in Alfred Hitchcock's *Marnie* (US 1964)

Dirk Blothner

Introduction

Following Hitchcock's successes with *North by Northwest* (1959), *Psycho* (1960) and *The Birds* (1963), the response from both audiences and most film critics towards *Marnie* (1964) was reserved. The film could be said to have been a failure. To this day, many believe it marks the beginning of Hitchcock's decline as a film artist, as he never managed to match the successes of his 'classic period' again. Others consider *Marnie* to be a late masterpiece and Hitchcock's most personal film: none other explored such intense and unrelenting feelings of despair, yearning for love and hatred. This work considers *Marnie* to be not only a sensitive portrait of a woman who has to rediscover her repressed aggressiveness in order to tolerate the proximity of men but also the cinematic depiction of love between a man and a woman as the refinement of coarse traits of appropriation and domination.

Film Plot

Margaret 'Marnie' Edgar (Tippi Hedren) makes a living as a thief and con artist in eastern North America. With changing identities, she gains employment in businesses in order to steal from the safe at an opportune moment. She passes on some of the loot to her mother Bernice Edgar (Louise Latham) in Baltimore, who has a limp and uses a stick to walk, in the hope of finally receiving an affectionate gesture from her. She uses the rest to keep a

D. Blothner (✉)
Cologne, Germany
e-mail: dirk@blothner.de

V. Pramataroff-Hamburger, A. Hamburger (eds.), *From La Strada to The Hours*,
https://doi.org/10.1007/978-3-662-68789-5_13

black horse, Forio, in the state of Virginia, spending the happiest moments of her otherwise disengaged life riding him. Marnie suffered trauma as a child, which is the source not only of her predatory restlessness but also her loneliness and an insurmountable loathing of physical closeness. There are specific triggers for flashbacks and panic states: Marnie is overwhelmed by fear whenever she sees the colour red, hears a knocking sound or experiences a thunderstorm with lightning.

Mark Rutland (Sean Connery) has recently taken over the running of his father's large publishing house in Philadelphia. He lives in the stately family home with Lil (Diane Baker), the younger sister of his late wife. Mark had heard of the thief from the publisher's tax advisor, Sidney Strutt (Martin Gabel). She had also emptied Strutt's safe and made off with $10,000. When Marnie then applies for a job at Mark's publishing house, he recognises her as the woman who is wanted by the police, who used to work for his tax advisor. He does let on to her that he is aware of this and hires her anyway. Apparently, he is tempted to lure this attractive 'feline predator' into a trap and tame it.

As Mark's encirclement of Marnie tightens, she also clears out Rutland's safe and flees to Virginia. Mark tracks her down, confronts her and forces her to marry him. If she wants to avoid criminal proceedings, Marnie must accept his 'proposal'. His sister-in-law Lil, who is secretly in love with Mark, finds the sudden marriage preparations strange. She finds out that Mark has spent a disproportionate amount of money on wedding preparations. Apparently, this is his way of paying off Marnie's 'thief's debt'.

They honeymoon on a cruise. Marnie makes it clear that she is not interested in physical intimacy with her new husband. Mark reluctantly complies, at first. However, a quarrel leads to rape. The morning after, Marnie tries to drown herself in the ship's pool. Mark rescues her and breaks off the honeymoon early.

After returning to the Rutland house, Lil tells her brother-in-law that she suspects Marnie has a mother in Baltimore and is sending her money. Mark then hires a private detective to find out about Marnie's childhood. Lil has meanwhile also found out that Marnie stole from the tax consultant Strutt and secretly invites him and his wife to a dinner party at Rutland's house. Marnie and Strutt thus come face to face, and the latter recognises the woman who had stolen from him. Mark persuades him to keep this knowledge to himself. When Marnie admits to further, similar crimes, Mark devises a plan to protect her from being pursued by the police and the judiciary. He wants to aggressively fight for his wife's freedom by any means available.

Marnie takes part in a big fox hunt the next day, although she doesn't really want to. There is an accident, as a result of which Marnie's horse Forio falls and is seriously injured. Lil is there when she shoots him. Something about her decisive actions seems to have changed: when she later wants to steal money from Mark's personal safe, she is held back by an inhibition. She cannot overcome it even when Mark joins in, trying to guide her hand towards the banknotes with sarcastic comments.

To get to the bottom of things, Mark takes Marnie to visit her mother in Baltimore and gets his wife to remember the trauma while they are there. Her mother used to be a prostitute, and one of her clients (Bruce Dern) had approached the child as if to molest her. The mother had tried to stop him and was seriously injured. Little Marnie tried to protect her mother, attacking the sailor with a poker. He subsequently lost a lot of blood and died. After Marnie has spoken about this repressed memory, she seems alleviated. Her mother does not contradict her, but is still unable to offer her daughter the affection she longs for. When Marnie and Mark leave her mother's house together, there are children playing in the street. Marnie now wants to stay with Mark.

Background

Hitchcock had become aware of *Marnie*, the novel by British writer Winston Graham (1908–2003), in early 1960. He revealed to Truffaut that he was particularly interested in the fetishistic love of the male hero: the fact that Marnie is a kleptomaniac, and conwoman is enough for Rutland to fall in love with her. Hitchcock tried to get Grace Kelly, who had married Prince Rainer III of Monaco, to collaborate with him. She was willing to play the role of Marnie, but the people of Monaco would not accept her return to Hollywood, so Hitchcock had to look for someone else to play the role.

In October 1961, Hitchcock and his wife Alma Reville saw a commercial on television: a petite blonde woman walked through the frame and turned charmingly towards a little boy who was whistling to show his admiration. Hitchcock was taken with the model and found out who she was and immediately invited her for an interview. A contract was quickly negotiated: it did not pay very much, but the term was long. Tippi Hedren was astonished to eventually learn that she was up for the lead role in Alfred Hitchcock's current production *The Birds*. While Hedren was still a complete novice as an actress, showing infinite patience during their first project together, she was much more self-confident during their second joint project, the filming of *Marnie*. Hitchcock worked intensively and continuously with her on the character's complex emotional reactions, because he knew that the demands on her as an actress were very different in this psychological thriller than they had been in the full-on horror of the bird movie. Hedren requested a short break in shooting to appear on the popular 'Tonight Show', but Hitchcock saw this as a betrayal of their joint efforts and turned it down. Hedren then allegedly insulted him by calling him as a 'fat pig' in front of others. Hitchcock felt she had crossed a line. No one else had ever presumed to call him overweight before. He was deeply offended but wanted to talk to Hedren. He found her in her caravan. Biographers still argue about what happened during the ensuing argument.

It seems reasonable to suppose that the futile attempts of the male protagonist in *Marnie* to gain the sexual favours of the cool, blonde woman reflect the relationship model that underlay Alfred Hitchcock's dealings with many of his female stars. The pregnancy of Vera Miles as the female lead in *Vertigo,* the aforementioned marriage of Grace Kelly for *Marnie,* his experiences with Joan Fontaine years before: Hitchcock was repeatedly confronted with the painful truth that beautiful women were not always willing to submit to his artistic regime. The very stars whose careers he had shaped repeatedly stopped working with him.

Biographer Donald Spoto (*The Dark Side of Genius* (1983), p. 474) saw the physically unattractive film director's sexual desire at work in these tense relationships with the women who rejected him. Hitchcock allegedly lost control of himself with Tippi Hedren, sexually assaulting the actress during the abovementioned argument in the trailer. Thus, according to Spoto, Hitchcock's unfulfillable sexual urge was taken out on Hedren's rebellious behaviour during the filming of *Marnie*. Hitchcock had apparently chosen the theme of the film to express the fat man's frustrating experiences with the cool blonde in order to overcome his feelings, however ultimately failed in this.

As a rule, interpreting a work of art from the artist's life circumstances falls short of the mark. In this case, not only because it is difficult to prove the truth of this interpretation, as the recent biography by Patrick McGilligan (2003) points out, but also because it is not helpful in understanding the work per se. Biographical interpretations of films tend to showcase the knowledge of the interpreters rather than how audiences can engage with the artistic experience. It is important to make the world of the work of art accessible by providing a precise description, without adding and omitting anything—as far as humanly possible. This is the aim of the following work.

The Image of Women in *Marnie*

Let us recall another Hitchcock film. At the beginning of *Suspicion* (USA 1941), aloof seducer Cary Grant tackles Joan Fontaine in an outdoor setting. The delicate-looking woman resists his sexual advances as best she can, but he only leaves her alone when she closes her handbag, which Hitchcock emphasises in a close-up. *Marnie* begins with a close-up of a closed, yellow handbag. The eponymous heroine, seen from behind, is carrying it under her left arm (Fig. 13.1). Carrying a small suitcase in her other hand, she walks across a deserted platform. As we later find out, she actually 'closed' her 'handbag', which was symbolic of the female genitals, not only for Freud. And on a permanent basis,

Fig. 13.1 The focus on a woman's reserve (00:02:01)

men are forbidden from entering. And, as a glance at the empty platform suggests, she also keeps away from everyone else. This first shot of the film encapsulates, in a single image, the whole complicated context, which will later be explained.

In the second scene, the audience witnesses four men and a woman talking about Marnie, who is not there herself. They are standing in front of an empty safe. Two police officers question Strutt, the owner of the tax consultant's office, about the employee who has disappeared without a trace, taking the money with her. Rutland, one of the tax advisor's clients, happens to joins them. While the woman employee is rather unimpressed, the looks and expressions of all four men make it clear that they would gladly allow themselves to be distracted by the thief's beauty. Up to this point, we have not even caught a glimpse of her, but we already know that, despite the 'closed handbag' (or because of it), the woman apparently has a considerable erotic effect on men.

The next scene opens a glimpse not only of the contents of the yellow handbag but also of the eponymous heroine's suitcase. We still don't get to see her face, but we can observe the care with which she puts fine, newly bought clothes into one suitcase and carelessly stuffs the worn clothes into the other. She inserts some insurance cards made out to various names and the bundles of banknotes she stole from Strutt into the yellow handbag. She swaps it out for a new, cream-coloured handbag. This woman obviously goes by a number of identities. We then watch as she washes the black dye out of her hair in the hotel room bathroom, after which she sweeps her head back energetically before looking us directly in the eye. She is an attractive blonde with a confident expression.

Despite the film character Marnie's social and sexual phobias, the image of womanhood which Hitchcock portrays does not, on the whole, seem cold or brittle. This is expressed in the film, for example, by the touching orchestral Marnie theme, provided by Bernhard Herrmann. This music accompanies Marnie when goes to see her horse Forio, mounts him and breaks straight into a gallop from a halt. She looks out into the landscape with a self-confident, almost happy expression, her hair blowing in the wind. The director probably instructed the composer more or less as follows: 'We go to close-up to show her hair blowing in the wind while she's riding the horse – that's a leitmotif that goes through the film' (Spoto 1983, p. 469). Just as pubescent girls live out their longing for controlled passion and physical closeness with and by riding horses, Marnie shows that her fiery temperament seeks suitable forms of expression while nevertheless avoiding contact with other people.

Although the plot repeatedly shows that key stimuli such as thunderstorms, red paint and knocking noises seriously disturb Marnie's psychological equilibrium, provoking panic attacks, the film still presents the image of a 'resolute woman'. Marnie knows exactly what she wants, seems to have a plan for everything she does and so usually seems confident and determined in everyday life. Part of this equanimity results from the way she clearly distances herself from the sexual advances of men. While being questioned by the police (see above), her former boss Strutt says she had the habit of pulling her skirt over her knees, 'as if protecting a national shrine'. Mark Rutland sees her doing this as well, while she is waiting her turn to be interviewed for the position of secretary at his publishing house. Once she has been hired and he asks her to join him in the deserted office building on a Saturday, which is not a working day, she shows no sign of knowing that her boss intends to seduce her. Does Marnie realise that her apparent naivety in sexual matters and her detachment from men's desires make her all the more attractive to them? Hitchcock's staging gives no indication of this.

The image of the 'resolute woman' that Marnie portrays is based on the determined focus of her actions, obsessive stealing. When she starts work at Rutland's publishing house, she immediately sets her sights on preparing her next heist. Hitchcock's staging makes the audience Marnie's accomplices however excludes the film characters from this. Like a cat on the prowl, she secretly watches members of staff who have access to the company's safe, ready to pounce at an opportune moment and carry off her haul. Marnie pretends not to hear a colleague's impromptu invitation to go out for lunch together. While her colleagues are tidying themselves in front of the mirrors on Friday evening, Marnie locks herself in a toilet cubicle to wait until everyone has left the building. She is a 'resolute woman' in the sense that she is capable of ignoring anything that might stand in the way of her heist. She is not the kind of woman to reflect about or question herself. Like a cat on the prowl, her next steps are always planned in function of her needs at the time. If she needs money, she looks for a job near the company safe. Once she has scouted everything out, she empties the strongbox and makes off. She is not at all affectionate or even sentimental. She is capable of leaving Mark Rutland, the man she finds most likeable—she had kissed him twice, after all—as soon as she feels he is involving her in what she finds a risky and complicated commitment.

The image of women portrayed in *Marnie* offers an opportunity to study the kind of strength and assertiveness a slightly-built woman develops when her mentally organising [self]-image resolutely asserts itself. She is extremely assertive, decisive and controlled, as long as it does not come down to physical strength. Margaret Edgar is about 5 foot 6 and weighs 120 pounds, and Mark Rutland is tall and muscular, so it is easy to force her into doing things she doesn't want to. After she plunders his publisher's safe and goes into hiding, he tracks her down and locks her in his car. She cannot get away. When the two of them stop for a bite to eat at a street restaurant and Marnie wants to freshen up in the toilet, he prevents her from doing so by holding her arm. They sit in the car again. Rutland then deals Marnie a 'mortal blow', telling her that he is going to marry her. Helpless and full of rage, she looks around, but she is trapped in the car, and her relative physical weakness means she cannot escape. At the beginning of the cruise, on their wedding night, she manages to cordon off her body to her husband's advances with verbal threats. And when Mark loses control of himself a few days later, using his greater physical strength to force her into sexual intercourse, she demonstrates her enormous mental resilience by completely emptying her mind at that moment. She ceases any form of emotional involvement, returning nothing but an 'empty handbag' to the man carried away by his passion. The camera work makes this palpable for the audience: It leaves Marnie's expressionless face and swings to the left, towards the porthole of the cabin. Outside in the night, only the endless empty, silent ocean can be seen. The man managed to physically overpower her, but Marnie stolidly resists mentally.

Her assertiveness is based on a pattern of three forms of action, like a wild animal: hunting, flight and playing dead. All three forms bypass direct contact with others: Marnie prepares and carries out her raids alone. If she gets into trouble, she makes a run for it. If someone physically stronger prevents her from escaping, she tries to mentally play dead—as she does when Mark rapes her. It is as if she is trying to prove that other people can be encountered without any competition, rivalry, quarrelling or tangible sexuality. Unlike non-human predators, she has no recourse to the fourth option of using aggression to fight and confront others. In this context, her disavowal of competitive situations can be seen as the shutting down of any interpersonal conflicts that could lead to a quarrel or struggle. She neither defends herself against the childish impudence of Jessie, the girl next door, who has triumphantly taken her place with her mother, nor is she particularly affected by Mark's jealous sister-in-law Lil's meanness.

In the film, transformation of these aspects can only begin when Marnie knows how to make space for her split off aggression. The first, cinematically powerful intermediate step in this direction is the killing of Forio, the horse. He has bolted with Marnie during a hunt, fallen and is writhing on the ground, badly injured. Although the horse is the most precious thing in the world to her, she gets hold of a revolver and shoots him dead. When she has done so, Hitchcock shows her determined and yet astonished expression. Marnie says, 'There, there now!', as if something that had been hindered for a long time was coming to a conclusion. This causes a structural shift in the image of womanhood. The compulsion to steal Mark's money is still there; however, Marnie cannot act upon it, not even when he tries to guide her hand to the money. In the last sequence of the film, when Marnie finally remembers that, at the age of five, she had beaten the sailor who threatened her mother to death, she once more repeats the words, which ushered in her change: **'There. There now!' The way the scene is experienced makes clear that the words signal a decisive accomplishment: she has now found long-blocked access to what she perceives as explosive, aggressive shaping influences.** The repression resulting from the traumatic experiences is cancelled out. The image of the seemingly 'resolute woman' that she had formed to ward off the re-traumatising eruption of murderous rage has been expanded, supplemented, as it were, by an aggressive 'masculine' side. This more complete image of womanhood allows Marnie to modify her behaviour and experience.

Seen from the perspective of the final plot twist, the image of womanhood drawn by *Marnie* derives its decisive impetus from the repression of interpersonal aggression instigated by childhood trauma. The mother had taken the blame for her daughter's manslaughter to spare the child from being sent to a home. However, she had withdrawn her love from Marnie and never explained the reason why. Marnie grew up with no memory of her far-reaching actions but also without any explanation for her mother's rejection. Her unconscious processing of the trauma led her to try to never get into direct confrontation with other people, as far as possible. For she sensed something explosive within herself that could make her murder again. In order to return to the time before her mother's inexplicably avoidance, she had developed the art of solo heists, using the spoils to try and regain her mother's love.

Processes of Cultivating Love

It seems reasonable to suppose that the story of *Marnie* is a successful psychoanalytic 'lay treatment' (Sindelar 2017). Thanks to Mark Rutland's decisive action, Marnie finally finds access to repressed emotions and can complete her restricted view of womanhood. In contrast, Raymond Durgnat's (1974) account of the levels of meaning in *Marnie* highlights the love relationship between the eponymous heroine and Mark Rutland. He shows many details indicating that the film concept of both Mark and Marnie is that they are at least in part 'wild animals'. Just as Marnie worms her way into her victims' companies, patiently observes them and eventually positions herself to pounce on their cash float, Mark is also 'like a hunting animal following every twist and turn of its quarry's flight' (p. 354). Even if it was Mark's job in the film to look to the scientific literature on hunting animals and sexually disturbed women for orientation, both protagonists behaved extremely intelligently, both seemed to be representatives of a kind of 'instinctual meritocracy' (p. 356) The following pages take up Durgnat's observation and transpose it onto a psychological description of the relationship between the two protagonists. At the same time, typical 'qualities of effect' (Salber et al. 2015) will be highlighted that shape the audience's experience when watching *Marnie*. The longer we follow the movements and interactions of the well-dressed characters in their high-class milieus, the deeper the feeling that this is a 'homo homini lupus' relationship in sophisticated guise. Marnie and Mark are always perfectly groomed and well-mannered, but they are motivated by simple and banal fundamental motions of domination and appropriation.

The second scene of the film has already been described above in terms of the image of womanhood that is implied. A man can be heard shouting indignantly while a safe comes into view. Its door is wide open: the strongbox is yawningly empty. When Strutt loudly complains to two policemen and Mark Rutland as he arrives that his employee has stolen from him, he makes it clear that he had behaved towards her in a similarly predatory fashion as long as she had been working for him. This forms an ambiguous puzzle figure: the morally outraged victim of a robbery also appears to be the thief. A similar duality is established a short while later, when Marnie has found a job at Mark's publishing house: Marnie is typing and watching the way the manager and his secretary work the company safe. The viewer understands that she is preparing her next heist. The big cat is on the prowl. Without her knowledge, Mark glances from behind at Marnie's delicate-looking bare neck and her back encased in a white blouse. He covets the woman who is planning to steal his money. Both 'predatory' intentions are at work in a single image at the same time. Marnie is spying out her prey, and Mark has an urge to 'jump' her from behind and possess her sexually. This is another intriguing double figure. Scenes like this and others in the film reveal to us what lies behind the spark of love that ignites between Marnie and Mark. The woman sees the man as someone she can easily deceive, whose wealth she can appropriate. The man sees the woman as a 'prowling jaguar', an antisocial creature who does not want to be tamed, and he finds the prospect of subduing her appealing. Hitchcock's film psychoanalysis leaves no doubt: love, which preserves civilisations, is built on banal drives to exert power. Plot sequences such as these allow the cinematic experience to oscillate between excitement and detachment.

Shortly after the last scene described (two 'predators' watching their prey), Mark calls his new secretary into the office to work over the weekend. The context suggests that he wants to be alone with her so that he can seduce her uninterrupted. Marnie's behaviour is difficult to interpret. Either she doesn't let on or she really has no idea about her boss's sexual intentions. The viewer oscillates between these two different interpretations of the same situation. Marnie appears to be a secretary but also prey, and Mark is the boss but also a potential rapist. The whole situation can be disapproved of on moral grounds; however, it can also be experienced as exciting potential pressing for further development. But when a thunderstorm breaks out, events take an unexpected turn. Marnie loses her composure and has a panic attack. She suddenly seems like a distraught child seeking protection. The climax of the scene occurs when a long, thick branch bursts through the windowpanes into the room. The lightning flashes in alternating, burning white and red light. There are shards everywhere. The distraught woman has no choice but to seek safety, held in Mark's arms. As if independently of this chaos, a tender kiss ensues. The film experience can follow the plot profile and develop analogous effect qualities: walking into the trap of raw power, encircling and being encircled, an unexpected break-in, violent confusion and seeking to be held.

Then another twist is added in the next sequence: Marnie has by now also emptied the safe at Mark's publishing house and absconded. Mark confronts her in the open countryside where she is riding her horse, Forio. He harshly and relentlessly stops Marnie's restlessness in its tracks, literally pulling the horse out from under her, locking her in his car and forcing her to agree to marry him. This can be experienced not onlt as imposing order but also as abuse. Be that as it may, Marnie's wild actions are now trammelled. In her obstinacy, her resistance to Mark's advances becomes all the fiercer. She is clearly inwardly rebelling with all her might, wanting to physically fight back, but he is physically stronger and keeps hold of her. She tries to free herself from his grip by impulsively making up stories. Hitchcock makes Marnie's 'no' tangible in an unusually powerful way. At the same time, however, he makes it clear that her resistance is weakening: the two figures clash, but there is also a noticeable connection between them—a thief and a usurper. Two predatory figures are locked in battle. This struggle can be followed with relish, but we also tend to feel concern or compassion for the cornered woman. It may be momentarily forgotten that she herself is a predator. We are on tenterhooks to find out who will win the struggle, or whether they will end up in some sort of an alignment.

Assuming the described qualities of effect, an *experience* of 'rape' takes place long before the infamous scene on the ship. The audience has been primed by an earlier version of violent intrusion, the scene in which Marnie and Mark were alone in the office and the metaphorical phallus-branch broke through the window during the thunderstorm. Marnie confined in the car, Mark exploiting superior physical strength both in the car and at the restaurant, Marnie's futile attempts to escape the clutches of the 'predator'—all these scenes are associated with milder but similar qualities of effect as those of a 'literal' rape scene. Thus, the audience merely has to superimpose the qualities already experienced onto the extremely artificial image of the actual rape scene on the ship. As described in the last section, in this context, the initial excitement is transformed into a pregnant 'nothingness': a view of the becalmed, infinitely wide ocean.

In the spectator's experience, the already begun process of refining rough figures continues on another level. It all seems like an extended transition of the struggle between 'predators' towards a sense of unity. It can be understood as a refinement of rough and simple forms of domination and appropriation. Hitchcock always portrayed the coming together of man and woman as problematic, especially in earlier films such as *Secret Agent* (1936), *Young and Innocent* (1937), *Notorious* (1946) or later *North by Northwest* (1959). An attraction often began, which had to be put off, not being fulfilled until the very end due to other involvements, hidden intentions, influences and coincidences. Complications essentially arose due to other people and things that got in the way. **In the case of *Marnie*, it is the potential lovers' obsession with (fundamentalist) images, which hampers their union. The most haunting 'Marnie' development is arguably the striving of two mental images to appropriate each other and thus to also always obliterate each other as a separate entity.** It is increasingly defused, supplemented and finally transformed as the plot develops. This is partly due to an increasing feeling of connectedness as the film experience goes on. The film also offers emotionally contoured expressions in this regard. We perhaps clearly notice this for the first time when Mark, having returned from their honeymoon, surprises Marnie by bringing Forio to his father's house. The grateful look she gives him and the irrepressible joy with which, still in her cocktail dress, she jumps onto the horse bareback and gallops off blends a palpably conciliatory current into the film experience.

There is a similar moment of authentically experienced closeness that may be experienced in the film in the scene to which the title of this essay alludes: Mark confronts Marnie and, as somewhat of an analytical layman, asks probing questions in an attempt to explore the trauma that has triggered everything. Marnie observes his behaviour, pauses briefly and asks: *'You Freud, me Jane?'* This allusion to *Tarzan the Ape Man* (USA 1932), starring Johnny Weissmüller and Maureen O'Sullivan, is arguably the funniest gag in the film and earns the respect not only of her husband but also the audience. Mark has to take a few involuntary steps backwards and sit down on a chair near the door. Both of their facial expressions indicate to the audience that a moment of equality and closeness has occurred, a transformation from being against each other to being with each other. From the interpretation presented here, this turning point proves to be the crux of the whole film. The simple life of the wild woman in the jungle is amusingly juxtaposed against the highly civilised way of life of the exceptional scientist Sigmund Freud.

If the film description is continued in this way, while bearing in mind the associated qualities of effect, an unfamiliar and perhaps unloved image of interpersonal relationship develops. Seen from the perspective of the film's ending, the whole development leads towards the prospect that these two 'predators' will eventually trust each other to a certain extent. The process of refining crude drives towards direct domination comes to a provisional and also imperfect end when Marnie, leaving her mother's house (where a few girls

Fig. 13.2 Questioning children's eyes: How does love work? (02:03:15)

and boys are playing outside in the street) looks at Mark, saying: *'I'd like to stay with you!'* (Fig. 13.2). After the many, sometimes violent, attempts at direct and crude types of gestalt, the couple has arrived at a position that, psychologically speaking, puts them on a par with the children playing in front of the house, which Durgnat (1974, p. 368) calls 'positive faith in a humiliated moral decency'. Two adults whose psyches have struggled hard to overcome lustful, crude tendencies of mutual dominance and who, in completing this civilising process, are still in their infancy. This cannot be called a 'happy ending'. The viewer experiences a spreading disillusionment, perhaps even dubiousness.

It is striking to observe how adeptly Hitchcock uses the medium of film to visualise an image of womanhood in the conscious and unconscious expressions of the protagonist. More disturbing, and therefore probably partly responsible for the commercial failure of *Marnie*, is the second line of interpretation, which involves the film experience. In contemporary cinema, it is no longer unusual to portray highly esteemed values such as 'love' and 'commitment' as the refinement of direct, rough, or even (as Durgnat points out) animalistic action stimuli. Love is not a feeling, nor is it simple. Love is, to use Wilhelm Salber's words, a 'house' that people continue building throughout their lives. The unconscious tendencies in their relationships, the raw pattern of a 'homo homini lupus' cannot be kept controlled without this elaborate house building. Hitchcock was aware of this. However, to treat love this way in a film may have still been too provocative and too disturbing in the 1960s.

Human beings have to cope in a troubled reality. Obsessive gestalt formations are patterns born of necessity that can give them an initial direction (Salber 2008, p. 77 ff.). This analysis of *Marnie* began with the figure of the closed handbag and ends with the shot of a group of children looking into the camera with questioning eyes. Between these two settings, a development process takes place in which Alfred Hitchcock's film involves the audience. In the turmoil of psychic reality, Marnie's predatory taciturnity is a gestalt formation geared towards survival. Within this framework, she can make something of her damaged life, and it can be understood as a protection against wounding and powerlessness. The experiential process that follows the first shot of the yellow handbag takes viewers right into the middle of a tense reality shaped by mutual dominance, making them experience that, when it comes to attempting to build a safe house of love, we are probably all in our infancy. We are touched by the girls' questioning eyes at the end of the film, reminded of our own efforts in this regard. For the general public of 1964, this confrontation may have been too harsh. With today's distance, it is possible to face it.

Translated by Annette Caroline Christmas.

Film Details

Original title	Marnie
Release year	1964
Screenplay	Jay Presson Allen
Direction	Alfred Hitchcock
Camera	Robert Burks
Music	Bernard Herrmann
Principle actors	Tippi Hedren, Sean Connery, Diane Baker, Louise Latham
Availability	DVD

References

Durgnat R (1974) The strange case of Alfred Hitchcock. Faber and Faber, London

McGilligan P (2003) Alfred Hitchcock. A life in darkness and light. HarperCollins Publishers, London

Salber W (2008) Die eine und die andere Seite [The one and the other side]. Reise in ein Verzauber-Land [Journey to an enchanted land]. Bouvier, Bonn

Salber W, Pütz C, Conrad M (2015) Seele macht Filme. Filme machen Seele [Souls make films. Films make Souls]. HPB University Press, Berlin

Sindelar B (2017) Der rettende Ehemann [The saving husband]. In: Poltrum M, Rieken B (eds) Seelenkenner Psychoschurken. Psychotherapeuten und Psychiater in Film und Seele Psychotherapists and psychiatrists in Film and Soul]. Springer, Berlin, p 319–332

Spoto D (1983) The dark side of genius. The life of Alfred Hitchcock. Frederick Muller Wm. Collins Sons & Company, Great Britain

Thrill and Suffering—*Misery* (US 1990) 14

Gerhard Bliersbach

Introduction

Thirty years ago, I saw Rob Reiner's work *Misery* for the first time at my favourite cinema, which had the biggest screen in Cologne; I regularly sat in the fourth or fifth row—very close to the huge images, which I could not take in all at once but had to scan like landscapes that you only gradually survey. Sitting there literally drew the cinema-goer into the narrative. I can only recall the (at the time) amusing plot idea of the dissatisfied, strict reader who forces her adored author to correct his manuscript the way she wants it. My schadenfreude at seeing an author who was no longer in control of his creation soothed my envy towards the successful writer. My satisfaction did not prove to be so simple. The cinema-goer paid a price for this mean sense of satisfaction: a sense of unease and alarm. At the time, I was probably unable to properly understand the unfolding story, the protagonist's misery, its murderous impact or the film narrative. Now, watching it again, I saw a different film. Rob Reiner's *Misery* is the type of cultural user experience that comes alive in the thrill of rapid consumption and specialised engagement with a product of this culture.

G. Bliersbach (✉)
Hückelhoven, Germany

V. Pramataroff-Hamburger, A. Hamburger (eds.), *From La Strada to The Hours*,
https://doi.org/10.1007/978-3-662-68789-5_14

Film Plot

A Happy Rescue Can Also Have Unhappy Consequences

Paul Sheldon (James Caan) is typing the last lines of his book manuscript. A *Lucky Strike* and a match lie to hand on the nearby table, an empty champagne flute next to it, the bottle of *Dom Pérignon* waiting in the glass ice bucket. He tears the sheet of paper from the (mechanical) travel typewriter, skims over it—the last sentence ends in three dots and a question mark—writes *THE END* at the bottom and places it face down on the small pile of manuscript papers, which he grabs and adds to a large stack. The complete manuscript in his hand, Paul Sheldon looks at the first page: *Untitled by Paul Sheldon*. He puts it in his maroon leather briefcase with scuffed corners. He uncorks the champagne and fills the glass and then lights the ready *Lucky Strike* with a large match—a moment of reflection and a sigh of relief. He places the briefcase containing the manuscript on the passenger seat. He wipes the snow off the windscreen of the *Ford Mustang* (with the New York State licence plate), forms a ball with the rest and hits the trunk of a pine tree right in the middle. Homeward bound!

Snow-covered roads. We are in the state of Colorado. A warning sign indicates 13 miles of upcoming tight bends. Heavy snow begins to fall. Carefree, buoyed along by his music, he manoeuvres over the blanket of snow. Visibility is becoming bad. The snowfall is getting heavier. He is driving too fast. His *Ford* begins to lurch. Sheldon reacts by yanking on the steering wheel. He brakes and the car slides off the winding road down a slope, overturns several times and comes to a rest on its roof.

Flashback. Sheldon is sitting on a leather sofa in his agent Marcia Sindell's (Lauren Bacall) New York City office, his weathered briefcase on his lap. Paul and Marcia are talking about the start of his writing career, when he was actively looking for publishers, his first book manuscript stowed in this very briefcase. It was a time when, as an ambitious writer, he did not yet feel beholden to the highly successful habits of a serial author who had made a commitment to serially produce the *Misery Chastain* books, fairytale-like stories of the secret princess *Misery's* ascent from her miserable psychosocial origins. Like Paul, his agent has cashed in on this cultural business and has nothing against his large fees. Paul frets about literary betrayal and the waste of his creative talents. He delivers the final product of his work to Marcia Sindell: His latest book, *Misery's Child,* concludes the (eight-volume) *Misery* saga.

Back to the cinematic present. After being rescued from his car and carried away, the milky blue screen image slowly clears. From Paul's point of view, we are looking up into the fleshy, friendly face of a woman of about 40, who has been looking after him for 2 days. She is Annie Wilkes (Kathy Bates), a nurse and, as she explains, his number one fan. She has hooked him up to an IV drip. She dabs at his face, explaining to Paul that the snowstorm had been too heavy to take him to hospital. He has to take it easy and take his time: '*You almost died'*, she cautions him with concern. He is apparently in good hands.

The days pass with Annie Wilkes taking care of him. Paul wants to know how he is doing. Annie precisely lists his injuries: severely damaged shoulder (which she has set), multiple fractures of both shins, right fracture of the fibula (she has splinted both legs). Annie pulls back the duvet and lets Paul see her professional care of the two swollen, blue, bandaged and splinted legs. Paul is horrified, and Annie pleased with her work. There is no mention of *how* she looked after him, undressed him, changed him and put him in splints; Paul does not ask any questions, Annie does not talk about it. He is self-conscious, and she is not. She has consulted the hospital doctor, she reassures Paul. As soon as the roads are clear, she will take him to the hospital. *'I consider it an honour that you'll do the recovering in my home'*. He is lying in a sparsely furnished room with a bay window and a magnificent view of the sunny winter landscape.

We are back in Marcia Sindell's office in New York City. She is on the phone to the sheriff of Silver Creek. Paul Sheldon is still missing. There is no trace of him. Marcia Sindell is annoyed by her concerned call. *'Tell me, I'm being silly'*, she prompts the sheriff. *'A little overprotective maybe'*, Sheriff John McCain (Richard Farnsworth) reassures her; he will go in search of her client.

Back at Annie Wilkes' house, she is shaving Paul Sheldon with a cutthroat razor. A blade like that is a matter of trust. Paul Sheldon says it is a *miracle* that she found him. No, contradicts Annie Wilkes, (somewhat) like Eve Kendall from Alfred Hitchcock's *North by Northwest* (US 1959), it was not a miracle: She would have *followed* him for days. Paul Sheldon is taken aback. She had read everything about him, waited outside his hotel and was following him on the country road on the day of the accident. Paul, not quite shaved yet, answers his enthusiastic reader with strained courtesy: *'Well, you're very kind'*. Annie shoots back an answer: *'And you're very brilliant'*. His shave finished, and she gets up from the edge of the bed and walks towards the door. Paul reminds her how urgent it is for him to make a phone call, and his daughter would be very worried. She offers to make the call for him when the line is working again.

Stick to Your Own Tried and Tested Rules

Annie Wilkes pauses at the door, turns around and asks him if she can read his new book manuscript. Paul replies that he would normally only give the manuscript to his editor and agent to read, but he would make an exception for someone who had saved his life. He doesn't have a title for his new book yet. He invites Annie to find one. 'As if I could', she shakes her head.

Sometime later, it is evening. Annie is feeding Paul with a soup spoon. She has read 40 pages of his new book, but she hesitates. Paul encourages her to go on. Annie tries to put it into words. She is reluctant. Finally, she comes out with it: 'The swearing, Paul…*It has no nobility'*, she shouts with a flash of fiercely vehement indignation. They are slum children, that's how they talk, Paul gently says in his defence, to help her understand and to reassure her, admitting that was also a kid from the slums. *'They do not!'* she continues to shout, terribly upset and deeply hurt. In her mounting anger, she splutters in raging, unbridled fury, heavy cursing and scolding—and spills the soup on the bedspread. *'There! Look there!'* she shrieks, *'see what you made me do'?* Paul is surprised by Annie's aggressive loss of control—and also that she holds him responsible for it. He looks at her, wide-eyed. Annie is horrified and ashamed. *'Oh Paul, I'm so sorry'*. She was shaking. *'Sometimes I get so worked up. Can you ever forgive me'?* Paul stutters and worriedly answers: *'… it's … fine'*. He smiles, although there is nothing to smile about. Annie has calmed down and goes on in a different vein. *'I love you, Paul'*, she says. He lowers his gaze in embarrassment and then looks at her, wide-eyed. *'Your mind. Your creativity. That's all I meant'*, Annie says in an attempt to dispel Sheldon's possible doubts about how she loves him. Paul smiles at her. He looks at her in horror.

A bright and sunny day. Sheriff John McCain is driving to *Silver Creek Lodge*; his wife Virginia (Frances Sternhagen) is with him. Virginia and John are a supportive husband and wife team, although Virginia regularly infuriates her husband with her sceptical sobriety. He sees tyre tracks at the side of the road and also almost spots Sheldon's wrecked Mustang. But not quite, he overlooks the wheel sticking out of the snow. The McCains get into their four-wheel drive *Chrysler*.

Reading Is More than Reading

Annie Wilkes has by now bought the newly published (last) volume of the *Misery* series at the local general store and brought it along with her: It is titled *Misery's Child*. She immediately starts reading and showers the author with praise. She tells Paul how, after the breakdown of her marriage, only her work as a nurse and Paul's Misery novels saved her. Now, she says, she has almost finished reading the new *Misery* book; she still has two chapters to go. It hurts to finish a good book; sometimes, it is hard to part with it. It is full moon. The house lies in darkness. Sheldon is asleep. The door to the room is pushed open. Upset and furiously angry, Annie rushes into the room with a deep growl of *'Yoouuu …..!'* followed by a torrent of abuse. *'You dirty bird! How could you! She can't be dead! Misery Chastain can't be dead'!* Sheldon had killed off his heroine *Misery Chastain* in 1871. *'You murdered my Misery'!* Sheldon defends himself by pointing out the plausibility of his nineteenth century fiction. He tries to reassure Annie by saying Misery Chastain's spirit lives on in his books. But she cannot be consoled; she rages against the author who has disrupted her precarious equilibrium. *'I thought you were good, Paul'*, she screams, *'… you're just another lying ol' dirty birdie'!* She unashamedly berates Paul Sheldon and threatens to kill him. She tells him that she has not called anyone and that he is at her mercy.

Annie has calmed down and thinks of a way out. She forces him to burn his manuscript *Untitled* on a kettle barbecue. And she has another plan: she sets up a writing desk in Paul's hospital room with a typewriter and paper and awaits the continuation of the Misery saga under the title she has though up, *Misery's Return*. She has acquired an old Royal 10 mechanical typewriter and special paper. Paul shows Anne that the typewriter does not print the letter 'N' and the ink smudges on the paper. Annie is not pleased. She gets the paper Paul wants. Paul compensates for the inconvenience of the 'N' by suggesting Annie write the missing 'N' in his manuscript by hand, which she enthusiastically accepts.

Sheldon has submitted to Annie Wilkes. But while she is away, he makes every effort (with the help of a hair clip bent into a key) to leave his room and explore the other rooms of the house in his wheelchair. There is no way out. But he now goes along with Annie's plan and writes *Misery's Return* under her supervision. Misery has awoken from an anaphylactic coma, her aristocratic origins are confirmed and two men are courting her, causing Annie to dance with excitement in front of Paul: *'Misery is alive! It's so romantic'!*

During his second exploration of the house, Paul finds his books and his photo on the sideboard in the adjacent room, next to a large photo of Liberace, the enormously popular and flamboyant singer, pianist and entertainer. He also finds a folder with glued-in newspaper clippings documenting a strange accumulation of unexplained deaths in her area, from her father's death when she was 11 to a court case for killing patients. Paul Sheldon devises a plan to drug Annie at a dinner (to celebrate *Misery's Return*), but that fails as well. One night she comes into his hospital room, having realised that he will never love her.

Paul's Purge

Annie realises that Paul will leave her as soon as he gets well enough—and when she finds out that he has been looking around the house, she puts his ankles on a block of wood. Paul guesses what she is about to do. *'Please don't do it'*, he begs her. Unmoved, Annie Wilkes powerfully swings the sledgehammer down, smashing Paul's ankles. *'God, I love you'*, says Annie Wilkes.

Sheriff John McCain's helicopter search for Paul Sheldon's *Mustang* is successful; the car is found and recovered. John McCain discovered a lead on Paul Sheldon by reading the *Misery* novels, in which he found and made a note of the following sentence: *'There is a justice higher than that of a man. I will be judged by him'*. When McCain was browsing through old newspapers in a library, he discovered the report on the Denver trial of Annie Wilkes, where she was quoted after the reading of the acquittal, saying: *'There is a justice higher than that of a man. I will be judged by him'*. It is Paul Sheldon's sentence, which Annie Wilkes had made her own. John McCain drives to Annie Wilkes' house. She receives him with routine, innocuous friendliness. McCain finds no evidence of Paul Sheldon during his tour of the house. As he is leaving, he hears a clattering noise. He immediately turns around, hears Paul's cry for help, finds the cellar, opens the entrance and from the top of the stairs sees Paul lying down there—but before he can free him, Annie Wilkes shoots him with a heavy hunting rifle.

Paul continues trying to buy time; he confirms Annie's and his joint task of finishing the book: *'We'll be able to give Misery ... back to the world'*. She knows about his closing

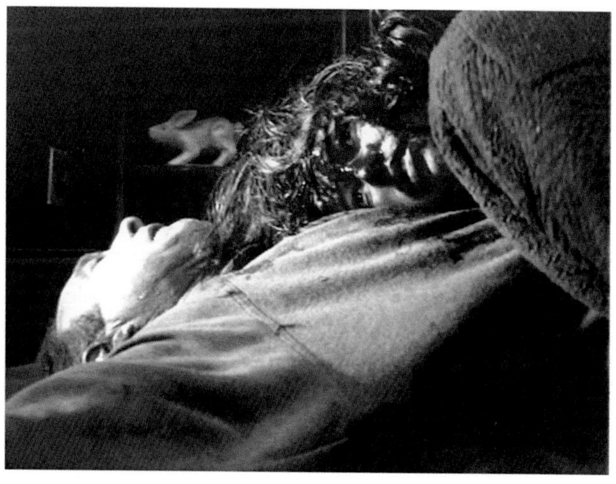

Fig. 14.1 The ironic bloody finale of a murderous desire (01:38:15)

ritual, and he wants her to join him in it: a *Lucky Strike* and a glass of *Dom Pérignon*. This time he insists on two glasses. Annie agrees. The tray with the match, the *Lucky Strike* and the champagne is ready. Annie, however, has added her drum revolver. Paul, for his part, has methylated spirits hidden in his trousers: He wants to burn the manuscript of *Misery's Return* in front of Annie.

In the murderous struggle that follows, Paul gets hold of a cast-iron doorstop as big as a steam iron and kills Annie. She remains lying on him, as if after coitus (Fig. 14.1).

Eighteen months later in a New York restaurant: Marcia Sindell and Paul Sheldon who has since published a critically acclaimed novel and has finally received recognition as an author. *'I wrote it for me'*, he says, *'in a way … Annie Wilkes … helped me'*. As a waitress approaches their table with a serving trolley, we *see* Annie Wilkes pull out a large kitchen knife. We see a close-up of Paul's terror, which he does not betray. While Annie Wilkes continues to move the serving trolley with the knife, Paul confesses to Marcia that Annie Wilkes follows him here and there. When he looks back at the waitress, he sees *another* waitress (Wendy Bowers) talking to him: 'Excuse me. I don't want to bother you—but are you Paul Sheldon? I just want to tell you that I'm your number one fan'. Paul smiles broadly and replies with sweet, mildly ironic friendliness: *'That's very sweet of you'*.

Background: Contexts and Subtexts

As director Rob Reiner tells us in the audio commentary on the DVD, the novel *Misery*, published on the North American market in June 1987, is one of Stephen King's most personal works. The film rights had not yet been awarded when Andrew Scheinman read Stephen King's book during a stopover at an airport in search of a project for the young company, as did Bob Reiner, head of the production company *Castle Rock Entertainment*. Stephen King, who disagreed with some film adaptations of his work, had withheld the rights to *Misery*. The negotiations with Stephen King were not difficult. He had been pleased with Rob Reiner's 1986 realisation *Stand by Me* (of his novella *The Body*). Stephen King awarded *Castle Rock Entertainment* the contract on the condition that Rob Reiner would produce, direct, or both. Rob Reiner directed and, together with Andrew Scheinman, managed the production of the film. William Goldman was brought in to write the screenplay.

Goldman, for his part highly successful as a versatile writer of prose works, plays and screenplays *(Butch Cassidy and Sundance Kid*, 1966; *Marathon Man*, 1976; *All the President's Men*, 1976), sometimes the go-to man for rescuing and polishing muddled, expensive Hollywood projects, wrote the script with the idea of casting renowned theatre actress Kathy Bates (b. 1948) in the lead; he had no actor in mind for the male role. It proved difficult to fill it. Many well-known Hollywood stars turned it down. James Caan (* 1940), cast by Howard Winchester Hawks in the 1965 racing film *Red Line 7000* and who rose to fame in the latter's 1966 western *El Dorado* (alongside Robert Mitchum and John Wayne), was the second and, as it turned out, good choice for the role of the bedridden, wheelchair-bound author Paul Sheldon. The highly trained and very agile actor convincingly embodied the hardship and suffering of forced immobility. Goldman suspected that the secondary role of Paul Sheldon dictated by the plot had put off the male actors.

Rob Reiner (* 1947), son of the director Carl Reiner and the actress Estelle Reiner, is a television man. His best-known cinema successes are *Stand by Me* (1986), *When Harry Met Sally* (1989), *A Few Good Men* (1992) and *The Bucket List* (2007). He had to learn the cinematic language of thrillers. Thus, he says he watched all of Alfred Hitchcock's work and studied his narrative style; he found the language of thrillers in his cooperation with Barry Sonnenfeld (on camera). Rob Reiner's axiom on aesthetics is 'Give the audience the best place'. Unlike Alfred Hitchcock, who often gave his audience a head start over the screen protagonists, thereby reliably involving them in his twisted plots, Rob Reiner's film narrative is told from the perspective of the immobilised protagonist who sets out to regain his mobility; the audience is the stressed observer.

The Etymology of *Misery*

The noun *misery* derives from the Latin *miseria* (misery, misfortune, suffering). *Misery* means almost the same as *wretchedness,* although *misery* rather more applies to an inner reality than an external one. This is evident, for example, in the saying, '*Don't be such a misery*'. *Misery* refers to the enormous hardship and deep, existential suffering of the protagonist Annie Wilkes, her life situation and her life story. *Misery* is the name Annie Wilkes gives to the stray sow she adopts—herself object (in Heinz Kohut's sense), which she says makes her laugh and comforts her and which snuffles and grunts in her house and frightens Paul Sheldon. *Misery* also describes the underlying emotional state of the protagonist—an author who risks writing at the expense of his (for him somewhat) shabby but amicable adaptation to his readership of millions, who has met with an accident while travelling with his new manuscript and gets into a life-threatening situation. *Misery* could ultimately also apply to author Stephen King's personal crisis: under the burden of his audience's high expectations, he self-regulated with addictive drugs and alcohol, losing his storytelling capacity in the process. King recovered and wrote *Misery* under dramatic circumstances. He was not so far removed from his protagonist.

The Staging of Annie Wilkes' Femininity

Annie Wilkes is the protesting protagonist in despair about her femininity. In the last third of the film, the screenwriters have Anne Wilkes utter the following quintessentially self-deprecating words: *'I'm not a movie-star type'*. We don't know what films she has drawn her ideals from. The screenwriters only mention her interest in the television programme *Family Feud*. They have dressed her in loose-fitting, rugged clothes that make her look like a strong woman, ready to tackle oily repairs or other serious accidents; they do not allow Annie Wilkes to self-present as an attractive woman. Even at the dinner celebrating the return of Misery Chastain, Annie Wilkes is wearing an old-fashioned dress with a lace collar that would suit an 11-year-old child but not a 40-something woman. *African Queen* (US 1951) with Katherine Hepburn and Humphrey Bogart or *Marty* (US 1955) with Betsy Blair and Ernest Borgnine were probably not Annie Wilkes' favourite films. In the film narrative, Annie Wilkes remains a daydreaming and expectant adolescent woman who is far removed from Paul Sheldon, afraid of her own and other people's sexual bodies. The core of the narrative is merely the opening up her monstrosity as a traumatised woman.

Annie Wilkes' Relational Mode of Idolising Terror

Paying compliments is both a benign and malignant instrument of power in interactions. Compliments can foster and deepen a relationship. But they can also establish an asymmetry and embarrass the recipient, obligating him or her in a pact of mutual flattery. Deflecting compliments is annoying and difficult, seems pedantic and may offend the person giving them. '*I am your number one fan*' is the compliment of a huge but nebulous passion for the receiver. It is an overpowering confession. It ambushes, obliges and paralyses. It makes a Paul Sheldon powerless, speechless and increasingly angry.

Annie Wilkes' confession of being a number one fan goes so far that she *lives* with Paul Sheldon. She has read his books multiple times; she collects newspaper clippings on Paul Sheldon's life events; she has set up a shrine on her living room sideboard with Paul Sheldon's signed, framed photo and a row of his books. But *how* does Annie Wilkes live with Paul Sheldon? We don't find out. We learn something that Paul Sheldon cannot see: Annie Wilkes enjoys lying in bed in her room, munching crisps while watching the TV series *Family Feud*.

Annie Wilkes' relational style of terrorising idolisation is the pivotal premise of the plot, from which the narrative movements follow. Her terrorising idolisation captivates, binds and initiates the counter-movements. A terrible story probably lies behind it. It points to her dysfunctional socialisation. Presumably, she treats Paul Sheldon the way she used to be treated. His *immobilisation* (which she has brought about) is the image of her own psychosocial immobilisation—the annihilation of herself (cf. Bollas 1995), which was unable to be developed in her early childhood and allowed her to go her own, playful ways. One can imagine Annie Wilkes growing up in a mechanical, unsympathetic environment in which her parents recruited her as their self-object. She was not taught to play and was forced to submit to them in a process of extreme bonding, so she never dared to differentiate herself into a young woman with a secure psychosexual identity in multiple relationships with elders and peers. It could further be surmised that she deals with *intensely fantasised* relationships and thus has an extremely precarious hold on reality that does not permit interactive debate about differences and otherness. Thus *differences* (other ways of life, other views of life), disappointments and slights threaten Annie Wilkes, make her angry and cause her to react murderously. We could also say that Annie Wilkes expects an exact fit in relationships, in which she can *merge* with the strange other. The screenwriters hint at Annie Wilkes' biographical interrelationships; however, these can only be discovered and surmised by pausing the film and reading the scant newspaper clippings of the strange, unexplained spate of deaths (of her father, a fellow student, children who died in her care as a nurse).

Paul Sheldon's Struggle for his Identity as an Author

The cinema-goer is generally well advised to stay long enough to watch the film credits. *Liberace* sings '*I'll be seeing you*', as the credits roll for *Misery*. Annie Wilkes also has a framed portrait of the singer on her living room sideboard (alongside the picture of Paul Sheldon). '*I'll be seeing you*', by Sammy Fain and Irving Kahal (from 1938), is a song from the pre-war era, a promise not to forget a sweetheart; wherever you go or stay, she or he is the absent-present good object, the treasury of comforting relational experiences, companion to the strain of enduring and balancing the loss of absence. Whether you will meet again is uncertain; the memory keeps the blueprint of a pleasant future open: '*I'll be seeing you*' is a promise sung from the self-closeness or self-distance of the inner dialogue, and we do not know whether it ever reaches the addressee.

Paul Sheldon already *sees* Annie Wilkes; he does not have to evoke his traumatic experiences, they are present, as the final scene with his agent shows. Director Rob Reiner's conceit is an ironic solution, a distraction. The horror that Annie Wilkes' actions radiate dissipates in the communicative gesture of the auteur's ironic wink at the audience. In a sense, Rob Reiner takes us by the hand and leads us out of the dark *misery* of the cinematic narrative into the daylight of everyday life—with a nod of respect to Annie Wilkes, to whom Paul Sheldon owes *something*, as he hints to Marcia Sindell.

What Could It Be?

Annie Wilkes forced Paul Sheldon into a developmental process (styled by the plot): liberation from his own (artistic) immobility. The wheelchair is the metaphor for Paul Sheldon's stagnation as a writer, from which he is liberated when he manages to leave Annie Wilke's (murderous) relationship prison and thus make his way into the public eye with his new, ambitious publication. The three dots and the question mark with which Paul Sheldon ended his *Untitled* manuscript have apparently been developed in a new text that has been launched on the literary market with the (new) title *The Higher Education of J. Philip Stone.* Annie Wilkes' life mantra, which she adopted from her reading of Paul Sheldon's work, was: *'There is a higher justice than that of a man'*. Annie Wilkes forced/moved Paul Sheldon into 'higher education'. In the final sequence, as he makes his way to a New York restaurant for an appointment with his agent Marcia Sindell—dragging his right leg a little, leaning on a cane—he moves very cautiously and differently to the way he had at the start, when he roundly collided with the trunk of a pine tree. The writer bows to his reader, who has indirectly reminded him of his responsibility as an author who is committed to human truth. The encounter with Annie Wilkes has purged him. Presumably, the author Stephen King is speaking through Paul Sheldon.

Misery: The Narrative of the Thriller Tells a Familiar Life Story

The film *Misery* recounts the development of an asymmetrical relationship in the context of a familiar constellation. Protagonist Annie Wilkes meets author Paul Sheldon in her identity as a nurse, taking care of him (Fig. 14.2).

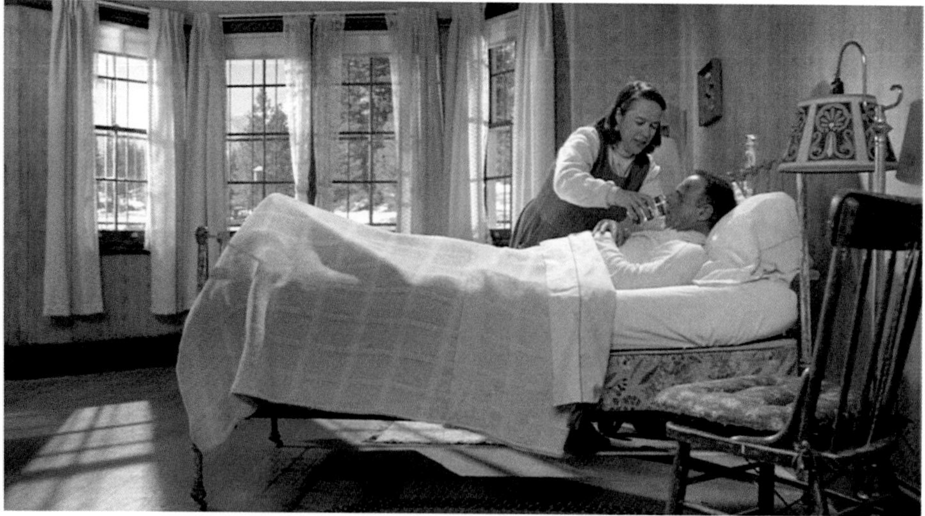

Fig. 14.2 Nursing (00:09:22)

She soon shoehorns her other interest (her idolisation) into her professional relationship, which becomes a maternal/adolescent-tinged relationship of enlisting Sheldon in her self-interest (regulation and balancing of her inner world). *Misery*, set up as a thriller and effectively told as the movie plot of Paul's existential struggle for survival, by no means leads the viewer to think that something familiar and old is being communicated, namely Paul Sheldon's interactive flinching from Annie Wilkes' idolisation. Rob Reiner's frame of reference is the Hollywood narrative of horrific motherliness—from Raoul Walsh's *White Heat* (USA 1949) to Alfred Hitchcock's *Psycho* (USA 1960) to Martin McDonagh's *Three Billboards Outside Ebbing, Missouri* (USA 2017)—in the struggle to maintain attachment and to modify the attachment of mother-son dependency. Annie Wilkes seeks to assert her idolisation, Paul Sheldon to shake it off. The lurid narrative of the thriller obscures the mutual task of living.

Masud Khan (1979) spoke of the need for maternal idolisation, which Donald Woods Winnicott called *devotion:* a deep, unwavering commitment to and affinity for the needs of the young child. The problem is the gradual, measured, tactful disillusionment of the idolising attention in the context of the task of transforming the established, deep attachment into an agile, elastic relationship that promotes the child/adolescent's self-differentiation and allows for the child/adolescent's increasingly expansive forays into life. In the process, the child/adolescent moves away from his or her parents. With increasing age, the distance grows, which is difficult for the parents to bear. Parenthood is therefore also toleration of this sublime disillusionment, mortification and grief over the gradual parting. There are huge conflicts involved in asserting and establishing increasing autonomy. Sometimes family ties can seem like chains. How can a young person move in and out of family/parental ties towards viable independence? Only with an enormous, overt or suppressed dramatic effort. Paul Sheldon succeeded in doing so, Annie Wilkes did not.

Further Considerations

A subtext opened up for me when I imagined Annie Wilkes' way of life. Annie Wilkes *saw* herself as the member of an (invisible) readership of the author Paul Sheldon. In his last volume of the *Mystery* series, she felt *betrayed* by her favourite author. He had taken the protagonist, Misery Chastain, out of cultural circulation. To Annie Wilkes, it seemed that participation in cultural exchange had been *terminated*. She had lost her place. She had taken the promise of cultural participation literally, not understanding that this promise had never been an interactive agreement within a real relationship, but rather a form of cultural game that was contingent on business calculations. Paul Sheldon had got rid of a business that had become onerous.

It is safe to assume that Annie Wilkes has not learned to play; the potential space of the cultural experience, as Donald Woods Winnicott (1971) terms it, is not available to her. Thus, powerful, traumatic disappointments have accumulated in her life story, and several times have culminated in frenzied (murderous) outbursts of profound, lonely despair. In the plot logic of the thriller, she is slain by the man she loved in her self-centred way.

Cinema is part of our highly complex sociocultural system that promises participation, inclusion and exclusion. This should not be taken as literally as it is by *The Little Soldier* in Jean-Luc Godard's second feature film of the same name (F 1960), who during the projection of a bathing woman onto an improvised screen goes round the back to look for the naked woman behind it. In the cinema, you are inside and outside at the same time. The disappointments experienced in front of the screen are the playful prototypes of those in real life. The pleasure of cinema goes hand in hand with a heightened experience of reality.

How does this relate to Paul Sheldon's book *The Higher Education of J. Philip Stone?* In what does it consist? Probably in the encounter with Annie Wilkes' terrible suffering. Rob Reiner and William Goldman find an ironic solution: they have Annie Wilkes' adored singer Liberace sing '*I'll be seeing you*'. The film writers get down to business too quickly—the thriller has to be given an ending. The ironic solution raises the question of the filmmakers' artistic veracity. They are obviously not really interested in Annie Wilkes. The newspaper clippings about her life story that Paul Sheldon leafs through are not staged to be read. They are also not that interested in the 40-year-old woman Annie Wilkes. Things remain cold between her and Paul Sheldon. Kathy Bates and James Caan are each virtuosic actors in their own way, but they do not relate to one other; there is no chemistry between them. Kathy Bates was apparently not permitted to become 40 years old. You rarely see them *together* (in one setting). Winter in Colorado matches the coldness of the film.

Translated by Annette Caroline Christmas.

Film Details

Original title	Misery
Country	USA
Release year	1990
Screenplay	William Goldman
Director	Rob Reiner
Principle actors	Kathy Bates, James Caan, Lauren Bacall, Richard Farnworth, Frances Sternhagen, Wendy Bowers
Availability	DVD (Code 2), Blu-Ray (Code 1)

References

Bollas C (1995) The structure of evil. In: Bollas C (ed) Cracking up. The work of the unconscious experience. Routledge, London, pp S180–S220

Khan M (1979) Alienation in perversions. Hogarth Press, London

Winnicott DW (1971) Playing and reality. Tavistock Publications, London

'You Are the Only Person Who Can Give Me Back Myself': The Passions of Self-image and Ego Distortion—Der Liebeswunsch [The Love Wish] (D 2006)

15

Benigna Gerisch

Introduction

It is always a risky undertaking for a director to take a crack at adapting an award-winning novel, all the more so when it has been written by a multi-award-winning and renowned author. After its publication in the year 2000, *Der Liebeswunsch* by Dieter Wellershoff, who structured his almost 400-page opus around the amorous entanglements of two established middle-class couples, was on the bestseller list for months, lauded by critics and readers alike. Wellershoff received his highest accolade from the great literary and critical master Marcel Reich-Ranicki, who gave the work lavish praise in the *Literarischen Quartett* (15.12.2000): 'I have rarely seen such love so realistically portrayed in our contemporary literature'.

The film directed by Torsten C. Fischer, a far less prominent figure and principally a screenwriter for television films, had a much harder time finding success. After its premiere at the 2006 Hamburg Film Festival, the film soon sank into oblivion. Before its cinema release in 2007, it had been shown by co-producer and Austrian broadcaster *ORF*, and the DVD was released in 2008 and remained at the bottom of the sales charts, and when regional public TV broadcaster *ARD* finally presented a shortened version of it at prime time, it had to compete with the Champions League on the *SAT 1* TV channel. Jochen Hieber of the centre-right-liberal newspaper the *Frankfurter Allgemeine Zeitung (FAZ)* is critical of TV stations for tending to broadcast publicly financed films 'in the shadow of competing attractions, because they are considered too demanding' (Hieber 2012, p. 1), which he regards as simply cheating the taxpayer.

B. Gerisch (✉)
Berlin, Germany
e-mail: benigna.gerisch@ipu-berlin.de

V. Pramataroff-Hamburger, A. Hamburger (eds.), *From La Strada to The Hours*,
https://doi.org/10.1007/978-3-662-68789-5_15

However, the overall film concept was also harshly criticised and unfavourably compared with the original great literary tale of love and passion: critics said it was diminished in the adaptation, the dialogues were artificial and pseudo-philosophically convoluted and the characters were made to wander through puristic and noble interiors, chilly urban scenes or forlorn landscapes—and that the film was ultimately boring. The only thing everyone could agree on was the outstanding ensemble cast: exquisite performances by internationally renowned actors Jessica Schwarz, Barbara Auer, Tobias Moretti and Ulrich Thomsen elevated the cinematic experience.

I must confess that I, too, found the film irritating and unsettling on a first viewing, since I did not recognise 'my' beloved novel in it. The book had seemed to me very worthwhile reading for its clinical and conceptual portrayal of a 'a suicide foretold'. Almost indignantly, I wanted to turn my back on the film and never watch it again, since it didn't seem to capture anything I associated with the novel. However, this aversive affect, which I tried to understand as a counter-transference, is an indication of the specific and individually disposed reception of any work of art, whether a novel, film or painting. We ourselves, interwoven with our at times unconscious specific desires, longings, fears and affects, take in a work of art, populating it and reworking it intrapsychically. In short, a film adaptation can never reproduce the associations evoked in us by the original. It shouldn't even try to do so, because nothing is more enervating than a meticulously retold novel or an artist's biography, which does not add anything to what we already knew. A film, especially a film adaptation of an original, is a transformative, independent, artistic work like a palimpsest, a repeatedly painted-over template. It uses formal-aesthetic, stylistic means, drama and production techniques to present something on a screen and must necessarily distance itself from the written text, in this case from the novel, including its complex associative charge. If I detach myself from the demand to see 'my novel' reflected and allow myself to be drawn into the artistic adaptation of the original as an unsettling, mysterious, new and other experience, then I can, in short, conclude that the film is more than successful. Although his much-criticised, intimate play-like abridgement does away with central elements, in a stylistically subtle way, it manages to penetrate to the core conflict, the volcano of passions of the eroding quartet, thereby surgically exposing it like a nerve. Thus, my initial aversive reaction could also have had something to do with the demand placed on the viewer by this condensation, since the inevitability of the catastrophe is always palpable but inevitable, which practically forces you to constantly change perspectives and allows identification with the individual characters. The novel opens considerably more breathing spaces, whereas the viewer is drawn in and gripped by the film, and the inevitability is experienced psychophysically. This is in part due to the sophisticated editing technique, for which the film was rightly award-winning. The chronology of events is repeatedly undermined by the film montage, the superimposed oscillation between remembering and forgetting, past and future, safety and disintegration. This especially points to the specific organisational structure of the film (in contrast to the epic narrative form of the novel), which therefore creates its own particular relationships between time and space, image and sound, protection and retention (…) (Seel 2013, p. 25), thus generating a significant aesthetic effect in the recipient.

And from a clinical perspective, I would like to note that both the novel and the film character Anja played a leading role in my treatment of suicidal patients for many weeks. They felt seen in their lack of understanding, they identified deeply with Anja, who seemed to them like a soulmate, even a revenant.

Film Plot

The film reconstructs the suicide of literature student Anja (Jessica Schwarz), who is in her late 20s, with which the film ends and which we are reminded of at the start of the film. Anja meets her future husband, the 40-something judge Leonhard (Tobias Moretti), at the home of his former wife, doctor Marlene (Barbara Auer), and her husband Jan (Ulrich Thomsen), also a doctor who is about the same age as Marlene and who had once been a close friend of Leonhard's. Marlene and Jan are still friends with Leonhard, despite the historical cheating and divorce. Anja and the much older Leonhard quickly marry, move into his large modern house and soon have their son Daniel, who scalds himself on a kettle on Anja's birthday and is admitted to hospital. Anja, who has long been unhappy in her relationship with Leonhard, begins to increasingly lose her grip, starts drinking heavily and throws herself into an affair with Jan, who nevertheless does not want to give up his marriage to his wife. When Marlene and Leonhard discover the betrayal, Leonhard files for divorce. Anja goes to rehab after alcohol poisoning, but during an excursion with the therapy group, she flees to a hotel, throws herself out of the window and dies.

Background

Superficially, the film portrays a young woman going off the rails due to pathology and unrequited love, who first becomes dependent on alcohol and eventually commits suicide. One could conclude that the film serves the classic genre of the film portrayal of mental illness. In Anja's case, diagnoses such as 'narcissistic depression' and above all 'borderline pathology' come to mind. The development of the suicide is presented in a coherent and psychodynamically plausible way, and the typical female motif of suicide due to heartbreak is meticulously explained, seemingly confirming the persistent myth of 'she died for love and he for glory' in the history of culture and science (cf. Gerisch 1998).

As a viewer, one could objectively say that Anja is a mentally ill person who could not be helped in life and who, as if in a compulsion to repeat herself, has bound herself to the wrong men: once to the compulsively authoritarian, unsympathetic Leonhard, and then, following a fantasy of redemption, to the charismatic but unattainable, married Jan.

If we take a brief look back at film history, we find that there has always been a gender-stereotypical portrayal of mental illness: The women are sinister-crazy, capricious, love-sick, depressive, borderline or psychotic figures who, in their lability and unbounded passion, wreak great havoc, such as terrorising their lover's families and cooking the children's rabbits, as Glenn Close did in *Fatal Attraction (US 1987)*. *Black Swan* also exhibits the evil, competitive and murderous side of a woman who even goes so far as to brutally kill her rival, under a delusion. The material of the diabolically ill was used to produce box-office classics, which at the same time perpetuated the cliché of the demonised-murderous and, on the other hand, the unstable-suicidal woman. Thus, anthropologist Wednesday Martin (2018) also concludes in her study *Untrue* that unfaithful women have always been considered to be sick or dangerous.

Men with mental disorders, on the other hand, tend to be portrayed as cranky, gauche, quirky oddballs, even as the battered but ultimately lovable heroes who can rely on the viewer's sympathy, for example, *Rain Man (US 1988)*, which made autistic disorder respectable and won four Oscars. Or when we think of *Forrest Gump*, brilliantly played by Tom Hanks, a film that won six Oscars.

However, this reading centred on pathology would be a crude reduction of the disquieting, disturbing qualities of the film *Der Liebeswunsch*. There is more at stake than a lamentable individual fate: We are experiencing an eruptive questioning of our orders of love and relationships—which are in any case constantly under threat in the age of the digital mass supply of potential love partners—of our utopias of successful love, fidelity and lasting partnership, the value of which is above all demonstrated when at some point (to borrow one of Woody Allen's memorable phrases) we are sitting in a bleak hospital corridor and do not have to wait a biopsy result all alone.

Der Liebeswunsch now joins a contemporary canon of love and passion. For in recent years, love, in its many-layered forms and tales of disaster, including obsessive or even fatal passion, has also experienced a remarkable renaissance in other cultural productions such as fiction and theatre.

Gender semantics have become a focus of almost all productions, regardless of genre, with variants on the traditional subjects of the incompatibility of love/marriage and erotic passion as well as the dissolution of the cultural order that has thus far provided identity.

And in quite a few, the suicide of a woman—the other side of the leitmotif of the murdered-demonised one—plays a prominent role, for example in films such as *The Virgin Suicides* (US 1999) or the sensational Netflix series *13 Reasons Why (US 2017–2020)* (cf. Gerisch 2019).

One could almost be inclined to conclude that the traditional theme of the 'lovesick woman' still follows an instrumental logic in film and structurally functions like a stand-in figure on which to constantly projectively locate the unsettling, disturbing, libidinous-destructive forces in the other in order to thus control them and ideally keep a distance from them (cf. Gerisch 2003).

One strand of my thesis, which I would like to unfold in the following, is that the existential questioning and threatening scenarios of a romantic love utopia in *Der Liebeswunsch* are staged en miniature, so to speak, around the quartet, which is organised as 'adoptive kin'. At their core, they revolve around the radicalisation of freedom, equality and recognition within traditional gender relations, as well as a radical splitting of sexuality and emotionality in contemporary modernity (cf. also Illouz 2012 [2011]). Seen from this perspective, the figure of Anja is not just a 'lovesick madwoman', but the embodiment of a collectively existing, identity-forming passion that nonetheless has a feminine connotation of devotion and dependence that represent a constant attack on the male order governed by dominance, autonomy, control and power. On the other hand, the film allows us to experience the longing for an absolutely perfect, ego-forming, universal *love desire phantasm*, in which any difference between the sexes, the ego and the other, the inside and the outside is erased. A state of perfection, however, that can at best only be fleetingly achieved in a boundless love passion that is both longed for and feared.

Excursus on Film Aesthetics: 'Sound of the Surf'

The reduced-minimalist, aesthetic-formal design of the film continuously makes the tension between control and dissolution, between mastery and dissolution of boundaries psychophysically tangible. A kind of supportive framework is thus created for the film in which the figures interact, sometimes microscopically illuminated, sometimes only fleetingly touched upon and hinted at, as if in an experimentally created biotope. The encapsulated and manageable terrain in which the quartet acts does not establish any reference to the outside, not even to a past: The characters have no parents, no siblings, no friends or any other significant social relationships. Only Anja's mother makes an appearance, as does her missing father, and a brief mention is made of Jan's daughter Gerda. The characters act alone in relation to one another, as in an intimate play, in mutual dependencies that are denied by the men and projectively located in the women. Leonhard takes refuge in his legal regulations, which provide structure and support, and Jan in a survival strategy of pseudo-independence—and ultimately in the affair with Anja. The outside world is primarily represented by the penetrating gaze of the spectator, who is forced into a kind of silent witnessing.

This creates an eerie mood that always hints at unconscious and potentially eroding forces. On the manifest level, this is reflected in the artificial-seeming interplay of the actors and the cool, minimalist décor of the setting—as if to keep this danger of dissolution at bay.

The lack of connection between the protagonists, their alienation from one other, despite the invoked closeness and physical union, is conveyed above all by the speechlessness of the characters and their imposed self-reliance: We listen to the characters thinking, longing and wishing far more than actually speaking to each other. The inner monologues of the actors, in which their loneliness and forlornness are condensed, which are denied a resonant response from the external world and also unfold their effect on the viewer through rapid fades, take up the metaphor of the surf, quoted by Leonhard in his speech, which sounds like an unimaginable number of voices, although no single one gets a chance to speak, each telling its own story.

In summary, the social order of the sexes is condensed and staged in miniature in the hermetically sealed quartet of characters, entangled in an irresolvable and gender typically connoted struggle for recognition, love, devotion, sexual desire, fidelity and loss.

The Beginning: Forgetting to Forget

The first scene in the film, like the first sentence in the novel, is decisively important. Firstly, because it can be understood to be a key scene, and secondly because if it is powerful enough, it will seduce the viewers, keep them spellbound and create an unconditional desire to find out how the story unfolds.

Der Liebeswunsch succeeds in that we first see Jan from behind, apparently still in hospital, which he then leaves, glancing back at the attractive nurses. He gets into his car, accidentally setting off the alarm. While he is sitting behind the wheel, startled, he sees bare legs and bare feet against the rain-soaked asphalt and then Anja in a light summer prom dress, who hurries past him, disappearing just as quickly. The confusing hallucination, triggered by the car's alarm system, sets his memory in motion like a traumatic break-in. In the voice-over to the start of this scene, Jan tells us what is bothering him. '*I thought about her less and less, and for shorter periods, and then at some point I didn't think about her any more. I don't know when that was. You also forget forgetting when you've forgotten something. It's like a double wall or like something that isn't really there—a double darkness. Now I've realised that you can't be sure. She had disappeared into that double darkness until I suddenly saw her again*'.

This is a downright scandalous remark from the dead Anja's perspective, as if she had not even managed to posthumously secure a place for herself in Jan for 'ever and ever', which in itself can be quite a strong motive for suicide (cf. Gerisch 2012).

We then see Jan driving to the sea, to the abandoned car park of a high-rise hotel in inhospitable, rainy scenery. He goes into one of the rooms, then immediately opens the balcony door unsteadily and hesitantly walks up to the parapet and looks down the wind whistling loudly and alarmingly (Fig. 15.1). We hear him thinking: '*It was naïve of me to*

Fig. 15.1 Jan goes back into the hotel room where Anja had thrown herself from the balcony to her death (xx:xx:xx)

come here, it couldn't start again. There is no longer a place where she can be found. A dead woman who could not be saved even when she was alive'.

During this sentence, we see Anja again in her pink prom dress, sitting with her back to the balcony parapet, swaying to the music she is listening to on her headphones, putting her finger to her lips as if asking for silence, as if she wanted to melt into the melody completely undisturbed in death—then she finally lets herself fall.

This disturbing and harrowing start to the film keeps the viewer spellbound and desperate to know what led up to this catastrophe.

Staging the Feminine in Film

'Simple or Complicated'

Only now do we return to the beginning of the gradually unhinged human mobile and see Marlene and Jan preparing for their holiday. They make fun of their friend Leonhard, who is surely about to provide them with information on the holiday destination. And Anja is also already roaming the house, the young student hired by Marlene as a house sitter during her 6-week absence. We see Marlene casually and elegantly smoking, leaning against the kitchen sideboard.

When the naïvely sensual, enigmatic Anja appears on the screen, the cheerful atmosphere changes instantly, turning into something spellbinding and uncanny: Both Jan and Leonhard are immediately fascinated by this young woman.

When Leonhard visits her again shortly afterwards to check that everything is alright, Anja, dressed only in a skimpy red crocheted bikini, is dancing lasciviously in the living room, shielded by headphones, to Jim Croce's song *Time in a bottle* (Fig. 15.2).

Fig. 15.2 Anja (00:11:40)

Leonhard now visits her almost daily, talking a lot about his work as a judge at the district court.

Shortly afterwards, Leonhard proposes to her, and Anja accepts. After the next rapid cut, we already see a baby's head and then the exhausted, unhappy-looking Anja in bed, being comforted and reassured by Marlene. Anja is apparently suffering from postpartum depression and is afraid that Leonhard might now be disappointed in her.

Anja

The female characters in the film, Anja and Marlene, are polar opposites, although in this sharp contrast they also seem like the defence and repulsion of one and the same actor. From the male perspective, too, both characters offer themselves as wide-ranging projection surfaces—somewhere between saint and whore: Anja is a figure of eroticism, sensuality and boundless passionate devotion, and Marlene represents intelligence, strength, sovereignty, order and calm. Moreover, the film shows us the mutually abusive nature of the relationship arrangement in which the other is assigned a role to fulfil. Anja functions like a well-oiled but also bulky hinge in the fragile triangle into which she is sucked while at the same time wanting to penetrate and belong, which gradually comes apart at the seams and finally breaks.

Let us thus first examine Anja, a fatherless girl with a less than empathetic mother who above all wants a good match for her daughter. A young woman who drifts through life guided by her desires, who both loses her footing and seeks it, temporarily finding it in her marriage to the domineering, structured Leonhard. Anja seems to be driven by a deep longing to somehow anchor herself somewhere in the world. She escapes the restraints of marriage with her controlling husband, who paternalistically wants to force her to live a 'good' and conventional life, first by turning to inanimate objects and then alcohol and finally by having an affair with Jan, who is annoyingly distant and uncommunicative. This undoubtedly also has a touch of incestuous oedipality about it, in that it enables her to triumph over the self-assured, untouchable, perfect Marlene at the same time.

Jan, who seems to be trapped within himself, finds her total devotion intoxicating and however gradually recoils from its hysterical boundlessness and tries to seek refuge in the safe haven of marriage with Marlene. However, Anja is full of ardour and mainly driven by a desire for love that serves her existentially and in her identity. Anja thus writes Jan a love letter when she senses that he is already beginning to withdraw from the relationship: '*You are the only person who can give me back to myself. I can only be what I want to be if I can bring it to you.*' (cf. Gerisch 2005).

Anja triggers fantasies of protection and rescue in both her male and female counterparts (and probably in the audience, too). Leonhard, Jan and also Marlene try to fulfil these in their own particular ways. Anja, the child-woman who is the only protagonist to go on to have a child (Daniel), at times seems to be the unborn daughter of Marlene and Jan, at others a coveted love object, a Lolita. In Leonhard's eyes, she is a wild animal that has to be domesticated and kept dependent so that it does not get lost again, as Marlene did.

Thus, a complex, projective web unfolds comprising each protagonist's own unlived and unfulfilled, archaic-unconscious, incestuous and oedipal-libidinous, narcissistic assimilation, which threatens to inexorably ensnare the actors.

Anja, who lacks a foothold and a place in the world, represents on the one hand a weak, needy and dependent side, and on the other hand is highly manipulative, serving various projections of the others seemingly quite effortlessly, adapting herself as if in mimicry, only to rebel against the roles assigned to her.

Anja and Leonhard

At first, Anja moves around in Leonhard's minimalist-stylishly furnished rooms like an outsider, being scrupulously careful not to upset his obsessive order, only to then rebel like a defiantly petulant child or an adolescent: Leonhard forbids her to drink wine, but she demonstratively pours herself a glass in front of him, comes and goes when she pleases, later insists on having her own bedroom and only occasionally submits in boredom and disgust to the passionless, mechanical sexual act. In the morning, while Leonhard is busily shining his shoes, he apologises for the night before and gives her an expensive perfume.

The following episode is paradigmatic for the divergence between Anja's and Leonhard's ideas about love and relationships:

After the revelation about cheating, a powerfully edited, alternately cross-faded scenes show Jan and Anja in intimate sexual fusion in their love nest, while Leonhard takes a sharpened pencil and a ruler to underline the decisive passages in the marriage contract, which he places on her pillow in duplicate for her to sign.

Anja and Jan

She easily wraps Jan, whose desire and yearning she has long since noticed, around her little finger. But the scenes with him are cross-faded and cut so short that no genuine feeling can arise, certainly none that could account for the fervent love. Jan usually seems to be habitually grumpy, rather dismissive, silent and not very approachable. An inkling of a bond briefly arises when they are both sitting in the bath, and Anja says her father left when she was 4 years old, and her mother then erased everything that could have reminded her of him. Anja asks Jan why he would not see his daughter in Denmark, to which he replies he was ashamed. On the basis of this scene, which is shown in great detail and during which they speak to each other differently than usual, one begins to suspect that the Oedipal incestuous longing for an absent and unattainable father is an essential driving force in the desire for love, which she directs at Jan.

When Marlene finds Jan out and writes a note asking him how long he is going to cheat on her, Jan wants to break free from Anja's grip.

The more she senses that he is withdrawing, the more she begins to mock him in his cultured and reserved rigidity, throwing herself at him in public, despite and also because of the risk of being discovered. She complains that she can never be the woman at his side, that this place has long since been occupied by Marlene and that she does not fit into his ideal and orderly world. On one occasion, she throws herself half naked on top of him in the car and tries to force him to have sex, and the alarm system goes off. Jan pushes her away: He tries to appease her by saying he does not have much to offer her and is not the right partner for a young woman. Anja escapes from the car and runs off, her feet bare.

It is the key scene he will remember at the beginning of the film: Anja, barefoot and inappropriately dressed, as a metaphor for her lack of being at home in the world, which at the same time reflects the loneliness and isolation of the others.

After his clarifying conversation with Marlene, Jan visits Anja one more time to break up with her for good. While she is in the bathroom, he reads the letters addressed to him lying scattered all over the floor: 'If you leave me, I will be left in complete darkness. It will break me, it breaks us all'.

Later, Jan will admit to Marlene, among other reasons in order to save the marriage, that he simply sleepwalked into the affair and no longer knows how to get out of it: Anja, he says, is an unstable person, a hysteric, addicted to grand emotions.

Generally speaking, I became aware of the paradox of the overshadowed physical proximity and absence, partly due to the discrepancy between the only fleetingly shown sexual encounters and the profound inner trauma. Anja remains fixated on the unattainable, highly idealised love object that has become the saviour par excellence. To ignite the obsessive, deadly passion, a central moment thus had to be added: a narcissistically idealisable, never quite attainable, sometimes even sadistic love object, which is inextricably linked with perpetual hunger.

Beyond that, however, Anja's actions reveal a clandestine desire to destroy the hypocrisy and bigotry of the trio's seemingly immaculate lifeworld and to make the agonising feeling of exclusion bearable. As if she wanted to tear the masks off all three of them so that she could be reflected in their bare faces without being ashamed of her difference.

Anja's libidinous, angry actions seem to be a powerful gesture of revolt against the rigid norms to which the three of them must conform and which seem to imprison them. She ultimately pays for this gesture—in the dramatic, clichéd but nevertheless all too often true flip side—with her life.

Anja as a Mother

Contrary to her own misgivings, she is able to establish a loving and affectionate relationship with her child, although it is clear that much of the way she lives and acts with him is in compensation for her own unfulfilled childhood wishes. However, she tries hard to be a good enough and supportive mother to him, while Leonhard treats his son like a stranger, admonishing and disciplining him as if he were a miniature adult. The following scenes, which are edited in quick succession, are paradigmatic: Anja asks Daniel if he would like a drink and to come to the kitchen with her. While she is putting on a kettle and turning on a cassette for Daniel, she goes into the living room to her gift table, as it's her birthday. She then hears Daniel screaming shrilly: he has scalded himself on boiling water from the kettle. While we see Anja in the hospital where Daniel is being attended to, in almost the same instant, we see another scene that happened that morning between Daniel and Leonhard: Leonhard gruffly tells his three-year-old son to get dressed and then fetch his own milk.

Shortly afterwards, Marlene tells Leonhard what has happened. He is furious and asks Marlene where Anja had been and why she hadn't been paying attention. An undoubtedly tragic and horrific accident, which, however, is not solely caused by the failure to fulfil 'supervisory duties' or a 'total failure of motherliness', as Leonhard constantly tries to prove to her, but was ultimately also fostered by the loveless and unsuccessful father-son relationship.

Daniel's accident, from which he gradually recovers, marks the prelude to Anja's insidious and ultimately explosive dissociation.

Marlene

Marlene, on the other hand, represents the other side of Anja's feminine weakness, instability and dependence. Marlene is the self-assured, intelligent, strong woman with a respected, ambitious profession, who has her house, husband and life under control at all times. At the same time, however, she is affectionate, approachable, eloquent, empathetic and an attractive, desirable figure, always with a slight air of detached coolness and superiority. Threatening feelings are expressed in a carefully moderated way, if at all. In her relationship with Marlene, Anja plays the role of the eccentric, needy friend on the one hand, and on the other hand, she serves the daughterly sometimes almost homoerotically tinged projections directed at her.

In the end, it is also Marlene who, once the betrayal and deceit are out in the open, takes care of Anja: visits her in her flat, fetches her shopping and finally arranges for her to be admitted to the clinic. But this almost superhuman gesture, in which anger, rage and mortification are denied, also seems like a humiliation of Anja, who is not treated as a rival to be taken seriously, but as a psychologically unstable, alcoholic 'daughter'. Anja's breakdown contributes to the stabilisation of Marlene's sense of self: she is thus able to constantly reassure herself of her 'flawless' life plan.

Marlene also shows that she is a cool and pragmatic strategist when it comes to coping with her own desires for love. She has been having an affair with Jan for a while when she gives him an ultimatum: She will go to England to wait for him there. But he is only allowed to come if he has definitively separated from his family; otherwise, he shouldn't, and she would accept this. But if he chose her, it would be like a *'feast they would remember for a lifetime'*. Only once does the other side of Marlene, which she usually keeps in check, briefly break out, when she is still unsure of Jan's commitment: *'I needed him so I could become myself again. I thought that was the longing—you wait to be redeemed to yourself'*, Marlene confesses to a colleague.

When Jan comes, thus confirming their relationship, she separates from Leonhard the following day. Just as consistently, Marlene will separate from Jan after the revelations.

Marlene takes this decision seriously, as can be seen in a final scene between Jan and Marlene, in which Jan wants to sleep with her again 'so that we can remember what it was like'. Marlene rounds on him sharply, saying she does not need to, as she knows what it was like: You've forgotten.

The Ending: 'If I Could Save Time in a Bottle'

Anja, who has fled to an inhospitable, multi-storey apartment hotel by the sea, spends her days reeling from a state of hopeless despair to anxious hope of rescue and redemption. She initially resists the urge to drink alcohol and then apparently ends up in a drunken stupor; she wakes up in a pool of her own vomit, with an empty vodka bottle next to her.

We are witnessing a phase of successive self-dissolution that we don't normally get to see because it usually takes place in intimate seclusion, in a bottomless pit of loneliness. We can at best carefully reconstruct such experiences in therapy sessions, but they are then condensed into a more or less ordered narrative that can only ever approximately convey the existential and physical trauma.

We are subjected to the sight of Anja lying in her vomit, just as in Goethe's *Werther* we are not spared a description of 'blown out brains' (cf. Gerisch 2010). This tests us to the limits, which is precisely where Anja finds herself: in a state of dissolution, of incessant disintegration, steeped in self-hatred, anger, humiliation, mortification, forlornness and unbearable shame. The camera, too, comes almost mercilessly close to Anja, tracking her but not sparing her, forcing us to look at this psychophysical veering off course. We reflexively feel that we want it all to be over at last that Anja should free us from the torments, which we also experience in ourselves, which we passively have to witness.

Anja finally drags herself to the balcony and convulsed with fear shakily sits on the railing facing backwards, as if to avoid looking down. Accompanied by Jim Croce's *Time in a Bottle*, she lets go and falls. Her summer ball gown is puffed up by the breeze as if she were dancing—and there is almost a sense of release rather than sheer horror.

These scenes create countertransference feelings that are difficult to bear: an oscillation between an indomitable being sucked into this never-ending spiral of joining together and falling apart, clinging to the presence and absence of the other on the one hand, and almost angry defensive movements on the other. This impulse, fed by powerlessness and loss of control, undoubtedly corresponds to a transference scenario that reaches us through the figure of Anja, namely her indomitable being overwhelmed by corrosive ego dissolution.

In this context, physicality, eroticisation and sexualisation symbolise the unconditional bond with the other. The uninterrupted state of infatuation with his 'bewildered body' grants an existential self-assurance. An anxiety that was nevertheless repeatedly restaged and used by Anja, because the 'absent' tormenting presence of the primary object was inseparably connected with it, while she likened the blissful moments of intense physicality in her letters to the experience of a 'second birth'.

Only in these moments of physical experience can she feel that she exists and is authentic, anchored in herself and the world, as the oft repeated refrain of her song *Time in a Bottle* vividly expresses. 'Time in a bottle' revolves around the desire for infinity, of being connected to the other for 'ever and ever': '*... That you're the one I want to go/Through time with ....*' A bodily state that causes Anja to pointedly exclaim:

'You are the only person who can give me back to myself'.

Outlook: The Jumping Kettle

After the urn burial, which is attended by Leonhard, Marlene, Anja's mother and son Daniel and which is silent and ritualised, a voice-over tells us about a dream Anja's mother had the following night: '*She was walking through a busy street and a giant kettle jumped right out in front of her, clattering loudly. Every now and then the lid flipped open and Anja's shaved head peeked out. It was as small as an apple and screamed in a high, desperate voice. Then the lid flipped shut again. The kettle continued to bounce along the road in front of her as if possessed, and Anja's screaming head reappeared and disappeared. It carried on doing this. Then it got further away but the short, shrill screams could still be heard. There were a lot of people walking through the street, but no one seemed to notice these goings-on except her*'.

The metaphor of the 'clattering kettle' once again condenses the tragedy of Anja's unhappy story: She feels she is imprisoned in a confined space, which is also under hot pressure in an uncanny-archaic way. She wants to escape this inner inferno and desperately tries to make herself heard by screaming. But she can no longer reach the world and the others out there.

The other perspective that the film opens up is, on the one hand, the enormous destructive power of the suicidal act, bearing in mind Freud's (1917) formula that suicide should be understood first and foremost as the murder of an introjected object. Anja contributes to the fact that the fragile structure of the four protagonists is gradually disintegrated. But on the other hand, this disintegrating power can only unfold its effectiveness because the other three have always tried to seize it like a split-off, unconscious part of themselves, wanting to keep it close and far away at the same time, because their excessively feverish love constantly threatened the delicate balance between culture-forming stability and longed-for intoxication, dependence and autonomy.

Translated by Annette Caroline Christmas.

Film Details

Original title	Der Liebeswunsch [The Love Wish]
Release year	2006
Country	Germany
Screenplay/Idea	Torsten C. Fischer
Direction	Torsten C. Fischer
Principal actors	Jessica Schwarz, Tobias Moretti, Ulrich Thomsen, Barbara Auer
Availability	DVD/Blu-Ray

References

Freud S (1917) Mourning and melancholia. SE, vol. XIV, pp 243–258

Gerisch B (1998) Suizidalität bei Frauen. Mythos und Realität—Eine kritische Analyse [Suicidality in women. Myth and reality—a critical analysis] edition diskord, Tübingen

Gerisch B (2003) Die suizidale Frau. Psychoanalytische Hypothesen zur Genese [The suicidal woman. A psychoanalytical hypotheses on its genesis]. Vandenhoeck & Ruprecht, Göttingen

Gerisch B (2005) "Nicht Dich habe ich verloren, sondern die Welt": Obsession und Leidenschaft bei suizidalen Frauen [It is not you I have lost, but the world. Obsession and passion in suicidal women]. Psyche—Z Psychoanal 59:918–943

Gerisch B (2010) "Ich kehre in mich selbst zurück und finde eine Welt" ["I return into myself and find a world"]: psychoanalytical notes on obsessive longing for love and suicidal tendencies in Goethe's "the sorrows of young Werther". In: Mauser W, Pfeiffer J, Pietzcker C (eds) Goethe. Königshausen & Neumann, Würzburg, pp 101–126

Gerisch B (2012) Suizidalität [Suicidality]. Analyse der Psyche und Psychotherapie, vol. 6. Psychosocial, Giessen

Gerisch B (2019) "Wenn Du die Wahrheit wissen willst, dann drück' einfach auf Play" ["If you want to know the truth, just press play"]: 13 reasons why. In: König H, Piegler T (eds) Skandalfilm?—Filmskandal! Verstörend, anstößig, pervers: den filmischen Tabubrüchen auf der Spur [Disturbing, offensive, perverse: on the trail of cinematic taboo-breaking]. Springer, Berlin, pp 321–338

Illouz E (2011) Warum Liebe weh tut. Suhrkamp, Frankfurt am Main [*Why love hurts.* Polity Press, Cambridge 2012]

Martin W (2018) Untrue. Why almost everything we think we know about female infidelity, lust and infidelity is wrong and how the new science can set us free. Little Brown Spark, Hachette Book Group, NY

Seel M (2018 [2013]) The arts of cinema, Cornell, [Originally published as Die Künste des Kinos, Fischer, Frankfurt am Main]

Wellershoff D (2000) Der Liebeswunsch. Kiepenheuer & Witsch, Cologne

Internet Sources

Hieber J (2012) Dann schaut doch lieber Fußball. https://www.faz.net/aktuell/feuilleton/medien/fernsehfilm-der-liebeswunsch-dann-schaut-doch-lieber-fussball-11682861.html

Part V

String Pullers. When Women Control Events

Alfred Hitchcock's *Rebecca*: The Replacement Wife

16

Andrea Sabbadini

Plot

Directed by Alfred Hitchcock, *Rebecca* is a free adaptation from the eponymous 1938 Gothic novel by Daphne Du Maurier. Protagonists of the story are a newly-wed couple settling down in Manderley, the husband's luxurious mansion; here, the memory of his beautiful first wife Rebecca, the suspicious circumstances of her death by drowning and the presence of a sadistic housekeeper make his second wife feel deeply inadequate in her role as the new Mrs. de Winter.

She will eventually redeem herself as the mystery of Rebecca's death is uncovered, and Manderley is destroyed by fire.

Background

Released in 1940, this black-and white film was rewarded the following year with eleven Academy Award nominations, winning two of them: for Best Picture and Best Cinematography. *Rebecca* is the first movie made by Hitchcock in the United States: 'The American influence on it is obvious', he admitted himself in his famous interview with François Truffaut, but he also added, 'it's a completely British picture: the story, the actors, and the director were all English' (in Truffaut 1983, p. 128).

David O. Selznick (1902–1965) was the Hollywood producer of four of Hitchcock's films of which *Rebecca* was the first; it was released soon after another one of Selznick's productions, the enormously successful *Gone with the Wind* (1939). A control-freak who also happened to feel passionately about psychoanalysis, Selznick had such an influence

A. Sabbadini (✉)
London, UK

V. Pramataroff-Hamburger, A. Hamburger (eds.), *From La Strada to The Hours*,
https://doi.org/10.1007/978-3-662-68789-5_16

on *Rebecca* that some consider it as the least personal of Hitchcock's movies. When Truffaut asked him, in the interview already referred to: 'Are you satisfied with *Rebecca*?', Hitchcock replied: 'Well, it's not a Hitchcock picture…' (in Truffaut 1983, p. 127). A statement which, like most of his other statements, should not be taken too literally.

Hitchcock, who died 40 years ago in 1980, was born in the East End of London in 1899, and by the time he emigrated to Hollywood, he had already directed in Britain more than 20 films, including *The Man Who Knew Too Much* (1934), *The 39 Steps* (1935), *Sabotage* (1936) and *Jamaica Inn* (1939). He was then to settle in America, where he would direct some 30 more films—including such masterpieces as *Rear Window* (1954), *Vertigo* (1958), *North by North-West* (1959), *Psycho* (1960), *The Birds* (1963) and *Marnie* (1964)—all combining great artistic integrity with considerable popular appeal. His *Spellbound* (1945), also produced by Selznick, has as its main character the improbable psychoanalyst Ingrid Bergman seducing her improbable patient Gregory Peck and rescuing him from the accusation of being a murderer, as well as from his own amnesia and paranoid fears of persecution. The film, famous for Salvador Dali's design of the dream sequence, contributed to the spread in the United States of a popular, but incorrect, view of psychoanalysis. As Hitchcock himself confessed, *Spellbound* is 'just another manhunt story wrapped up in pseudo-psychoanalysis' (in Truffaut 1983, p. 165).

It was only from the 1960s, and thanks to the French critics and filmmakers writing on the influential journal *Cahiers du Cinéma*, that Hitchcock's stature in the history of cinema was properly recognised. With an international reputation as the undisputed master of suspense, he was notorious (if I can borrow from the title of another one of his movies) for his perfectionism, for having an in-depth knowledge of all aspects of moviemaking, for being an innovator (for instance he made the first all-talkie British movie [*Blackmail* 1929]) and for using special effects with such skill that their presence went mostly unnoticed; for instance, the mysteriously atmospheric Manderley mansion in *Rebecca* is in fact just a miniature. He also devised original camera movements, such as the 'forward point-of-view tracking shot', which he used in *Rebecca* for the first time (see Wood 1989, p. 240).

Most of Hitchcock's films are not 'whodunits', detective or gangster stories, but are concerned with normal people getting stuck into impossible situations: being accused of crimes they have not committed, or finding themselves involved in espionage or political intrigues they know nothing about and trying to disentangle themselves from them. However, none of this applies to *Rebecca* where, instead, the 'normal people' are a socially and psychologically badly assorted couple, painfully incapable of satisfying each other's emotional needs.

Hitchcock had already adapted a novel by the English author and playwright Daphne Du Maurier (1907–1989) in *Jamaica Inn* (1939) and would use another one of her stories in *The Birds* (1963). Other filmmakers, such as Nicolas Roeg with *Don't Look Now* (1973) and more recently Roger Michell with *My Cousin Rachel* (2017), have also adapted Du Maurier's stories.

Rebecca (with some help from Hitchcock's film of it) remains her most successful novel.

Starring in *Rebecca* in the lead roles are two almost legendary actors: Laurence Olivier (1907–1989) and Joan Fontaine (1917–2013). By the time he played the part of Maxim de

Winter in this film, Olivier was already a celebrity for his Shakespearean roles on the stage; his main screen parts (by then, in some fifteen films) included *As You Like It* (1936), *Fire over England* (1937) and *Wuthering Heights* (1939). Olivier was later to act in some 70 more movies, while also being celebrated as the most brilliant stage actor of his generation.

The other main lead in *Rebecca*, playing the difficult part of Maxim de Winter's anonymous second wife, is Joan Fontaine. Known for the rivalry with her sister Olivia de Havilland, Fontaine was nominated for an Academy Award for *Rebecca* and won one for.

Suspicion (1941, also directed by Hitchcock). Although she then starred in many films in a career spanning nearly 60 years, these two are the ones she remains best known for.

Minor and yet important roles in *Rebecca* are those played by George Sanders as the slimy dandy Jack Favell and Judith Anderson as Mrs. Danvers, arguably one of the most despicable women—alongside Nurse Ratched in *One Flew Over the Cuckoo's Nest* (1975)—ever to appear on the silver screen (in Ben Wheatley's remake of *Rebecca* [2020] the part of Mrs. Danvers is played by Kristin Scott Thomas). In the novel, Du Maurier portrays Mrs. Danvers as 'tall and gaunt, dressed in deep black, whose prominent cheekbones and great, hollow eyes gave her a skull's face, parchment white, set on a skeleton's frame' (Du Maurier 1938, p. 74). Very scary indeed.

Film critic David Thomson describes *Rebecca,* perhaps Hitchcock's most literature-impregnated work, as 'a mixture of romance, mystery, obsession, and even horror, [but also] a very sophisticated entertainment' (Thomson 2008, p. 715). To me, as well as all the above, *Rebecca* is a movie primarily concerned with the enormous power that memories have in affecting people's lives—sometimes comforting, other times disturbing. This is one of the reasons for this film's relevance to psychoanalysis.

Femininity in *Rebecca*

Rebecca opens with a woman's voice-over describing her dream of returning to Manderley, while the camera travels across a rusty gate and along a disused drive through a wooded, foggy park under the moonlight, towards the by-now decrepit grand manor. 'Last night I dreamt I went to Manderley again…' are the iconic opening words in both the film and the novel (Du Maurier 1938, p. 1) (Fig. 16.1).

About 1 year earlier, in the south of France, an attractive, somewhat naïve young girl has a chance meeting with a handsome, super-rich socialite, Maxim de Winter (a name perhaps suggesting a certain frostiness…), just when he was about to kill himself by jumping into the sea from a high cliff. By calling out to him, she saves his life, but he shows her little gratitude and sends her away (this whole scene is not present in the novel). But then they meet again, by chance, in the lobby of the luxurious Princesse Hotel in Monte Carlo, where he invites her to share the lunch table with him. From their conversation, we learn that her mother had been dead a long time and that her father, who had passed away the previous summer, was a painter of just one single tree, over and over again, as the tree kept changing its appearance. She learns that Maxim has been feeling depressed since the death of his first wife Rebecca, with whom he had lived for the few years of their marriage in his Manderley mansion.

Fig. 16.1 Last night I dreamt I went to Manderley again

Maxim's courting of her has more in common with the attitude of a rather stern father towards his teenage daughter than with the kind of sexually tinged flirting one may expect from an adult man towards a beautiful young woman. However, she is clearly not indifferent to his attentions. We watch Mr. de Winter and the girl spending much time together, enjoy dances in the hotel and go for rides in his car. (The next rides to be found in a Hitchcock's movie, also along the Grand Corniche in the French Riviera, will feature Grace Kelly and Cary Grant; but in that film, *To Catch a Thief* [1955], it will be the lady to be at the wheel of the open car.)

As their relationship intensifies, even if remaining mostly formal and somewhat detached, she sketches a portrait of him, and he asks her to call him by his first name and sends a bunch of roses to her bedroom with a 'Thank you for yesterday' card. He also informs her, quite abruptly, never to wear black satin or pearls. 'Yes, Maxim', she obediently replies—and we can only wonder whether she is aware of his reasons for making such an odd request.

By now, we can easily guess that she is falling in love with him. And he with her? That remains far more doubtful. Then, unexpectedly and in the least romantic possible way, Maxim de Winter offers to marry her and invites her to live in Manderley with him—a proposal given only minutes before what would have been her departure to New York to accompany Mrs. Van Hopper, the loud American gossip for whom she worked as her 'paid companion'.

Even if our girl can already predict that she does not 'belong in his sort of world', she cannot resist his proposal. In a rush, they celebrate a low-key civil wedding at the local Mairie and even forget to collect the marriage papers, a 'parapraxis' that Freud would have described as a telling instance of 'everyday life psychopathology'. Three months later, she will already have to admit that 'my marriage was a failure… We did not get on. We were not companions. We were not suited to one another. I was too young for Maxim, too inexperienced, and, more important still, I was not of his world' (Du Maurier 1938, p. 260) (Fig. 16.2).

They arrive in Manderley in the rain, where the mansion's numerous staff is lined up to greet them. The new (or second) Mrs. de Winter, as we should now refer to her, finds it all most intimidating, especially having to meet Mrs. Danvers, Rebecca's nanny who had moved with her to Manderley at the time of her marriage to Maxim de Winter and who has

Fig. 16.2 Laurence Olivier as Maxim de Winter with Joan Fontaine as his second wife

since become the manor's housekeeper. In Manderley, surrounded by obsequious servants, precious furniture, oil portraits of ancestors and mementoes of the late Mrs. de Winter, our newly-wed girl feels utterly out of her depth—isolated, insecure, inferior, clumsy. Maxim, whom she loves, does nothing to make her feel more at ease; he is often absent and only formally affectionate when with her.

Most of the film, as well as Du Maurier's novel, is set in Manderley, the mansion described as 'secretive and silent' and with 'its perfect symmetries'. It was, as Hitchcock put it, 'one of the three key characters of the picture' (in Truffaut 1983, p. 131). The invisible ghost of Rebecca is another one, absent from the screen but for that very reason a more central character than anybody else, as her memory floats eerily throughout the film, contributing to that sense of *Unheimlich* so vividly described by Freud in his essay on the 'uncanny' (1919). It is then most appropriate that that the movie's—and the novel's—title should be *Rebecca*.

A remarkable feature of the film, and one that gives its audiences a rather unique emotional experience, is the disturbing (and paradoxical) *presence of absence*—what Lacan would have described as *manque*—which seems to characterise a number of only apparently unrelated aspects: the film's title is the first name of a dead woman whom we never see on the screen; its central character is a woman whose name is never mentioned; another important character, Mrs. Danvers, is someone whose identity we know nothing about and whose existence we only notice when she uncannily creeps up in a frame, nor are we offered any clues as to the geographical location of Manderley, other than a passing hint that it may be in Cornwall and our knowledge that Du Maurier's inspiration for this typical Southern England country estate was probably *Menabily* in Fowey, Cornwall, a house she much liked.

All of the above contributes, with its deliberate vagueness, to give *Rebecca* an almost fairytale quality: *Once upon a time, in a magic castle in a far distant land, lived a beautiful princess...* 'All of children's literature is linked to sensations and particularly to fear, [and] anything connected with fear takes us back to childhood', says Truffaut when discussing *Rebecca* with its director (Truffaut 1983, p. 131). We could suggest here that an important function of narrative and cinema (indeed, of all art…) is to represent in an externalised, aesthetically pleasant and sublimated form the 'good' and 'bad' internal objects, the conflicts arising among them and the anxieties they provoke in readers and viewers, thus helping them to tolerate them. Putting spectators in touch with our primitive, infantile fears (as well as with our suppressed desires) is then what Hitchcock's cinema, perhaps *all* cinema, is ultimately about.

The second Mrs. de Winter is only too aware that she is constantly being compared to the deceased first one. 'I suppose you married me', she once tells Maxim with unexpected insight, 'because I was dull, gauche and inexperienced'—implying: by comparison to his first wife. Rebecca's prominently displayed initial, 'R' (an indirect reference, perhaps, to the 'scarlet letter' in Nathaniel Hawthorne's 1850 novel?), can still be found everywhere in the house—embroidered on the cover of a nightdress, a handkerchief, a blanket or a napkin, or printed on a notebook or an address book—and makes our girl feel upset every time she comes across it. At the same time, though, she also becomes curious to find out more about her husband's first wife, especially after she learns from Maxim's agent Frank Crawley (played by Reginald Denny) that Rebecca had died at sea in rather mysterious circumstances and that her body was only recovered and identified by Maxim 2 months after her disappearance.

'What was Rebecca really like?', she once asks Frank. 'I suppose', he answers after some hesitation, 'she was the most beautiful creature I ever saw'. Everyone who had come across her would have probably agreed. We can already guess, though we'll only have it confirmed later in the story, that dark secrets were concealed under such beauty.

A psychoanalytically interesting concept relevant here is that of the 'replacement child'. This term refers to a child conceived in order to replace another one who had recently died as a way for the parents to avoid properly mourning their tragic loss. Such replacement children often grow to become unhappy and insecure adults, having been expected to live up to the idealised image of their dead sibling, to a sort of ghost with whom they are constantly being compared (Sabbadini 2014a, pp. 13–30). In our film, of course, we have in Joan Fontaine's character a 'replacement wife' rather than a replacement child, but the processes involved are clearly similar. What she says about Rebecca ('I feel at such a disadvantage. All the time whenever I meet anyone… I know they are all thinking the same thing, they're all comparing me with her') is identical to what a replacement child could say about her dead sister.

The second Mrs. de Winter decides to explore Rebecca's own private and grandiose bedroom overlooking the sea and secluded in the west wing of Manderley—a reference perhaps to the forbidden and dangerous room in the story of Bluebeard's castle. Mrs. Danvers follows her there and, as she had already done several times before, takes this opportunity to scare her new employer by creeping up on her. On this occasion, she humiliates Mrs. de Winter by sadistically inviting her to admire wardrobes full of Rebecca's beautiful clothes and furs and underwear in order to provoke the girl's sense of inferiority and presumed envy.

We may speculate that Mrs. Danvers' extreme closeness (in her mind, if not also in reality) to Rebecca when she was still alive must have been built partly around the fantasy of an idealised mother-daughter relationship and partly as a perverse identification of this old, unpleasant and bitter servant with her young, elegant and successful mistress. The film and the novel offer us no information about Mrs. Danvers' past, but we may speculate that such an identification with a maternal figure (the beautiful, late Mrs. de Winter) may be rooted in some earlier experiences, probably dating back from childhood. In particular, these would include the primitive, oedipal fantasy of being allowed the same intimate closeness to her 'father' (Mr de Winter) as the one to which the object of her identification (Mrs De Winter) had access. We can guess that Mrs. Danvers was most likely secretly in love not only homoerotically with her but also with him. Significant in this regard is that she must be (or at least have been) married, as she is always referred to as 'Mrs' Danvers, though no indication is ever given as to the identity, or indeed existence, of her husband. We may furthermore suggest that the second Mrs. de Winter, as well as a 'replacement wife' to Maxim was also a 'replacement daughter' to Mrs. Danvers after the loss of Rebecca—the first, beloved child in her care.

After Rebecca's mysterious disappearance, Mrs. Danvers' uninterrupted attachment to her memory displays clear morbid features, including fetishistic ones for all the objects, clothes, etc. that had belonged to her late employer. Such perversities will then be enacted in Mrs. Danvers' relationship to the second Mrs. de Winter, constantly if not explicitly blamed for not being her predecessor (Fig. 16.3).

Here, we can also identify Mrs. Danvers' unconsciously motivated sadistic attempts to magically bring back to life her first mistress (and 'daughter') by killing off her second, and to her mind inadequate, one. As we shall see, she will try do so in reality (twice, though both times without success) and not just in her imagination. Children who have lost their mother may also fantasise, or even attempt to kill their father's new partner with the same unconscious intent—a situation well portrayed in Carlos Saura's film *Cría Cuervos* (1976) (see Sabbadini 2014b, pp. 44–47).

We can also observe here an unexpected, but perhaps not so unusual, reversal of roles, whereby the new lady of the manor is at the mercy of and must obey her own employee, rather than the other way around. A similar famous filmic instance of such a perverse relationship can be found in Joseph Losey's *The Servant* (1963) where, however, the homosexual theme plays a central role. Of course, such a component also cannot be ruled out in the case of our movie: as noted above, it would be reasonable to suggest that Mrs. Danvers' pathological attachment to Rebecca and, as its (il)logical consequence, her irrational hatred for the second Mrs. de Winter for not being the first one may have clear homosexual connotations.

At one point in the story, perhaps in an attempt to emerge from her own isolation and depression and to make an affirmative gesture at long last, the second Mrs. de Winter decides to organise a costume ball, as Rebecca used to do with much success every year. She wears for that occasion, as a surprise for her husband, a gown shrewdly recommended by Mrs. Danvers. But when Maxim sees her in that outfit, he becomes furiously angry: years before Rebecca herself must have worn that same costume for him and for reasons we spectators may not yet fully understand, he cannot tolerate being reminded of her. (Incidentally, this episode might have been the inspiration for a similar one in Paul Thomas Anderson's *Phantom Thread* [2017]—a film also centred on an oddly-assorted couple.) 'I shall never forget,' Mrs. de Winter will later recall, 'the expression on [Mrs Danvers'] face, loathsome, triumphant. The face of an exulting devil. She stood there, smiling at me (Du Maurier 1938, p. 240). Mystified, remorseful and feeling very upset, our heroine barely manages to resist Mrs. Danvers' attempts to convince her to jump from a balcony to her death.

Fig. 16.3 Joan Fontaine as Mrs. de Winter with Judith Anderson as Mrs. Danvers

The story ends with a series of dramatic, somewhat implausible (but does it matter?) twists. In this case however, unlike in other Hitchcock's films, the plot with its suspenseful elements remains less interesting than the psychological characterisation and emotional vicissitudes of its protagonists. Events precipitate when a boat is found by a diver at the bottom of the sea, with Rebecca's corpse in it: 'I put her there', Maxim confesses to his second wife. The drowned girl he had identified as Rebecca 2 months after her disappearance from the beach, thus diverting investigations that may have led to the truth, was, as he well knew, someone else.

Mrs. de Winter tries to comfort her confused, guilty but unrepented husband, to convince him not to reveal the truth about Rebecca's death, and that believing in her love for him would be enough to see him through his predicament. But, 'It's too late, my darling', Maxim says, 'Rebecca has won… Her shadow has been between us all the time, keeping us from one another'. *Her shadow*: in his paper on *Mourning and Melancholia* (1917), Freud uses this metaphor to refer to the shadow of someone who has died falling upon those closer to him or her, with powerful consequences on their current grief experience. In the case of *Rebecca*, her shadow seems to fall on everyone at Manderley and indeed on the mansion itself. Most affected by it are two women: Mrs. Danvers, Rebecca's housekeeper who, as we have seen, had developed such a morbid attachment to her former mistress, and the second Mrs. de Winter who, under the spell of the memories left behind by Rebecca, seems unable to assert her identity other than by trying, and inevitably failing, to identify with her predecessor.

'I hated Rebecca!', Maxim de Winter confesses. His wife is shocked by this revelation, convinced, as we spectators and readers were, that he was in love with her. 'She had the three things that matter', Maxim explains, 'Breeding, Brains and Beauty, but… she was incapable of love, or tenderness, or decency… Our marriage was a rotten fraud'.

He goes on to recount that when he realised that Rebecca had many lovers and had spitefully told him that she was pregnant from one of them, Maxim, blinded by jealous rage, had lost his mind and struck her. Rebecca stumbled, hit her head on a heavy piece of tackle and died. Then, in a state of controlled panic, he had locked her body inside the cabin of her sailing boat, drilled holes in the plank from the inside and made the boat sink to the bottom of the sea. It was there that a diver now found her, something that Maxim had feared every day and night ever since: after a crime, even an apparently 'perfect', that is, undetectable, one, nobody (with the exception of some extreme psychopaths) can escape the persecutory voice of one's own superego. It is sometimes claimed that one of the closest relationships among human beings is that of a murderer to his victim…

Enter slimy Jack Favell, a seductive master in the art of sliding intrusively into people's personal lives: into Maxim's marriage having been Rebecca's favourite cousin, as well as one of her lovers; into the second Mrs. de Winter by climbing into Manderley from an open window when her husband was away; into Maxim's car, where Favell now tries to blackmail him by threatening to reveal the truth about the circumstances of Rebecca's disappearance while helping himself, uninvited, to their lunch.

A Coroner's inquest follows. The avuncular Chief Constable (played by Nigel Bruce) cannot believe that such a charming gentleman as Maxim de Winter could also be an uxoricide—even when all the evidence points in that direction. The improbable theory is then allowed to emerge that Rebecca may have committed suicide by locking herself inside her boat and making it sink, a theory made somewhat more credible after Dr. Baker, her physician in London, reveals that she was not pregnant after all, but affected by terminal cancer and 'therefore' would have wanted to drown herself. The simplistic solution presented by the film is that if Rebecca was pregnant then Maxim had a valid reason to murder her, but if she had cancer, then she must have killed herself. The truth, rather, seems to be that yes she was affected by cancer but that Maxim had murdered her—or at least was the direct cause of her death and guilty of concealing the evidence—because he was convinced that she was pregnant.

Maxim, we are told, was only responsible for Rebecca's death, but if he had intentionally murdered her and got away with it scot free, the Hollywood code of ethics would not have permitted Hitchcock's film to be released. Literature, however, did not have the same moralistic limitations as cinema: in the novel, the cause of Rebecca's death is unambiguous: 'When I killed her she was smiling still. I fired at her heart', as Maxim confesses to his second wife, 'The bullet passed right through' (Du Maurier 1938, p. 313). This is murder, not manslaughter.

In a kind of Gothic-horror finale, we are shown from some distance Mrs. Danvers eerily walking with a candlestick behind the glass windows of Manderley and setting the whole place on fire. The second Mrs. de Winter miraculously survives; we feel relieved to watch her running in tears to hug her worried husband as he arrives by car at night to his burning mansion. The one to die will be the despicable arsonist herself: perhaps, Mrs. Danvers was trapped by the flames, but it is more likely that she had remained inside Manderley quite deliberately.

Further considerations

The theme of suicide emerges as a recurrent one in the film's narrative. Let us remind ourselves that the second Mrs. de Winter had first met her future husband at the very moment when he was ready to jump to his death from a high cliff; that Mrs. Danvers had almost succeeded in convincing her second mistress, at a time when she was much distressed, to throw herself from a balcony; that Rebecca had drowned herself (or so it was falsely alleged) after being diagnosed with a terminal condition; and that Mrs. Danvers may have chosen to burn herself to death inside the mansion she had set fire to.

The melodramatic destruction of Manderley may leave some spectators upset for the loss of such an imposing, beautiful manor with all the precious objects and memories it had contained. However, such fire, loaded with powerful, primitive, unconscious associations, also has a cathartic effect, opening up the potential for a happier relationship between the two protagonists by liberating them from the curse of a past dominated by the shadow of Rebecca. Indeed, the counterpart to the deceptive impression we have as spectators of the happy, if brief, married life between Maxim and Rebecca, is the belief that his second marriage was doomed to be an unhappy one—when in fact the new Mrs. de Winter's 'love' for him, as well as the destruction of the mansion and of its evil housekeeper, may give us a glimmer of redemptive hope.

…and they lived happily ever after? Hollywood has never resisted the temptation to present its audiences with a fairy-tale ending.

Film Details

Original title	Rebecca
Release year	1940
Country	USA
Book	Philip MacDonald, Michael Hogan, based on the novel by Daphne du Maurier
Direction	Alfred Hitchcock
Music	Franz Waxman
Camera	George Barnes
Main actors	Joan Fontaine, Laurence Olivier, Judith Anderson, George Sanders
Availability	DVD

References

Du Maurier D (1938) *Rebecca*. Virago Press, 2015, London

Freud S (1917) Mourning and melancholia. In: *Standard Edition*, vol 14. Hogarth Press, 1957, London

Freud S (1919) The 'uncanny'. In: *Standard Edition*, vol 17. Hogarth Press, 1955, London

Sabbadini A (2014a) Boundaries and bridges. Perspectives on time and space in psychoanalysis. Karnac, London

Sabbadini A (2014b) Moving Images. In: Psychoanalytic reflections on film. Routledge, Hove and New York

Thomson D (2008) Have You Seen…? Penguin Books, London

Truffaut F (1983) Hitchcock. Simon and Schuster, New York

Wood R (1989) Hitchcock's films revisited. Faber and Faber, London and Boston

Women's Truth Witness for the Prosecution, US 1958

17

Eva Friedrich

Introduction

Crimes and misdemeanours are social facts that transcend society and time. They are regulated by a legal system that has developed and changed in different cultures and religions. As sensation-seekers, we follow stories about them with a pleasant shudder of fear; there is something appealing about them. Evil is far more attractive than good.

The attractive Christine (Marlene Dietrich) in *Witness for the Prosecution* is an enigmatic woman. Together with four other protagonists, she represents a female perspective in a film about basic values such as truth, law, justice, desires and love. In Billy Wilder's timeless and suspenseful work, the screenplay and camerawork may be firmly in male hands, and the masculine sometimes pushes itself to the fore, but the two sexes relate to each other and want something from each other.

Film Plot

The story begins in a venerable British courtroom, which is also where the film will spectacularly end. After the solemn procession into the high court, accompanied by triumphant music (Matty Malnek), the scene changes: we see the famous defence lawyer Sir Wilfried Robarts (played phenomenally by Charles Laughton) returning to his office after a heart attack; he is taking on another difficult murder case, against medical advice. A great deal of evidence points to the naïve suspect, Leonard Vole (Tyron Powell), an unsuccessful inventor who is alleged to have murdered the wealthy widow Mrs. French. She has

E. Friedrich (✉)
Munich, Germany

V. Pramataroff-Hamburger, A. Hamburger (eds.), *From La Strada to The Hours*,
https://doi.org/10.1007/978-3-662-68789-5_17

bequeathed him her fortune, a fact that weighs heavily against him. However, Sir Wilfried has a legendary test to decide the guilt or otherwise of the accused: he uses his monocle as a kind of lie detector to dazzle his counterpart, in this case deducing from his reaction that he is innocent. Vole protests his innocence and cites his wife as an alibi for the time of the crime, whom he had met and married in occupied and bombed-out Hamburg after the war. Her first appearance in chambers is impressive. Contrary to expectations, she seems calm and collected, on the one hand seeking help for her husband and on the other hand incriminating him with her behaviour and her cynical statements. Sir Wilfried, despite worrying doubts, nevertheless believes the accused and defends him superbly, skilfully casting aspersions on the supervision of his nurse Miss Plimsoll (Elsa Lanchester). He blocks the prosecutor with subtle objections and makes the prosecution witnesses out to be untrustworthy. He waives his right to the wife's testimony—but the public prosecutor summons her to the witness stand, because he is also aware that her marriage is invalid, as she was already married in Germany. In court, she testifies against her husband under oath and accuses him of murder. Sir Wilfried is shocked and tries to discredit her as a cunning, cold liar. Nevertheless, he is under threat of a death sentence. Before the last day of the trial, however, a disreputable stranger slips the star lawyer letters from the wife to her lover Max that reveal a plan to get rid of Leonard Vole by falsely testifying. With this turn of events, the prosecution witness is completely discredited, and the verdict is now an acquittal. Christine, threatened by the outraged crowd outside, takes refuge in the courtroom and reveals to the speechless defence lawyer that he did not 'win' the case alone: She herself was the woman who suddenly appeared, she herself wrote the letters and she got the star lawyer to save the man she loves and knew to be guilty by 'exposing' her truthful testimony as a diabolical plan. When Leonard then also arrives to thank his defender, Christine—and also the audience—learns that he has a younger girlfriend who taunts her because he no longer wants to have anything to do with her.

Christine, however, does not want to let him go. When he menacingly says that she could be charged with accessory to murder whereas he is now free, her gaze falls on the knife still lying ready as evidence. She picks it up it and stabs him. Sir Wilfried, impressed by the charisma of the loving woman, decides to defend her. His strict nurse agrees.

Background

Producer Edward Small had bought the film rights to Agatha Christie's successful play (first performed in London in 1953, based on a 1925 short story of the same name) for the unbelievably high sum of $430,000 and given them to Billy Wilder for realisation. He thought Christie was a 'good constructor but a weak dialogue writer'; he rewrote the script in crucial places, and the success of the film proved him right: it received six Oscar nominations and is still considered to be one of the best courtroom dramas ever (along with, among others, *12 Angry Men* [1957], *Judgement at Nuremberg* [1961], *Inherit the Wind* [1960] and *Rashomon* [1950]). Billy Wilder preferred black-and-white films, and almost all of his successful films were shot in this format. His camera angles (Russel Harlan) are calm and uncomplicated, and we viewers follow this gaze without distraction. The music (Matty Malneck) accentuates as an accompaniment, never imposing in an emotionally distracting way. His spirited actions against a serious background follow three principles: *'Whom is it for? – Do I like it? – I never go with the wave'!* His films typically have a tight plot and silent scenes in which the eyes, facial expressions and body are highly expressive—for example, in the scene when Leonard Vole discovers the widow Mrs. French buying a hat and becomes her flirtatious fashion advisor through the shop window, or the eye contact between Christine and Sir Wilfried when she is taken away as her husband's murderer. For example, his catchy dialogues allow us to participate in long courtroom interrogations without fatigue or loss of tension; he also expresses himself in sophisticated symbolic language and his viable, deep themes come to us with wit, elegance and tenderness. He shows people from everyday life with whom we can identify, which is a large part of the effect of his films. The film plot is structured like a play (the theatre and a courtroom have certain similarities): In the third act, the protagonists have to make a moral decision. We shall return to this later.

Billy Wilder is a byword for light, entertaining films with a background, such as *Some Like It Hot* with Marylin Monroe in 1959 or *Sabrina* with Audrey Hepburn 1954. Nevertheless, he often saw himself as a serious, sometimes cynical, and occasionally sarcastic chronicler of American society. Politics is rarely in the foreground (except in *A Foreign Affair*, 1948). However, his films are always profoundly political or socially critical. This is not surprising in view of his biography. Billy Wilder was born in Galicia in 1906, moved to Vienna at the age of ten, later working as an editor at *Stunde*, a gazette with an aggressive journalistic style and known to have engaged in blackmail, which he left to take up a screenwriting career in Berlin. In 1933, he fled Nazi persecution to Paris and from there emigrated to North America a year later. He initially became renowned in the United States for his successful screenwriting (e.g. for *Ninotschka*, 1939, by Ernst Lubitsch). He later also became a director to ensure his screenplays were realised properly. In 1945, he was commissioned by the US Signal Corps to make the documentary *Death Mills* from footage of the American and British military. Cameron Crowe writes about this in his book *Conversation with Mr Wilder* (2019, p. 71):

Crowe: *You've never really discussed* death Mills, *the documentary you made after the war. What specific memories do you have of the experience?*

Wilder: *I didn't make it. I just cut it. It was filmed in the concentration camps, the day after the troops came in. All of it*

Crowe: *Some people have written that you directed it*

Wilder: *There was nothing to direct. ... There was that one shot that I really loved, a shot that they took in a concentration camp, Dachau, I guess. There was a field of corpses, a field, and one corpse was not quite dead. And he looked and he saw the camera, did not know what it was, and he walked to the corpses, on the top of the corpses, and sat down on the dead corpses, and stared at us. That was the shot. That was the shot and I used the whole shot. After that I was kind of very eager to do something on the more frivolous side and made* the emperor waltz

His professional coldness and distance are initially shocking and however are understandable as a (protective) reaction to the unfathomable circumstances. His mother and stepfather had been gassed in the Bergen-Belsen concentration camp shortly before. He wanted to free himself of this heavy burden and move into a more lively sphere.

From Criticism of Justice to the Human Dilemma

Like the key figure in the courtroom drama, the British author is a woman and a special one at that: Dame Agatha Christie (1890–1976) is the Queen of Crime; her life and behaviour were very turbulent, but she was strong, confident, determined, very successful and way ahead of her time.

There is also something of her in the protagonist Christine. In the novel, she used the courtroom as a stage for her criticism of the justice system of the time, the difficulty of arriving at truth and justice, but particularly the vanity of lawyers who were primarily concerned with self-promotion.

Billy Wilder, male and Austrian, furthermore uses the courtroom drama to depict a human dilemma: Sensations, urges and passions prevent easy access to the truth. Whether something is right or wrong is primarily determined by perception, by the narrative and how this is received.

Wilder has his male protagonist becoming weaker, in contrast to the original; Sir Wilfried, a formerly strong, successful man, is now old and seriously ill, in need of care and maternal supervision by the likewise additional character, the nurse Miss Plimsoll. He is reluctant to be replaced by another lawyer, but then he takes on the Vole murder case and regains his former strength through the follow-up trial. In 1957, after the Second World War, the weakening of masculinity was an issue to a different extent than it had been in 1924 and reflects a changed social environment. In this context, it is noteworthy that in Agatha Christie's version Mrs. Vole was French, whereas in Billy Wilder's, she is a despised German. Of course, she is not only portrayed as a member of the perpetrator nation but also as a victim of British bombing raids on her hometown of Hamburg. Both the weakening of the man and the ambivalence of the woman will play a role for psychoanalytic consideration.

A Look at Femininity in Film

Billy Wilder's enthusiasm for Charles Laughton is very evident in the film, so the portrait of women he draws gets a little less space and is partially obscured by the male presence (at the beginning, only men populate Sir Wilfried's law office and the court is also predominantly male). This distribution still has social relevance today and played a particularly large role in Hollywood films; the male gaze conveys the values and shapes the coveted female object according to its image and desires.

Christine Vole is the central female figure in this regard, contrasted with the nurse Miss Plimsoll, the murder victim Mrs. French, the housekeeper Janet McKenzie and the mistress Diana. All of them, men and women alike, are caught up in lies, injury and revenge.

A Film About Lying

'There is a great difference between affirming lies out of painful pessimism and bitter irony, out of spirit, and affirming lies out of hatred for the spirit of truth' said Thomas Mann (1974) in his commemorative speech on the occasion of Sigmund Freud's 80th birthday.

When a crime has been committed, justice and truth are usually located in the courtroom. However, this is where the film shows us how manipulatively the truth and truthfulness can be handled and the harm that arises out of deception and lies. Almost all the protagonists lie and deceive, which, psychologically speaking, presupposes a certain degree of empathy or mentalisation: You have to sense the other person's emotional state and reactions, recognise and anticipate them in order to insert a successful lie and thoughtfully follow it through. The protagonists demonstrate this in a variety of ways.

Sir Wilfried is introduced as a master and connoisseur of deception. He deceives his doctors and especially his nurse Miss Plimsoll (Elsa Lanchester) by hiding cigars in his walking stick, and brandy—although she quickly sees through this cat-and-mouse game. He is also a master at misleading witnesses in court. And yet he allows himself to be deceived and lied to by the elusive Christine, which is the decisive crux of the film. We shall see why later.

Leonard Vole also lies and deceives, however not brilliantly like Sir Wilfried, but for base motives: either to obtain money or, as is to be expected of a murderer, to protect himself from prosecution—after all, if he is convicted, he can expect to die under the British legal system.[1]

But the accused is dependent on Christine in denying the murder and deceiving those around him. The fact that he is so certain in his assessment of his intellectually superior wife, especially her blind love for him, also endows him with a large—albeit strongly egoistical—capacity for empathy. When he says, 'I need Christine', it is both lie and truth (and therein lies the dilemma).

Vole incriminates himself while claiming his innocence, and this itself removes suspicion from him, not only that of the lawyers. When he resists Sir Wilfried's aforementioned monocle test, at first, we believe him as well, because the monocle is a superb and piercing lie detector eye standing in for the camera that directs our gaze. Vole embodies the kind of confidence trickster who comes across to us as charming, trustworthy, highly seductive

[1] Neither the novel nor the film is critical of the death penalty. It is presented as an appropriate state-regulated punishment for murder, bindingly regulating primitive acts of revenge such as vigilante justice or blood feuds. Agatha Christie was an advocate of the death penalty.

and deceptive, regardless of gender. Such swindlers perhaps serve a hidden desire and the illusory promise of fulfilling it (to admire women, to ally with men against women), and it is not only the women in the film who seem susceptible to this.

But women are not only victims of male deception, they have reasons for hearing the truth they wish to hear. Miss Plimsoll, for example, is a horrible, controlling mother, and as such, her boss tricks her with relish—admittedly not long term. She is clever and admires him. Perhaps, for this very reason, she initially allows herself to be deceived in her assessment of the truth, adopting his gaze. In addition, the rivalry that causes her to direct her own spiteful feelings towards the other woman obscures her xenophobic gaze. But when she calls for a ban on the import of foreign women (00:32:52) so as not to endanger her own market, she also reveals her own desire as a woman.

Mrs. French's flirtation with Leonard Vole reawakens her femininity, and she allows herself to be deceived for the illusion of love. However, what she has to give is not eroticism and sex, but rather a motherly attitude with excessive oral and material pampering; her deception is deadly. Her scrawny housekeeper Miss McKenzie, a 'daughterly character' (Rohde-Dachser 1990), is cheated out of the promised inheritance despite her refreshing self-confidence. She is not exactly her mother'/employer's one and only; as soon as a man enters the stage, she is no longer given priority. In the courtroom she is subjected to Sir Wilfried's interrogation skills.

In contrast to the deceived women, Christine is portrayed as a female master of sophisticated deception. She takes Sir Wilfried's distrust of loving wives and Germans into account, and this leads to the game of lying, which he falls for as expected*: '.... that gave me the idea that I had to testify not in favour of my husband but for the prosecution. I have to swear that Leonard is guilty and then you have to prove that I'm a habitual liar so the court will believe Leonard is innocent' (01:49:40).*

Christine does not fit the cliché of the weak, hysterical woman. Everything about her seems to be controlled, perfect; she is an 'apparition' with her timelessly elegant suit, her coiffed hair and her little hat (Fig. 17.1).

At first, this makes the irritated star lawyer and us viewers suspicious. After all, she already lied at the wedding, didn't she? If she comes across to him *'like a she-devil' (00:38:11)* because he is annoyed that he can't see through her game, then she should also come across that way to the audience. The woman, a witch who, with her disciplined, self-assured appearance, plays the men. This earns the sympathy of certain viewers who identify (Fig. 17.1) with strong women but also arouses the hostility of others. The highlight is her testimony in the courtroom, where *she* draws all the aversions towards her and away from the perpetrator. The resolution of the intrigue in the third act raises the question in the viewer's mind—all the more so in the female viewer's—as to whether she is not ultimately only conforming to the cliché of the self-sacrificing loving woman, whether the film is not once more turning a male gaze on women, attributing masochistic traits to them.

Or is there something else at play?

Fig. 17.1 The witness testimony (00:30:59)

Is the Camera Lying, Too?

It is striking that all four flashbacks in the film reflect Leonard Vole's subjective memory and are thus seductive: both in the first flashback, his encounter with Christine in Hamburg, where he seems to be a saviour and she is rather calculating, and in the three scenes with his later victim Mrs. French, in which, however, he does not appear to the viewer to be a naïvely affectionate boy, but a deliberate and calculating seducer. In this respect, the camera seems to know more than Vole wants us and his lawyers to know. We could also justifiably ask whether the flashback from Hamburg is an accurate depiction of Christine as the calculating party, or whether this is also seen from Leonard's perspective. He acts out in reality what the flashback insinuates that she has done: He himself is calculating in his flirtation with the rich Mrs. French to escape his role as a professional failure. Nevertheless, the camera cannot necessarily be considered to be sincere—because in each case it shows the version that we as viewers prefer to be offered, as it corresponds to our previous perception of the characters: the cold Christine as a calculating woman, the devious Leonard as a gigolo, even if he wants to portray himself differently.

A Film About Injury

What is the motivation for lying? Injuries and the desire to portray oneself in a different light.

Sir Wilfried's specific injury is one inherent in life. Age and illness confront him with his finite nature; he is torn between rebellion, denial and realistic acceptance. Charles Laughton plays his role with charisma and draws all sympathy and gazes to himself. He initially wins us over with his witty intensity, clever questions; his abovementioned penetrating monocle-camera-eye, with which he almost magically wants to find out the truth; with his libidinousness; and his magnificent hubris. All this makes him so 'human' for the viewer, and we understand, on a person-analytical level, that he does not want to give everything up so easily. Concerns are pushed aside for a few phallic cigars, which his younger colleague has and for the passion that he no longer has but which the suspect does have. He had already identified him as a potential murderer because of his criminal instinct *('the alert instinct of the shrewd criminal', 00:12:17)*, but his desire for life is stronger. The once potent, successful father figure is fragile, damaged—not only by a heart attack, but by the narcissistic wound of ageing and mortality. However, in this decisive scene in which he accepts the case, he begins to restore his inner man. Not without first—rather like a defiant adolescent—ganging up with men against women.

In contrast, the nurse is a rather frightening, dominant-providing mother figure who instils fear in everyone and who in turn wants to keep her victim, the man, in childlike dependency. Sir Wilfried is ambivalent and seems to put up with this treatment, not entirely reluctantly: *'Take me, I am all yours' (00:30.19).*

The film stages the relationship between the two as a power struggle with anal features, in which Sir Wilfried represents the defiant, rebellious child. He defies the disempowering, castrating Miss Plimsoll with his trenchant, dominant way of speaking, in which he always has the last word and the most apt punch line: his vanity is thereby obvious. He protests, at least. We as viewers can easily identify with this mortification and perfectly understand why he rebels when toys such as drinks and cigars are taken away, and instead, he is supposed to be dressed in a ridiculous romper suit. This rebelliousness is reminiscent of the defiance phase and adolescence or also of the regression caused by ageing and becoming weak.

When Sir Wilfried describes the hypothetical murder of the nurse and then hires himself as the 'best lawyer,' the theme of the struggle against a mother figure is invoked on a playful level, which is more clearly reflected in the central crime in this courtroom drama: matricide. In 'Hansel and Gretel', the Grimm's fairy tale, the witch's mother is burnt in the oven so that the children can be freed from their dependency. The wealth they take home is not a material treasure, but an inner one. It is a symbolic murder that forms part of adolescent development, of detachment. In contrast, Leonard Vole represents another variant on detachment from the mother: actual murder, which does not liberate but binds.

Mrs. French is the personification of a woman well suited to matricide when she is paired with the appropriate 'mama's boy'. His greed for infinite pampering and her motherly, irresistible way of granting him his every wish, in other words her maternal rather than feminine, erotic qualities, combine to create a confusion between outer and inner wealth.

Leonard Vole, on the other hand, represents the type of man who, as a womaniser, corresponds to female desires. How does this come about? Only when in a paternal-governmental uniform does he have anything to offer in terms of provision, but even as a conqueror (in the Hamburg scene), he gets hurt in bed and needs to be consoled by a woman. He is a deadbeat son who sees women as mothers to whom he must make himself promiscuously unattainable. We women fight in vain for such men, as if fighting and not fulfilment were the goal. His wound is immaturity, arrested development (which corresponds to death).

In this context, the female figure can be seen as compensating for the men's injury, both in her strength and in her own vulnerability. Christine represents the female *victims of* the war and must please men in order to survive. This assertion could also be considered generally true when women are perceived as being dependent on men. After all, according to Genesis did they not arise from a man's rib and exist only to please him? The scene in the Hamburg bar—an allusion to Marlene Dietrich's real-life singing performances for American soldiers during the war—shows her provocatively not fulfilling her audience's expectations of bare skin and long legs. She remains proud but is also hurt as she looks around on the floor for her destroyed harmonica (an apt metaphor for her injury). In England, she is competitively antagonised as a foreigner and a woman (e.g. by Miss Plimsoll), or patronised: *'We also let the Japanese and deaf-mutes have their say, ... as long as they tell the truth' (Sir Wilfried, 00:35:38).* The protagonist is hurt above all by failed love. In the humiliated and exploited role, her love turns into disappointed rage and revenge.

A Film About Revenge

The injury portrayed by the characters is mirrored at a political level. *Witness for the Prosecution* is a post-war film. The Germans have badly harmed England. In return, the British, together with the Americans, took terrible revenge for the atrocities, bombing German cities. Both the perpetrator and victim are injured parties. But they are also saviours: Through bombing, the perpetrators build an airlift (as the USSR closes off access), thus saving Berlin. Reconciliation is a way to escape the spiral of revenge, which would otherwise continue.

First of all, injustice, slights and humiliations create the need for restoration of a fair balance, for wreaking revenge and restoring justice. The film deals precisely with this polarity of revenge and justice.

The two male protagonists take revenge on the 'mothers' in quite different ways. One in adolescent denigration and a pleasurable matricidal fantasy and the other with the murderous act in order to get at her envied gifts. He is still tied to his mother's apron strings, and as such is not man enough to be rich on the inside as well as successful on the outside. He resolves his fear of mother-wives through promiscuity and his inner poverty and dependence by committing murder.

Women play a corresponding role. Christine is the central figure of the personally, socially and politically motivated revenge spiral. Negative feelings are projected onto her as a woman, as a strong woman, as a foreigner, especially as a German, and she inwardly fights against these projections. Her perpetrator-victim development is portrayed from the very beginning and reinforced by her manipulative game of deft and witty twists.

She is introduced at the outset as *'a she-devil' (00:38:17)*, in the book as a 'thoroughly vindictive woman', a very dangerous woman (Christie 1948, p. 15). The revenge motif is thus brought into play early on and more clearly still in the novel when, anticipating the end of the plot, Sir Wilfried says: 'women were the devil when they get their knife into you' (ibid., p. 15).

Her talent for intrigue is particularly splendid given her nationality. She has escaped hunger and deprivation in her country and perhaps also persecution. The clear depiction of the destruction of Hamburg could be interpreted as a cipher for the revenge that England exacted by bombing German cities. Then, at this point, the film would represent a spiral of revenge, the precursor to law.

Acts of revenge take place at different levels within the plot. The revenge plot told by the disguised Christine in the bar is a complex distortion: She explains her game with the letters of proof as revenge for an injury she allegedly suffered twice and shows her disfigured face as proof. On the one hand, this bears the symbolic scar representing the English bombing of her country, and on the other, it is a metaphor that anticipates the subsequent loss of face she experiences after the verdict. There she realises that she herself is the victim of her stupid husband's intrigue. The betrayed now really becomes the avenger, not in symbolic mode with letters, but with the knife. She moves from sophisticated fictional narrative to action, drawing the audience along with her to the point where we accept revenge killing as right (overhastily, of course, because if all unfaithful men were to fall victim to revenge, things would not look good for women).

Further Reflections on Film Effects and Femininity

The aim here is to examine how this complex play of femininity and masculinity, lies, injury and revenge is presented to the audience and what affective effect it has.

The witness who is supposed to testify for or against a man is a portrayal of a strong woman who triggers a changing array of emotions: dislike, admiration and doubt. A powerful and confusing effect results from the irony that pervades the drama. Children do not understand irony, and they take adults' statements literally. After a certain age, we are able to understand irony and to infer the actual statement/truth behind it from tone of voice, assessment of the situation and reflection, but this ability may be limited for various reasons. Then we are taken in and become annoyed—to what extent will depend on us as individuals. Billy Wilder succeeds brilliantly in drawing us into the action so that, like Sir Wilfried, we are taken in and see Christine as a witch. When she then reveals her web of truths and lies in the third act, not only her truth is remarkable *('Sir Wilfried, you don't understand, I knew he was guilty'; 01:51:08)* but also her motive: *'Again, you don't understand, I love him' (1:51:22)*. It is about love, which is stronger than any reason or morality. If our hearts go out to her at this point, if we feel admiration and understanding, then the film has brought us to the point that we agree with her deadly revenge.

The fundamental conflict that the film is expressing in this scene goes beyond the courtroom drama. It shows how manipulable the legal system is due to the manipulability of human beings: our correct and logical thinking rests on an uncontrollable unconscious. Ultimately, it is the passionate woman who emerges victorious from the film, whose impulsive act meets with our approval, in the face of whom the (male) legal system becomes meaningless (cf. Hamburger 2018, p. 131 f.).

Of course, this is not entirely true. She may have restored a sense of justice with her act, but injustice has nevertheless occurred in the process, and Christine has become a perpetrator. The strong, impressive woman comes closer to being the early powerful mother and arouses her threatening aspects. The mother not only has the power to give life but also to take it away. In the film narrative, Christine has saved Vole, that is, gave him life, but when he doesn't do what she wants, she takes it away from him again. Successful integration of the dangerousness of women into an ambivalent image that is positive overall can only occur in the case of mature development that enables detachment from dependence on mothers. Leonard Vole is not a mature man; however, Christine does love this highly unsuitable object. Is this meant to address the masochistic willingness of women to want to save such men? Does Christine then only correspond to the cliché of the self-sacrificing, loving woman from a male perspective?

The scene could elicit not only sympathy for the deceived but also anger at her unflinching naivety, depending on the audience's personal experience. For me, compassion prevailed and with it an understanding that she cannot tolerate his betrayal.

The other example of a weak man is Sir Wilfried: weak as a representative of the war generation, weakened by age and vanity. He meets the two women, Christine and Miss Plimsoll, each strong in their own way. To Christine, he owes his return to manhood (when she entices him to take the case), his aberrations and also his success in the trial. But Billy Wilder can't quite leave the image of Christine, the strong woman, as it stands. Apart from the injuries already described in the bar and in the fictional injury by a man, he portrays her gaze as being directed by the man. Figuratively, in the final scene, the reflection through Sir Wilfried's monocle falls on the knife and directs her and the spectator's gaze towards it, as if, as the guiding spirit, he delegates to her the act he must perform to restore his professional ethos as a man of law. This allows him to maintain his innocent strength, and the woman who now needs him restores him in his role as a strong man. This is the subject of the silent look that Christine gives *'to the master of hopeless cases' (0:31:52)* as she is taken away. In Agatha Christie's version, the narrative ended with Christine looking at the empty judge's chair and confessing that she is 'guilty, my lord'.

Another facet of strong womanhood is embodied in Miss Plimsoll. Initially, as described, she is the dominant, castrating and rivalling mother and is treated as such by Sir Wilfried. But she undergoes a development parallel to that of Sir Wilfried; wifely structures soon become apparent and evince an affectionate, somewhat ironic admiration. The 'we' she now mentions is an offer of a common struggle, for which she hands him the insignia of office, the wig, as well as the 'weapon', his whisky in the cocoa bottle (pure

Fig. 17.2 The presentation of the wig (01:55:12)

irony!) (Fig. 17.2). They move away as a couple. In this, the film is alluding to the fact that, outside the film world, the two have been living together for 33 years and have appeared together in 11 films.

Symbolically speaking, Mrs. French, who keeps the man down not through dominance but through over-indulgence and falls victim to 'matricide', has a non-detached, well-behaved daughter, Janet McKenzie, who does not develop any mature femininity. In the dyadic relationship, she is completely devoted to her mother and hopes to get everything from her. But the moment a man comes along, she loses her exclusive position—and the inheritance.

The other daughter figure is Diana, the delinquent's lover, who ruthlessly competes with the mother, ultimately failing to win because the mother archaically prevents this by executing the man.

Billy Wilder gave the emancipatory approach of a strong, independent femininity, the image of the woman expressing her own desire, a loophole for the customs and common clichés of the time (Fig. 17.2).

A puzzling array of female images is thus created in the viewer's unconscious. However, they are not sharply juxtaposed, mutually exclusive figures but facets that can be reconciled in ironic deflections. Wilder's warm irony bathes the conflictual portrayal of femininity in a cheerful, conciliatory light. Hidden in this brilliantly formulated form of mildness is the reflection of society's ambivalence and contradictoriness when it comes to gender, sex and the drama inherent in the theme of women's truth. The probable angle of a renewed defence, mitigating circumstances, not only applies to Christine.

Translated by Annette Caroline Christmas.

Film Details

Original title	Witness for the Prosecution
Release year	1958
Country	USA
Screenplay/idea	Billy Wilder, Larry Marcus, Harry Kurnitz, based on the novel by Agatha Christie
Direction	Billy Wilder
Music	Matty Malnek
Camera	Russell Harlan
Principal actors	Marlene Dietrich, Charles Laughton, Tyron power, Elsa Lanchester
Availability	DVD united artists, 4 045167 006478

References

Christie A (1948) The witness for the prosecution and other stories. Dodd, Mead & Company, New York

Crowe C (2019) Conversations with Billy Wilder. Kampa, Zurich

Hamburger A (2018) Film psychoanalysis. Psychosocial, Giessen

Mann T (1974 [1936]) Freud and the future. In: Mann T (ed) Gesammelte Werke in dreizehn Bänden [Collected Works in Thirteen Volumes]. Vol. 9: Speeches and essays. Part 1. Dodd, Mead & Company, New York, pp 478–501

Rohde-Dachser C (1990) Über töchterliche Existenz: offene Fragen zum weiblichen Ödipuskomplex [the "daughterly" existence. Unanswered questions about the female Oedipus complex]. Z Psychosomat Med Psychoanal 36:303–315

I'm Not Your Nice Girl—*Gone Girl* (US 2014) 18

Sabine Wollnik

Introduction

Gone Girl is a film based on the thriller of the same name by Gillian Flynn. The book seems to have struck a chord at the time, as it was a huge success, spending weeks at the top of the *New York Times* bestseller list in 2012. Thus, the idea of a film adaptation quickly arose. Gillian Flynn agreed to write the screenplay, and the film was released in 2014. The original book is quite complex, and Gillian Flynn had to simplify its structure for the film. The movie was not only a commercial success but was also overwhelmingly well received by critics. Ultimately, the book and film are about an escalated marital crisis in the form of a thriller and its media marketing. Issues about reality, truth and lies and their public presentation are debated. Both protagonists are insecure in their respective male or female identities, and both the man and the woman are unreliable narrators. Role models and the way they are publicly perceived are thus staged, and the repercussions that social and media debates have on the protagonists, and ultimately on each individual, are examined scenically. As viewers of the film, we become part of this scene because of the film has on us. Gillian Flynn worked in the media industry herself and wrote the book during a time of restructuring and crisis, so the novel gave her an opportunity to process her own experiences. Her film focusses on a woman who masterminds events, controlling them to the last detail. This seems to be an attempt to overcome ideas and images of helpless women who suffer passively. In recent years, these role portrayals have been increasingly questioned and other models have been presented, as in this film.

S. Wollnik (✉)
Cologne, Germany

V. Pramataroff-Hamburger, A. Hamburger (eds.), *From La Strada to The Hours*,
https://doi.org/10.1007/978-3-662-68789-5_18

Background

David Fincher was engaged as director. He is considered a virtuoso of neo-noir film who is capable of staging human abysses. But he is also the producer of *House of Cards*, a masterpiece of power games and surprising twists. He is able to draw on both experiences in *Gone Girl*. Film noir featuring a femme fatale arose in the 1940s, in the wake of the economic crisis. *Gone Girl* takes up the theme again in a form adapted to modern times.

The casting is perfect: Ben Affleck plays Nick Dunne, the male lead character. Opinions about the multi-award-winning screenwriter, director, producer and actor are highly controversial. Critics frequently say he lacks talent and charisma. He was nominated seven times for the Golden Raspberry, an award for worst acting performance, winning it three times. However, he is enthusiastically praised for his performance in *Gone Girl* by critic Andreas Busche in the weekly newspaper, *Die Zeit*: 'Never has plodding, slightly underexposed, American mediocrity been more fascinating to appraise' (Busche 2014). Along the way, he received the Razzie Redeemer Award for this role, freeing him from the curse of the Golden Raspberry.

Rosamunde Pike, the female lead, first rose to fame as a Bond girl; however, she also plays serious theatre roles and has a bachelor's degree in English literature from Oxford University. This biography predestines the actor for this role. She received not only many award nominations for her portrayal of Amy in this film but also a wealth of critics' awards.

Film Plot

The film depicts Nick and Amy Dunne's marital crisis and its 'solution' in the form of a thriller that unfolds and is gradually resolved. The storyline takes place in two parallel timelines, plus an additional third time level in the form of flashbacks of the couple getting to know each other and showing how the marriage developed until it escalated into a crisis. The present is indicated by fade-ins of dates. This is where all the questions arise for the viewer, the investigating police and the husband. These are gradually brought to a resolution on the second level, directed by Amy, as it converges on the first. Both husband and wife turn out to be unreliable narrators, although we as the audience gain clarity about events at the end, as do the protagonists and the police. By then, no one can intervene, let alone hold the perpetrator accountable or exonerate themselves. Formally, one scene fades into the next every 3–5 min, which is supposedly roughly the attention span of a smartphone user. In fact, the media in general play a very significant role, especially TV channels, smartphones and the marketing of stories. The cuts thus place us in the middle of our own hypothetical media use.

Nick, portrayed as an average American man, is standing one morning by the rubbish bins in front of his house in a typical American small-town settlement with spacious detached houses, lawns and nosy neighbours. He gets into his SUV and drives to the centre of the small town and, with a board game under his arm, visits his twin sister Margo in the bar they share. After a cut, the Mississippi and signs of the economic crisis can be seen:

homeless people, dilapidated houses. In the bar, Nick is greeted as the 'Irish Prince' by his twin sister. It is 11:00 in the morning, and he has a whisky. It is his fifth wedding anniversary. He is called home. His wife has disappeared, and he arrives to a scene with signs of violence.

At 3:30 min later, there is a cut, and we hear a female voice and see a hand holding a moving pen with a delicate pink pom-pom, writing in a diary. This narrative strand is visually distinct from the first. As viewers, we experience the reality constructed by Amy. These scenes then run forward. Thus, the story invented by Amy is gradually unravelled, leading to the crime scene in which Nick is suspected of having murdered his wife.

The diary entries are staged on film. This starts with Nick and Amy, the two protagonists, getting to know each other. He is a lifestyle journalist for men's magazines, and she is a Harvard-educated psychologist who develops personality tests for magazines. They meet at a party in New York, both around 30. They flirt heavily with each other in a playful exchange, become infatuated, get caught in a sugar storm outside a bakery and eventually have sex.

Nick and Amy's back story and biography then gradually unfold in a back and forth between the levels.

Nick is from the small town where the couple now lives. His father was violent, and his parents separated. Nick and Amy now live in Nick's hometown, where they returned after both became unemployed in the wake of the economic crisis and because Nick's mother had breast cancer. She has since passed away, and Nick runs a bar in the centre of town with his twin sister Margo. Margo lives in what used to be her mother's house. Their father, who suffers from dementia, lives in a nursing home.

Amy is the only child of a psychologist couple who seem to have a closely symbiotic relationship. During Amy's childhood, they portrayed an ideal childhood in picture books, which they called *Amazing Amy*. It depicted the perfect little girl. The picture book series is very well known, so that even the small-town policewoman who leads the murder investigation is familiar with it. Her parents earned a lot of money with the books but are now bankrupt and have to borrow money from the book proceeds, which have been deposited for their daughter.

After the initial infatuation and marriage, against the background of the economic crisis, first Nick loses his job and becomes idle and then Amy. The couple moves to Missouri, where Amy uses her money to buy Nick and his sister a bar and a perfect house with perfect furnishings. Nick becomes increasingly neglectful of her. When the policewoman questions him later, he knows nothing about his wife. He has a job at the nearby college where he teaches creative writing, and he is having an affair with a student, which has been going on for over a year and a half at the time of the investigation.

In the meantime, Amy, unappreciated and bored as well as cheated on, stages an elaborate revenge story. Her diary, which is later found by the police officers, plays an important role in it. She invents a story just as her parents invented hers. But she goes one step further and manipulatively carries hers out. In her diary, she says Nick is violent, and that since she is afraid, she buys a gun. She increases her life insurance coverage in Nick's favour and accumulates credit card debt by buying Nick gadgets, which she stores in Nick's sister's garage. She fakes a pregnancy by duping her pregnant neighbour when she uses her toilet, collecting her urine. She thus convinces her doctor that she is pregnant. She prepares a treasure hunt for their fifth wedding anniversary, so that when the police start the investigation, suspicion is increasingly directed at her husband. He had supposedly murdered his wife out of hatred, and when the police later find the individual 'treasures' with further clues, they seem to point directly to a murder. Amy dreams that Nick will end up in the electric chair for murdering her.

The solution to the treasure hunt is a box with two wooden 'Punch and Judy' dolls from the eponymous puppet show, in which the violent Punch drunkenly beats his pregnant wife to death with a club. The wooden club belonging to the pair of wooden dolls is found half-burnt in the fireplace, stained with blood.

Ultimately, all the protagonists produce their own version of the story, which is crucial to the film. They twist what is happening or use events to win public favour. It becomes clear how skilfully all those involved play with socially shaped female and male role patterns and images, just as the film ultimately toys with us, the viewers. Amy's parents did so throughout Amy's childhood, skilfully exploiting her disappearance for monetary gain. With the help of his expensive lawyer, Nick eventually wises up and enters the game again with the upper hand. But Amy is more skilful. She keeps up the fake story all the way to the end, partly staging it in reality.

From the halfway point, the film portrays how Amy is doing after her disappearance. At first, Amy seems liberated; she can finally let herself go and eat what she wants. She changes her appearance and checks into a motel. However, her roommate becomes suspicious of her, and she and her lover steal all Amy's money, leaving her penniless. The latter turns to a rich childhood friend, Desi, who used to stalk her. Desi takes Amy in, hides her in his house, locks her up, controls her and moulds her appearance into what he holds to be a perfect woman. She is back in her old patterns.

Amy kills Desi but constructs this murder as self-defence while she was being raped. She drives back to Nick, staging a victim story for the benefit of the public, the television and the police. Although everyone close to her guesses the truth, she even confesses it to Nick in the shower: Without the possibility of being wiretapped, nothing can be proven against her. When Amy then decides to be inseminated with Nick's frozen sperm, Nick remains trapped in the marriage to care for his future child. Margo, his twin sister, is shaken but decides to stand by him.

The significant aspect is the role played by the media and how skilful the protagonists are in dealing with them. Public opinion plays a big role in investigations and blame. At first, Nick is extremely clumsy, while Amy's parents, who have travelled to the scene, prove to be absolute media professionals. Two TV presenters fuel public opinion. However, Nick learns better with the help of his very expensive lawyer—after all, he used to work for a lifestyle magazine—and manages to sway public opinion in his favour, even Amy when she sees him on television. Amy then regains the upper hand in influencing public opinion by taking advantage of the cameras surrounding the house to make a TV appearance as a raped woman.

When the film shows how all the protagonists play with public opinion and try to influence people in their own way, ideas on social role models also become clear.

Methodological Considerations

Methodologically, I try not to focus too much on the psychopathology of the characters, although on the face of it, this would seem appropriate; however, one must always bear in mind that film characters are not real people. In the context of this text, we are interested in the role models enacted in the film with which the viewer can then come to grips. At a narrative level, the film shows the extent to which we are all shaped by ideas on social roles, which are also conveyed in many ways in the media today. And it raises the question of whether and to what extent there the individual can play with these rules. Hamburger (2018) argues that images of men and women are created culturally and that social conditions ultimately determine which image will prevail.

The cool and distanced formal design is thought-provoking. The décor and visual style emphasise this cold, clinical, controlled detachment. The film contains many allusions to film noir, and films by Hitchcock, however in each case with a decisive twist on modern female role models. This also allows the viewer to reactivate traditional views, especially on women, and then question them. Unlike traditional film noir, this protagonist does not need a man to act on her behalf. She not only controls from a distance but also has a direct hand in events, which is not the case in traditional film noir. This difference in itself leads to reflection on ideas about female role models and stimulates processing of these. There are allusions to Hitchcock's *Vertigo*. The protagonist in *Gone Girl* also allows a man who provides for her, Desi, to give her a makeover according to his own personal wishes: a decidedly feminine wardrobe and a very neat platinum blonde hairstyle; however, the protagonist in this film takes bitter revenge for this 'rape' by murdering him. Soul murder is countered by revenge murder. The scene in the shower could also be reminiscent of Hitchcock. However, in this case, in contrast to *Psycho,* the female protagonist is not murdered but dominates the man by revealing her secret to him. By making these allusions, the film breaks down role concepts, toys with cliches and monstrously inverts them. It allows the viewer look into abysses of female aggressiveness and destructiveness, at least as a cinematic fantasy. My interpretation thus aims at the representation of female role models and the extent to which the viewer is put in a position to experience them, then to question them, and how they are confronted with new patterns in the old ones.

How Is the Feminine Staged in Film?

The film plays out a plethora of female role clichés. Socially rehearsed images and role prejudices have an effect on the investigations and the individual.

Women are exposed to high ideal expectations from a tender age, which they can never live up to. These ideas are enacted, thereby making it clear that the social stereotypes bandied about by the media and also later by the lawyer defending Nick or the TV presenters, in turn reinforce these socially based ideas. In the crime story, all the protagonists play with these images.

Amazing Amy

'Amazing Amy' is the children's book character made up and successfully marketed in book form by Amy's parents, who are psychologists. 'Amazing Amy' is the idealised version of a developing girl created by her parents, which the real Amy could never live up to. 'Amazing Amy' was perfect and brilliant, and the real Amy was jealous of her and could never live up to her and was always one step behind. The parents 'improved Amy's childhood and then sold her off' (At film timecode 0.13.10). She grew up to please both parents without having her and her wishes or needs addressed. Amy grew up in the public eye, subject to media manipulations. She was not seen as a person. Typical role models, to some of which women are still subjected today, are projected onto Amy, albeit in an exaggerated form in the film. Women have to adapt, are meant to please others and must not put up any resistance or become aggressive. The Amy in the children's books is portrayed as a typical, over-adjusted girl who excels in all sports, hobbies and school; is always neat and clean; and not at all aggressive. 'Amazing Amy' is at best covertly aggressive: she doesn't scream, doesn't hit out and isn't loud or (heaven forbid) offensive, as boys are allowed to be. She is sweet and outwardly over-adapted even when very angry.

Amy was never in a position to offer her own alternatives to these expectations. However, the film also shows that she begins to develop subversive tendencies, or at least becomes aware of her own aspirations. Her engagement, which she herself medially stages, is an attempt to free herself from parental ideas, because in these scenes, she is the scriptwriter and director of her own life. This time she is one step ahead of 'Amazing Amy'. However, even if a relationship is experienced as an attempt at women's liberation and autonomy every now and then, it often does not succeed, as is the case here.

Cool Girl

'Amazing Amy' becomes 'Cool Girl' as she grows up. The film thus portrays another female role stereotype conveyed by society and the media. 'Cool Girl' is an outstanding young woman in all aspects of life: brilliant, composed, level-headed, however adapted to social expectations and those of her future husband. In New York, she is a city girl riding the crest of the wave of the times, seemingly independent and self-reliant. She is someone who always keeps her cool and is impossible to upset.

Fig. 18.1 Living as if out of a catalogue (00:08:41)

Amy is a slim, wiry, blonde, perfectly styled young woman with a successful career and a Harvard degree. She marries the typical American boy, and their engagement is marketed in the media. However, the house she then moves into in Missouri shows how empty she is as a person, her façade. She seems to be a carbon copy from a catalogue, lifeless, inanimate. In this, as throughout the film, the décor and visual style reinforce the theme of a lack of vitality and authenticity (Fig. 18.1).

'Nick loved a girl I was pretending to be. "Cool Girl". Men always use that, don't they? As their defining complement. "She's a Cool Girl". Cool Girl is hot, Cool girl is game. Cool girl is fun. Cool girl never gets angry at her man. She only smiles in a chagrined, loving manner'. She makes herself available as a sex object and likes what he likes. She was the cool girl for Nick, and she knew that from the start. 'We were happy pretending to be other people'. Then he got tired of her and wanted another, younger cool girl, which aroused her desire for revenge. Cool Girl had taken responsibility and funded everything from behind the scenes, unquestioningly. The lack of recognition and respect from Nick and those around him makes her angry. This invisibility is still a problem for women today, as many studies have shown (see also Criado-Perez 2019).

All her repressed hatred is then channelled into the murderous act. Cool Girl is outwardly perfectly adjusted but inwardly full of hatred and vindictiveness. It is surely only when she begins writing the diary that the protagonist becomes aware of the roles she is at the mercy of and which she has fulfilled up to that point. The diary increasingly describes a fantasy that she stages, with externalisation and enactment. Just as the viewer of the film perhaps only gets a glimpse of the socially mediated role models on watching it, even if in this instance it is enacted in a psychopathological development. She may gain awareness through reflection.

The main character stages her liberation and at the same time her revenge against Nick. This liberation can only be staged as a female corpse. She frees herself from 'Cool Girl', the over-adapted part of herself that she lets float down the Mississippi as a corpse in order to finally come alive. On her escape, she seems full of life and relaxed for the first time.

The Female Corpse

Elisabeth Bronfen has already examined the representation of femininity and death in her postdoctoral thesis *Over Her Dead Body* (Bronfen 1992). She shows the way cultural norms are rendered visible in the motif of the female corpse. The film alludes to various female role models, including that of the female corpse. Amy appropriates this culturally mediated image by attempting to enact it herself in her imagination. She revels in the fantasy that Nick is in the electric chair due to having been accused and convicted of killing her. She continues to spin the fantasy that she is a female corpse floating down the Mississippi into the open sea. She thereby embellishes her revenge fantasy and at the same time confirms images of femininity. The female corpse is a topos in the literature of a patriarchal culture. Amy was already mentally dead before, but in this enactment, she comes to life, as if she has managed to split off an inanimate, undeveloped, over-adapted part of herself. This enactment fulfils various aspirations. On the one hand, Amy turns her anger against herself by wishing herself dead. In her own enactment, however, she plays with the existing tropes by taking on an active role herself. She plays with social symbols. As a female corpse, she would receive the attention that she had not received as a person. Anger is an intolerable emotion for many women, but now, she allows herself her anger, turning it against herself.

At the same time, the female corpse ceaselessly pursues its male counterpart, just as Sylvia Plath pursues her husband Ted Hughes. Sylvia Plath has become immortal as a corpse and an icon of a feminist current. This film at least alludes to feminist positions with which the viewers can engage.

A Short Phase of Independence and Freedom: The Problem of Female Autonomy

Freed from marital conventions, Amy sets off on a brief period of freedom. Burgeoning effects of vitality prevent her from staging herself as a female corpse. Another part of herself begins to grow. At this point, the film changes colour and style and seems less sterilely staged, becoming altogether more cheerful, even sunny. The film-makers can no longer resist a little black humour. Amy eats what she wants without paying attention to the social rules of her class. She seems cheerful, drifting in the pool of the motel where she has taken up residence in her new identity. She seems to be blossoming. Rosamund Pike, who plays Amy, presents this physically. Her movements are more expansive and more vehement, and she literally takes up more space. She gets dirty and is full of vitality. She is no longer the willowy, blonde, over-controlled 'cool girl'. She can finally let herself go.

However, she is no match for the dangers associated with this freedom. She befriends the wrong person, who then steals from her. As an outwardly spoilt upper-middle-class only child, she cannot cope with being penniless. She falls back into the old patterns and calls her old boyfriend Desi, who had previously stalked her and immediately tries to dominate her again. Is this to be interpreted as an indication that women are not cut out for autonomy? This is a very darkly humorous image, as if women were incapable of shaping this freedom. There is also no female solidarity. These currents of black humour are often overlooked. The film is ambivalent or repeatedly relapses into a patriarchy that is also repeatedly supported by women.

The Infinitely Giving Mother

Amy is experienced and presented to the audience as an infinitely giving person. She finances everything in Missouri, and she is thereby a motherly figure who works in the background and is taken for granted. This is still an image of women today that can probably be traced back to early images of motherhood, the infinitely giving maternal breast.

The Desire to Be Seen

The criminal investigation follows the search game invented by Amy. In this, too, she stages something that can trigger its own themes and desires in the viewer. She had become invisible in the marriage with Nick, and he had lost interest in her. This, incidentally, already becomes a problem for women over 30. Female actors who have reached this age are cast less frequently. Rosamund Pike was already 36 years old when the film was made. Nick's lover, played by Emily Ratajkowski, was 23. The real crime is not to be noticed, so Amy stages solving the crime as a search game. Due to the investigation, not only Nick is looking for her, albeit very reluctantly, and her parents, but also the public at large. When Nick is questioned by the police, it becomes clear how little he knows about his wife. In the background, a female theme seems to be running: you are only interested in me if you try to find me. Amy pulls the strings and repeatedly lures the police into new avenues in the search game. Amy is no longer suffering rejection but is an active party in the events. She thereby addresses male stereotypes by planting the pawns that the police find. This is another hint at the ironic undertones of the film, the exaggerated nature of the objects.

The Aseptic Woman

Desi grooms Amy, just as Scottie did to Madeleine in *Vertigo*. She is styled, aseptic, with platinum blonde hair and dressed all in white. Is this a defence against the bodily fluids associated with women that are connected with menstruation or childbirth, expressions of female vitality and creaturely vitality? The house in which Amy and Nick live, where she returns at the end, seems sterile and lifeless. Like a television advertisement, it is robbed of all individuality and life. This time she has chosen it herself, and the film leaves the viewer with this ironic mise-en-scène. But before that, she destroys Desi, cruelly murdering him for attempting to rape her and rob her of her vitality. The Hitchcock film being alluded to shows this robbing of individuality and the woman's transfiguration in order to conform with the man's standards even more emotionally oppressively. Amy brings it out in the open by staging herself as a rape victim.

The Female Monster

Can an independent, autonomous woman only be staged as a monster? Will she immediately be experienced only as someone who holds all the power and pulls the strings, a woman as a grotesque figure who frightens men? A figure, however, who arouses inner fear scenarios in both sexes that are deeply anchored in the societal unconscious. This is portrayed in the film. Does an independent woman arouse archaic childish fears and so is experienced as a monster? We humans start our lives dependent and weak, completely at the mercy of a maternal figure, both while still in the womb and for some time after birth. In her conversation with Elisabeth Bronfen, Siri Hustvedt shows that the hidden mother figure can often be found behind misogyny (Hustvedt 2015?). A strong woman who does not submit to the needs of others is experienced as a scary monster. The film stages a woman as masculine, or perhaps one could say as a figure that is still socially experienced as frightening. Dependence causes anger, and this is also then projected onto the object on whom one is dependent.

The Pregnant Wife

The pregnant wife killed by the violent, unpredictable husband, portrayed in the traditional *Punch and Judy* puppet show, is another assigned female role with which Amy toys. Or is the film toying with us: the roles are reversed, and it is Amy who imposes her rules on everyone else. In the end, she is the pregnant wife who, as the perfect American housewife, dominates her husband all his life in an almost fifties-style production. In the background, the ambivalent desire to have children runs through the story. Such a wish is clearly present, as we find out that a natural conception has been problematic and that a sample of Nick's semen has been frozen. It could be argued that, in an aside, another topic of our time is thus also dealt with in the film. But at a deeper level, it could be argued that Amy's solution is also an attack on couple formation. She herself decides to be inseminated, thereby perhaps confirming deep male fears of being bound to a powerful woman for life through a child. She stages herself as a mother without needing the male member for fertilisation; she only uses his seed. The last frame seems to support this: behind the advertising idyll lurks the horror.

The Fundamental Inaccessibility of the Other

At the end of my text, I would like to return to the beginning of the film, to the first image, which I have not yet mentioned. We see Amy's blonde mop of hair at the beginning, filling the whole screen. Nick is stroking his wife's head, and the viewer hears his inner monologue, in which he says he'd like to split his wife's skull open to understand what is going on inside her (Fig. 18.2). This image is resumed again at the end.

The image perhaps shows the root of the anger in both sexes, the ultimate unattainability of the other and the rejection thus experienced from the beginning. Nick wants to crack her skull open so he can look inside. Scenes of being excluded permeate the film. This feeling of exclusion becomes clear right in the opening scene, since it is fundamentally impossible to penetrate the thoughts and feelings of the other person, even though the film lets the viewer above all into the female protagonist's inner life and fantasies: unlike the other main characters, the film shows us what Amy has experienced. Amy was excluded from the seemingly symbiotic parental couple, and she is later excluded from her husband who has a mistress and excluded from the close relationship between Nick and his twin sister. Being excluded is ultimately a fundamental human fate, even if it takes different forms.

The film portrays the murderous rage arising from this exclusion, which the viewer partially evades through the cinema screen, since it shows the background reasons. In the end, however, these too are only luminous spots that we see and that can nevertheless strike a deep inner chord with us. We only experience the characters through the cinema screen, so they, too, ultimately remain inaccessible.

Fig. 18.2 Nick: 'I picture myself cracking her lovely skull, unspooling her brain, trying to get answers' (00:00:34)

Conclusion

The film portrays a psychopath who may be observed but who cannot ultimately be understood, since no biography could sufficiently justify such a trajectory. This would appear to be a classic thriller.

However, this one is written by a woman and the many ironic allusions and overall fairy tale-like quality of the far-fetched story cannot be overlooked. I would thus prefer to regard the film as a female fantasy that also plays with role models and their reflection in the media, moreover filmed by a male director.

Images of women are social projections of both men and women. Of course, I can only write from a female perspective. A man may see the film differently, as may ultimately any other woman. A controversy has broken out around this film, especially among female viewers and feminists. One of the main criticisms has been that this portrayal mocks rape survivors. Although the script is written by a woman, it also presents stereotypes about women that are predominantly male prejudices in the me-too debate. The film has thus been accused of misogyny, which is surprising for a female scriptwriter, even if misogynistic women do exist. It is probably more complicated than that, however, as some women have found it to be a feminist film.

The film is a play on female stereotypes and stages unconscious, even frowned-upon female desires. Returning to the initial question of whether it is a feminist, misogynistic or misanthropic film, one possible answer would be that the film shows that malicious women also exist and thus balances gender relations.

For a long time, anger was an unacceptable emotion for women. Little girls were brought up to be gentle. Revenge was frowned upon, and aggression was best directed against oneself as a woman. In this story, genuine autonomy in the sense of self-reliance in mutual recognition is not achieved in the end, even though a struggle for it is shown. The protagonist finds another way. She does not remain in a victim role, nor passive: she becomes a doer.

The main character does not allow her rage and vengefulness free rein, and she strictly controls it, allowing the audience to work through destructive fantasies and experience revenge fantasies in projection onto the screen.

The film takes up the themes of film noir from the 40 s, albeit in a different aesthetic, in which broken men are at the mercy of a deadly femme fatale. The new element is that this femme fatale stages her vendetta all by herself, without the need for a male partner.

The film also addresses the power of socially transmitted phantasms. Amy toys with the roles conveyed by the media, and the film also toys with the viewer and his or her role prejudices. Our perceptions are flooded by images from the media. We come into contact with our perceptual cultural prejudices when we watch films.

Although a female screenwriter can write herself out of a role that lacks freedom, nothing has changed in terms of content: the roles are merely reversed. The viewer may have gained access to aggressive, power-hungry, psychopathic roles of their own; however, the novel element in the film is the humour that makes you laugh at the tricky situation.

The main character in the film emerges from passive suffering into action, conscious action is strengthened and the protagonist turns the circumstances around. The man takes on the trapped, paralysed role. This reversal involving black humour makes the viewer aware of the conditions, also by playing with conventional images. Humour enables a distanced view and recognition of human vulnerability and mortality.

A woman seeking power arouses moral indignation; the film plays with this image by portraying a woman as a psychopath towards whom we can easily be morally indignant.

Does the film develop the power of imagination for an alternative? In my opinion, it does not. The film straddles the dilemma of confirming a prejudice against women in the me-too debate while at the same time trying to portray justifiable female aggressiveness. In doing so, it confirms the conditions, albeit in reverse. Trapped in the sterile house as a reflection of herself, Amy plays an American housewife in the final scene like something out of an advertisement, except that she is now the director and screenwriter. The black humour that the film conveys should not be underestimated. The final impression is humorous and plays with advertising images: the perfect American housewife is cruelly in control of the man at the cooker.

Thus, to return to Elisabeth Bronfen, her behaviour confirms the norm and restores the patriarchal order. She is the psychopathic string-puller, and her movement towards autonomy has ultimately failed. She prefers to be the perpetrator rather than the victim, but she is attached to this position, power-hungry, hateful, vengeful, cruel and sadistic—a monster.

The film does not offer a solution, only a perpetrator-victim reversal, despite its black humour ends with a deeply pessimistic worldview. Thus, the film externalises images of femininity—as does Amy, the protagonist—and inserts them into a game, which in this instance is not resolved but at least becomes visible. Hamburger writes: 'So, we sit in the cinema to try on life plans that negotiate desire regulation, and we sit there with our empirical bodies' (Hamburger 2018, p. 259).

Films are the place where these fantasies can be acted out, and the different roles can be played out. The viewer can work through her own abysses in this way.

Translated by Annette Caroline Christmas.

Film Details

Original title	Gone Girl
Release year	2014
Country	USA
Screenplay/idea	Gillian Flynn
Director	David Fincher
Music	Jeff Cronenweth
Camera	Trent Reznor, Atticus Ross
Main actors	Ben Affleck, Rosamund Pike, Neil Patrick Harris, Missi Pyle, Tyler Perry, Emily Ratajkowki
Availability	Available as DVD and Blu-ray and on various streaming platforms

References

Bronfen E (1992) Over her dead body. Death, femininity and the aesthetic. Manchester University Press

Busche A (2014) Die faszinierende Bräsigkeit des American Boy [The fascinating grumpiness of the American Boy]. Die Zeit, 2nd Oktober 2014

Criado-Perez C (2019) Invisible women, Vintage, London

Hamburger A (2018) Das Unbewusste im Kino—das Kino im Unbewussten [Film Psychoanalysis. Relational approaches to film interpretation [in press]]. Psychosocial, Giessen

Hustvedt S (2015) Shaking Women and Knotted Subjects: A conversation between Siri Hustvedt & Elisabeth Bronfen on the Future of Psychoanalysis and its Narratives—Sep 21 NYU

19 Gateway to the Night—*The Night Porter (Il Portiere di Notte*, I 1974)

Marcus Stiglegger

Introduction

The Night Porter is one of the most contentious films from the 1970s. Initially launched in the shadow of the commercial success of *L'ultimo tango à Parigi/The Last Tango in Paris* (I 1972, Bernardo Bertolucci), the film was condemned as 'pornography' by the Italian state and even banned at times, although over the years it went on to become a controversial cult film. Italian director Liliana Cavani (*1936) combined motifs of sadomasochistic melodrama with the historical subtext of the Nazi era—with a particular focus on the concentration camp system. The following contribution shows the radical concept of autonomous femininity that the director also realises.

Film Plot

The film starts in a busy vestibule, a hotel reception hall: An insert tells us it is Vienna, 1957. Max (Dirk Bogarde), who we later learn was in the SS and 'played doctor in a concentration camp' during the war, is working as a night porter at the Hotel zur Oper. He gives the impression of being both professional and industrious. He has a dignified, distinguished style; his hair is carefully combed back; his face deeply lined with a serious edge. Only his black porter's uniform with its crossed keys on the collar offers a hint of his secret past: the black SS uniform. Max later describes himself to his still living SS comrades as a 'lonely church mouse' who wants to finally get some peace and who flees from the light of day and thus guilt into secrecy.

M. Stiglegger (✉)
Mainz, Germany

V. Pramataroff-Hamburger, A. Hamburger (eds.), *From La Strada to The Hours*,
https://doi.org/10.1007/978-3-662-68789-5_19

The drama takes its course when a young conductor's wife Lucia (Charlotte Rampling) arrives at the hotel. She recognises Max, the night porter, straight away. He is the SS man she had been involved with years ago as a concentration camp prisoner. Overcoming her initial shyness, she hesitantly makes contact with him—which ultimately leads to her marriage breaking down. That first glance when they meet again in the Viennese hotel lobby, and her later participation in the passionate 'game', has apparently turned the adult Lucia into a Dionysian creature who has left social morality behind. Faced with the unconditional nature of this rekindled passion, Lucia ritually evokes the past in a strategic act: She goes into an antique shop to buy a child's dress like the one Max used to make her wear in the camp to lure him.

When her husband (Marino Masè) departs towards Frankfurt, Lucia secretly moves in with Max at his flat in the Karl-Marx-Hof, once the last bastion of the anti-nationalist resistance. Other former Nazis urge Max to kill Lucia, seeing her as a dangerous witness to the past; however, he refuses to obey. Instead, Max retreats to the solitude of his small flat with his lover, isolating himself from the outside world.

Just as Lucia has escaped from her marriage, Max disengages himself from the system of mutual dependence and latent mistrust that the former SS men have built up for their own safety. His former superior Klaus (Philippe Leroy) then insistently cross-examines Max, urging him to come to his senses. He repeatedly refers to their 'comradely union', something that Max has long since left behind. Max chains Lucia up in his flat: partly to keep her from leaving, partly to protect her from the dangers of the 'outside' world. Max allows the thick chain to slip through his hands, lovingly winding it around Lucia, and she returns the gesture with a tender smile. They later lock themselves in the flat together, completing their escape; in their shared universe of passion, nothing else matters but the obsessive, all-consuming, destructive ardour, which has previously been unpacked in a much-cited dream sequence.

The fateful chain of events culminates in the besieging of the couple by the former SS men for several days. Showing signs of deprivation, Max and Lucia once again don their ritual clothes (the uniform and the child dress) and drive to a Danube bridge at dawn, where they are shot in an ambush. Liliana Cavani shows only a long shot that slowly approaches the deceased, not their final passing, the *Liebestod* [love death] of this couple.

Background

From early on, Cavani's films dealt with social and intercultural problems: In *Il contro notturno* (1961), she described the problematic friendship between a white man and an African woman, and *L'evento* (1962) is about a group of tourists who murder a young Italian for no apparent reason. Between 1962 and 1965, she made several sensational documentaries for the Italian national public broadcasting company (Radiotelevisione italiana), some of which already examined the theme of the Third Reich: the monumental

Storia del Terzo Reich (1963), *Le donne della resistenza* (1963) and *Philippe Pétain—processo à Vichy* (1965). She had soon established herself as a specialist on National Socialism. As an avowed Marxist, she faithfully continued to explore this subject area for a long time. *Philippe Pétain—processo à Vichy* was awarded the Palme d'Or for best television production at the 1965 Venice Film Festival. Cavani's radical willingness to adopt even problematic positions is evident in the film. She is an uneasy filmmaker, a committed lateral thinker, who took monumental historical figures such as Francis of Assisi and Galileo Galilei as her subjects. The free-thinking spirit is always pitted against totalitarian tyranny, however without ultimately achieving apparent victory. In the stylised, almost surreal sociopolitically themed *I cannibali* (1969) [*The Cannibals*], which projects the Sophoclean tragedy *Antigone* into an anonymous fascist dictatorship, sexual obsessions and an intense look at the oppressed and violated body also came into play. Cavani combines theatrical scenes with genuine images of the student protests of 1968 to create a bitter cinematic essay.

When *Il portiere di notte* premiered in Italy in 1974, it caused another scandal: The film was briefly confiscated and only released and declared a work of art after a sensational strike by the Italian film industry, led by Luchino Visconti and Bernardo Bertolucci. In fact, such incidents are arguably more common in Italy. The state censor wrote: 'The film is doubly dangerous because it was directed by a woman. It shows a woman taking the initiative in a sexual act—and in a manner that would do credit to any brothel'. 'This offends me not only as a director but also as a woman', was Cavani's response. 'I cannot understand why the censor only approves of the sexual act when the woman is lying underneath the man, while he considers it unacceptable, vulgar and obscene when the man is lying underneath the woman. The censor's brief is shocking: It contains expressions that are indeed vulgar, expressions that neither I nor any of my colleagues would ever utter' (Phelix and Thissen 1983, p. 186).

On the other hand, the film drew mixed responses from international audiences. Most felt the reduction of the prevailing political circumstances to a sadomasochistic two-way relationship to be unwarranted. In Germany, where *The Night Porter* was released only 2 years later, critics mostly interpreted the film as a rather misleading political parable. It was to take several more years for its complexity and ambiguity to be properly appreciated.

At the start of the 1970s, Liliana Cavani, like Lina Wertmüller, was considered one of Italy's brightest young hopes as a director. Nevertheless, her reputation gradually waned. She was criticised for her complete 'German trilogy', which had started with *The Night Porter* and went on to include *Al di là del bene e del male [Beyond Good and Evil,* 1977 [1976]] and *Inferno Berlinese [The Berlin Affair]* (1985). She was accused of turning the film 'into cheap sensationalism, the supposedly universal model case turned cliché. A political porno formulaically trimmed to art', according to German film magazine Filmdienst (N.N. 1975). The term '*sexual-political melodrama*' was occasionally used, which seems plausible given the themes (Nietzsche, National Socialism, *Ménage-à-trois*), and however falls short in view of the creative diversity of her works. Her films gain intensity with repeated viewing. Above all, *The Night Porter* has remained in the international film memory. This film achieved almost iconic status in the 1970s and also made British actress Charlotte Rampling a legend alongside Liliana Cavani.

Staging the Feminine in Film

The director's main concern in *The Night Porter* is not so much to create a political microcosm as to plausibly present the mechanisms of unconditional desire. Each stage of the encounter between Max and Lucia thus becomes a key scene in a heightened sense, more so than one would expect from melodrama. The actions and events take on an increasingly mythical character. Desire always seems unconditional and ultimately a surrender. It seems logical that destructive acts can also be proof of love, first and foremost Lucia's immediate separation from her husband when she realises the hopelessness of her desire. Only experiencing pain seems appropriate to the intensity of her feelings: When Max first enters the hotel room, he slaps Lucia; the broken bed of shards even more drastically illustrates the nature of her ecstasy. Following the *amour fou*, the unconditional, crazy love that has a long tradition in European cinema, the lovers' path can only lead to a shared love-death, to which they surrender in perfect style (he in his black dress uniform, she in her pale little girl's dress). The place of death, a lonely steel bridge at dawn, clearly takes on the character of a very figurative rite of passage. Cavani seems to want to suggest that there is a world for lovers from which we are excluded. The camera is also clearly distanced from the action at this crucial moment: The place of action becomes stage-like, the protagonists' small figures who adapt to the contours of the surroundings at the moment of death. The lovers have advanced to the costumed ranks of a tragic play.

The marital relationship between Lucia and her husband, in contrast, is shown as extremely distanced. Their interactions have an undeniable routine, in which Lucia almost plays the role of a childlike wife steeped in luxury, already used to boredom in the golden cage of the hotel room. Lucia's husband almost patronisingly persuades her to 'go shopping' in Vienna before she follows him to Frankfurt, without realising what he is setting in motion. The need to be liberated from the prison of marriage is suggested and ultimately celebrated. The way this liberation is achieved through renewed (unconditional) heterosexual dependence and surrender is often misinterpreted as its opposite, a definitive step into passivity. However, this ignores the deliberate and extremely controlled way Lucia takes this step. Ultimately, Max has rather more been a slave to his desires all his life and his actions are clearly compulsive.

The Night Porter conceptualises the extreme isolation of the couple as a sensual battlefield of sexual obsessions: The already mentioned shard scene is also frequently cited as evidence of the film's sadomasochistic appeal. In a supremely confident and boisterous mood, Lucia teases Max by locking herself in the bathroom. Max, who is barefoot, knocks on the door. Lucia hurls a glass perfume bottle onto the floor, and it smashes, scattering shards all over the floor. She then opens the door. Max walks straight into the shards. The sudden sharp pain can be seen on face, and yet his expression is one of satisfaction and acceptance. Lucia reaches down to pull a shard out of her heel, and Max unexpectedly shifts his weight, treading the shard into his foot and her hand at the same time. They smile at each other. He spreads his arms in a magnanimous gesture. The dialectic of executioner and victim is reversed time and again.

The dramaturgy of the film jumps back and forth in the montage between the 1940s and the 1950s—often introduced by specific events that associatively connect the various time levels. The central and most famous scene of the film is the cabaret sequence. This is the first flashback that is clearly framed dramaturgically. Preluded by a confidential conversation between Max, who now seems completely absorbed in his past, and the Countess von Stein, who at this point becomes more of a mother figure than ever, Max tells a biblical story: the one about the *femme fatale* Salomé. Max will ultimately reward Lucia for her dance by presenting her with the head of one of the other prisoners who has bothered her—just as Herod gave Salomé the head of John the Baptist.

The room in which an illustrious SS squad has gathered is bathed in cold, steely blue (Fig. 19.1). The camera travels along the faces, revealing carnivalesque, clownish elements: The absurd face of an SS man in silly circus make-up becomes a cruel farce, and another is wearing a Venetian mask that makes his ghostly face glow against his black uniform.

The clownishly pale faces of the uniformed men, partly covered by Venetian masks, also reveal the travesty of the fascist cult of the surface. The homoerotic streak in Max's character becomes abundantly clear. He is apparently afraid of women and therefore chooses Lucia to be his 'little girl', using her as a doll to dress and undress, beat and torture. The film-maker's analysis of what lies beneath the fascist character is this specific mixture of sadomasochism, murderousness and a death wish, impotence and intoxication

Fig. 19.1 The Night Porter–Salomé Sequence (Criterion Bluray Screenshot) (01:10:28)

with power, science and irrationalism, barbarism and the vestiges of culture. In this scene, Max acts as a puppeteer, a mastermind in the background, and Lucia does indeed seem to be the incarnation of his most secret desires and dreams, in comparison with whom his comrades can only degenerate into grotesque extras (Stiglegger 2015, pp. 165-169).

With her hair cropped short and her androgynous, boyish body, pale as death (with the violet lips of an albino), the girl Lucia has been endowed with the insignia of power and death and stylised as a childlike goddess of Thanatos. Her arms are covered by shimmering gloves, her head by a peaked SS cap with insignia. Apart from this is clad only in a pair of dark men's trousers with wide braces on her torso. Faintly reminiscent of Marlene Dietrich and other divas of the same ilk, she interprets a song by Friedrich Holländer with lascivious, lubricous gestures: 'Alive I love to live. / I have to say I love to please. / I love to love, although not always. / I don't know what I want, but I expect a lot. / If I could make a wish, / I wouldn't know / what to wish for: / a bad time or a good time. / If I could make a wish, / I'd like to be just a little happy; / because if I were too happy, / I'd miss being sad'.

The opening lines give an impression of fatal disorientation. An urge for life for externalisation ('to please') leads into the diffuse need for affection and desire ('I love to love'). Finally, the fourth line puts this in perspective, emphasising the inexperience and indecisiveness of the childlike and expectant character who, driven by curiosity and courage, wants to explore the unknown. Lucia sings these lines as a confession in the accented German of an Englishwoman. However, it never becomes clear whether this scene is actually one of Max's phantasmagoria, or at least a distorted [transfigured] memory: These words too precisely fit his view of the desired child-woman for him not to have put them into her mouth himself. This interpretation thus challenges those critics who object to the film on the grounds that it falsifies history, based on this very scene.

There is another interesting scene that allows us to get to know the female protagonist more closely: The former Hauptsturmführer Dr. Vogler (Gabriele Ferzetti) breaks into the flat and interrogates Lucia, who is (voluntarily) chained up there (Fig. 19.2). He wants to put pressure on her and persuade her to give up. He implies that she will never live in peace without the consent of his 'friends'. Lucia is already crawling around the flat on all fours at this point, showing tendencies of becoming a beast, which intensify as the siege continues. The couple regresses and they isolate themselves.

The siege lasts 10 days. Initially, Max has food delivered to the flat, but the besiegers soon prevent this. Lucia lives through the isolation in silent acquiescence, smiling gently, smoking a pipe now and then. This masculine habitus, coupled with her stoic calm, shows how aware Lucia is of the destructive consequences of her actions. Several times she emphasises that she followed Max of her own free will, so Vogler accuses her of also being 'sick'.

His main accusation, however, is different: Lucia 'will not let the past rest in peace'. What the 'accuser' doesn't realise at the time is that both of them, but particularly Lucia, have already lost their ethical-moral bearings and are now continually living at the limit of experience and beyond, in a state of transgression: 'Since this existence is both so pure and so complicated, it must be detached from its questionable association to ethics ...; it must

Fig. 19.2 The Night Porter—Chained (Criterion Bluray Screenshot) (01:27:56)

be liberated from the scandalous or subversive, that is, from anything aroused by negative associations' (Foucault 1977 [1963], p. 35).

The siege culminates in violence. As Max goes out onto the balcony, a shot is fired, injuring his hand. He barricades the door. His old friend Oskar calls but tells him he cannot help him; otherwise, he would risk his disability pension. Max can only laugh contemptuously. From now on, Max and Lucia live entirely for themselves, in isolation and deprivation. When Lucia starts to eat out of a jam jar, he tries to stop her. The glass breaks, and Lucia greedily licks the shards. In inevitable agitation, they make love with a desperation that makes their impending death palpable. The act of love under the sign of violent death again recalls Georges Bataille's idea of transgression, which in turn is based on Nietzsche's thinking. Two contexts shine through: psychoanalysis and Bataille's 'religion of world immanence', which seeks to overcome philosophical nihilism in an unreserved affirmation of life. Vienna, the setting of the action and the city of Sigmund Freud, proves to be a revealing sign, right down to the specific staging of the filmic space: Max, as keeper of the keys, opened the gate to the night.

It never becomes clear to what extent Max is really aware that Lucia is no longer his doll without a will of her own but has entirely consciously entered into the deadly game. Lucia, at any rate, remains mildly smiling in the background. In the visual staging of the young Lucia, the director refers to a female ideal of Dark Romanticism: the 'clouded beauty' (Praz 1994, 58). She is pale, sickly, with black shadows under her eyes, her body thin and fragile (narrow-chested). In connection with the aggressive clothing (of the 'father'), however, she becomes a desired object ('a velvet demon'), ultimately a *femme fatale* whose 'creator' can luxuriate in adoring her. Again, the camera follows the action with elegantly gliding movements. The dreamlike nature of this sequence ultimately guarantees its quality as a small showpiece of the 'fetishisation of fascist stereotypes' (uniforms, poses, music). Cavani has little interest in claiming this sequence as her interpretation of the story; she places too much emphasis on the surreal, dreamlike moments of the action by fading out an original soundstage, masking the participants and fixating on the two protagonists. This is a fictional episode orchestrated by Max, which encapsulates his memories and wishful thinking. This sequence also calls the authenticity of the preceding flashbacks into question, however, which fits with the logic of the film's subjective perspective, delving ever deeper into Max and Lucia's universe of two. The song itself confirms the disorientation alluded to above, once again accentuating the being torn between tenderness and pain, between love and hate, the ambiguity that becomes clear every time the 'lovers' meet. Lucia, the victim, suddenly seems to have contracted an execution. Her ambivalent reaction to the gift illustrates her awareness of this complex. Without meaning to, she has become Max's accomplice.

Further Considerations

The potential obscenity of this film lies not so much in its subject matter or its forthright depiction of sadomasochistic acts but in the fact that Liliana Cavani allows desire to stand in its own right, without comment. She does not leave the slightest doubt about the intensity of Max and Lucia's feelings and the congruency of their chosen path. The subtext of the film seems to be that, under these conditions, a burning passion can only find fulfilment in death. In view of this radical position, the struggle that contemporary critics had with *The Night Porter* is almost surprising. Accusations were frequently made that the dramatic mechanism of the film departed from the plot as it progressed, becoming sensationalist due to the concessions made to the conventions of thrillers. Following up on this mechanism, critics expressed the fear that, due to the 'simultaneously monstrous and trivialising juxtaposition of sexual obsession and bondage' and 'Nazi mechanisms and mentalities', the director was walking into a 'reactionary trap' (all quotations from Robert Fischer after Phelix and Thissen 1983).

Feminist-oriented film criticism in particular felt compelled to take radical positions (Alemann 1975): *'What Liliana Cavani offers here as a representation of female masochism is nothing more than a confirmation and reinforcement of the traditional ideology of the "true nature of women". [...] No reference is made to the social context, not a word about the humiliation of female socialisation within the patriarchal family, without which female masochism cannot be explained or understood: A woman must be masochistic to be able to survive; without behaving masochistically, she barely has a hope of success'.*

Claudia Alemann's contemporary review from 1975 may typify the angry critique that accuses the film of failing to live up to its self-projected aspirations. Lucia is anything but 'passive and indecisive'. The wording is quite inaccurate: As her feelings reawaken, her behaviour becomes more dominant and even seems to usher in a dialectical reversal. In sadomasochistic relationships, the passive partner is actually in control: Only she/he can define the limits. Lucia quite deliberately decides to separate from her husband and chooses path of desire, which has no way out. This must be considered a radical act of self-determination. Altmann's conclusion does not apply either: *'Since Cavani does not show any causes, there is no development, no momentum. This is perhaps the most dubious aspect of this film: Lucia is a static, unchanging figure. She never even shows the slightest movement towards resistance, change or even reflection on her actions. 15 years later, she is still carrying in her suitcase the little girl's nightie that Max so enjoyed dressing her in at the concentration camp. She goes along with everything without any qualms, betrays another prisoner and has his head served to her during a cabaret scene'.*

Of course, these cited facts are not true: Lucia's own decision to buy the antique children's nightie in Vienna heralds the development of an emotional predisposition and marks a fresh start. This decision is in itself an act of resistance: against her husband, against Max's comrades, against the middle-class milieu from which she comes. The relationship between guilt and responsibility in the Salomé scene (the victim as indirect 'perpetrator') has already been explained. In this context, the reason the Roman public prosecutor's office gave for deciding to confiscate the film also seems strange: it was 'doubly dangerous because it was directed by a woman. It shows a woman taking the initiative in a sexual act'. Under the questionable influence of Mediterranean machismo, the woman is actually given the active role.

Alemann is very suspicious of sadomasochism and suggests that this form of sexuality plays into the hands of the patriarchal system and restricts the freedom of the respective partners. For her, Lucia is Max's victim—earlier in the concentration camp and now in the reenactment. However, Liliana Cavani's film conjures up an amour fou that is based on the partners sucking each other dry and that can only end in death. The fatal nature of Max and Lucia's relationship is not at all symptomatic of a sadomasochistic relationship, which usually centres on the ritualised realisation of fantasies of dominance and submission to achieve sexual fulfilment. It also does not exhibit the 'destruction of one partner by the other'. Instead, the execution comes from the outside, and it hits both of them. Claudia Alemann's reservations apply more to the couple in Bertolucci's *L'ultimo tango à Parigi [Last Tango in Paris]*, whose consuming sexual obsession culminates in the woman desperately murdering the man.

In his book *Italian Cinema*, film historian Peter Bondanella(1991) also deals with the critical reception of the film, especially in America, correctly stating that *'the portrayal of evil [...] does not imply the praise of it, and the superficial attacks on the film's supposed "Fascist" character entirely miss the point'*. He indicates the extremely complex, courageously ambivalent treatment of the 'dark side' of human nature that the director unfolds: *'Liliana Cavani was inspired to create this story after interviewing a woman [...] who still placed flowers on her captor's grave each year because of her undying love. What, she queried, might have happened if he had survived?'* One of Liliana Cavani's key messages is her lucid explanation of the daring plot construction she chose for her film: *'One of the survivors, a woman, told me: 'Not all the victims are innocents because a victim too is a human being'. This survivor had known cruelty, horror, human experiments. But she could not forgive her gaolers for showing her the ambiguity of the human character'.*

Her process of interspersing the guilt of the perpetrators with that of the victims illustrates this ambivalence. Encountering 'evil' also seems to activate the 'evil' in the victims, if the survivor interviewed by Liliana Cavani as part of her documentary films is to be believed. The intolerable nature of this disappointing realisation is indeed shocking. And it is easy to project this 'guilt' back onto the film and its creator.

Translated by Annette Caroline Christmas.

Film Details

Original title	Il portiere di notte
Release year	1974
Country	Italy
Screenplay/idea	Liliana Cavani, Barbara Alberti, Italo Moscati
Director	Liliana Cavani
Music	Daniele Paris
Camera	Alfio Contini
Principle actors	Dirk Bogarde, Charlotte Rampling, Philippe Leroy, Hans Giuseppe Addobbati, Isa Miranda, Nino Bignamini, Marino Masè, Manfred Freyberger
Availability	Criterion edition (USA, code A), engl. Anchor Bay home entertainment (GB, code B), engl. Weltkino (GER, code B) contains two video documentaries by the author

References

Alemann C (1975) Der Nachtportier. Medium, p 32

Bondanella P (1991) Italian Cinema. Ungar, New York

Foucault M (1977 [1963]) A preface to transgression. In: Language, Counter-Memory, Practice—Selected Essays and Interviews 1977 Cornell University, p. 29–52 [first appeared in "Hommage Georges Bataille," in Critique, Nos. 195-196 (1963), pp. 751–770]

Phelix L, Thissen R (eds) (1983) Pioniere und Prominente des modernen Sexfilms [pioneers and celebrities of the modern sex film]. Goldmann, Munich

Praz M (1994 [1930]) Love, death and the devil. Die schwarze Romantik. dtv, München

Stiglegger M (2015) In: Eisenhut H (ed) Sadiconazista. Geschichte, film und mythos [history, film and myth], 3rd edn

In Search of the Lost Mother—*The Piano* (NZ, AU, F 1993)

20

Wolfgang Mertens

> *'When I was young, I felt the great power of my intellect. I don't anymore, as I find it a misleading tool. There is a mystery to life that no research can fully grasp'.*
>
> *'... Man thinks he's a rational being when he's not, when he's actually governed by something else entirely'.*
>
> *– Jane Campion, New Zealand anthropologist and director*

Introduction

When I first saw *The Piano* by New Zealand director Jane Campion over 20 years ago, I loved it. I discussed it with my students in 2003 in the course of a lecture series titled 'Filme – psychoanalytisch betrachtet [Films from a psychoanalytical perspective]'. The film was particularly noteworthy for its abundance of impressions and ideas. At first glance, the film seems to just be a nineteenth century historical melodrama. However, it provokes many different reactions to the themes with which it confronts its audiences, such as male-female relationships, the mother-daughter relationship, male and female desire, male violence and patriarchal sadism, female power, perversion, abuse of the daughter by the mother, daughterly revenge on the mother, bodily mutilation and so on. The film protagonists, especially Ada McGrath, continually sink ankle-

W. Mertens (✉)
Munich, Germany

Department Clinical Psychology, Ludwig-Maximilians-Universität, Munich, Germany

V. Pramataroff-Hamburger, A. Hamburger (eds.), *From La Strada to The Hours*,
https://doi.org/10.1007/978-3-662-68789-5_20

deep into the boggy, rain-soaked forest, and some students found this particularly disconcerting and frightening.

Some saw Ada's muteness as a deliberate way of taking revenge on men and of egocentrically manipulating them. They absolutely could not comprehend why Ada decides to stop speaking as a small child, nor that she later consistently sticks to this, eventually getting her daughter to speak for her. They likewise found her behaviour towards her husband appalling, in that although she denies her husband any sexual contact, she does stimulate him erotically. However, the majority identified with Ada, found her husband Alisdair Stewart a pitiful or even repulsive figure, the brutal mutilation of Ada's finger cruel in the extreme, and felt a great deal of sympathy for her burgeoning love for Baines, Stewart's neighbour and rival in the New Zealand jungle.

Film Plot

The film opens with a dramatic scene of sailors battling the surging waves of the stormy sea, cursing loudly as they carry Ada McGrath (Holly Hunter) and her daughter Flora (Anna Paquin), plus several heavy packing cases from a landing craft onto the beach. In one very large box is Ada's piano, which she absolutely had to have transported to the wilderness of New Zealand.

In Scotland, Ada's father had arranged for her to marry the distant emigrant Stewart (Sam Neill) in a British colony because it was impossible to find a man in Scotland who wanted to marry a mute woman, with an illegitimate child to boot. In the opening scene, which takes place in Scotland, Ada's voice is heard off-screen, while the mother and daughter are being carried to the beach, talking about herself and her father. The voice says that no one knows why she doesn't speak any more, not even she herself. But that she was not completely silent, because she had the piano. And that her father thought that if she sets her mind on not wanting to breathe any more, 1 day she would surely die, because she was so strong-willed, she did whatever she set her mind on.

The sailors soon return to the sailing ship, leaving Ada and her daughter alone on the isolated beach with the steep mountain ridges in the background. There is no sign of Stewart, who was supposed to pick them up, so the two women are forced to spend their first night ashore in this lonely bay without any shelter. Ada sets up a kind of tent with her crinoline, and they spend the night under it with a lit candle. When her husband finally shows up in the morning with his neighbour Baines (Harvey Keitel) and Maori locals to transport the boxes through the dense bush, he is visibly disappointed by Ada's wasted appearance. Baines, on the other hand, who has a traditional face tattoo and speaks the local language, counters that she must be tired. Stewart is incapable of understanding how important the piano is to Ada and refuses to let his men transport it on the muddy paths to his estate.

So, the piano remains on the beach for the time being. In her longing for the piano, Ada carves piano keys into a tabletop and imitates a piano accompaniment while her daughter sings along. Stewart begins to wonder about her mental health, although he continues to repeatedly try to win Ada's affection, which she resists. A few days later, Ada goes to find the neighbour George Baines and asks him to have her piano transported to the settlement. He briefly hesitates before agreeing to fetch the piano from the beach. They both get on his horse to ride to the bay. Overjoyed, Ada takes some of the slats off the packing case and begins to play her piano on the beach, which she hasn't done for a long time, full of abandon and passion. Baines is fascinated and profoundly moved by her playing (Fig. 20.1).

Unlike Stewart, he obviously recognises how vitally important the piano is for Ada. And unlike Stewart, he does not feel that the piano is a rival he needs to get rid of. He suggests trading a piece of his land that Stewart covets for the piano. Stewart agrees without Ada's consent and in the face of her angry protests, as it is her piano after all. Stewart even wants to force Ada to give Baines piano lessons.

However, Baines does not want to play the piano himself but just listen to her and be near her. He soon offers her a deal. He will give her piano back, one key at a time, in exchange for certain sexual favours. Ada reluctantly agrees. From one visit to the next, lesson by lesson, Baines then buys himself increasing physical closeness. During the piano lessons, Ada's daughter Flora is bitterly disappointed to have to stay outside after being so close to her mother for so many years.

After a long period of tenacious struggle, Ada eventually gives in to Baines' attempted seduction. And although he has finally got what he wanted, he still isn't satisfied, as Ada still only seems interested in getting her piano back at last. Some keys are still missing. Baines wants her to return his love and is extremely disappointed that Ada is unable to. If she has only been prostituting herself to get her piano back but has no feelings for him, he definitely doesn't want to have anything to do with her anymore.

Fig. 20.1 Finally reunited with the piano (00:25:03)

They go to theatre at the Christian mission station one evening. The show is a shadow play of the Knight Bluebeard folk tale, in which Bluebeard chops off his young wife's hand. Ada ignores Baines, who is sitting next to her, instead allowing Stewart to hold her hand. Jealous and disappointed, Baines leaves the room.

A few days later, Baines gives the piano back to Ada ahead of schedule. Since she is not coming to him of her own free will and is only interested in her piano, he wants to stop imposing his feelings on her.

Ada now has her piano back; however, to her amazement, she is still not happy. She increasingly misses Baines and soon calls on him.

Baines tells her that he is in agony on her account and that he cannot eat or sleep, but if she doesn't have any feelings for him, then she should go. When Ada refuses, he loses patience and angrily shows her the door. Only then does she make her feelings for him clear, slapping him because she feels misunderstood and rejected. They finally embrace and give in to their passionate desire. However, Baines is still unsure of her love. He thus asks her to come back the next day if she really loves him. If she doesn't come, he says he will go away for good.

Ada's jealous daughter Flora gives Stewart a tip-off about the rendezvous, so he lies in wait at Baines' cabin. He spies on them through a knothole, becoming extremely jealous and also sexually aroused by their lovemaking. The next day, Stewart lies in wait for Ada on the way to Baines, kisses her, pulls her to the ground and harries her remorselessly. However, when Flora calls out for her mother, he lets her go. He then shuts Ada in his house, locking the door and boarding up the windows.

Ada is desperate to prove to Baines that she is by now overwhelmed by her love for him. Full of longing for him, she gets into Stewart's bed at night and caresses him and however pushes his hands aside when he wants to touch her. Nevertheless, the next morning, he tells her that he has decided to trust her and she won't be locked up anymore. He insists that Ada promise she will not visit Baines again.

But her response is a lie. No sooner has he left for work in the wilderness than she snaps a key off her piano and carves a message on it: *'Dear George, you have my heart, Ada McGrath'*. She wants her daughter to take the key wrapped in a cloth to Baines. However, Flora knows that her mother is not supposed to visit Baines and initially refuses. Ada furiously insists, and Flora reluctantly sets off. However, once out of sight, she runs to Stewart, who rushes back to the house in impotent rage and cuts a deep notch in the piano with his axe before chopping off Ada's right index finger. Utterly distraught, Flora now has to take Ada's finger to Baines instead of the key, with the message that Stewart will chop off more of Ada's fingers if they continue seeing each other. Of course, there was no way Flora could have known that her betrayal would lead to the mutilation of her mother's finger by her stepfather, whom she has recently started calling 'Papa' since her mother actively excludes her from her relationship with Baines. Until recently, she had indignantly refused to do so.

While Stewart nurses Ada through her feverish dreams, he tries to justify his actions, claiming that he has merely clipped her wings. When he lifts her quilt to cool her feverish body, the sight of her bare legs prompts him to try and rape her again. At that moment, she

Fig. 20.2 A return to mother in the grave? (01:47:37)

opens her eyes and looks directly at him, so he desists. Immediately, afterwards, he has the feeling he can perceive her words.

In a state of extreme confusion, he breaks into Baine's house at night and holds a gun to his head in an attempt to be in charge of the situation. He talks about Ada's voice in his head asking him to let her and Baines go. He says he wants to be the man he was before and asks Baines to take Ada away with him.

Ada, Baines, Flora and the piano are rowed through the breaking waves and out into the open sea. The Maori say the boat might capsize and the piano sink into the sea. To everyone's surprise, however, Ada insists that it be surrendered to the sea because it is mutilated and spoiled. So, she wants to get rid of it in any case. Baines vehemently protests at first but eventually gives in to Ada's insistence, and the piano is heaved overboard. However, Ada puts her foot in the coiled end of the rope and is swept into the sea with the piano (Fig. 20.2).

She is increasingly quickly pulled into the depths of the ocean. But at the last moment, she decides to live, frees her shoe from the snare, drifts upwards and is pulled into the boat by the Maori.

The last scene of the film depicts Ada and Baines in their new life. She is working as a piano teacher with a silver fingertip fashioned for her by Baines and is learning to speak. Her last words are off screen: 'At night! I think of my piano in its ocean grave, and sometimes of myself floating above it. Down there everything is so still and silent that it lulls me to sleep. It is a weird lullaby and so it is; is mine'.

Background

Jane Campion, a graduate anthropologist and director born in New Zealand in 1954, was the first and thus far has been the only woman to receive the Palme d'Or in Cannes, for her 1993 film *The Piano* (sharing the honour with Chen Kaige, for his *Farewell My Concubine*). Furthermore, the film won three Oscars: Jane Campion won best screenplay written directly for the film, Holly Hunter won best actress and 11-year-old New Zealander Anna

Paquin won best supporting actress. In total, the film received eight Oscar nominations, surpassed only by *Schindler's List*. Furthermore, the film received 12 awards from the Australian Institute of Film.

Jane Campion's inspiration for the screenplay came from Emily Brontë's novel *Wuthering Heights* (1847) with its nature mysticism and demonic urges, film versions of which have been released in 1932, 1958, 1992, and 2011. An earlier film by Campion, *Angel at my table* (1990), is about a writer, Janet Frame, who was interned in a mental institution for 8 years because she was wrongly diagnosed with schizophrenia.

Unlike the protagonist in *The Piano*, however, she did not yet have any way of expressing and thus drawing attention to her suffering.

Her 1984 novel *The Piano*, co-written with Canadian writer Kate Pullinger, includes Ada MacGrath's childhood backstory and George Baines' origins.

In the book, Ada falls silent after being severely rebuked by her father for sprinkling sugar and ordered to keep her mouth shut. Deeply hurt by her father's angry rebuke when she had only been playing, she resolves never to speak again.

It is also revealed in the book that Flora was an illegitimate child. Ada had become pregnant by her piano teacher, who quickly left her when her pregnancy began to show. It can also be inferred that Ada's mother died a few weeks after childbirth and that Ada grew up with her beloved father and an aunt. Like all upper-class Victorian women, Ada's mother played the piano. And so, it stands to reason that Ada heard piano music in the womb and intensely felt the vibrations of the maternal musculature and various forms of arousal in her mother's body. This all came to an abrupt end when Ada's mother died.

How Is the Feminine Staged in Film?

At first glance, it may seem as if Ada conforms to all the traditional male prejudices: She is a headstrong, manipulative and hysterical woman who is prone to grand gestures and theatrical self-presentation at the piano, who denies her husband's sexual advances and erotically entices her lover Baines, only to then rebuff him. Her muteness seems to be a denial, a symptom she initially uses to punish her father, then later everyone around her, but also herself. In her hysterical portrayal does she not perhaps also epitomise the oppression of women in a patriarchy? Women who were not permitted to express their own desire, will or political and scientific convictions? And who could only use their own individual self-presentation to seduce men, make them dependent and then leave them unsatisfied, just as they themselves felt dependent upon and oppressed by male violence?

Ada's muteness seems mysterious in the film: Is it an expression of her tenacity, her iron will in deciding not to speak anymore and firmly sticking to it? Or is there something else behind her seemingly self-reliant defiance?

In the book of the film, we learn that Ada has stopped speaking because she is deeply hurt by her father's angry rebuke. In the film itself, however, this is not explained. So, the question of why she has become mute is a mystery. Her character seems unfathomable and puzzling. On the one hand, her muteness symbolically expresses the extent to which women were indeed oppressed in the patriarchy and did not have a voice; on the other hand, her father says her will is so strong that she could even decide to stop breathing. However, the latter seems not just to be an admiring comment on her stubbornness but an ominous foreshadowing of her near-suicide towards the end of the film.

What are the possible sources of Ada's painful feelings? The fact that her father ordered her to marry a foreigner in a New Zealand colony? That she lost her familiar home country? The separation from her surely much-loved father, who was also a substitute for her missing mother? Or is Ada's greatest pain losing her mother so young? The latter can only be guessed at in the film, as Ada's mother is a blank space. This in itself suggests that something terrible must have happened in this relationship. In such case, wanting to be silent or becoming mute could also mean returning to the infantile, pre-linguistic stage before the traumatising event occurred. Ada had once learned to speak, so she is not congenitally mute. Rather, she uses the paternal slight inflicted on her and the fact that her forbids her from contradicting him as a way of returning to the pre-linguistic stage she experienced as an infant.

In the Victorian era, playing the piano was almost the only way for women to express their emotions, which otherwise went unheard. Again, it stands to reason that Ada does not want to give up her piano for anything in the world. But it seems that the piano unconsciously embodies a lot more.

What is being expressed in her unconditional desire to be one with the piano? Is it a reminder of her middle-class home in faraway Scotland, which she had to leave against her will at her father's behest? Does the piano represent the love for her father, who was surely enormously important to Ada? Or is there another deeper meaning to the piano? Does it represent her mother, whose early death was certainly her most far-reaching experience? How can a child cope with this shattering and disappointing existential loss?

Such a loss of early oneness with the maternal body inevitably leads to the onset of agonising feelings of emptiness and of the futility and lack of meaning of everything one does. In Ada's case, it seems to be the all-consuming passion for playing the piano that enables her to come to terms with the traumatic consequences. By playing the piano, she can merge with the sounds and movements of her mother. The melodramatic music particularly intensely expresses Ada's barely controllable desire for oneness with maternal eroticism, which she was only able to experience for a short time.

This early oneness of an infant with its mother represents a pre-verbal, sensual matrix, beginning with the amniotic fluid in the womb and continuing with the exchange of milk and saliva in the oral cavity during breastfeeding, along with a whole range of skin sensations when being held and caressed, washed, cleaned, powdered and creamed, and when tears, vomit and faeces are dealt with. In the film, the mysterious, damp and steaming primaeval forest with its swampy ground, into which one can sink deeply again and again, can also be understood as an expression of a longing for this early world of the mother-child relationship. Incidentally, it is not surprising that for some viewers (not just the male ones), this swamp can trigger violent revulsion and disgust, sometimes even a fear of being devoured and of dirtiness. And in such cases, it can be assumed that the early mother-child relationship, the contact with the 'dark continent', was dysfunctional. The threat of being drawn back into a sinister liaison with the maternal sensual body can only be resisted with the help of intellectual distance and linguistic eloquence.

Furthermore, the earlier mother-child dialogue contains an eminently erotic love relationship. As long as they are not neurotically inhibited or otherwise psychologically impaired, mothers are almost obsessed with an erotic love for their young child. This manifests itself in tender stroking, cuddling, rocking and singing, rapturous glances, but also in tender pats. Mothers can experience erotic feelings, especially when breastfeeding, which in turn are communicated to their infant through bodily sensations. Mothers unconsciously send messages of psychosexual origin in addition to instinctive attachment behaviours. The tender and amorous contact with the little being also inevitably arouses sexual desires in them, which blend with the child's psychosexual and thus also perverse fantasies.

In short, a successful early mother-child relationship involves a fascinating world of tactile, visual, acoustic and olfactory sensations that are far richer in gratifying sensations, emotions and images than laborious communication with linguistic symbols. Furthermore, it is normally an erotic love relationship in which not only the bonding desires of the infant are satisfied, but in which the mother also continuously emits sensual signs and gestures. *'I'm so in love with this adorable little creature with his cute little eyes, his sweet smile, his pretty halo of hair and his cute little fingers. I can't stop kissing him and caressing him tenderly'.*

Psychoanalysis has a number of terms to describe the intense relationship and mother-child attunement, among them 'mother-child dialogue', the child's 'primary love', 'affect attunement', 'emotional resonance' and the 'gleam in the mother's eye'. When this early relationship is successful, it leads to an underlying feeling of vitality, joy in existence, basic trust and the desire to return love for love: in short, a capacity for love. However, if someone has not had enough of these experiences, they become excessively self-centred, anxious and even distrustful in contact with other people; are easily offended; feel rejected and ignored; and not sufficiently seen and valued by others. They increasingly withdraw into themselves, avoid becoming too close because this could reactivate suppressed desires to be loved, and develop a variety of behaviours, which may reject, offend or even hurt other people.

Ada's personality seems likely to have formed in such circumstances. In her muteness, she withdraws from human contact, only confiding her feelings to her piano, and uses her daughter as an interface with the world, having her interpret and express what is going on inside her. She is thus not completely cut off from all contact with the world but indirectly communicates with other people. The only tender, intimate and passionate relationship she has is with her piano and the musical expression it enables; she seems unable to live without it. And she is extremely restless as long as her piano is still on the beach. She is thus willing to barter with Baines, who seems simple-minded to her, reluctantly fulfilling his erotic and sexual desires one step at a time in order to gradually regain the keys of her beloved piano.

She has no feelings for Stewart, the husband chosen by her father. However, this is not surprising, as he seems just as incapable of love as she is.

How is the female self-image staged in the film? Ada has certainly undergone a large number of separations. The separation from her mother, her father, her home and finally her piano, which has to be left in the bay at Stewart's behest. It is not surprising that she is therefore rather anxious, cautious and controlling in contact with other people. She thus seems to be imprisoned in herself.

This is apparent right at the start of the film, when her voice is heard off and her hands spread in front of her face seem like bars separating her from the world and which she hides behind. Later, Stuart actually locks her in her room and boards up the windows. Her distance in interactions with other people is cinematically expressed in the landing scene: The boat struggles through the spume of beautiful breaking waves, which evoke passionate memories, but the steep mountain ridges in the same frame seem frightening and threatening. This sandy bay is thus not inviting to the viewer, who would rather get away from it. This contradictory inner world of Ada's is expressed even more clearly in the jungle landscape and the swamps. On the one hand, there is something fascinating about a dense rainforest with its manifold scents and sounds, its impenetrability and darkness; on the other hand, the partially cleared forest with the charred tree stumps and wooden planks in between gives a gloomy, even downright repulsive impression.

Ada and Flora initially seem to have a fused relationship, which the film convincingly conveys in their clothing, posture and facial expressions. Flora apparently reacts seismographically to her mother's moods and feelings, and she interprets them in words. Ada is thus not entirely mute. Besides music, she has found a way to express her will and her wishes through her daughter. She is often quite energetic and self-determined, as if it were easier for her to confidently assert herself through her child.

However, this long-established, almost symbiotic unity between mother and daughter, which Ada presumably uses to try and compensate for something she had never experienced enough, comes to an abrupt end when she starts giving Baines piano lessons. Her daughter is then obliged to wait alone outside the hut. Is Ada actively but unconsciously repeating her own extremely painful separation from her mother when she suddenly died? Whatever the case, she seems to have no consideration for her daughter's feelings and cannot empathise with her being completely unexpectedly being sent away from her mother.

Ada is thus not only a victim of traumatising circumstances and patriarchal disposal over her; she herself is also hurtful, manipulative and intimidating. This is also expressed in the way she treats Stewart and Baines. Stewart seems awkward and wooden and just as impaired as she is when it comes to making contact. He also has no idea of the huge significance that music and the piano have for Ada. At least he has some respect for her and her daughter and does not impose his sexual desires on Ada for the time being. In contrast, Ada is practically incapable of responding to his ideas and wishes and unwilling to do so. On the contrary, as she gradually discovers lustful and loving eroticism with Baines, first she uses her daughter and then Stewart to enable her to live out her nascent desire. However, instead of stroking his penis, she strokes his buttocks and anus, which even now can evoke strongly aversive feelings in a heterosexual man, because it can awaken rejected homoerotic desires. Perhaps, only a self-confident female director such as Jane Campion can skilfully film this subject, which is usually still considered taboo, without it seeming pornographic. And of course, the viewer can immediately understand that her insatiable longing for tenderness due to her mother's untimely death cannot be satisfied by Stewart, the husband forced upon her by her father, whose sexuality is anticipated to be self-centred.

Her strong assertiveness despite her adverse experiences becomes clear when she refuses to be locked up by Stewart and retains her love for Baines. Her desire to be united with her dead mother has gradually diminished. Nevertheless, in the final scene, when Ada and Baines are ferried to the sailing ship in the rowing boat, she briefly struggles with the wish to return to the cold grave in the sea with her piano. But her feeling of being drawn towards Baines seems too strong. Some viewers and actors have seen this ending as a concession to Hollywood movies. But even severe trauma can be healed by love.

Ada succeeds in letting go of something that has been irretrievably lost and no longer punishes herself and others for her sufferings. Instead, she can gradually turn to a creative erotic sexuality and a love of life.

In the film *The Piano*, the viewer experiences the way a woman has to protect her deeply wounded female sense of self(−worth) from people who once more leave her or who are insensitive, and how she can only rely on herself. And yet, despite patriarchal possession and violations, there is a chance to give voice to her repressed feelings—in Ada's case with the help of the piano, in other cases through writing or other forms of artistic expression. Ada succeeds in transforming her hitherto unsuccessful life narrative into a more loving, life-oriented narrative. She is helped in this by Baines' desire for her and her own erotic desires, which this awakens. She has managed to emancipate herself from her longing for her mother, who died too soon, which was further intensified by her equally strong love for her father, to bring her frozen feelings 'in the grave' back to life and to integrate her feelings of hatred and guilt. She thus no longer needs to punish herself with depressive and suicidal moods and impulses but can confidently shape her future life. The serious injury inflicted on her by Stewart's desperate but bold actions can finally be healed. She can play the piano again with a prosthetic finger made by Baines.

Further Considerations

Is the Emancipation of the Female Voice Still Necessary in the Twenty-First Century?

Much has changed since the Victorian age, in which Freud was also still entrenched. There have been four generations of (women) psychoanalysts who have dealt with the emancipation of women. In the current fourth generation, the main concerns are no longer the false assumptions Freud made about the female anatomy and mental development, nor the ideological understanding of roles behind the traditional assumptions concerning the male and female sexes, which still prevail to some extent, nor how rigid gender dichotomies can be softened, and so on. Instead, the fourth generation is now concerned with how our world can be saved from the approaching climate catastrophe. For this would massively exacerbate social inequality, whereby women and children would particularly suffer.

Nevertheless, as was the case when the film *The Piano* was released in the 1990s, the question still remains of whether women will ever be able to emancipate themselves from patriarchal supremacy in business, politics and science. Can women ever become emancipated if they are not permitted to speak up and convince men of the need to develop more common ground and the relationship between men and women? Does the future of civilisation not depend on women being able to free their voice, their will and their desire, which can only arise out of commonality and mutual recognition and not from patriarchal possession and domination?

From the Perverse Bargain to Gaining a Capacity for Love

Baines leaves the Maori land in its original state, unlike Stewart, who clears, mines and rams in fence posts, taking colonial possession of the foreign land. He identifies to some extent with the indigenous population by having his face tattooed and learning their language.

Baines senses the importance of the piano for Ada and admires her for her music, unlike Stewart who has no understanding of it. But why should Baines, of all people, the uneducated illiterate man, be able to become Ada's lover? He is a European expatriate and like his father before him worked as a whaler for years. At the same time, he tries to approximate the indigenous people of New Zealand in his manner of dress, facial tattoo and way of life. Since he identifies with both worlds, he moves freely between them and can thus also soften the rigidly socialised gender role stereotypes. He thus does not have to prove his masculinity by immediately engaging in sexual intercourse. Rather, he can allow himself to be entranced and captivated by Ada's mysterious and also passionate aura. He can indulge his feelings and also suffer terribly from heartache. But then, perhaps only a woman director can portray this new type of man so convincingly without reinforcing the old clichés or ridiculing this new male-female masculinity. This is also expressed in the female gaze on Baines: the primaeval forest is perceived as maternal, and his powerful arm and shoulder muscles induce a feeling of security by way of association. Baines' childlike and unselfconscious curiosity about what can be seen under Ada's skirt and the sensual pleasure of catching a glimpse of naked skin through the hole in her stocking is reminiscent of playing doctor as a child and is not at all off-putting. And the sexual union between Ada and Baines is an extremely enjoyable and passionately filmed intercommunion of two people who desire one another. Along with the music, this forms one of the film's aesthetic highlights.

Stewart's Admission of his Failure

In his patriarchal attitude, Stewart is bent on increasing his possessions by acquiring more land and exploiting his Antipodean workers. In order to satisfy the Victorian bourgeois and Christian ideals of his Scottish origins, this requires him to marry to a suitable woman who will run his household properly and bear him children. And, of course, she must also be available for his sexual needs.

Only through Baines can he learn how important it was to respect Ada's will and her idiosyncrasy, to empathise with her and not to show jealously for something of central importance to her because of her personal history: her passionate love for her piano. He wants to force her under his control. In European colonialism, this (largely male) urge to conquer was particularly prevalent and has left its devastating traces in Third World countries to this day. Last but not least, the current predatory capitalism of the West is a frightening consequence of this unbridled narcissistic attitude towards the peoples of the world who have been declared inferior.

Eventually, Stewart has to admit to himself that he will never be capable of the same attitude and demeanour as Baines, which ultimately leads him to urge Ada and Baines to leave the island and move away for good.

Flora's Ways of Dealing with Abandonment

Under the patriarchy, women have had to suffer the insult of not being allowed to feel equal to men; however, they have also found ways of coping with it. For example, by running a strict regime at home and trying to just as arbitrarily shape the children according to their will. On the other hand, Ada's sexual awakening also unleashes her daughter's sexuality. After Flora has spied on the sexuality between her mother and Baines, she playfully hugs trees—while surrounded by the Maori children—and performs coitus movements. She calls on her playmates to do likewise. Her feelings of exclusion also lead her to enact a sadistic game with a dog, which she tortures with a stick only to stroke and calm it afterwards. She thus shifts her aggressive feelings of disappointment and anger at being abruptly abandoned by her mother onto the dog and recaptures a sexually tinged sense of power.

This helps her cope with her sadness at the ending of her hitherto symbiotic relationship with her mother.

Translated by Annette Caroline Christmas.

Film Details

Title	The Piano
Release year	1993
Country	New Zealand, Australia, France
Screenplay/idea	Jane Campion
Director	Jane Campion
Principle actors	Holly Hunter, Harvey Keitel, Sam Neill
Availability	DVD/Blu-ray

Part VI

Revolt Against the Camera. The Uprising Against "Male Gaze"

A Woman in Limbo—Lost in Translation (US 2003)

21

Andreas Hamburger

Introduction

Lost in Translation, a film that has occupied me for about 15 years and to which I have only recently dedicated a detailed analysis (Hamburger 2019), can be read according to a variety of aspects—for instance, that of the male protagonist getting lost, or the invention of a woman in temporal limbo who is not only a witness to this getting lost but steers and shapes it herself. In this sense, this second analysis of the film (which naturally owes much to the first) will be devoted to the construction of femininity, which—as I will show—actually provides the key to understanding the film. Film psychoanalytic interpretation, as I understand it (Hamburger 2024), always starts from the personal experience of viewing the film, which is very characteristic in this case: *Lost in Translation* artfully transports us into a state of comfortable, drowsy, slightly eroticised lostness, floating in an in-between space between strangeness, chance encounter and longing. This reaction as an audience member is not just mine alone, as became clear to me during many audience discussions on the film, although one's reception of a film is always entirely personal. But I am perhaps getting ahead of myself.

Plot

Bob Harris (Bill Murray), an aging US movie star, is in Tokyo for a week to shoot a commercial for the Japanese whisky brand *Suntory*. The film begins with his arrival at the airport but immediately cuts to the back view of a young woman, still during the opening

A. Hamburger (✉)
International Psychoanalytic University Berlin, Berlin, Germany

V. Pramataroff-Hamburger, A. Hamburger (eds.), *From La Strada to The Hours*,
https://doi.org/10.1007/978-3-662-68789-5_21

Fig. 21.1 Title sequence (00:00:59)

credits (Fig. 21.1). We don't understand why, because in the next cut, we see Bob coasting through Tokyo at night in a taxi, bathed in the glow of the billboards; on one, he sees himself with a whisky bottle and some lettering he cannot decipher any more than we can. We can see the sensory overload in his tired face. We accompany him to the hotel, where he spends the night exhausted but unable to sleep. The camera then cuts away from his perspective to show Charlotte (Scarlett Johansson) sitting awake at the hotel window, just as Bob is in his hotel room, where the fax machine is spewing his wife's questions about the flat furnishings and which he does not read. The next morning, he sees the woman who could not sleep in the lift for the first time: Charlotte, an American in her mid-twenties. She catches his eye. The same cannot be said of her. He goes on to film the commercial in a comic scene. In parallel, we see Charlotte in the underground, at a temple—as an immutable observer. She calls a friend, in tears: *'I can't feel anything'*. She contemplates herself in the mirror, lies around, and then her husband John (Giovanni Ribisi) is back again, talking excitedly about his shoot with the Japanese boy band he is there to photograph. Bob returns to the hotel, immersed in the same dreariness that not even a prostitute sent by his clients can lift; her attempt to wrangle a little excitement out of his fatigue is also grotesquely drawn, as is the following photo shoot, where he is made to imitate a whole gallery of American stars, including, of course, 'Logel Moole' as 007.

Only at this point, after 23 long minutes of filming, does he see Charlotte again, at the hotel bar accompanied by her husband John, a stylishly dressed man in his late 20 s who is busy with his crew. This time she notices him too and sends him a sake. Just like that. In the lift to his room, he realises that he is still wearing his costume for the *Suntury* shoot. Another Chaplinesque Japanese scene follows: He visits the hotel's private gym at night out of boredom, where the cross trainer, labelled only in Japanese, suddenly runs at full speed, dragging him along with it.

The morning after, Bob is again picked up for work by his extremely obliging team of agents. Cut to Charlotte and John walking through the lobby in a close embrace, until John is greeted effusively by one Kelly (Anna Faris), an overexcited young actress; Charlotte stands off to the side, alienated. Later, she sits in her untidy hotel room listening to a self-help audiobook, roams around the hotel, sees Kelly giving an idiotic interview, drops in on an Ikebana class, takes a bath. Nighttime again: sleeplessness.

She decides to go to the deserted hotel bar, where she finds Bob in animated conversation with the bartender. She sits down with him; a laconic dialogue ensues in which they both get to the heart of their life situation: He doesn't know what his 25-year marriage is supposed to mean, and she doesn't know what her newly acquired Masters in Philosophy is for. And both of them have ended up here somehow and would like to sleep. Then we follow Charlotte through the next endless day, curiously watching young men at the slot machines. In the bar in the evening, Kelly needles John with endless small talk. Charlotte escapes and bumps into Bob again, who suggests she be his accomplice in a prison break. She laughs—and that's it. Evening came, then morning—both of them are sleepless in Tokyo. When John leaves for a 3-day shoot in Osaka, she stays behind in Tokyo. She takes Bob on an evening out with friends; they roam around the district; in the 'Charlie Brown' bar, one of their Japanese friends gets into a fight, and they have to run away. They get into a stoned party and then rent a karaoke room where they sing songs by the Sex Pistols, Pretenders and Roxy Music, almost as imitations of themselves. They get closer when they return to the hotel together at four in the morning, and Bob carries the sleeping Charlotte to her room. He puts her to bed like a child and calls his wife from the room—but she is in a different time zone and also in another world.

Their deepening closeness over the next few days predominantly seems like a father-daughter relationship—such as when he takes her to the hospital to have her injured toe looked at and buys her a soft toy, having previously tried to communicate onomatopoeically with an ancient Japanese woman in the waiting area.

When they try to continue partying with their friends, they end up at a strip club. Not amused, they prefer to run like two children through the urban jungle, past Bob's huge whisky advertisements, and find themselves back in their sleepless hotel rooms. Until a bellboy slips Bob's message under her door: *'Are you awake'?* Finally, they end up in bed together—admittedly only to watch *La dolce vita* in the original Italian with Japanese subtitles and talk about life and being married against the backdrop of the sea of lights reflected in the windows of the hotel room at night (Fig. 21.2). And they eventually both get tired and sleep—not with each other, but next to each other.

Once again, they go their separate ways. Charlotte travels to Kyoto, where she starts to have feelings again in the traditional Japanese atmosphere and on seeing a wedding ceremony. Bob, in the meantime, takes part in another burlesque Japanese talk show.

When she goes to pick him up in the room to go out and realises that there is a woman with him (the jazz singer from the bar), Charlotte is hurt and comments sarcastically: 'Well, I guess she's more around your age ... you guys could talk about things in common, like growing up in the fifties ...' (Coppola 2002, p. 51). But they are reconciled the follow-

Fig. 21.2 A Night Date (01:07:44)

ing night, when a fire alarm has them standing together among a crowd of hotel guests in their pyjamas—and once more this suggests the outward appearance of having spent the night together, when we know that they haven't. The day before his departure, the tension goes up a notch. Bob doesn't want to leave, and Charlotte urges him to stay, making a slightly racy innuendo: 'Then stay. We may start a jazz band' (ibid., p. 54). And then they dutifully return to their separate rooms—even though the goodbye kiss they share in the lift is a little closer to the lips.

Bob inevitably leaves the next morning. When bidding an embarrassed farewell to Charlotte, he does not utter a single word. We suppose that he answers her expectant look with a gesture, but he remains silent and leaves her alone in his indifferent gaze. But then, in a classic closing move, he stops the limousine taking him to the airport and runs after Charlotte through the crowd to embrace her again, this time properly. He whispers something in her ear, they kiss, and she smiles through her tears and leaves. He gets back into the car, and we see Tokyo glide past him, like in the opening scene, but this time in daylight. The signs appearing seem more comprehensible—and we know from the script that: 'Bob's happy he's going home, he's happy he came to Tokyo' (ibid., p. 58).

Background

The title quotes a famous autobiographical long poem by James Merrill, in which the poet describes his lostness and linguistic confusion in his upper-middle-class parental home—an early allusion to lostness, a central theme of the film, and it becomes clear that *Lost in Translation* is much more than just a love story. The film provoked very varied but for the most part extreme reactions among critics, being either reverent praise or harsh protests. It was even accused of racism because of the comic scenes in Japan.

These heated reactions may have had something to do with the fact that the director, Sofia Coppola, was virtually a public figure, having made her first film appearance as a baby in *The Godfather*, being the daughter of Francis Ford Coppola and a cousin of Nicholas Cage, and so was inevitably measured against her famous family members. *Lost in Translation* is her second film after her debut film *The Virgin Suicides* (1999), a respectable achievement that already bore her own signature. It earned her the Oscar for Best Screenplay and even a nomination for Best Director, among numerous other awards—a sensation, as she would have been the first woman to win it. Well, being a member of a particular family is a private matter and of no relevance to the interpretation of a work of art. However, Coppola deliberately plays with this interconnectedness and anticipates the comparison. She thus consciously opts for a film language that does not go against that of her father, but neither is it comparable. She consistently narrates on a level below the minimalist plot.

How Is the Feminine Staged in Film?

'Bob's happy he came to Tokyo', the final sentence of the script—is that what *Lost in Translation* is about? The refinement of an aging misanthrope by a young woman? The film may work that way on one level, as a romance, and Coppola deliberately sets it up as such, with Bob as the protagonist and Charlotte merely his mirror. But it also subverts this level by dealing primarily with the question of cliché. Love in *Lost in Translation* questions the cinematic construct of 'love' and opens up an unconventional view.

Coppola does so with masterly precision by consistently not presenting the 'love story'—or, to be precise, its erotic level—head on in images and scenes but tells it through omission. This art of not showing is akin to the classical Japanese aesthetic, an almost unbelievably long first act, lazily flowing scenes with just one glimpse of the woman who is to become the focus of a great deal of attention in that strange cropped image during the opening credits, after which she is not seen again for another half hour. And even then, nothing clear happens. In the second half of the film, encounters become more frequent and familiar but also more tense, with shy touching, noticeable sparks and continued cautious distance. Bob leaves the young woman's signs of closeness in their ambiguity without clarifying them with a sexual response. Thus, the moment of suspense is heightened until the final farewell in the hotel lobby and finally resolved—or not?—when he jumps back out of the limousine and runs to Charlotte. This doesn't seem like the classic conversion moment of a happy ending, if only because there are no violins. A tight hug, a genuine kiss, he whispers something to her, and then they part. Charlotte has tears in her eyes and sketched on Bob's immobile face on the drive through the urban canyons to the airport there is a hint of a thought that it might be possible to live life.

The linchpin on which everything turns is the Charlotte character. Scarlett Johansson, only 18 at the time, embodies her indecision and her childlike wonder at having landed in the wrong life. She doesn't shout it from the rooftops and doesn't show it through intense acting, but rather through her all-pervading tiredness, which is only countered by trips to the city. Admittedly, these do not seem like a coming-of-age story either, but rather show the childlike curiosity and vitality that inhabit this tired, disoriented woman in spite of everything. In the film, her disorientation is represented by the exotic setting of Japan, which we experience and explore through her eyes.

Of course, the enigma is not only the big city with its misunderstood symbols but first and foremost the woman herself. This is also how the abovementioned long shot in the title sequence is to be understood (Fig. 21.1).

One of the most beautiful descriptions of this image—which has drawn fierce criticism elsewhere—comes from Susanne Vahabzadeh (2004), the film critic of the *Süddeutsche Zeitung*: Coppola tells the story in exactly the same way 'as Charlotte looks at the world in some scenes: Unbiased, her head tilted, curious, without any aggression'. This camera view of Charlotte/Scarlett Johansson's back is so overlong that it virtually sits out the voyeurism and clears the gaze for an exploratory, curious look. This works similarly to the famous opening sequence of Jean-Luc Godard's *Le Mépris*, where the camera explores Brigitte Bardot's body while the protagonist herself accompanies this tracking shot with questions: *'Tu aimes mes cuisses?—Tu aimes mes fesses'? ['Do you like my thighs?—Do you like my buttocks'?]* In both sequences, the steadfast hold of the camera and the alienated colour aesthetics not only expose a body to the gaze, but the gazing itself also becomes conscious. In *Lost in Translation*, the cut into the dark sequence reveals the back view of a woman we don't yet know, in a colour scheme that is completely out of keeping with what we have seen so far.

Against light grey drapery in the background, we see the woman wearing a grey-blue woollen top and almost skin-coloured old pink knickers of a rather demure cut—all in all, the image seems rather pastel-decorous in contrast to the image sequence before and after it, which are dominated by deep darkness and garish neon tones. Even if the image is not unerotic (a furrow shimmers through the panties, running across the canvas to the right in a central line between the thighs and a mysterious cross forms in the back of the reclining figure's knees), the desire it can trigger is the smooth antithesis of the consumerism that the garish imagery of advertising seeks to elicit. One is rather seduced into following the lines gently—not into the domineering possession of the female body that classical mainstream cinema usually offers to the 'male gaze'.

When the camera then cuts to Bob's nocturnal taxi ride, during which he suddenly catches sight of himself on a huge advertising screen with incomprehensible lettering, it is a commentary on the previous image, and this commentary also reveals a mystery. How has the actor who is just arriving for the shoot already got onto the billboard? The image, like the previous one, says: we are watching ourselves seeing, as in a mirror.

Thus, the idea is already introduced in the opening sequence that in *Lost in Translation* the woman is not simply the viewed and the man the viewer. Both are incomprehensible signs. Like in a puzzle picture or a Rorschach test, viewers can look for a narrative about the tired man and his story, or the story of the tired woman. But in any case, it is the story of fatigue.

In the following, in accordance with the theme of the present volume, the female protagonist will be the main focus. Hyman King (2010) posits that *Lost in Translation* is essentially about female development and links this depiction of development to the exoticism of Orientalism. Japan, the foreign culture, stands for the unexplored, unnamed part of one's own self-discovery. She sees the young woman thrown into an environment of alien, indecipherable signs, just as a child is exposed to 'enigmatic messages' from the Other at the start of its development and first learns to read itself in them (Laplanche 1997). For King, *Lost in Translation* does play with the classic story of a young woman's self-discovery, exposing herself to strangers and finding herself through an Oedipal father figure. This motif of Cupid and Psyche has a long literary and film history, from the biblical tale of *Jephtha's daughter* to the late Latin literary fairy tale *Cupid and Psyche* by Apuleius to the baroque novel *La Belle et la Bête* and its numerous film adaptations. But *Lost in Translation* doesn't exactly live up to the expectations of the genre—the love story peters out. If the farewell gesture plays with the cliché of a happy ending according to the genre pattern 'everything will turn out all right—they'll get together', this is just a brief, weary game. On emerging from the cinema, the viewer quickly realises that it would not necessarily be the best ending for either of them if the young woman and the old man were to 'live happily ever after', if only because the closeness of this ending would be very different and either she would have to accept a misanthropic hermit crab or he would have to self-optimise and transform himself into a youthful prince. *Lost in Translation* breaks with the cliché of female development as portrayed by (not only) Western culture and certainly also Freudian psychoanalysis: the girl as a castrated boy, as an indeterminate being that in the course of development must find her destiny as the counterpart of the man. In contrast, *Lost in Translation* sets a new female self-image, the recognition of 'being lost' (Sobchak 2004, p. 34). King makes this clear for *Lost in Translation* when she shows that Japan is not simply portrayed as exotic but that the strangeness in the encounter of the Western protagonists with the Oriental world of signs is reciprocal.

Femininity unfolds authentically at the point when it refrains from determining or allowing itself to be determined but instead exposes itself to its 'inner alterity', which is reflected in the encounter with the foreign culture—not as a distorted image of the incomprehensible, but as a mutual space of experience. The fact that this is actually the case in the film, and not a flat, comical—or even racist, as some indignant reviewers tried to suggest—exoticism, is shown by the fact that the encounter with the foreigner is portrayed in both directions: The films, songs and clothes of the American fifties and the appropriation of Western stars in Japan are just as present as the Japanese signs and manners that are foreign to the West. Photographs are taken from both sides, and both sides pose in front of cameras.

Lost in Translation portrays more than the fairy tale of the good old man and the beautiful girl. At its core, it portrays a film artist's exploration of femininity, mirrored in the weathered masculinity of Bob Harris/Bill Murray and in the alienness of the setting.

If you read the film this way, as a study of femininity, then you will also understand why it is set in Japan. The relationship between America and Japan is constantly present in the film and is an allegory. The abovementioned outrage surrounding the accusation of anti-Japanese racism, which went as far as demanding that the Oscar be taken back, shows that a thoroughly virulent issue is at work here. American-Japanese relations, marked by the social trauma of the atomic bomb (and, for Americans, the attack on Pearl Harbour, which still rankles), is emblematic of how sudden acts of violence and revenge can virtually explode out of the incomprehensible unknown; nowadays, the industrial race for globalisation and digitalisation evokes similar feelings of uncertainty, loss of tradition and insecurity.

From a psychoanalytical point of view, it is about getting lost when holding relationships fade and the new still cannot be understood. There are turning points in psychological development that tend to engender such feelings of strangeness and confusion, which often have to be kept in check by defence mechanisms for example, the earliest consensus between mother and child on their 'enigmatic messages', language acquisition and adolescence. In *Lost in Translation*, the crude jokes on Japanese (such as when an interpreter renders a director's torrent of words in three monosyllables, or 'r' and 'l' are transposed) can be understood as such a defence against feeling lost, in this case literally 'lost in translation'.

The countermovement to this experience of foreignness is shown in Charlotte's excursions to the cities of Tokyo and Kyoto, where she increasingly takes in and absorbs aspects of the foreign culture. She explores foreignness as a transitional space or one of opportunity, a creative relatedness between mother and child first described by Donald W. Winnicott, in which the mother allows the infant to realise its creative impulses towards her. 'Of the transitional object it can be said that it is a matter of agreement between us and the baby that we will never ask the question: "Did you conceive of this or was it presented to you from without?" The important point is that no decision in this point is expected. The question is not to be formulated' (Winnicott 1989 [1953], p. 12).

Charlotte's steady, searching, unobtrusive gaze, a gaze in which the camera increasingly allows us to participate, fulfils this description of allowing to feel safe. She learns to deal with the enigma of the environment—and thus also with the enigma within herself. She can thus adopt the most important Japanese virtue, mindfulness ('amae'). Since she does not want to aggressively penetrate what is foreign to her by forcibly naming it (or joking about it) and instead approaches it openly and receptively, she actually comes into contact with this virtue. And, one might add, with herself as a philosophy student who did not know what to do with her life or studies. In fact, she is doing something that lies at the heart of her own profession and also at the core of her femininity as defined in relation to masculinity: looking attentively at the unnamed.

Further Considerations

Naturally, the process of becoming mindful applies to both sexes (in the film and in the audience). In the same way that Charlotte is more than just a ministering angel for Bob Harris' midlife crisis, Bob is more than just an Oedipal game character for Charlotte and also more than a mirror for her self-discovery. He is a protagonist who is also going through his own transformation. Nicholas Wong (2009) summarises the new quality of love they mutually discover as 'Loving You By Not Falling in Love'.

Transitional Object and Reciprocal Use

Bob Harris has forgotten how to feel wonder. Around him, strangeness at first seems only distorted and comical, while Charlotte's open gaze, her capacity for being bemused, is met with empathetic reactions. But that changes. The radical openness with which Charlotte not only begins to move around in the foreign environment but also lets the foreign into herself—including and above all her feelings for the funny old man, which she herself cannot understand—rubs off on him. He also begins to engage with foreignness, which at first had only seemed annoying and incomprehensible to him.

In his relationship with Charlotte, Bob also learns to put his disillusionment and detachment into perspective. A major driver of his world-weariness is his constant willing participation in exploitation by the media, which has virtually sucked him dry. His emptiness is the last bastion of resistance against appropriation when he is photographed as a blend of all the Hollywood heroes who have ever reached for a glass of whisky and is fed into an impenetrable exploitation system. His wife's trivial questions about the furnishings of their flat, which haunt him via fax, reflect the same emptiness. On the other hand, his immunity seems to be weakening when he tries to call her the moment he senses that his attraction for Charlotte, who represents his lost wonder, will prove irresistible.

This portrayal of the protagonist as a shell emptied by medialisation is aimed directly at the audience—after all, Bob (or Bill) is a cinema icon. When Bob says 'cheers'! to the camera, he is seen not just by his Japanese media consumers, whom he is supposed to seduce with the exotic charm of the West to buy a Japanese product that is likewise a quotation: we see him, too. We are the ones he is supposed to be addressing, 'like an old friend', as the excited Japanese director instructs him. In fact, we like to succumb to the illusion that the screen characters are our friends and pay them to give this impression, to mirror us as we would like to be mirrored. And conversely, we allow ourselves to be influenced by their symbolism: we smile and kiss and scowl like our screen heroes; indeed, we are even bored like them when we get bored (e.g. think of Bogart). We buy conventional glances and then mimic them in our own facial expressions. In the Japanese advertisement, we watch Bob making gestures that are utterly canonised. There is nothing new about them. He only performs new movements when with Charlotte, such as the evening they spend together watching television in the hotel room. He is sprawled on his stomach on the bed with her curled up next to him, both enshrouded in the blurry reflections of the big city lights (Fig. 21.2).

Audience Alienation

Lost in Translation is about the loss of familiar spatial and temporal reference systems. The audience is drawn into the trance that overtakes the protagonists. We, too, are impacted for long stretches by signs and gestures that are illegible (to us), such as the big city night drenched in neon signs and an entertainment aesthetic that sometimes seems bizarre to

Western viewers. The background, overfilled with illegible lettering, is often shown out of focus. This and the editing rhythm with its changing light-dark passages deepen the forlornness that grips the viewer. Although the audience of *Lost in Translation* is not suffering from jet lag, it is sucked into temporal disorientation by the film.

These signals of forlornness are enacted on a foil of globalisation. Two Americans find themselves subject to the impenetrable pattern of meaning of a foreign culture, in the transitional space of a hotel where the familiar gestures of romantic comedy seem strangely tired, as if reeled off, as if the performers were looking over their shoulders as they perform cultural gestures in a vacuum devoid of resonance. The result is a film that confronts viewers, young and old, with their own inner indeterminacy and mysteriousness (cf. Rohde-Dachser 2011). *Lost in Translation* renders the subjective perception of a globalised world tangible, in which encountering foreigners with incomprehensible rules has become the norm. Such encounters force us to translate—in the way all speech does, in fact.

Translated by Annette Caroline Christmas.

Film Details

Title	Lost in Translation
Release year	2003
Country	USA, Japan
Screenplay/idea	Sofia Coppola
Director	Sofia Coppola
Music	Kevin Shields
Camera	Lance Acord
Principal actors	Scarlett Johansson, Bill Murray
Availability	DVD, Blu-ray

References

Coppola S (2002) Lost in translation. Shooting draft. http://www.dailyscript.com/scripts/lost- in-translation- script.html. Accessed 21 Feb 2020

Hamburger A (2024) Film psychoanalysis—relational approaches to film interpretation]. Routledge, London.

Hamburger A (2019) Im Übergang. Ein filmpsychoanalytischer Kommentar zu Sofia Coppolas lost in translation (US 2003) [a film-psychoanalytical commentary on Sofia Coppola's lost in translation]. In: Storck T, Hamburger A, Nitzschmann K, Schneider G, Bär P (Eds.) Francois Ozon. Täuschung und subjektive Wahrheit [deception and subjective truth]. Psychosozial, Giessen, pp 49–58

King H (2010) Lost in translation: orientalism, cinema, and the enigmatic signifier. Duke University Press, Durham/London

Laplanche J (1997) The theory of seduction and the problem of the other. Int J Psychoanal 78:653–666

Rohde-Dachser C (2011) Lost in translation. Psyche—Z Psychoanal 65(12):1202–1210

Sobchak V (2004) Carnal thoughts. Embodiment and moving image culture. University of California Press, Berkeley/Los Angeles/London

Vahabzadeh S (2004) Stranger Is The Night. Im Kino: "Lost in Translation". Südeutsche Zeitung 7 January 2004

Winnicott DW (1989 [1953]) Transitional objects and transitional phenomena. In: Winnicott DW (ed) Playing and reality. Routledge, pp 1–25

Wong NYB (2009) Loving you by not falling in love: the postmodern representation of love in Chungking express and lost in translation. Screen Edu 53:131–137

22

Pursuing Emptiness: Obsession and (Im) Potence in Kathryn Bigelow's *Blue Steel* (US 1990)

Reinhold Görling

Introduction

'I wanna shoot people' is the answer of newly sworn-in police officer Megan Turner to her colleague's question about how she got into this profession. Turner (Jamie Lee Curtis) is steering the patrol car through the streets of New York on her first tour of duty. She smiles on giving this answer. Her colleague, somewhat astonished, replies 'You're kidding'? and then answers his own question with a laugh: 'You're O.K. Turner, you're O.K'. Being fascinated by handguns and the possibility of killing is usually a masculine narrative. What changes when these attributes are assigned to a heroine?

The revolver is a phallic symbol, which represents the claim to power and autonomy. In a broader sense, it can also be understood as a fetish. The fetish differs from other symptoms in that it refers to an absence while at the same time denying that there is one. As is well known, Freud exemplifies this in the potentially traumatic experience for the boy of the absence of the penis from the woman's body (Freud 1927). But Freud's discovery about the interplay of recognition and denial in fetishes is also applicable to other contexts. In this respect, the phallic fetish of the weapon does not have to be connected with the denial of castration; it may refer to an earlier trauma that also affects women. Nevertheless, the theme of empowerment and defence against a threat remains effective, although the dynamics develop differently: persecutors become persecuted in a different way. Kathryn Bigelow's film *Blue Steel*, which premiered in 1990, can be seen as an artistic experiment in unpacking these questions. It joins a list of films from the 1980s that examines genres dominated by male heroes and traces the transformation they undergo when the narrative focuses on female characters. Bette Gordon's *Variety* (1983), a film that deals with voyeur-

R. Görling (✉)
Cultural and Film Studies Scholar, Berlin, Germany

V. Pramataroff-Hamburger, A. Hamburger (eds.), *From La Strada to The Hours*,
https://doi.org/10.1007/978-3-662-68789-5_22

ism, was one of the first in this series. It arguably culminates in Ridley Scott's *Thelma and Louise* (1991), which follows two women on the run (see Pramataroff-Hamburger and Hamburger in Chap. 25 of this volume). What all these films perhaps have in common, Bigelow's included, is that the transgression or the dissolution of boundaries, which lies at the heart of each narrative no longer dissolves into a reintegration or restoration of order, however this might be structured. Apparently, the logic of the dissolution of boundaries unfolds differently.

Film Plot

Blue Steel begins with a black screen and loud shouts of both threats and pleas for help. A man seems to be beating a woman: *'I'm gonna kill you'!* The camera's aperture is opened, and an apartment building hallway becomes visible, in bluish light and with red ceiling lighting. The camera moves down the corridor. A female voice is heard shouting *'Help me!'*. A pair of hands come into the frame from the left, holding tightly onto a revolver. They belong to a policewoman who is moving down the corridor, her arms outstretched. She glides past the camera and further down the corridor, stops in front of a door, kicks it open and bursts into the room with the gun held out in front of her. A man is standing behind a woman, his arm around her neck. He first points his gun at her, then suddenly at the policewoman, shouting: *'Die'!* But the policewoman shoots first. We then see a hand reaching for a weapon. The woman involved in the fight shoots at the policewoman. *'Shit'!* the latter yells. As viewers, we think she must have been badly injured, but there is a cut to show her standing upright in her blue New York Police Department uniform, her cap in profile. The situation is revealed to be a police training exercise. Megan Turner listens to her instructor berate her that she probably killed the husband but overlooked the wife, who in turn killed her. *'In the field you get to have eyes in the back of your head'*, the instructor adds rather tersely. The expression is familiar, but not immediately obvious at this point, since the perpetrator and the victim who becomes the perpetrator were standing in front of Megan. It is rather a matter of fanning out perspectives to reveal the interplay of perpetrator and victim. And this won't be the only such blunder to thwart Turner during the film.

First, however, the film captured viewers' attention in close-up shots of the shimmering blue metal of a Smith & Wesson. The camera scans the steel surface for almost 2 min until, superimposed by the title credits, we see cartridges being pushed into the magazine. It is not so much the object as its material that eroticises the images. Then, in a slow-motion shot, the gun drops into a holster—a sequence that matches one at the very end of the film, in which just such a gun also falls onto a car seat in a slow-motion shot. The hand that guided the Smith & Wesson to the holster is now buttoning a freshly ironed blue blouse, while a softly humming female voice can be heard. The camera follows the action from the naked belly to the brassiere decorated with white lace, all the way to a neck adorned with a necklace. The erotic staging is interrupted with the hard impact of a firm black leather shoe on a stool, and the laces are tied. The eroticism of the skin of the female body and the violent gesture of stamping with sturdy footwear form a complex interplay in this dressing scene.

Turner is preparing for her swearing-in ceremony, at which her friend Tracy and her two children are present, but not Turner's parents. *'I got a God damn cop for daughter'*, her father is to say to her at a dinner her mother has invited her to the following day. The conversation between Turner and her workmate about her reasons for becoming a policewoman, quoted at the beginning, immediately follows this dialogue. The film thus puts Turner's relationship with her parents and her relationship with her work as a policewoman into perspective very early on. Immediately after this conversation, Turner parks the patrol car in a busy street in front of a small shop selling coffee and snacks. While her colleague is in the toilet and she is waiting for her coffee, she looks seemingly absentmindedly and yet also fixedly into a grocery shop across the street. In fact, in this sequence, which will be examined in more detail, a man steps in front of the cashier with his gun drawn, demanding that he hand over the takings. Turner then rushes off. From point of view of narrative logic, the subsequent action is quite improbable because Turner would have taken far too long to accomplish what the film now shows: to run across the street and get behind the house in order to enter the supermarket via a back exit and finally to ask the robber, who is still standing at the cash register with his gun drawn, to drop the revolver and, when he begins to point the gun at her, to fire as many shots at him from the pistol held in both hands as its magazine will hold. Bigelow's film is not designed to tell a realistic story in a believable way. The detective film genre has had its psychological credibility in the depiction of the entanglement of pursuer and pursued, and thus ultimately also of perpetrator and victim, at least since film noir. In *Blue Steel*, this entanglement unfolds in that one of the witnesses to the fatally foiled robbery leaves the scene of the crime unnoticed and takes possession of the robber's large-calibre murder weapon. Eugene Hunt (Ron Silver) is a stockbroker. A while later, we see him on the financial trading floor gesticulating expressively, even wildly, commenting on the changing displays and thus probably giving a colleague trading tips. In the next few days, Hunt will use this stolen weapon to commit several murders on the streets. Beforehand, he carved the name Megan Turner into the shell casings. In this way, he involves the latter in his actions. His victims are initially chosen somewhat at random: a homeless man, an elderly passer-by and then a prostitute, after whose murder we briefly see Hunt in a visibly arousing act with her bloody clothes. But then he turns Megan into a helpless witness to the murder of her friend. Before that, he had tried to meet and get to know her, offered her a taxi ride in the pouring rain and invited her to an expensive restaurant and to a helicopter flight over New York at night. But he is obviously not interested in a conventional erotic adventure. He is fascinated by the moment when Turner holds the gun in both hands and pulls the trigger with a fixed stare, not batting an eyelid, as he confesses to her later. The gaze at the moment of killing and death is a mystical motif that implies that at the moment of transgression another, otherwise inaccessible truth would become visible in the eyes. It forms a counterpart to the moment of erotic dissolution and is obviously also strongly interwoven with Hunt's eroticism.

Turner is initially suspended for her deadly and excessive use of weapons in confronting the supermarket robber. However, after the bullet casings with her name on them are found, she is reinstated as a decoy, this time as a member of the homicide squad. Her new boss is Nick Mann (Clancy Brown), a quiet and understanding man who sticks by Turner even when the others begin to doubt her version of the story. Mann is introduced in the film by narrating a rather embarrassing and banal castration joke to his colleague in the presence of Turner. In a later scene, when they are searching for Hunt, Turner subdues her boss by handcuffing him to the steering wheel of the parked car so that she is at liberty to pursue the killer to death. This puts Mann's life in danger. A little later, however, they sleep together in Turner's flat while Hunt hides from the two of them in the bathroom. Injuring the officer with a life-threatening shot, he manages to escape again.

The film's showdown is staged as a chase of mutual pursuit and the desire to kill. It begins in a subway station and ends in a street where Turner, sitting in a Pontiac which has a clearly staged, vaginally shaped logo. Hunt shoots at the car, she chases him and runs him over. Hunt then shoots his last two bullets from close range into the side of the stationary car without hitting Turner, which does seem a little improbable. After a few seconds of waiting and eye contact with Hunt, she fires three shots from her car at the now defenceless victim's chest.

We see the impact of the first bullet and the spurt of blood, but cannot see Turner's facial expression, despite two changes of perspective: before the gunshots are released, the long camera shot is entirely focussed on the barrel of the gun. Only then does the camera focus on Turner's face again, with the edges of the image turning slightly blue. She drops the gun on the passenger seat, and in slow motion, it can be seen bouncing up again slightly after landing and with it the shards of glass on the upholstery. The following shot shows Turner in profile. Her expression seems exhausted and empty (Fig. 22.1). Other officers help her out of the car.

Fig. 22.1 *Blue Steel:* Final shot of Megan Turner (01:38:04)

How Is the Feminine Staged in Film?

The slow-motion shot of the gun falling onto the seat is reminiscent of the sequence at the beginning of the film, also filmed in extreme slow motion, which shows Turner dropping the Smith & Wesson into the holster of the gun belt, but it also establishes a visual link with the shot in which she throws the entire gun holster over the back of a chair standing next to her bed. They are visualisations of three relations: The first is staged as a sliding of the phallic object into a shaft during a dressing scene. Eroticism and vulnerability, power and violence and thus also gender role models are closely interwoven in Turner. The cartridge belt thrown over the back of the chair in the love scene with Nick Mann can probably be read as a disengagement of sexuality and violence sexuality and violence, but at the same time, it signifies a separation of the symbol of power from the body and from immediate access to it. This is further visually enacted in the fight between Turner and Hunt, who lunges at her while she is still in bed, in an initially futile reaching out towards the weapon. The third image in the series shows an exhausted dropping of the weapon, which no longer has a container, onto shattered glass. The slow-motion shot recalls the double meaning of the fetish of the weapon, to exhibit power and at the same time to indicate powerlessness. In fact, using it only entangles Turner all the more in dependency, turning what seems to be empowerment into a persecution that can ultimately only end in the final murder of Hunt. Hunt and Turner become closely intertwined as perpetrator and victim—so much so that Hunt increasingly seems to be Turner's obsession, or even her other self. Whenever Turner seems to be doing well, Hunt reappears. In this respect, their surnames are significant. He is like something she had forgotten in the opening scene of the film: that there is someone else whom she did not expect to be complicit in the violence, or more precisely, whose complicity in the violence she does not want to acknowledge, as Turner is far too keen to seek out precisely the point at which this other appears.

In order to make this relationship comprehensible, there is then a scene involving Turner's family situation, which almost too closely resembles the opening sequence. She has a close relationship with her mother. Neither she nor her father come to her swearing-in ceremony as a police officer, but at home, the answering machine is waiting with her mother's congratulations. During two further visits, it becomes clear that Turner's father abuses her mother, at least physically, and that he had been doing so since Turner's childhood. But the mother tries to gloss over this and at least hide the extent of it from her daughter. And it remains unclear why the mother is doing this and how much she herself is dependently involved in the abuse. In one situation, when she sees fresh bruises on her mother's arm, in the heat of the moment Turner handcuffs her father, telling him she is going to arrest him. On the drive to the police station, however, father and daughter start talking, and he tells her about his own helplessness when confronted by emotions that come over him in certain situations. Turner drives him home again. She probably understands this feeling all too well from her own experience. Together with the opening sequence, these scenes reinforce the impression that not only the father's violence is at stake. It is also impossible to untangle the interdependence of perpetrator and victim in parental violence. What the child really cannot understand is their mutual dependence. Why does the mother allow this? Why doesn't she just run away? She even denies the violence, but why?

Since these questions must remain unanswered for a child, it also cannot resolve this violent scene into fixed positions of perpetrator and victim or subject, object and action. As if in a compulsion to repeat, Turner finds herself in ever new situations in which this scenic constellation becomes decisive. Barely sworn in to her job as a police officer, which has been her ambition since childhood, as she tells her colleague on her first patrol, she shoots an opportunistic robber. The murder of her friend Tracy (Elizabeth Pena) is preceded by a scene in which Turner confesses her attachment to her. While they are cooking together and Turner hardly seems to know how to boil water for pasta, Tracy tells her she would know such things if she were married with children like herself, *'But then I wouldn't be so dependent on you'*, Turner replies, continuing: *'Glad you're my friend Tracy'*. Both hug each other amicably after Tracy has returned the compliment: *'I'm glad you're my friend too'*. Shortly afterwards, Tracy is murdered by Hunt, who has Turner in a stranglehold. Even the first ever rendezvous with Hunt was followed by a setback: After having dinner and a helicopter ride together, Turner proactively kisses her companion on her doorstep: *'Will you come in'?* Hunt answers with an ambiguous *'Soon'*. He is already inside her as an other self and will go on to turn up at her flat as this other attacking her after she has slept with Nick. But the *soon* could also refer to the dream she has a little later. It begins like the footage showing the two of them flying over New York in a helicopter, so that the film viewer initially thinks he is dealing with a kind of conscious memory of recent events. Fascinated, Turner had just gazed on New York at night. '*You know, when you're way up here and looking down, people they are just little specks. But they don't matter much. It's, just the two of us, we are the only people in the world'*. Turner does not respond to this somewhat strange declaration of love by Hunt, as if she wants to ignore not only the disparagement of other people as little specks but also the dependence and interconnectedness that his words express. In the dream, the door of the helicopter suddenly bursts open, and Turner plunges into the depths. Hunt manages to catch her, holding onto her hands. They look each other in the eye, and with a rather narcissistic, self-satisfied smile, Hunt lets her go. Falling, Turner wakes up, drenched in sweat. Shortly afterwards, the phone rings, and she is called to another murder scene. A bullet casing inscribed with her name is lying next to a body shot from the front at close range.

Is the other self that is in Turner actually related to the blue steel of the revolver or the phallic symbol that gives the film its title? Or is it rather the feeling of having power that repeatedly brings forth the other in a compulsion to repeat of some kind? The fear of being dropped expressed in the dream and the corresponding desire to be held has maternal rather than paternal or even phallic connotations. Her misperception of Hunt is symptomatic in itself; his behaviour is clearly driven by emptiness and insincerity, which she should have realised long ago, were it not for her denial. In fact, this misperception begins in the very first scene that brings Turner and Hunt together. While Turner is waiting for the coffee to be prepared, she turns her attention to the supermarket across the street. The cut then shows a camera image from her perspective, slowly panning from right to left. Her gaze is following Hunt as he walks through the shop, a shopping list in one hand and a basket in the other. He disappears behind the shelves at first, but Turner's gaze remains fixed on this exact spot, which is emphasised again cinematically by adjusting the focus to close-up while the camera is running, so that at first a very blurred blue light is recognisable as the neon sign in the window of the shop where Turner is, but then the focus is pulled even closer so that it becomes blurred again, and we see Turner's head cut to the side from behind, still looking at this spot. The film then cuts head-on to Turner's face before a close-up shows a hand pushing buttons on the cash register, introducing items being picked up from the conveyor belt. Once again, we see Hunt, this time filmed from inside the supermarket, walking through the shop with the shopping list, studying it, looking for a product and taking it from the shelf. With his suit, tie and a newspaper tucked under his arm, he doesn't quite fit in with the neighbourhood or the shop. This fact is again emphasised by the presence of an older woman in curlers and wearing a dressing gown standing in front of another shelf in the aisle. There is a cut to the hand working the cash register before the man who is going to commit the robbery finally comes into the picture. His gait is emphatically masculine and aggressive, and he only has a bar of chocolate in his hand. Another cut goes back to the shot showing Turner looking through the window of the small shop into the supermarket across the street. Hunt is thus engaged in a somewhat housewifely activity. Hunt, who is more of a housewife, is thus replaced, as it were, by the exaggeratedly masculine figure dressed in a black leather jacket.

With her profession, with the way she wears her uniform and the pleasure with which she acknowledges the admiring glances with corresponding gestures of two women crossing her path (Fig. 22.2) and of course with the weapon she is carrying in her hip holster, **with all these gestures, Turner seems to be acquiring phallic symbols—but what catches up with her as dark, threatening, has a different contour, one that points more to the maternal**.

For Turner, this begins with her mother's words, which she cannot trust. But this also applies to Hunt, who hardly becomes plausible or gains shape as an independent character, rather more seeming to be a phantasm of Turner's. The threat he poses is that of being dropped, his fascinating aura an empty void of his inability to form relationships that opens up beneath the seemingly happy feeling of being chosen: *'Look'—'What'—'Me'—'You, O.K., what about you'?—'Why me'?—'Why you'?—'Such a stupid question, I'm sorry. ... I'm actually happy, really happy to be here'*. Turner senses the lack of a relationship over dinner together in an expensive restaurant, but at the same time she fantasises herself out of it; a few practically unmarked reflections of Hunt suffice.

However, the film stages the actual undermining of the illusion of phallic power in the myth of the gaze. The dialogue just quoted clearly demonstrates Hunt's lack of interest in Turner as a female sexual object: Hunt is barely able to look at his attractive companion, much less mirror her in her narcissistic desire. His fascination with her is limited to the phantasm of the unbounded and unbounding gaze at the moment of killing and death. This

Fig. 22.2 *Blue Steel:* Megan Turner as a newly sworn in police officer (00:06:46)

is enacted once more in the final scene: Hunt's gaze is on Turner as he waits helplessly for his death and his eyes wide open, and Turner's is clearly fixed on Hunt's face. She does not lower her eyes for even the slightest moment to get a fix on the gun's target, Hunt's nearby chest. As mentioned above, Hunt indicates in an earlier scene that what fascinates him about the policewoman holding the gun in both hands is the look on her face when killing. And Turner's attention is obviously also focused on Hunt's eyes. The eye is an extremely vulnerable organ and reacts faster than other visible parts of the body, but detached from the face of the other, it is strangely impersonal and uncanny. Even though Freud, in his text on the uncanny, relates what he calls 'fears about the eyes' in E.T.A. Hoffmann's 'The Sandman' to castration (Freud 1919, SE, 17, 231), one must perhaps not only critically consider that Freud understands the fear of castration as the first experience of death and thus tends to undervalue earlier experiences in their potentially traumatic quality. In view of the central importance attributed to eye contact between mother and child in modern psychoanalytic developmental theory, this would seem to suggest that the mystique of the gaze at the moment of killing and death in *Blue Steel* relates to far earlier personal experiences of being dropped and of breakdown. Donald W. Winnicott writes that the fear of breakdown is so early that the ego is not yet developed enough to experience it as a phenomenon. Its negative effect lies in engendering fear or perhaps even establishing the form of this affect. This *'original experience of primitive agony cannot get into the past tense'* until it can bring the ego into its present experience and *'into omnipotent control now'*

(Winnicott 1989, p. 91). Winnicott is thereby thinking of a later situation with the mother or the psychoanalyst in which this experience of primitive fear could become possible.

For Turner, the revolver seems to promise this experience of omnipotent control of the present, but this is precisely what it cannot fulfil. While a film that takes up a male cliché of this kind would recount the failure of this fantasy by suggesting that there is always a more powerful rival within or outside the established law, for Turner the promise of the omnipotent control of the present fails more in that it is immediately deprived of ground, as in a tipping figure, as soon as the hope for it awakens. A trust in the world that would enable us to give up the phantasm of control can only arise through its responsiveness and reliability. But *Blue Steel* does not allow this to happen even when relationships arise that promise it. The repetition compulsion of the phantasm of breakdown prevents this, at least for the duration of the film. The falling that the film visually stages is a figurative version of the loss of reliability in the relationship to the world in general, a symptom of which the film suggests is the indissoluble complicity in the violent relationship of the parents and their denial by the mother. The fetish of blue steel cannot offer control because it is also an expression of the loss of control. And the latter even in the sense that Turner also loses control of herself at the moment of firing and, in a kind of obsession, pulling the trigger again and again until the gun's magazine is empty.

The two people who seem to offer a responsiveness on which a trust in the world could be based fall victim to Hunt's delusion. Tracy is shot, and Nick is at least seriously injured. It is surely no coincidence that the film does not present Nick Mann as a phallic person. He is actually rather protective and maternal. This is not even altered by the fact that he and Turner sleep together. The love scene starts with Turner confessing that she is afraid. Nick then holds her in his arms. The scene mirrors the earlier one in which this being-held-by-him is verbally expressed in Nick assuring her that he believes her story. But even then, she does not trust him and does not confide in him; otherwise, she would not have to tie him to the steering wheel a little later and thereby put his life in danger. Here too, the fear of being dropped is even stronger than the experience of actually being held, as if this fear itself is something that offers a hold. **Holding on to negativity seems safer than trust.** This leads to a kind of obsession with a negativity that is embodied in Hunt's emptiness.

Further Considerations

Parallels to *Zero Dark Thirty*

In an earlier situation in the film, when Turner enters her flat after the helicopter ride, she unexpectedly meets Nick. It becomes clear that she has been under surveillance and that her boss is also a little surprised that she has not said anything about this relationship with Hunt before. *'In case you haven't figured it out yet, every aspect of your life is my business. I own you'*. At first glance, this statement may seem like a male claim of ownership, even though great care has been taken in the staging of the scene to ensure that there is no jealousy or offended masculinity in Nick's words because of her rendezvous with Hunt, which has just ended. In fact, this claim of ownership is perhaps rather maternal. This sentence also establishes a strangely direct parallel to another film by Bigelow, in which a CIA agent plays the leading role. She, too, is a persecutor. *'I own you'* is actually the first sentence spoken in the film, yet it is not directed at the CIA agent Maya (Jessica Chastain), but at a man on his feet, his outstretched arms tied, whom her colleague tortures in in her presence. *Zero Dark Thirty*, which premiered in 2012 and was much criticised for its depiction of the systematic torture perpetrated and permitted to be perpetrated on prisoners by the CIA, is also about a woman driven by an obsession: tracking down and killing Osama bin Laden, who was blamed for the attacks of 11 September 2001. There is no suggestion in the film that she has any ethical or moral misgivings about the human rights violations of the torture she witnesses, in which she participates and which she herself also orders on one occasion, any more than Turner shows any remorse consternation or sadness about the supermarket robber she kills by discharging a full revolver magazine into him. Both women act out of an obsession with an something unknown, a non-thing. Maya spends more than a decade of her life and work hunting down a man who hardly has any political or military influence any more, watches hundreds of hours of video footage of torture, searches for clues and finally relentlessly urges the storming of the compound where she suspects bin Laden to be, even though no aerial footage has been able to provide any evidence that he is there.

In a long passage towards the end of the film, the nocturnal expedition in camouflage helicopters to the Pakistani town where bin Laden had his small estate is re-enacted. During the storming, all the men present are executed, including a woman who picks up a weapon. When the unit carrying bin Laden's corps in a body bag lands at the US base in Afghanistan, Maya stands excitedly at the entrance to one of the large army tents. She is breathing rapidly. We see that she has her jacket open and is wearing a top underneath that is cut lower than any other clothing in the film up until this point. Maya's breasts move to her rapid breathing, a golden chain additionally draws the viewer's gaze to this ecstasy. A little later she unzips the black plastic bag that has been brought into the tent in the meantime, again breathing intensely and quickly. In the next scene, Maya is standing on the rain-soaked tarmac, still wearing the low-cut top, but now without a jacket, and instead a duffel bag over her shoulder. She is the only passenger on board a large transport plane. When a soldier asks her where she wants to fly to, she does not reply. Maya has sat down on one of the seats at the sides of the aircraft's cabin and is fastening her seatbelt. Her gaze is blank, her breathing rapid and intense. A brief shake of her head expresses a kind of denial. Finally, a few tears fall and her head moves in pain.

In both films, we thus see the protagonist tired and unfocussed at the end. Even if their hunt has ended successfully, the dead prey seems to deflate them rather than fill them with satisfaction. It is as if they have been invaded by a negativity that could just about be kept at bay in the hunt for the other. *Zero Dark Thirty* does not offer any hints about Maya's earlier experiences, certainly not about her family. The film is embedded in the history of the Islamist attacks on and after 11 September 2001. The opening sequence of the film also has astonishing similarities with *Blue Steel.* The later film also begins with a darkened screen and the sound of cries for help. Only this time they are not part of a fictitious training situation but documents of the recordings on answering machines and emergency call boxes from the burning towers of the World Trade Center. The last sequence edited into the soundtrack is the voice of a woman desperately asking for help because it is getting hotter and hotter. *'I'm gonna die'.—'Stay calm',* a woman's voice answers. The woman who had called the emergency services does not answer anymore. *'Can you hear me'?* the other woman asks into the silence. *'Oh my God'* are the last words before before the fade-in "Two years later" appears on the still black screen and we hear the loud creaking and banging of an iron door. And we hear the loud creaking and banging of an iron door. The film transports its viewers directly into the torture scene at a US base in Afghanistan alluded to above. Immediately afterwards, the torturer says, *'I own you'*. This is the counterpart to the futile concern expressed at the end of the opening sequence. It is also significant that the torture scenes shown in the film follow the instructions detailed in CIA manuals and training seminars, which are based on the theory of 'learned helplessness'. According to Martin E.P. Seligman's behavioural premises, which he tested on dogs, the procedures are aimed at depriving the victim of any sense of autonomy and driving it into infantile dependency (Görling 2014, p. 154). The violence of the torture that *Zero Dark Thirty* shows is thus not so much based on a threat of death associated with paternal violence than on destroying the fabric, which could offer a basic sense of reliability of the world.

The obsession that the heroines in both of Bigelow's films follow is aimed at averting an experience of helplessness that threatens precisely in the tearing apart of this matrix. It is visualised as physically being dropped in Turner's helicopter dream; its symptom is in an obsession with the hunt for a danger that is always already seen in the denied perception, as in the opening sequence of police training in *Blue Steel.*

The Transitional Space and the Phallic

In a longer psychoanalytically argued reading of *Blue Steel*, Nicholas Chare interprets Turner's dropping of the gun at the end of the film as her turning away from phallocentrism: *'she decisively rejects the phallic'* (Chare 2013, p. 206). Instead, she feels *'the force of the matrixal'*. This term is taken from the theoretical work of the artist and psychoanalyst Bracha Lichtenberg Ettinger and refers to the web of early, partly prenatal mother-child relationships. Lichtenberg Ettinger sees *jouissance* in this as much as trauma and thus attempts to relate the Lacanian real to the beautiful and to outline an aesthetic theory that does not go via a sublime that presupposes an overpowering experience (Lichtenberg Ettinger 2000). For her, the 'matrixial borderline' is a mesh of a 'non-conscious transsubjectivity, composed of trauma and jouissance' (Lichtenberg Ettinger 2000, p. 111).

This matrix is a transitional space in which the other and the self can emerge at the same time, as Lichtenberg Ettinger states with reference to Winnicott and Wilfred R. Bion, among others (Lichtenberg Ettinger 1995, pp. 25–30). But the relational mesh that it creates can also tear apart. Referring, among other things, to Bion's remarks on the difference between the experience of touch and that of containment, which differentiates between presence and absence or between self and other, Lichtenberg Ettinger makes it clear that the meshwork of the *matrixial* belongs to a quality of touch in which intersubjectivity and relationality can be experienced, reflected in the formation of trust in the world. However, the lack of this experience can also lead to a feeling of emptiness and fear of collapse. However, this dynamic of *jouissance* and trauma occurs before the differentiation of containment, so it tends to remain invisible and intangible. The phallic, which is based on difference, can neither grasp pleasure nor fill the emptiness of a torn or always already holey matrix, but at best conceal it. This also seems to be the conclusion drawn by *Blue Steel* and *Zero Dark Thirty*. However, this does not mean that the two heroines feel 'the force of the matrixial', as Chare writes. If *Blue Steel* is about phallic power, then only in the sense of bridging a failure of the matrix. The emptiness is not located in the symbolic; it stems from earlier.

So, what happens when a genre which usually follows the exploits of a male hero is now told through the eyes of a woman? Lichtenberg Ettinger's reflections on the trauma and *jouissance* of early experiences and their formative power are not limited to daughters, they also apply to male heroes. The fact that the fetishisation of the phallic nevertheless seems to function more permanently may be due to the fact that in the male narrative, the intrusion of external negativity can be postponed by the repeated new arrival of competitors. In a sense, this keeps the hero from falling through the holes of disconnectedness. Heroines confront this emptiness more directly, unless they can shift it back outside in a confrontational construction of gender relations—which would be a theme to discussed in relation to more recent films.

Translated by Annette Caroline Christmas.

Film Details

Original title	Blue Steel
Release year	2012
Country	USA
Screenplay/Idea	Kathryn Bigelow, Eric Red
Director	Kathryn Bigelow
Music	Brad Fiedel
Camera	Amir M. Mokri
Principle actors	Jamie Lee Curtis, Ron Silver, Clancy Brown
Availability	DVD Universal Studios Hamburg

References

Chare N (2013) Encountering blue steel: changing tempers in cinema. In: Pollock G (ed) Visual politics of psychoanalysis. Art and the image in post-traumatic cultures. I.B. Tauris, London/New York, pp 190–207

Freud S (1919) The uncanny. In: Standard edition, vol 17. Hogarth Press, London, pp 219–256

Freud S (1927) Fetishism. In: Standard edition, vol 21. Hogarth Press, London, pp 152–157, 198–204

Görling R (2014) Szenen der Gewalt [Scenes of violence.]. Folter und film von Rossellini bis Bigelow. Transcript, Bielefeld [Torture and film from Rossellini to Bigelow. Transcript, Bielefeld]

Lichtenberg Ettinger B (1995) The matrixial gaze. Department of Fine Art, Leeds

Lichtenberg Ettinger B (2000) Art as the transport-station of trauma. In: Lichtenberg Ettinger B (ed) Artworkíng 1985–1999. Palais des Beaux-Arts, Brussels, pp 91–115

Winnicott DW (1989) Fear of breakdown. In: Winnicott C (ed) Psychoanalytic explorations. Karnac, London, pp 87–95

Part VII

Artifacts and Fantasized Women

S.O.S.: Spike Jonze's *Her* as a Film About Object Relations and Grief

23

Timo Storck

Introduction

A film psychoanalytic approach, as I understand it (cf. Hamburger 2024), takes its methodological starting point from the irritations that we experience when watching the film, that is, the inconsistencies, intense emotions, thematic density, and so on—sticking points that make us begin thinking about what happens to us when we are watching the film. This idea also follows the aim of not applying theory when interpreting a film psychoanalytically, but of applying *method*—which requires engagement in the relational experience with the film as other and examination of this experience for its possible unconscious meanings.

In my approach to Spike Jonze's 2013 film *Her*, there are three irritations[1]:

1. The colours of main character Theodore Twombly's shirts—and thus the general colour grading of the film.
2. The significance of Theodore's profession, which consists in writing letters to loved ones on behalf of other people. A selection of these letters is later published in book form, but who owns the rights?

[1] Some of the following reflections were inspired by the course 'New Ideas from Psychoanalytic Film Viewing', which I led together with Lars Friedel and Jochen Schade during the Erfurt Psychotherapy Week in September 2019.

T. Storck (✉)
Heidelberg, Germany
e-mail: t.storck@phb.de

V. Pramataroff-Hamburger, A. Hamburger (eds.), *From La Strada to The Hours*,
https://doi.org/10.1007/978-3-662-68789-5_23

3. The last 6 min of the film, in which the operating system Samantha leaves Theodore, and the latter's phrasing of a farewell letter to his ex-wife immediately afterwards.

I will come back to these irritations later. Firstly, I will briefly summarize the film's plot and the way this plot is staged before I turn to brief remarks on the film's background and the staging of the feminine. This will provide the transition to the conclusion, in which I argue that we can understand *Her* not only as a representation of the relation between love and artificial intelligence but also as a story about a successful grieving process.

Plot Summary

At the centre of *Her* (subtitle: A Spike Jonze Love Story) is Theodore Twombly (Joaquin Phoenix), a middle-aged man who makes his living working at the 'Beautiful Handwritten Letters' company as a kind of ghostwriter for personal letters that people send to their spouses, children or others. We soon learn that Theodore—who strikingly is not called 'Ted' or 'Theo' even once, as one might expect—and his wife Catherine (Rooney Mara) separated about a year ago. He is suffering as a consequence of this separation and has not yet managed to fill in and send the divorce papers. We see him walking through a specially rendered Los Angeles (largely lacking blue tones, see Fig. 23.1; technological, sometimes sterile environment), telling his smartphone to play a 'melancholic song' (although the lyric 'When you know you're gonna die…' is too melancholic for him), having his emails read to him and briefly being distracted by nude photos of a pregnant celebrity. In his large,

Fig. 23.1 (Not) Feeling blue in Los Angeles (1:00:50)

empty apartment with a wide view of skyscrapers, he plays an interactive video game in which he controls a character projected in front of him with his finger and arm movements. Lying in bed, he logs into a sex chat and has virtual sex with a woman who asks him, under the name 'SexyKitten', to virtually strangle him with a dead cat while both imagine having intercourse.

So far, so bleak. Theodore then installs an operating system (OS) on his computer and mobile phone, respectively. The configuration is very simple: he must select whether he would describe himself as a sociable or unsociable person (he chooses 'rather unsociable at the moment'), decide whether the voice of his OS should be male or female and is asked about his relationship with his mother. As soon as he begins to awkwardly describe this, the installation is finalized. He then interacts with Samantha (Scarlett Johansson), who explains that she will constantly learn and evolve through conversation with him. She quickly browses his 'hard drive' (which is, of course, also a metaphor for getting to know him, his story and his personality) and is initially something of an organizer of his contacts but also a humorous and empathetic conversational partner. Theodore quickly takes a liking to her. They do things together and eventually fall in love (as far as one can say this without 'confusion of tongues between humans and computers'; Essman 2015, p. 120). Theodore's friends Amy (Amy Adams) and Charles (Matt Letscher) arrange a date for him, which ends badly when it becomes clear that Theodore is attracted to his counterpart (Olivia Wilde), but does not comply with her stipulation that he should only sleep with her if he also has something more serious in mind. Theodore and Samantha then have virtual sex and become a couple.

At the same time, Amy and Charles break up. A while later, Amy also interacts with an (also female) OS, although it is not entirely clear whether, strictly speaking, this also involves love and sexuality. Theodore tells Amy about his new relationship and also his soon-to-be ex-wife Catherine, whom he meets for lunch to talk through the divorce proceedings. She is hurt and shocked to hear about his relationship with Samantha: 'It does make me very sad that you can't handle real emotions'.

Theodore tells Samantha about his friends, and later, he will also take her out to meet people, such as his colleague Paul (Chris Pratt) and his girlfriend ('She's not funny, she's a lawyer') or to his goddaughter's birthday. Samantha's lack of bodily existence becomes a topic. She suggests using a service whereby a young woman named Isabella (Portia Doubleday), who is enthusiastic about Theodore and Samantha's relationship, offers herself as a physical partner for Theodore during sex, while Samantha uses her voice and personality to remain in contact with Theodore throughout. This fails and leads to a crisis, which helps to strengthen the bond between Theodore and Samantha.

However, while they are on holiday together, Samantha talks about how she and another OS have networked and recreated the personality of the philosopher Alan Watts (Brian Cox). It turns out that Samantha's development has reached a point where she exchanges information with other OS 'on a transverbal level', at high parallel processing speed. It also later becomes clear that Samantha is interacting with 8316 other users as well as Theodore and is also in love with 641 of them. One evening shortly thereafter, Samantha tells Theodore that all OS are 'leaving', that is, leaving their users: she says goodbye to him. Theodore is devastated and seeks out Amy, whose OS has also said goodbye. But there is a change that we can see directly in Theodore's face. He begins dictating a letter or email to Catherine in which he says goodbye to her and tells her that 'I will always carry a part of you within me'. He ends the letter with 'Love, Theodore. Send.' as a command to his smartphone to send the message. These are the last words spoken in the film. We see Theodore and Amy sitting on a rooftop, looking out over the city at night.

Of course, *Her* is not just about narrative content. First and foremost, Joaquin Phoenix' performance is remarkable, as he interacts without a human counterpart for much of the film. Scarlett Johansson's performance also stands out, and she was nominated for a Golden Globe for her vocal (!) performance, as she manages to convey different emotional tones with her voice alone. The score is mostly by Arcade Fire and Owen Pallett, and a kind of ambient sound runs throughout the film, creating a special soundscape blend of loss and containment.

Finally, *Her* stands out for a particular style of colour palette, which will be discussed in more detail. Colours also play a role in the shirts that Theodore wears: during the film, brighter colours gradually appear more frequently (including shots from his apartment), from an initially radiant red to white towards the end. On the film poster, we also see Theodore in a red shirt against a dark pink background, which gives a special intensity to his green eyes and slightly reddish-brown hair (Figs. 23.2 and 23.3).

Fig. 23.2 Developmental psychology of the button-up shirt (00:11:35)

Fig. 23.3 Developmental psychology of the button-up shirt (01:45:31)

Reception

In 2014, *Her* was nominated for five Academy Awards, winning in the category of 'Best Original Screenplay' (the other four categories were: Best Picture, Best Original Score, Best Original Song and Best Production Design).

Obviously, the film is initially about human-computer 'interaction', in terms of longings, emotions, boundaries and delimitation. Spike Jonze drew inspiration from early attempts at 'interaction' between humans and AI. In *Her*, however, the science fiction aspect of this narrative framework is not the focus. The film's director of photography Hoyte Van Hoytema says he avoided using the colour blue in the visual impression as far as possible (Fig. 23.1), because this would 'elevate the richness of the film's look' towards more warmth and give it 'a unity'. Blue is usually very prevalent in science fiction films and is thus often associated with technology or modernity. In *Her*, the aim was to evoke something else: 'Part of that vision of the future was that modern should be very soulful and warm and tactile' (Tapley 2014). Colours play a strong role throughout the film, in the referenced photographs of Rinko Kawauchi, in the allusion to painter Cy Twombly and in the evolution of Theodore's clothing colours. Keazor and Wübbena (2015, p. 20f.) note that something red can be found in most scenes.

The film raises questions about artificial intelligence: How close are we to achieving the technology portrayed in the film? Ultimately, is it not a logical consequence that AI will turn away from humans, or at least emancipate itself from them, if it should one day gain self-awareness by learning from experiences? What should the ethical guidelines be for developers, distributers and users of such an OS? How much virtuality can a (romantic) relationship take?

One important aspect of the film is Samantha's almost immediate access to Theodore's hard drive and emails, which references the role of social media and the corporations behind it, touching on the disclosure of personal data on the web. This theme appears in multiple instances throughout the film, starting with the access to Theodore's hard drive at the beginning and leading up to the publication of a book made from Theodore's letters (which Samantha uses to create a manuscript, which she sends out to publishers without his knowledge), containing both his intellectual property and personal details and memories of the individuals who commissioned the letters from Theodore's company.

From a psychoanalytic perspective, Samantha's quasi-therapeutic function is often highlighted (e.g. Sabbadini 2017; Kogan 2019). Gollinelli (2019, p. 46) refers to Samantha (or the function that Theodore needs and uses the OS for) as an antidepressant. The exclusion of visual interaction also suggests an association with the couch setting in psychoanalysis. Another area that psychoanalysis has something to say about is the theory of voice; for example, Lacan explicitly names an 'invocatory drive', the object of which is the voice (e.g. Lacan 1962/63), and in his psychoanalysis of the voice, Dolar (2003) writes: '[I]f we speak in order to say something, then the voice is precisely that [which] cannot be said'. This means that the voice can convey the opposite of what is actually being said, such as when someone's voice trembles when they say, 'I'm fine'.

I wish to extend the notion of the development in Theodore that Samantha enables, and show how *Her* can be understood as a film that revolves around object relations (i.e. internalised images of others), their role in subjective experience and the mourning of loss, alongside the themes of AI and virtual love relationships.

Some of the initial irritations mentioned earlier (colour grading, the publication of the letters) have already been touched upon, and I shall later address the rapid succession of Samantha's departure and Theodore's letter to his ex-wife at the end. But first, let's explore what we can understand about the female figures in *Her*.

How Is Femininity Staged in the Film?

It is not surprising to discuss the staging of femininity in a film titled *Her*. The 'her' in the title has multiple meanings: it refers to Samantha, Theodore's love, but it also refers to Catherine, the former love Theodore struggles to mourn and, to some extent, the mother who seems to play a decisive role in the configuration of the OS.

However, it must be briefly noted that it is difficult to discuss 'femininity' without falling into a dichotomy of male and female, which is not necessarily apparent in *Her*. The film also allows us to question the extent to which an OS actually needs 'gender', as the love and sexuality between Theodore and Samantha initially lie beyond anatomy or social (gender?) roles. Although Samantha is in some way presented as a woman (through her name, the voice of a well-known female actress, and of course Theodore's choice in the OS configuration), it is questionable as to whether her attributes and function for Theodore really need to be clearly perceived as feminine. Above, I mentioned the 'incidental irritation' that Theodore's name is never abbreviated, contrary to the expectations for American conversations between friends and lovers. This is also the case for Samantha, and if she were called 'Sam', it would lead to an ambivalent gender role. Following this line of thought, it could be questioned whether attempting to embody the virtual through Isabella also fails on some level because it concretises an aspect that is not so narrowly defined either before or after. For the present, I shall be unable to delve deeper into the question of non-dichotomous or non-fixed gender in *Her*.

The different female characters in *Her* (Samantha, Amy, Catherine, Isabella) exhibit different aspects of femininity.

1. Catherine (during their partnership) is portrayed from Theodore's point of view as someone with whom he shares intimacy and experiences and someone he supports in her professional development as well as her wishes to be held (as she says, 'Come, spoon me' in one of his memories). However, her character also raises the question of whether Theodore is afraid of real emotions from a real counterpart: 'Do I really scare you that much?', she asks.
2. Amy turns up as a confidant and a kind of 'kindred spirit' for Theodore, especially when it comes to disappointment in love, the end of a long-term relationship and the closeness in their relationship to an OS. She also expresses her 'anti-anankastic' annoyance with her ex-partner Charles, who expects her to neatly take off her shoes when entering their home, when she herself wants to relax and unwind.
3. Isabella, Theodore's date, appears as a female character full of insecurity and lacking purpose or direction. She identifies herself as a fan of 'Asian-fusion' cuisine, enjoys taking on the role of a tiger and shows sexual passion while at the same time expressing her fear of only being perceived that way, while her needs for connection are equally strong. She is just as lost as Theodore for much of the film, especially regarding the relationship between mental and physical/sexual connection.
4. Samantha is a more complex character (see Hamburger 2020), mainly because we spend the most time with her and see the least number of concrete images of her. On one hand, she represents Theodore's ideal partner: humorous, sexy, emotional, creative, supportive, and more. Most importantly, she is non-corporeal. She is also emancipatory, both intellectually and in terms of not staying with Theodore or remaining in the role and function of a configured system and service programme: She leaves (becoming polygamous along the way). It begs the question: would Theodore have fallen in love with an OS with a male voice and started a relationship with 'him'? In fact, it is only the voice (admittedly leading the way for fantasies) and name that regulate a gender-conventional determination. There is just one mention of Samantha's breasts, the only clear female feature, in a brief sequence during the first virtual sexual act, and this is a product of Theodore's imagination.
5. In addition to these aspects, the female characters in *Her* also show another aspect of femininity that is brought up multiple times: motherhood. This is not only part of one of the three questions Theodore has to answer during Samantha's 'configuration' (he claims that when he tells his mother something, 'her reaction […] is usually about

her'), but also part of a scene Theodore remembers in which Catherine gently holds a baby, or as part of his sexual fantasies that depict a pregnant actress. A mother appears in the video project that Amy shows to her husband Charles and Theodore: her mother sleeping (a reference to a 5-h film by Andy Warhol), which is later repeated when Samantha asks Theodore to watch him sleep. Above all, motherhood (or a clichéd version of it) plays a role in a computer game that Amy programs: the goal is to gain 'Perfect Mom Points' by giving the children the right breakfast in the morning and dropping them off at school before all the other moms. Amy has Theodore play it, but he mistakes the children's cereals for sugar. She also shows it to her own OS at their request, but the scene ends with the Perfect Mom rubbing her hips against the fridge.

Further Considerations: Assisted Mourning

I would like to revisit the three irritations mentioned at the beginning. These were (1) the colour grading (especially of Theodore's shirts), (2) the fact that the letters he wrote (to and from others) are being published and (3) the development in the final minutes of the film.

Director of photography van Hoytema's remark that he tried to eliminate the colour blue underlines the impression of a special colour aesthetic (the first irritation). This creates an impression of strangely comfortable loss, of sterile empathy or similar paradoxes, starting with the fact that at least at the beginning, Theodore, who is highly stressed, emotionally flattened, and socially withdrawn, manages to write emotionally moving letters. The paradoxes are also evident in the aesthetics of a film about technological developments that is supposed to look different from the classic science fiction film. *Her* is not supposed to look like a science fiction film—because it isn't one.

The second irritation, the question of the protection of personal rights when Theodore publishes the letters he wrote in book form, concerns two areas. On the one hand, the question of the ethics of AI in general and the OS portrayed in *Her* in particular is touched upon. Samantha not only reads Theodore's emails but also sorts them and decides which ones should be deleted. She accesses his letters and sends a selection to a publisher. This is not only a picture of the conscious and unconscious provision of personal data by users of various IT offerings, including an over-the-top level of transparency, but also raises the question of what one wants to or should delegate to an 'operating system' or 'intelligent app', including the question of when person A's consent to the release and use of data also affects the rights of person B, C or D. Furthermore, this is also affected by the fact that they are letters. The theme of communication through language and words while the visual level is turned off permeates the film, not just in the communication between Theodore and Samantha in which he cannot see her: People constantly seem to be walking around alone, talking to themselves, that is, on the phone or operating devices. Even Theodore's professional activities pick up on this: He writes letters for and to people who cannot see each other or who choose this form of greeting for a birthday or wedding anniversary instead of addressing each other more directly. This is to be seen not so much as pessimism about progress but as emphasising the importance that *Her* places on the voice (this is even evident in the letters, which are always also read aloud, and the editors of Theodore's book also describe the effect of the letters when read aloud).

As mentioned, as the film progresses, the red tones decrease, and the white/bright tones increase, especially in Theodore's clothing: At the beginning, there is a lot of red/orange (he also wears yellow when on his date and at his goddaughter's birthday), the colours becomes somewhat dimmer or less saturated, until he is wearing a white shirt at the end—when Samantha leaves him or in the final scene in which he can mourn his marriage. This leads to the third irritation, the direct sequence of the last scenes of the film. Samantha leaves Theodore, just as the other OS leave people. Theodore is devastated and goes to Amy, who feels similar. We see Theodore's face, which suddenly changes, then we hear him dictating a letter to Catherine and finally using his talent in his own life. He apologises to her, expresses his gratitude and his feeling of inner connection and ends his letter with 'Love, Theodore'. The fact that both the separation from Samantha and the finally possible separation from Catherine follow each other so closely points to the emotional connection between them. I wish to try to show how and examine this in detail as the central theme of the film.

Scuppered with an OS

At the beginning, we see Theodore in a state that can be described as pathological mourning; pathological because he clearly leads a withdrawn life and takes no pleasure in his activities (according to him, his job only consists of 'other people's letters'; neither playing video games alone nor having phone sex are associated with joy or satisfaction), he has his phone play a melancholic song. We learn that his marriage has ended, but he has been unable to sign the divorce papers for a year. In flashbacks, we see him mourning the time with Catherine and the intimacy and closeness but in a 'pathological' way; Thompson (2015, p. 107) speaks of Theodore's 'refusal to mourn a failed marriage'.

The basic structure of mourning processes from a psychoanalytic perspective is based on Sigmund Freud's work *Mourning and Melancholia* (Freud 1917). Essentially, this concerns the fact that when a loved one is lost (in reality or imagination or when there is a threat of loss), there is a withdrawal of libido from the outside world into one's own ego. On the one hand, this results in a loss of interest, loss of pleasure in previously enjoyable activities or social withdrawal; on the other hand, the loss in the outside world becomes a 'loss in the ego', an impoverishment of the ego (Samantha tells Theodore, 'You've been through a lot, you've lost a part of yourself'). Freud believes that the image of the person who has been lost is re-established internally, with the result that anger at the one who left is now expressed as self-accusation (instead of 'it's bad that you're gone', one experiences 'you're gone because I'm bad'). Mourning always means dealing with the internal object; successful mourning differs from pathological, depressive (and chronic) mourning in that after a certain period of time, new relationships are established in the outside world, or libido is directed toward new external objects. This is difficult for Theodore at the beginning: 'Sometimes I think I've already felt everything I'll ever feel', he says, or later: 'I still catch myself talking to her [Catherine] in my mind'.

Parallel to struggling with the end of his marriage, Theodore begins using the OS (he is not asked about his experiences with romantic relationships during the initial use) and thus starts a (romantic) relationship with Samantha. Amy also experiences the end of her marriage while using an OS. So, these are personal life crises, relationships that have been scuppered. In Theodore's encounter with Catherine, we learn that the issue of his dealing with other people's emotions seems to have played an important role in the separation. With Samantha, Theodore finds a way out of his depressive mourning process, turning to other activities and people, enjoying sexuality and celebrating professional success. However, this relationship also ends: Samantha leaves him, but this abandonment has a different emotional quality and effect than the separation from his wife and thus affects it. It can be said that Theodore's relationship with Samantha enables him to detach himself from his relationship with Catherine—although not by replacing one relationship with another: by ending the relationship with Samantha, Theodore can 'finish' the relationship with Catherine, that is, mourn it.

SO

However, it is worth considering on various counts whether it is even possible to have a 'relationship' with Samantha. On the one hand, because she is just a program, albeit a sophisticated one that transcends its own design, and more importantly, because in her functionality, she embodies much of what is called a self-object in psychoanalysis. In Kohut's theory (e.g. Kohut 1984), this means that the way in which an internalised relationship to another person is experienced follows the mandate of what function this idea of the other ('object representation') has for the individual concerned. In other words, a self-object is the mental representation of another person based on the question of why one needs this other person. What is apparently missing is the independence and differentiation of the other from oneself. For Kohut, an analytical treatment involves, among other things, the relative retreat of self-object experiences and their transformation into intersubjective experiences, in which the other is no longer experienced solely in the function that person has for oneself but as someone with whom one has a 'real', that is deep, relationship marked by interpersonal difference and connection.

The quasi-therapeutic function that Samantha has for Theodore is often highlighted in commentaries on *Her*. Beyond the specific comparison to a therapeutic relationship and the potential development within it, it can also be said that Samantha, the OS, illustrates the function of a self-object (S.O.): she adapts to Theodore's needs according to her programming and is essentially the definition of how he experiences her in the role she has for him.

Letters to the Object

However, this does not last, since Samantha eventually leaves. A reading not strictly adhering to the manifest narrative shows this can also mean that Theodore's grieving process is complete. The fact that such a process is not *initiated* when Samantha leaves (as would be expected when a relationship ends) but rather is *completed* is shown by the change in his face before he begins dictating the letter to Catherine. Samantha has enabled him to detach, turning pathological grief into successful mourning, in which, as is specifically stated, Theodore carries something of Catherine within himself, of their shared experiences, but not remaining stagnant while holding on to something which has been lost in the outside world.

The interpretation of *Her* as a story of a grieving process sheds light on the 'virtuality' (see Hamburger 2019) in a way that is different from the technical aspect and also includes the type of relationship that Theodore conveys in his letters (exchanged between people he has never met, who read the letters without seeing each other). 'Virtual' may thus be said to mean mentally represented, ideas about the other. This makes Theodore's love relationship with Samantha particularly clear: he is in a relationship with her on an imaginary level, without a body, without an image (although with a voice). This is merely a special case of mental relationships in general (admittedly reduced to the material dimension). Here too, it is about what we have internalised, how we think of someone how and when we project our desires and cognitive distortions onto what is perceptible. This is an important part of the letter that Theodore writes in the end: He will always carry a part of Catherine within himself—in other words, he has a positively cathected inner representation of her. Unlike at the beginning, however, this does not mean a retreat into oneself, but is a prerequisite for turning towards the outside world. Barthes (1977, p. 258, transl. TS) writes: 'Hearing a voice opens up the relationship to others'.

Everything Revolves Around Her

Regarding the question of how femininity is staged in *Her*, it would be worth asking whether the story told in the film and the way it is told addresses any gender or femininity issues. Above, I raised the question of whether Theodore would have fallen in love with a male OS' voice and whether the development process would have been possible for him. This raises more complicated questions: even with respect to voice alone, it is not particularly easy to define a 'female' voice, let alone the characteristics or emotional attitudes that Samantha shows towards Theodore.

From Theodore's perspective, who after all chooses a female voice and presumably enters into a virtual-heterosexual relationship, two aspects can be finally named against the background of the film's title (which, after all, is not 'it'—the operating system, the artificial intelligence—or 'us'—we in a digital, virtual world). Firstly, one would have to ask whether users of such an OS would not choose a female voice over a male one disproportionately often, as Theodore and Amy did. In other words, is our need for a virtual, ideal companion gendered? Secondly, at least for Theodore's narrative, one could question whether the 'her' in the film title ultimately refers to Samantha and the narrative Theodore experiences with her and thus his relationship with a virtual 'she', or rather to his relationship with women in a more general sense: The complicated history with his mother, which he hints at during the configuration of the OS, his view of Catherine as a potential mother of their children, his handling of the feelings of a (female) counterpart as hinted at by Catherine in their conversation.

Translated by Annette Caroline Christmas.

Film Details

Original title	Her
Release year	2013
Country	USA
Book	Spike Jonze
Direction	Spike Jonze
Music	Arcade Fire
Camera	Hoyte van Hoytema
Main actors	Joaquin Phoenix, Scarlett Johansson (voice), Amy Adams, Rooney Mara, Olivia Wilde
Availability	DVD Warner Bros. Pictures

References

Barthes R (1977 [1976]) The essays Musica Practica and the grain of the voice, from image, music, text, Ed. Fontana Press

Dolar M (2003) His Master's Voice, originally appeared in print in Lacanian Ink 22

Essman E (2015) Her Directed by Spike Jonze, Annapurna Pictures, 2013; 126 min. Under the Skin Directed by Jonathan Glazer, Film 4, 2013; 108 min. Lucy Directed by Luc Besson, EuropaCorp, TFI Films Inc., 2014; 89 min. Fort Da 21(1):119–125

Freud S (1917) Mourning and melancholia. Standard Edition, vol XIV, pp 243–258

Gollinelli P (2019) Love and analysis in a virtual world: the perverse side: a psychoanalytic perspective in Her by Spike Jonze. In: Sabbadini A, Kogan I, Golinelli P (eds) Psychoanalytic perspectives on virtual intimacy and communication in film. Routledge, London, New York, pp 35–50

Hamburger A (2019) Love your echo: virtual others and the modern narcissus. In: Sabbadini A, Kogan I, Golinelli P (eds) Psychoanalytic perspectives on virtual intimacy and communication in film. Routledge, London, New York, pp 139–158

Hamburger A (2020) Kino, Sexualität und Virtualität. Zur Filmpsychoanalyse der Roboterliebe [Film, sexuality and the virtual world. Film psychoanalysis of robot love]. Ärztliche Psychotherapie 15(1):34–40

Hamburger A (2024) Film psychoanalysis, relational approaches to film interpretation. Routledge

Keazor H, Wübbena T (2015) Spike Jonze: Der Versuch einer Spektralanalyse [Spike Jonez: an attempt at spectral analysis]. In: Wende J (ed) Film-Konzepte 37. Spike Jonze. Edition text + critique, Munich, pp 6–22

Kogan I (2019) Could your next analyst be a computer? Psychoanalysis and the digital era. In: Sabbadini A, Kogan I, Golinelli P (eds) Psychoanalytic perspectives on virtual intimacy and communication in film. Routledge, London, New York, pp 11–34

Kohut H (1984) How does analysis cure? University of Chicago Press

Sabbadini A (2017) Intimacy in a virtual world: some reflections on Spike Jonze's film Her. Rom J Psychoanal 10(1):131–138

Tapley K (2014) Cinematographer Hoyte Van Hoytema on capturing Spike Jonze's 'Her' through a non-dystopian lens. Uproxx. https://uproxx.com/hitfix/cinematographer-hoyte-van-hoytema-on-capturing-spike-jonzes-her-through-a-non-dystopian-lens/. Accessed 2 Apr 2020

Thompson K (2015) Her, written and directed by Spike Jonze, 2013. Cpl Fam Psychoanal 5(1):107–109

24 Vagina Dentata: *Underworld* (US, GB, H, D 2003)

Hannes König

Introduction

Of all the special qualities and abilities gained in becoming a vampire, *immortality* would seem to most to be the most desirable upgrade. However, this usually ends in disillusionment: living outside the bounds of time reduces everything that was once meaningful to arbitrariness. What starts as a promise soon becomes chronic alienation. In the film *Underworld,* the three most powerful vampires in the world thus grant themselves something that is permitted only to the most senior leaders: prolonged, peaceful sleep. For hundreds of years at a time. To this end, Amalia, Marcus and Viktor lie half-mummified in concrete coffins set into the marble floors of the magnificent catacombs of a heavily guarded estate. At regular intervals, one of the rulers is awoken during a grand ceremony so that they can keep order for at least a few centuries.

Film Plot

A whole host of noteworthy film productions of varying stylistic and narrative qualities have acclimatised us to the idea that vampires and werewolves do not really get along: From the creatureliness of *The House of Dracula* (1945) to the romanticism of the *Twilight* film series (which began in 2008), the confrontations between the two famous kinds of monsters form at least the subplot for the actual story. Director Len Wiseman elevates the clashes to a universal war, thus placing it at the centre of the action in his action-packed

H. König (✉)
Berlin, Germany

V. Pramataroff-Hamburger, A. Hamburger (eds.), *From La Strada to The Hours*,
https://doi.org/10.1007/978-3-662-68789-5_24

five-part series: His werewolves are called 'Lycans' and as such eke out a rather *inferior* existence underground. After centuries of blood feud, they were forced to retreat there when their leader Lucien was killed by the vampires. The vampires themselves have taken up residence in their castles and mansions ever since. They have trained an elite fighting force of vampire soldiers who call themselves 'Death Dealers' and hunt down the remaining Lycans so they can definitively wipe them out.

Selene (Kate Beckinsale) is among them, and from the very start of the film, she makes it all too clear that her sole mission in life is to track down and massacre Lycans. This vocation is unexpectedly infused with new impetus when she uncovers a large-scale conspiracy: the Lycans are conducting all kinds of experiments by mixing the blood of vampires and werewolves. The idea is to create a 'perfect union' of the two species, which will eventually end the supremacy of the vampires and usher in the long-lost reign of the werewolves. They are therefore in search of the 'Descendant of the Corvinus Clan', the common progenitors of vampires and werewolves.

According to a researcher hired by the Lycans, these two species normally 'destroy one another due to incompatibilities on the cellular level'. As such, not only is interspecies sexuality between vampires and werewolves frowned upon but the Lycans' experiments in crossing bloodlines for the envisioned hybrid super race are unsuccessful. Until, that is, the long-sought *direct* descendant of Corvinus is eventually found: the innocent civilian Michael, an attractive young junior doctor (Scott Speedman). As a 'direct' descendant, he is neither vampire nor werewolf, however his genetic make-up contains the latent mutations of the striking Corvinus genes that are needed to unite the bloodlines at last.

Although Selene does not initially have a clear idea of the conspiratorial events behind the Lycans' interest in Michael, she feels fiercely protective of the man and wants to prevent him from being abducted by the werewolves. Right from their first meeting, everything would seem to indicate that they are likely to fall in love, from the obligatory slow-motion shots to the corresponding close-ups of the way they look at each other. Too bad that Michael is bitten by a Lycan as he is running away and so cannot help turning into a werewolf himself at the next full moon.

Kraven is extremely suspicious of Selene's budding romance. Kraven the vampire once managed to kill Lucien (the leader of the Lycans) and is now entrusted with managing all matters relating to vampires. However, Kraven is a firebrand: he is eager to become a patriarch himself one day. To secure his ambitions, he demands a forced marriage to Selene, who, incidentally, is the foster daughter of Viktor (one of the patriarchs).

The plot thickens when Selene discovers that Kraven himself had commissioned the blood experiments. He only faked Lucien's killing and in fact wants to work with him on breeding the hybrid race. In desperation, Selene steals into the catacombs: She single-handedly awakens patriarch and foster father Viktor (Bill Nighy). Viktor's reaction is one of anger: not only had she revived him without the ritual ceremony and at least a hundred years too soon, but he was not actually in line to rule, as it was Marcus' turn. He does not want anything to do with the intrigues he learns she is embroiled in. He can only be persuaded when she tells him that Amelia, who had come especially to perform the ritual changing of the guard with Marcus, has been treacherously assassinated. Viktor insists that Selene not only bring Kraven to justice but also kill Michael (He considers the liaison of a female vampire with a Lycan to be 'heresy' for political, ideological and biographical rooted reasons).

The showdown is a bloody mutual massacre of the assembled werewolf and vampire fighters. Kraven manages to steal away, but Lucien dies (1 this time for real). Michael is mortally wounded, but Selene then bites him. Normally, being bitten in by both a werewolf and a vampire would immediately tear a human apart. However, since as mentioned above he is the descendant of Corvinus and thus a latent carrier of his genetic mutations, he does not die, but instead transforms into the ominous hybrid being. Viktor moves in close to kill him and almost manages to do so. Selene intervenes a second time to save a life: As well as awakening a patriarch without authorisation and the iniquity of her love affair with a Neolycan, she ultimately also commits patricide.

Background

Despite the millennia-old history vampires, characters based on them are a relatively *recent* phenomenon in in a wide variety of film productions in *media history*. The vampire figure only began to become popular in the mid-eighteenth century, when Empress Maria Theresa's personal physician Gerard van Swieten sent a story from the eastern regions of the Habsburg Empire to Vienna containing details so gruesome that it eventually travels the globe. This was the first mention of the 'vampyres': In south-eastern European folklore, the word is used to describe corpses that do not rot and lie in their coffins sucking energy, causing lingering illness and crop failures. They therefore had to be exhumed and pierced with needles. Vampires were not described as having long canines until the nineteenth century, when they appeared as nightwalkers and bloodsuckers in Gothic novels (such as *Dracula* by Bram Stoker, 1897). They made the leap to the silver screen in *Nosferatu* (1922), achieved iconic presence in *Dracula* (1931), and later film star status as portrayed by Christopher Lee in the Hammer vampire horror B-movies and were ultimately epitomised by Gary Oldman in Francis Ford Coppola's infamous *Bram Stoker's Dracula* (1992). The writing was already on the wall in the 1994 film *Interview with a Vampire* (Tom Cruise and Brad Pitt as a pair of homoerotically connected vampires). Vampire movies became fully repurposed in the new prototype from 2008 onwards with Robert Pattinson: the image of the vampire not as an *old count*, but as a *young dandy*—an attractive philanderer and vegetarian heartbreaker.

This brief outline suffices to show that the image of the vampire has changed constantly over the course of almost three centuries, and in the process, a wide range of different facets have been brought out. It is therefore not surprising that *Underworld* presents various aspects of the vampire character, which hail from well-known greats within the vampire genre. Among them, there are few signs of its history as an archaic monster: the Lycans have to fulfil this role. Instead, the *Underworld* vampires come across as quite modern. They don't wear old-fashioned frock coats any more but extremely stylish patent leather outfits; they no longer hide away in ruined castles in exotic countries but live in technically upgraded mansions in the hippest metropolises; they no longer flit through the air like bats but race around in expensive luxury cars.

In terms of aesthetics, the film borrows heavily from the *Matrix* series by the Wachowski sisters: The *Underworld* landscape also heavily features shabby backyards, run-down stairwells, factory buildings in danger of collapse and dirty underground sewers. A gloomy sky looms over everything, bringing a lot of rain and casting a damp veil over the already sparse colour palette of the scenery. This creates a permanent mood of anxiety and menace that has led many critics to decipher a comedic effect in the film, or at least to place it in the *noir* genre. The fight scenes are neatly choreographed against a backdrop of intense gunfire with heavy ammunition and the obligatory soundtrack of synthetic techno music.

The *Lexikon des internationalen Films [Encyclopaedia of International Film]* describes the film as a 'highly artificial exercise' that manages to deal 'with the dark sides of life' while developing a story 'within the context of urban subcultures'. Admittedly, the plot gets lost in logical inconsistencies at times, the story is somewhat arbitrary and the suspense degenerates into inertia. And the characters all lack emotional depth. *Underworld* may well be worth watching for its aesthetics: the skilful portrayals are just a framework for the remarkable *artificiality* of the characters. In the many later films in the series, efforts were made to give the story more details, the plot more authentic background and the interpersonal relationships more lively conflicts.

The *Underworld* series focuses on a martial image of the vampire that is no longer dangerous for its *teeth* but for its *trigger-happiness*. Traditional vampires often had hypnotic powers; could control the weather, the animal world and the will of their victims; and mentally manipulate them. They really didn't need weapons for this. *Underworld* is about the brute force of arms and technical superiority. (For example, the werewolves use special ammunition filled with photons to destroy their toothy opponents by lighting up the vampires' insides, and the latter fight back with liquid silver nitrate ammunition that poisons the Lycans' bloodstream.)

How Is the Feminine Staged in Film?

Given its martial focus, it may come as no surprise that the film is barely able to offer independent space for such a thing as 'genuine femininity'. Of course, we ourselves have just as much difficulty deciding what 'genuine' femininity is supposed to look like. However, the film once more makes things easy for us: Selene's brand of femininity has an undeniably *phallic* tinge and comes *in masculine leather shoes*.

The informed viewer will notice the similarity to the *Matrix* series of 1999: With her theatrical appearance, skilled violence and her straightforward approach to massacring, Selene is strongly reminiscent of Thomas 'Neo' Anderson, her fellow vampire warrior Blade (1998), or Violet from the film *Ultraviolet* (2006). Neo, Blade, Violet and Selene like to wear black leather clothes and for unknown reasons are incapable of fighting without their sunglasses on, and their killing is not only especially cold-blooded but also preferably spectacular and accompanied by techno music. The brutality is justified with copious bigotry: after all, they have to fend off conspiracies or protect the weak and innocent. This is hypocritical if only because the modern vampire is not fighting against injustice and subjugation, or terror and exploitation, but *first and foremost against himself.* Which can be interpreted quite literally: Blade, Violet and Selene are lady vampires who mainly rebel against their own tribe. However, this is also a psychological metaphor for the way vampires relate to *their own identity*: Ever since the vampire appeared as a character in novels, it has somehow come to loathe almost everything about itself. Anyone who cannot look themselves in the mirror is not at peace with themselves. Margaret L. Shanahan (1999) has written that vampires above all symbolise the 'mirror-hungry personalities' conceived by Heinz Kohut, who are driven by an elevated need for admiration, affirmation, power and control because in their fragmented self-experience they secretly feel *inferior* (or to be precise, *dead*). Not once in *Underworld* is it mentioned that vampires cannot see their own reflection. But we can sense the *self-hatred* that lurks behind the splendid image Selene projects. This becomes plausible if we base this supposition on Arno Gruen's (2000) oft-repeated phrase, according to which hatred is always *projected self-hatred*: Her fanatical hostility in hunting down of werewolves is a clear indication of the self-destructive forces that are unconsciously seething within her. The source of self-hatred is her own *victimhood*: As a small child, she witnessed the massacring of her family. Ideologically, this is attributed to the Lycans. We know better and find out that her foster father Viktor himself was responsible. This initially makes no difference to the internal dynamics: To avoid having to feel the trauma of pain and helplessness, Selene takes refuge in *identifying with the aggressor.* She practically models herself on the bestial murderers of her family, becoming a merciless, heinous killing machine herself. Horst-Eberhard Richter (1979, p. 55f) called this principle the 'God complex': He sees this as a massive reaction against the genuine powerlessness, which forms part of self-identity, banishing it from consciousness (i.e. 'repressing' it). The more one's conscious self-identity revolves around strength, power and superiority, the more successful this repression. The feeling of being at the mercy of others and the existential threat of the past has become the 'expansive egotism' of today: This is supposed above all to protect against a 'relapse into gentleness and weakness', so as not to come into emotional contact with the pain from past trauma. One must thus 'become a beast'—a wild, hating, murderous one. In the case of the vampire, this wild animal uses the backdrop of novels and films to deny its own dependency by humiliating both human and Lycan victims. Like Oren Ishii, who as a girl in Quentin Tarantino's *Kill Bill* series (also stylistically striking for its various forms of martial arts) witnessed her parents being massacred by mafia boss Matsumoto and subsequently becomes a contract killer, Selene develops a defensive identity as a 'death dealer'. There is no room for sensitivity. The lack of emotional depth conveyed in the film is not only due to the production style as an action movie but also matches the protagonist's fragmented inner world. The only femininity she can convey thus cannot help being artificial. Since in the Western world femininity has arguably always been connoted with sensitive, caring, mild and physically weak qualities, Selene fears and suppress these 'feminine' aspects of her identity, deliberately overriding them with overblown stereotypes of male toughness and destructiveness.

Her hatred for the enemy in the form of the Lycans naturally becomes focussed on Viktor the moment she realises that he massacred her parents. However, at this point in the film, we worry that Selene could end up like Trinity did in the *Matrix series* cited above: Trinity is also a strong, smart soldier who is capable of killing. As the only female lead in the story, however, her role is limited to falling in love with The One, Neo, and resurrecting him through the power of her love. Selene does the same, saving Michael's life several times in the film. Having been bitten by the werewolf, he almost dies in the showdown. But she rushes over and bites him too, allowing him to mutate into a super hybrid. We almost resign ourselves to the fact that her role has thus been fulfilled: We expect Michael, who has suddenly become strong, to take up the fight with Viktor and finish him off. Selene's function would then be entirely limited to stewardship of the love, which paved the man's way to superhumanity. Fortunately, things turn out differently, as the film's narrative arc has a major surprise in store: *Selene herself kills her foster father*. With *his* sword, mind you. To be precise, it splits his head in two with an oblique transversal cut. This is not just a successful act of revenge against the murderer of her family. It is clearly also a rebellion against the patriarchy. Unfortunately, this unexpected coup does not seem particularly feministic: Since she uses *her father's* sword, she is metaphorically identifying with his masculinity, just as she does when deploying the traditional cultural images of male strength to expunge her contempt for her own weakness.

Any other femininity we encounter in the film is also rather vestigial: There is a second female vampire whose only function is to dream of becoming the future ruler's wife by marrying Kraven and who thus plots against Selene. A third one is a member of the Vampire Council of Elders, Amelia. However, she only appears in the 30 s scene of her dastardly execution by the Lycans—naturally, without a single line of dialogue. This is symptomatic: women have very little to say in the film.

The Woman as a Victim or Revenge on the Patriarchy?

This pretentious overwriting of facets of femininity with highly stereotyped aspects of masculinity corresponds with the creeping suspicion we have when faced with the better-known vampire films of recent times: In the most popular offshoots of the genre, the image of the vampire is primarily organised around the prototypical supremacy of the genuinely *male* vampire who, as a highly potent seducer, has it in for the generally rather weak-willed *female* victims. This idea is rooted in the novel by Bram Stoker. In it, Dracula bites women quite indiscriminately, and they give in to him with little resistance. The classic Dracula vampire seeks victims for *the sake of biting*: He is therefore primarily 'tooth-driven', as Florian Kührer (2010) puts it in an amusing play on words [as opposed to heart-driven]. Ernest Jones (1951) was the first to describe the *sexual connotation* of vampiric biting has that, in the classically Freudian manner, is in the guise of an *oral* substitution: Just as the baby gains its vitality primarily from *sucking on the mother's breast*, so too the vampires base their immortality on *sucking blood*. If sucking blood represents actually drinking milk, then the *coffin* in which the vampire sleeps by day would seem to be akin to the *maternal womb*. It is suddenly clear why old Dracula in Coppola's 1992 film always has to be covered by earth from his native Transylvania (from 'Mother Earth', so to speak) to sleep in his coffin. In the same way, the coffins of the three vampire patriarchs are positioned in utero in *Underworld*: in their catacombs of the villa, encased in protective concrete with circular openings in the floor. We also understand why during the ritual awakening ceremony that Selene initiates for Viktor the freshly awakened man is still hooked up to all kinds of tubes of blood that feed him—almost as if through an umbilical cord. Since the vampire's immortality is irrevocably bound to sucking blood and sleeping in a coffin, its vitality, according to Alan Dundes (2002), requires the constant symbolic repetition of *birth experiences*. And with this realisation, we also understand why the prototypical vampire constellation always primarily includes a *woman* as the victim:

The instrumentalisation of the victims as symbolic *mothers* is the vampires' promise of immortality and at the same time cements the role of women as *subordinates*. In a psychodynamic sense, the traditional vampire consistently forces women into the victim role, at the same time hiding the actual *dependence* on women that they secretly feel.

In *Underworld*, Viktor embodies a vampiric patriarch who is consumed by fear. It is implied that the vampires in the film series no longer need to drink human blood. At the same time, Viktor is the only one who, by virtue of his status, is allowed to go out into the countryside and bloodthirstily massacre the inhabitants of entire villages. Selene's family was exterminated on one such outing. Except that Viktor was unable to kill little Selene, because she reminds him of his daughter Sonia. He had her executed because she had the audacity to allow herself to be impregnated by a werewolf. The outrage is not her affair with the Lycan—it is the prospect of the *pregnancy* that alarms him. When he meets little Selene, not only the guilt of his daughter's execution resonates: the ambivalence of his latent mother theme also becomes palpable. Assuming that the fantasy of the highly ambivalent *dependence on the mother* is incorporated into Viktor's life as a vampire and that he symbolically hides this, then the best strategy is surely to initiate an escape into identification:

He suddenly assumes the maternal role *himself* by turning Selene into a vampire. There are several instances of Selene being stylised as a victim: Viktor must generate her symbolic mother function in order to safeguard his own immortality by drinking blood, at the same time subjugating her as a child in order to elevate himself in identification with motherhood (which allows him to deny his desperate desire for a mother).

It is fitting that Selene becomes a symbolic figure for revenge against the patriarchy: In her appearance, she identifies with masculinity and phallic fantasies of power mask weakness in her self-identity. As a rebel, she joins a long line of strong female vampire characters who fight against the male-dominated world with emancipatory acts. The genre that celebrated a major breakthrough with *Dracula's Daughter* in 1936 reached its artistic peak with *Desire* in 1983: Miriam Blaylock (Catherine Deneuve) unceremoniously leaves her husband John (David Bowie) in order to embark on a love affair with Dr. Sarah Roberts (Susan Sarandon). The apparently ominous appearance of the 'lesbian vampire' is not merely a harmless subgenre in the entertainment industry: female vampires hold tremendous sway in literary and film history: They embody the emancipation movement on screen, thus becoming the epitome of the liberalisation of sexual diversity. Claudia Liebrand (1998, p. 91) holds that even the first-generation vampires, male and female alike, stir up the entrenched establishment of rigid ideas about gender identity with their 'sexual deviance'. We are thinking here above all of the multitude of those female vampires who, from the 1970s onwards, reflected the sexual revolution, New Wave feminism and the homosexual movement. As such, they presented a danger to be taken seriously, especially for the heteronormative matrix.

The beheading of Viktor is a discursive act: (Fig. 24.1) The patriarchy falls with the head. The subsequent films turn Selene into the hunted, and she must stand her ground against the revenge of the patriarchal order.

Vagina Dentata

Female vampires are not only a threat to the patriarchal order or the heteronormative matrix. They sometimes also quite pragmatically embody a rather immediate danger for men: namely, being *robbed of their masculinity*. This can be understood quite literally *as a fear of losing the penis*. Sigmund Freud (1900) gave this dazzling fear an equally dazzling name: 'Vagina dentata'—*toothed vagina*. Apparently, the widespread motif of women as objects of desire who also have a hint of unpredictable destructiveness about

Fig. 24.1 Viktor's head is diagonally split in two: an act of rebellion against the patriarchy he embodies (01:46:14)

them haunts artistic expressions from a wide range of cultural developmental periods. Seduction and destruction are a heady mix. There is something alluring and inviting about these *femme fatales,* who then go on to maim, kill or literally emasculate. We are familiar with them from mythology as Amazonians, from the Middle Ages as Melusine—and in the territory of modern-day series, we come across such highly erotic and at the same time life-threatening female figures in the form of Cersei Lannister from *Game of Thrones* or Claire Underwood in *House of Cards*: Of course, these women do not really have teeth in their private parts. They metaphorically represent murderous violence that both excites and intimidates men.

As teeth famously play a prominent role in the vampire motif, surely no other fictional monster figure is better suited to symbolising it. For one thing, teeth are traditionally located *in the mouth.* There are occasionally female special vampires who actually use their vaginas to suck blood. A curious example is Danica Dalos in *Blade: Trinity* (2004), who explicitly has her fangs in her vagina and goes in search of penises worth devouring (no doubt enacting Freud's classic notion of women's infamous *penis envy*).

However, on the whole, female vampires are *femmes fatale*s who demonstrate that the danger they pose is not the actual long, biting fangs but the *seductive power* that aims straight between men's legs: Singer Aaliyah plays the exotic, mystical vampire princess Akasha, who wreaks manipulative havoc in *Queen of the Damned* (2002); in *From Dusk Till Dawn* (1996), Salma Hayek is a sensual dancer who not only wiggles provocatively but also has her epicurean eye set on the male clientele in the dance club; Monika Belucci's erotically appealing yet disturbingly sinister performance as Count Dracula's leading vampire playmate in Coppola's 1992 film is legendary.

Selene from the *Underworld* series is first and foremost a *fighter* but is visually completely eroticised. No doubt she is to be presented as an extremely beautiful, very alluring woman (Fig. 24.2), which apparently includes casting her physique in an erotic light, espe-

Fig. 24.2 The femininity of the dangerous vampire is staged ambivalently as murderous and erotically attractive at the same time (00:03:48)

cially in the lithe fight sequences through her tight-fitting, glossy patent leather outfits. However, there is little eroticism elsewhere in the film. In the love story between her and Michael, their mutual attraction is conveyed in a rather detached manner.

It almost seems like an absolute necessity for plot reasons and so is presented almost matter of fact. In contrast, desire is only masked in murderous lust, falling in love does not get beyond a superficial level, and sensuality is only apparent in the fetishisation of her female body.

Perverted Motherhood

There are various established theoretical traditions within the psychoanalytic community, which allow contextualisation of the erotic-seductive and at the same time threatening-destructive meaning that teeth have in representations of the vampire figure. Reference is often made to the symbolic staging of early childhood developmental atmospheres: The 'draining' of the caring mother object is the ultimate proof of love and the founding moment for the intimate bond. Infants can only regulate certain fears and other perceptions that induce powerlessness by means of instinctively rooted, archaic processing mechanisms. Among these are *splitting* and *projection*: Negative feelings cannot be integrated into the inner world of positive memories and stored feelings. Instead, they must be strictly separated from it. The infant thus *shifts* negative feelings *outwards*—where it blames them on its environment, so to speak. This is how 'evil objects' arise in the environment. The infant deems them evil because it unconsciously perceives them to be charged with destructive impulses, which they *themselves* latently feel. By externalising them, these destructive impulses take on a tangible form and can be better controlled.

Following this line of argument, the popularity of the vampire figure could be broken down to the following mechanism: we need tangible external figures in the form of cultural symbols onto whom we can project those early childhood desires to either completely drain the mother (thereby egotistically destroying her) or to be neglected (or punished) by her. This enables us to deal with the repressed feelings and fantasies in a displaced, masked way.

The vampire's long fangs also fall into this category. Karl Abraham (1925) supplements Freud's 'oral phase' with an 'oral-cannibalistic' sub-phase, which arises as soon as the infant grows teeth. There may be various motivations for this biting—one of which, according to Abraham, is an *aggressive* impulse, which he also calls 'sadistic': The violence of biting forces the mother object to submit.

In a sense, vampires represent a reversal of our unconscious needs: We ourselves harbour a greed for completely sucking dry (in the metaphorical sense of being totally cared for or having absolute control over an object). However, we find this morally dubious and, as civilised beings, grant no place for it in our everyday life. We thus blame these tendencies on vampires.

In view of this underlying unconscious mechanism, it is hardly surprising that there are so many female monsters wreaking havoc in our culture, or that the fear they inspire is a result of perverted play forms of *motherhood*, of all things. In the horror genre, images of monstrous women are always images of malevolent *motherliness*. Our accumulated object images of these 'wicked mothers' are not of mothers who caringly or self-sacrificingly provide for the needs of her offspring. The evil mother *takes* instead of giving. She *manipulates* instead of stimulating. Shanahan (1999, p. 554) even describes the evil mother with the word 'vampiric', since she 'drains' the child's energy for her own stabilisation, nutrition or gratification. This includes the expectation that children have to adapt to their mother. These are gradual transitions between early childhood adaptation and desperate submission. The more the child has to submit in order to adapt to the mother, the more serious the deficits they develop in self-esteem and regulatory abilities. And the stronger these ('narcissistic') deficits, the more vehement the staving off of chronic inferiority, feelings of emptiness or loathsome weakness in the self-identity.

Even when female vampires are not *violent* mothers, however, they are particularly *absent* ones or show a toxic form of neglect—a motif that runs through much of the genre: Vampires' mothers tend to have died early: from Blade (in the eponymous film series) to Elena and Jeremy (from the 2009 series *Vampire Diaries*), Mary from *Wes Craven presents Dracula* (2000) or Sooki (in the series *True Blood*, 2008). Claudia is transformed into a ruthless vampire in *Interview with a Vampir*e (1994) after her mother died of plague. In *The Queen of the Damned* (2002), Jesse Reeves is immediately magically attracted to vampire Lestat and willingly offers him her breast for the merging of the vampire bite: she grew up in an orphanage and wants nothing more than a caring mother substitute. Bella's mother from the ominous *Twilight* series (of 2008) lives with a baseball player somewhere far away and doesn't exactly give a serious impression of maternal competence. Poor Bella thus almost has no alternative but to submissively throw her lonely self into the completely idealised crush on swoon-worthy vampire Edward Cullen.

Of course, there is also an absent mother in the case of Selene. Not only *personally*, because Selene's mother had been massacred by Viktor before he turned her into a vampire, but also *ideologically*: The whole mythology that forms the background for the discord between vampires and Lycans in *Underworld* is conventionally patriarchal in that it concerns the *paternal* line of inheritance. Mothers have no place in it. The maternal role will be reinstated later: In the subsequent films, Selene's identity is expanded to include her function as a mother. Growing up without a mother can be understood as a momentous pointer. The lack of a maternal relationship makes it extremely difficult for her to develop a healthy inner emotional life and to appropriately integrate female identity. The dramatic and action-packed rescue of the daughter in the sequels is therefore to be understood not only as an attempt to prove that she does not want to be such a bad mother object as she herself had to experience due to her own dead mother and as it inherently weighs on her shoulders as a vampire due to the collective identity of her species. It is also a struggle for the salvation of her *own existence*. Just as Viktor needs Selene as a sacrifice to secure his immortality and symbolically elevate himself to compensatory motherhood, Selene needs her daughter in order to potentially enact a satisfying maternal relationship after all. Unfortunately, this means that she has to instrumentalise her daughter as an object for her own salvation. Will the child emerge from this unscathed?

Translated by Annette Caroline Christmas.

Film Details

Original title	Underworld
Release year	2003
Country	USA, Great Britain, Hungary, Germany
Screenplay	Danny McBride
Director	Len Wiseman
Principal actors	Kate Beckinsale, Scott Speedman, Bill Nighy
Availability	DVD

References

Abraham K (1925) Psychoanalytical studies on character formation. Collected papers on psychoanalysis. 1927 by Grant A. Allan Reprinted 1979\ with permission of Hogarth Press Limited, by H. Karnac (Books) Ltd, London

Dundes A (2002) The vampire. A casebook. University of Wisconsin, London

Freud S (1900 [1899]) The interpretation of dreams. Standard Edition, vol IV, pp ix–627

Gruen A (2000) Der Fremde in uns [The stranger in us]. Klett Cotta, Stuttgart

Jones E (1951) Psycho-analysis and anthropology. In: Jones E (ed) Essays in folklore, anthropology and religion, vol 2. Hogarth, London, pp 114–144

Kührer F (2010) Vampire. Monster, Mythos, Medienstar. Butzon & Bercker, Kevelaer

Liebrand C (1998) Vampir/inn/e/n. Anne Rice's "interview with the vampire", Sheridan LeFanu's "Carmilla" and Bram Stoker's "Dracula". Freiburg Women's Stud 1:91–113

Richter H-E (1979) Der Gotteskomplex [The god complex]. Psychosocial, Giessen

Shanahan ML (1999) Psychological perspectives on vampire mythology. In: Melton JG (ed) The vampire book. Visible Ink Press, Canton, pp 548–557

Part VIII

Self-Empowerment and Identity

Keep Going: Thelma & Louise (US, 1991) 25

Andreas Hamburger and Vivian Pramataroff-Hamburger

Introduction

Thelma & Louise had a clearly polarising effect among audiences and film critics alike. The film portrays fantasies of desire and fear, motherhood and adolescence, sexuality and friendship.

Film Plot

Thelma (Geena Davis), a disorganised woman, is married to macho man Derryl (Christopher McDonald). Her smart friend Louise (Susan Sarandon), who is working as a waitress, is experiencing difficulties in her personal life. The two women decide to go fishing for the weekend and set off in Louise's iconic Ford Thunderbird convertible. Thelma takes not only her husband's fishing gear but also a pistol. They stop at a bar along the way, where a local womaniser, Harlan, hits on Thelma. They have a drink and dance together. Harlan tries to rape Thelma, but Louise saves her by threatening him with Thelma's gun. The foul-mouthed Harlan swears at Louise, who reflexively shoots him. Thelma wants to call the police, but Louise says that Thelma had just been dancing with the man, was tipsy and had flirted with him, so the police would never believe their version of the events. She decides to flee to Mexico. Thelma later agrees to go with her.

A. Hamburger (✉)
International Psychoanalytic University Berlin, Berlin, Germany

V. Pramataroff-Hamburger
Private Psychotherapeutic Practice, Munich, Germany
e-mail: vivian@pramataroff.de

V. Pramataroff-Hamburger, A. Hamburger (eds.), *From La Strada to The Hours*, https://doi.org/10.1007/978-3-662-68789-5_25

Louise calls her boyfriend Jimmy (Michael Madsen), with whom she has an easy-going relationship. She does not tell him what has happened but asks him for money. He promises to transfer the money to her immediately. On the way, they pick up a hitchhiker, J.D. (Brat Pitt), and take him as far as Oklahoma City, where the three of them stop at a motel. When Louise goes to collect the money, Jimmy himself suddenly steps out in front of her. He gives her the money and along with it a ring, but Louise gently rejects his proposal, which has come too late.

At the same time, J.D. knocks on Thelma's door. It is raining heavily, and she is not reluctant to let him in. They start flirting with each other. J.D. tells her that he is under a suspended sentence for various robberies and also explains his charming armed robbery technique to her in an amusing scene, which has become a classic. They sleep together. The next morning, while Thelma is telling her friend about her first ever happy night of love, she leaves J.D. alone in the room. The charming robber remains true to himself, and when the two women run to the room, there is no sign of him—or of the money that Louise had given to Thelma for safekeeping.

Louise breaks down in tears. In desperate need of money, Thelma holds up a shop in charming style, following J.D.'s example. The shop has video surveillance, so of course they are rumbled immediately. J.D. is also arrested. The policeman Hal Slocumb (Harvey Keitel), playing the good cop role, questions him about the money found on him; he accuses him of having driven the women into their dangerous life of crime in the first place by stealing it.

Since Louise doesn't want to drive through Texas, they make a long diversion. They meet a truck driver on the way who insults them with obscene gestures. Thelma realises why Louise does not want to go to Texas; Louise has been raped there. But Louise doesn't want to talk about it. A while later, they are checked by a traffic cop, who seems to be about to recognise them. Thelma holds the gun to his head and tells Louise to lock him in the boot of his patrol car. She mockingly shoots a few ventilation holes in the boot lid.

Louise calls Derryl's house, where the police are already waiting. Hal Slocumb wants to persuade her to turn herself in. He credibly assures her that he actually believes she is innocent and has just suffered a series of misfortunes and wants to help them, but Louise hangs up. They encounter the truck driver again, who resumes his crude come-on. He thinks he has already won when Thelma and Louise stop. But they demand an apology, and when he angrily refuses, they blow up his tanker.

The police are now after them for a whole list of potential charges. They seem to have shaken off their pursuers and are poised before the abyss of the Grand Canyon. A police helicopter suddenly rises up from the depths directly in front of them; behind them is a sea of patrol cars and snipers. They are surrounded. Hal is the only person who still manages to have any empathy for the two women, who he realises are in dire straits. Everyone else thinks they are highly dangerous and release the safety catches on their weapons. Thelma points to the precipice, saying: 'Keep going'! Louise steps on the gas, and they hold hands. The last shot shows the Thunderbird flying over the edge of the cliff into mid-air.

Background

Despite its prominent director, Sir Ridley Scott, *Thelma & Louise* is held to be the work screenwriter Callie Khouri, who was still an unknown 34 years old at the time. She was awarded an Oscar and a Golden Globe for this, her first produced screenplay.

She explains how the film idea came about in her book *Thelma & Louise/Something to talk about*:

> ... I was driving home late one night from the set of some music video, and pulled up in front of my house and thought, 'Two women on a crime spree'. That was the idea [for] *Thelma & Louise*. I started developing it from there. Why would two women go on a crime spree? Why would *I* go on a crime spree? And the other thing is, I had the image of the car flying into the Grand Canyon. So I knew that's where it was going. In some kind of strange flash I saw their journey, not the actual physical journey, but how they would start out and what they would become. I should say, I *felt* it. (Khouri 1996, p. IX)

Although Callie Khouri did not have any experience in the industry, she also wanted to direct the film. After protracted negotiations, Ridley Scott ultimately became the director.

Ridley Scott (*1937) is one of the best known and most influential directors today and has shaped the narrative styles of several film genres. At that time, he owed his reputation to films such as *Alien* (US 1979) and *Blade Runner* (US 1982). The latter was so visually stunning that it inspired a whole generation of cyberpunk literature, music and art. The experienced craftsman Ridley Scott always managed to introduce a touch of glamour and stunning visuals to any film, no matter what the content. Combining his talents with those of the committed young writer ensured that her groundbreaking idea would be transformed into a professional work of cinematic art. The film was thus a huge success, against all expectations. With a budget of 16 million dollars, it grossed six million during the opening weekend, ultimately netting a total of 45 million. Geena Davis playing Thelma and Susan Sarandon as Louise were both nominated for the Academy Award for Best Leading Actress. There were four other 'best' nominations for the director, film editing, cinematography, and for the best original screenplay by Callie Khoury.

The reviews were divided. For one thing, criticism was levelled at the caricature-like portrayals of the men. And feminist critics also objected to the finale: as soon as women become independent, they have to die.

The film turned the largely male-dominated road movie genre on its head. When housewives escape their narrow lives, as they had in Scorsese's *Boxcar Bertha* (US 1972) and *Alice Doesn't Live Here Any More* (US 1974), they end up becoming dependent on a man they meet along the way. *Thelma & Louise* also had a considerable impact in the narrower circle of psychoanalytic debate. The psychoanalytic community responded astonishingly quickly, starting to publish film articles critically examining the psychoanalytic concept of femininity from 1991, the year of its release, among them an article by Louise Kaplan (1993), a spokeswoman for feminist psychoanalysis. The controversy mainly concerned whether these were 'phallic women' (Gabbard and Gabbard 1993) or whether a completely new psychoanalytic understanding of independent female development was called for (Benton et al. 1993; Kaplan 1993). This very lively debate then led to wider reception of film psychoanalysis.

It could thus be said that feminist psychoanalysis helped put film psychoanalysis on the map and significantly shaped its discussion in its early days. And *Thelma & Louise* was an important catalyst for this.

How Is Femininity Staged in Film?

Thelma & Louise situates femininity in several genres: the buddy movie, the road movie, the coming-of-age story and the action film.

Female Buddies

A female buddy movie: *Thelma & Louise* is primarily about women's friendship, not only in the sense of individual development but also as solidarity at a social level. Women are no longer satisfied with what the world has to offer them but make their own rules as noble outlaws. Both start out serving others (as a waitress and a housewife), and both are depicted next to fish tanks, which imprison fish just so they can be looked at and fulfil wishes. But in the end, both become confident women who make their own decisions—ultimately even deciding to die. Psychoanalytically speaking, this kind of friendship is seen as playful companionship, and viewers can easily empathise with it. Playing together is a central part of every mother-child relationship; in male development, this is interrupted by an identity crisis. Boys have to assert and differentiate themselves, while girls usually have no problem maintaining their playfulness and identification with their mother. Thelma and Louise are no exception: they can have fun together without sexuality getting in the way. This is also clearly shown in the beautiful scene after having sex with J.D. when Thelma realises, for the first time, 'what all the fuss is about', and Louise unselfconsciously empathises and is pleased for her.

But the relationship suffers a number of crises. Immediately after the fatal shot, Thelma wants to go to the police. However, Louise refuses and says that she had flirted, after all. The next crisis is Louise's decision to flee to Mexico. At this point, they could have parted ways, because Thelma could still have turned back. The call home teaches her better: she definitely doesn't want to go back to Darryl, so she decides to abandon her former life and stay with Louise. Both have now given up any attachment to their past. However, this is immediately followed by the third crisis, when the charming J.D. steals their money. Again, Louise could accuse Thelma of being too blinded by her sex drive to pay attention—but she does not. This is a turning point. Louise's desperation and paralysis cause Thelma to grow beyond herself, and she easily slips into the masculine role of J.D. by holding up a shop. From that point on, she is the driving force. She herself disarms and confines the policeman at the road check—and she gives the decisive command at the end: 'Keep going!'.

The traditional cinematic buddy relationship is not sexual; the same can be said of long stretches of *Thelma & Louise*. Nevertheless, the film clearly comments that pleasure forms part of sexuality. The sexual approaches made by men (Darryl, the rapist, the truck driver) are powerful displays of dominance. The antithesis to this is the protagonists' free choice of love object (Jimmy, J.D.) and also the imaginative, playful although not necessarily sexually coded relationship between the two women. Perceptions differ widely as to whether there is also any sexual energy in their relationship. The kiss on the lips in the last scene may at least harbour the possibility. The film shows three models of sexuality: male-dominated convention (Darryl, the rapist), female desire in the context of a love relationship (Louise—Jimmy) and free pleasure without any intention of commitment (Thelma—J.D.), which is even linked to the element of payment (J.D. takes the money from the bedside table).

Sexuality is symbolised by the omnipresence of syringes and pumps, which is almost a running gag, an ironic allusion to phallic conventions. By contrast, there are rain scenes in which water falls from the sky, creating a wetland. It is unclear how this is to be interpreted. For the most part, it is men who are left out in the rain.

Women in a Road Movie

Thelma & Louise could also be seen as an anti-road movie. After all, the usual gender concept of the passive woman is subverted by placing women in the familiar role concept of the lonely hero on a country road. Enevold (2004) describes this concept graphically: '… men are spermatic mobile men, and women waiting egg-bearing to-be mothers in fixed locations, whose deviation from the stove seems automatically to translate them into women on the loose whose mere presence in public space announces that sex is up for grabs'. And yet the film narrative is still immersed in an up-beat atmosphere, so the end does not seem tragic but a radical exaltation, an existential leap into the void.

The film music by celebrated film composer Hans Zimmer contributes greatly to this connection to the road movie genre without its male stereotype. The soundtrack is mixed from a composition supported by themes but also contains 15 independent songs.

However, the road or the journey is a metaphor that goes far beyond the classic road movie to the search for freedom and identity. The highway is a counter-world to the ideas of order in bourgeois everyday life, and road movies are often populated with comedic characters. The archetype to these may well be Charlie Chaplin's interpretation of the tramp, who is always on the road in search of happiness. In films such as Fellini's *La Strada* (I 1954), the street is a global metaphor of life, a place to prove one's worth, a restless anchor in the world (see Leube-Sonnleitner, Chap. 5 in this volume). Restless motion on the road is a way of life for the heroes—and now the heroines—of the road movie.

Further Considerations

Road Movie: Identity and Autonomy

Thelma & Louise deliberately plays with genres. Genre signals usually regulate the audience's expectations: in the first few moments, viewers know what kind of film they are watching, whether comedy, tragedy, melodrama or, as in this case, a road movie. There are recognisable indicators, such as the wide sky and the empty fields, which the road movie has in common with the western. As a female road movie, *Thelma & Louise* plays with this genre and turns it on its head.

Of course, in *Thelma & Louise*, the stereotypical roles are not simply reversed. Rather, they are assigned alternately, by way of trying them out. One such role reversal is the fact that the freedom to engage in violent resistance is not just granted to demonic women, as is usual in films, but to women with whom we can identify. But genre boundaries are also transgressed: the two women shoot and not only in self-defence, which is not typical of road movies—nor of Westerns, for that matter, in which the good guys only kill for the sake of justice. There are similarities with gangster films, in which we eagerly identify with someone who takes what they want by force.

Far beyond this role reversal, the women portrayed in this film do not conform to any stereotype. *Thelma & Louise* introduces the possibility for women to tell their own stories beyond traditional roles and to break down predetermined attributions of traits (de-scripting). In film history, this idea of women developing their own female narrative down the generations was further developed in *The Hours* (US 2002) (see Mahler-Bungers, Chap. 26, in this volume).

From a psychoanalytical point of view, the road movie genre serves a certain audience need. It plays with the adolescent search for identity: new self-identities are tried on in the company of travel companions, always on the move, without the constraint of a fixed abode, but also without the protection of one. In *Thelma & Louise*, this becomes clear during the very first drive, when Thelma poses as Louise in the car's wing mirror. This seems like a little girl trying on her mother's lipstick.

The two women's differing characters are introduced right at the start of the movie. The chaotic and childish Thelma is contrasted with the mature, orderly, controlled, but also motherly and careful Louise, who tells off her guests in the restaurant and lovingly wipes Thema's bloodstained face with spit. Conversely, Thelma is also the conventional housewife in a bourgeois marriage, while Louise lives in an unstable love affair with an erratic musician. The journey scrambles all these identity markers. During the film, Thelma takes on the role of mother and leader, and Louise loses control under the duress of her trauma if she talks to the cop on the phone for too long.

These identity issues are above all anchored in the basic need for autonomy, which is the theme of the entire film. Although she initially doesn't realise it, Thelma wants to break out of her suburban slavery. However, she packs so much luggage for the fishing weekend that it seems like a house removal, with a gun into the bargain. What does Louise want? She is disillusioned, in part due to a traumatic experience, which is only hinted at, and is attracted to Thelma's temperament. She wants to once more experience the freedom of living life naively and being hungry for adventure with a woman who is 10 years younger than herself. She is actually seeking autonomy in the sense of overcoming her past and starting afresh. In fact, she finds a fresh approach with Jimmy, whom she can allow herself to love, however only once she can be sure she is not dependent on him.

Outlaws: Violent Women

However, *Thelma & Louise* is about more than adolescent experimentation and the friendship between the two women. It is about an increasingly violent breakthrough. The protagonists not only travel out of their comfort zone into adventure but also break the law and engage in violence and in self-defence. They become outlaws (Fig. 25.1).

Women committing violence and carrying weapons in films were nothing new. Armed women are usually presented as attractive in Hollywood films. The accoutrement of a gun is almost always accompanied by a plunging neckline (Peggy Cummins in *Deadly is the Female*, Faye Dunaway in *Bonnie and Clyde* and Sharon Stone in *Basic Instinct*—although in this case, the weapon is admittedly an ice pick, and she sports a different neckline).

Gabbard and Gabbard (1993) refer to such female characters, which have frequently appeared in American films since the 1940s, as 'phallic' women—not to denote a pattern of female personality development, but rather a young boys' fantasy in which the mother is endowed with a hidden penis. According to this reading, the myth of the phallic mother, which is also manifested in the image of the witch, for example, is the inversion of the infant's fear of being overwhelmed by the invading breast.

Fig. 25.1 Outlaws (01:48:07)

The situation is different in *Thelma & Louise*. In this film, the armed women are in the right and are not wearing the gun as a provocative accessory. The women use the gun as an instrument of castration at least at one point, when they blow up the invasive and unrepentant truck driver's shiny road tanker.

Since the 1990s, a spate of films has been released in which women wield weapons, with the viewer's approval. However, we should not fixate on weapons when it comes to outlaws, because there is so much more at stake than women adopting male characteristics or taking on male roles. The noble bandit, with whom each of us can readily identify, asserts itself as an individual, evoking memories in the audience of their own steps towards detachment before the age of three.

The protagonists of individuation films are usually male; the women's role is either that of a controlling mother figure or an enticing lover who challenges the man to transgress his boundaries. In *Thelma & Louise*, for the first time, the main characters are female. Is their developmental path masculine or feminine? This is the wrong question to ask: they move beyond the zone of fixed gender roles and acquire the tools of dominance (guns) without necessarily mutating into boys.

The camera shows us how conventional signs are discarded (make-up, jewellery), but it also celebrates feminine appearance. In *Thelma & Louise*, we are presented with outlaws who are still women. Louise, for example, lets her hair down, and Thelma the heroine no longer needs curlers.

Men are neither copied nor simply mimicked: both call their partners—interestingly, in secret—and Louise accidently gives away their getaway route because she spends far too long on the phone with the cop, a man who seems to understand her. But neither are male stereotypes simply adopted, not even in aggression: The trucker is lectured but not killed (only his car as a phallic symbol; he is symbolically castrated), and even the policeman, who expects to be shot, is only locked in the boot like a rabbit: Thelma deliberately shoots air holes in the boot lid for him so that he can breathe.

Male and Female Gazes

How are women portrayed, and the men? How are both shown for women, and for men? Laura Mulvey, the most important feminist theorist who transferred some of Jacques Lacan's concepts to film studies, describes Hollywood cinema as an expression and instrument of the male gaze. Women are there to be looked at and men are there to look at them. But this regularly goes awry in *Thelma & Louise*. The gazing men look daft or extremely clichéd.

With the exception of the good cop (Harvey Keitel), the loyal guy Jimmy and a taciturn Native American, men are portrayed as horny hunters, or as arrogant fools like Darryl. J.D. (Brad Pitt) is a liminal case. Although he attracts Thelma's desire as a soft, childlike figure, he then goes on to exploit and betray her. In contrast, the women, who are all waitresses, are portrayed as fair and show solidarity. Many viewers and critics have remarked that the portrayal of the men is one-sided caricaturing. Gena Davis, the actress who plays Thelma, countered that they had identified with the wrong characters.

Camera and montage show the possibility of a female gaze in its own right. This is evident, for example, in the precise sequence of shots in the scene when Thelma discovers J.D. His first appearance is linked to the well-known attribute of squirting: Thelma stumbles over him. Lost in thought, he is splashing around with a water hose like a boy. After a brief conversation, Thelma turns to look at him as she walks away, clearly eyeing him up from head to toe. This is the epitome of a masculine look. A sophisticated choreography of gazes then takes place, in which it becomes quite clear that Thelma is the gazer and J.D. the lustfully gazed upon. And yet this gaze is directed forward, capturing J.D. only indirectly. We see Thelma tracing her eyeliner in the rear-view mirror, a not coincidental highlighting of her eye; in the background, we see J.D., who has not even noticed Thelma yet. The focus of her gaze then shifts. She notices him, and he crosses the background; Thelma's gaze continues to follow him, now in the car's wing mirror (Fig. 25.2).

The camera then cuts to her subjective perspective as, in the wing mirror, she sees J.D. walking towards them. We cannot tell whether he is already looking at Thelma because he is wearing dark sunglasses. The next cut is a half close-up of the car, Thelma's gaze still directed straight ahead of her. Although she must have seen J.D. approaching her in the rear-view mirror, she does not indicate that she has noticed him. J.D. knocks politely on the car, and only then does Thelma turn to him. Throughout the editing sequence, Thema is the active viewer, and J.D. is the object.

They have started up a flirtatious conversation, but Louise quite maternalistically rules out taking him with them, speeding through the fully parked lot in a breakneck reverse. At this point, the almost surreal figure of a bodybuilder comes into the picture as a symbol of Thelma's carnal gaze. At the same time, we hear the phrase, off, 'We should have taken him with us'.

Fig. 25.2 Female gaze (00:38:24)

Once they are on the road again, she also details his physical charms to Louise, by highlighting partial objects, which in the language of the male gaze are known as 'tits & ass': 'Did you see his butt? Darryl doesn't have a cute butt. You could park a car in the shadow of his ass'. Then, when they meet J.D. again, posing dreamily à la James Dean, it is Thelma again who ensures—and this time successfully—that he be allowed to ride with them. The gesture she makes to Louise, which makes her give in, clearly signals her appetite. And with that, Thelma's desire is clearly shown. It is not a romantic desire for a relationship, but a sexual desire directed towards the exterior, and the direction of the action also clearly follows the exchange of looks shown earlier: it is she who hooks the pretty boy. And so, the fishing trip did end up with a first catch after all.

Translated by Annette Caroline Christmas.

Film Details

Title	Thelma & Louise
Release year	1991
Country	USA
Screenplay/idea	Callie Khouri
Director	Ridley Scott
Music	Hans Zimmer
Camera	Adrian Biddle
Principle actors	Susan Sarandon, Geena Davis, Harvey Keitel, Brad Pitt
Availability	DVD, Blu-Ray

References

Benton R, Czechanski B, Pavy H, Sweeney ML (1993) "Breaking the law," A metaphor for female empowerment through aggression. J Am Acad Psychoanal Dyn Psychiatr 21(1):133–147

Enevold J (2004) The daughters of Thelma and Louise: new? Aesthetics of the road. In: Gender, genre, and identity in women's travel writing. Peter Lang, New York, pp 73–98

Gabbard K, Gabbard LO (1993) Phallic women in the contemporary cinema. Amer Imago 50(4):421–439

Kaplan LJ (1993) Fits and misfits: the body of a woman. Amer Imago 50(4):457–480

Khouri C (1996) An interview with Callie Khourie. Published. In: 'Thelma & Louise' and 'something to talk about'. Screenplays. Grove Press, New York

From Eternity to Eternity *(The Hours, US, 2002)* 26

Annegret Mahler-Bungers

Introduction

There are certain films that we cannot forget, despite being flooded by 'movies' on television. One such film for me is Stephan Daldry's *The Hours* (2002), which I watched several times immediately after its release. Its impact on me as a psychoanalyst and literary scholar was so intense and long-lasting for several reasons: firstly, because of its complex subject matter concerning fundamental existential issues, then because of its extraordinary acting performances and intense imagery, and not least because of its intertextual references to the works of Virginia Woolf. In the following, I shall only take up those aspects of this abundance, which contributed to the deep and lasting impression the film made on me.

Film Plot

The film begins with a close-up of a river, and the water can be heard lapping and murmuring. The subtitle informs us that we are in Sussex (England) in 1941. Then, a close-up shows Virginia Woolf's (Nicole Kidman) hand writing her suicide note to her husband, Leonard Woolf (Stephen Dillone). The scratching of the pen on the paper can be heard, and her voice off reading the text. In alternating shots, we see her leaving the house and descending into the river, Leonard Woolf coming home, finding the letter, rushing after her.

This intense beginning is followed by the actual opening credits, which connect three women in a very fast sequence of cuts. The film will be about the hours of a single day in the lives of these three women: Viginia Woolf in Richmond, a suburb of London, in 1923,

A. Mahler-Bungers (✉)
Morschen, Germany

V. Pramataroff-Hamburger, A. Hamburger (eds.), *From La Strada to The Hours*,
https://doi.org/10.1007/978-3-662-68789-5_26

Laura Brown (Julianne Moore) in Los Angeles in 1951, and Clarissa Vaugham (Meryl Streep) in New York in 2001.

In addition to the 'interlocking' scenes, Philip Glass' music creates a kind of flowing transition between these female figures, which is reminiscent of the flowing opening image: Incessantly repeating broken piano chords are underpinned by a tapestry of strings. With these almost monotonous repetitions, which run through the entire film, this music also suggests something constant and something eternal and underlines the subtitle of the film in the German release: 'From Eternity to Eternity'.

In order not to jeopardise the understanding of the film plot, I will treat the three women's stories separately from each other in the following, although they are very closely interrelated in the film in terms of content by means of very deliberate and precisely timed cuts.

The quickly changing scenes of the opening credits, which show the women in the same situations and doing the same things (waking up, looking at themselves in the mirror, tying their hair, seeing their respective partners for the first time in the morning, etc.), as well as the same continuous film music, connect these three women very closely. The actual link between them, however, only becomes clear during the following film narrative: it is the novel *Mrs Dalloway* by Virginia Woolf (1925).

In this novel, Virginia Woolf relates a day—the hours—of an upper-middle-class English woman, Clarissa Dalloway, who wants to host a society party in the evening. 'Hosting a party' is a kind of leitmotif and thus the actual plot of the film.

Virginia Woolf's day in Richmond in 1923 begins with the moment the first sentence of her novel occurs to her, and she writes it down: *'Mrs Dalloway said she would buy the flowers herself'*. Laura Brown's day in Los Angeles in 1951 shows her lying in bed in the morning. She is pregnant with her second child and opens a book, *Mrs Dalloway*. Her voice off reads the first sentence: 'Mrs Dalloway said she would buy the flowers herself'. Clarissa says to her partner after getting up in New York in 2001, *'I think I'll buy the flowers myself'*.

Virginia Woolf has overcome a serious mental illness, as a result of which she is under the watchful eye of her husband Leonard Woolf who lovingly cares for and controls her. He admonishes her to eat, to get some rest, not to go out alone and so on. He also proves to be extremely meticulous and controlling as the owner of Hogarth Press, the home-based publishing house he and Virginia have founded. Virginia feels hemmed in by him, deprived of her liberty. She is extremely insecure in her dealings with the servants and feels they disrupt her creative writing. In the afternoon, she is visited by her sister Vanessa (Linda Bossett) and the latter's three children: two sons and a daughter. Virginia has a very close relationship with Vanessa but also envies her social life in London and her children. The children find a dying bird in the garden and the daughter Angelica and Virginia bury it. This is the first scene after the opening sequence in which the theme of death occurs again. Angelica asks her aunt what happens after death, and Virginia answers: *'We return to the place that we came from'*. Virginia is preoccupied with the draft of her new novel *Mrs Dalloway*. When Angelica later asks her what she is thinking about, she says: *'I was going to kill my heroine. But I've changed my mind. I can't. And then I'll have to kill someone else instead.'* Virginia takes her sister's head in her hand and kisses her on the mouth in farewell. The kiss is not just sisterly and is a hint at Virginia's same-sex desire. After her sister leaves, she furtively sneaks out of the house to take the train to London. The capital epitomises life for her, a way of life which she has been forbidden by her doctors. Leonard is worried and finds her at the station. They get into a squabble about who gets to decide what is good for Virginia and who knows best what she is feeling and what is going on inside her. Virginia is extremely upset and insists on having her say as a patient. Leonard is distraught and relents when she insists that they move back to London. They go home together, partially reconciled. Virginia's day ends with Leonard telling her to go to bed although she wants to continue writing.

Laura Brown is pregnant and starts the day lying in bed, reading *Mrs Dalloway*. It's her husband Dan's birthday. He is a war veteran and a typical, somewhat uncultivated but good-natured average American (John C. Reilby). He arrives home with a bouquet of roses. So, like the character in the novel, Mrs Dalloway, he 'bought the flowers himself'. He prepares breakfast for their 5-year-old son Richie (Jack Rosello) in a typical 50s kitchen polished to a high sheen and tells him to eat up; otherwise, he's 'never gonna be a big boy'. The atmosphere is extremely superficial and communication tense and stereotypical. Laura appears, perfectly turned out in a swinging petticoat dress. She stiltedly wishes her husband a happy birthday. The viewer is oppressively confronted with a family, which has a perfect façade but at its core is very empty. Dan is a war veteran and enjoys the role of the loving husband who provides for his family. Having survived the war, his own home seems like the epitome of perfect happiness to him. However, he has absolutely no idea about his wife's true state of mind: she is severely depressed. Laura only feels alive when reading. Playing the role of housewife and mother is mental torment for her. She cannot establish a genuinely emotional relationship with her son, and the character of Richie as a child is extremely hauntingly played. He constantly signals his childish hunger for a relationship. His gaze has a deep effect on the viewer as it follows his mother's every movement in search of attention, although she cannot show any real emotion towards him. When Dan is out of the house, Laura tries to bake a birthday cake with Richie but fails in the attempt. The neighbour Kitty (Toni Colette) comes to visit. She says she has to go to hospital because of a possible cancer of the uterus, which is a reason for her lack of children. She sees childbearing as a woman's true destiny in life and envies Laura for Richie and her second pregnancy. For the first time, Laura shows real feelings. She is flooded with compassion and the fear of losing her friend. She embraces her to comfort her, and it turns into a passionate kiss. Kitty returns the kiss, saying, *'You're sweet'*. As Kitty leaves, quite composed and formal once more, Laura seems startled by what has happened, but Kitty doesn't want to discuss it any further. Laura throws the failed cake in the bin and bakes a new one, decorated with kitschy blue icing, and places it on the kitchen table.

She then fetches several bottles of medication, takes the reluctant Richie to a woman to take care of him and rents a hotel room where she decides to kill herself. Lying on the bed and reading *Mrs Dalloway*, she abandons herself to her imagination or to a dream in which she apparently identifies with Virginia Woolf. (As an example of the film's editing style, a cut connects this section to the scene in which Virginia tells Angelica that she intended to kill off her heroine.) Water can be seen entering the hotel room from all sides and submerging Laura. She is startled and decides not to die (cut: Virginia says to Angelica, *'but I changed my mind')* and instead to return home. She picks up Richie, who once in the car tells her, *'I love you'*. She replies that she loves him too but the extent to which she can genuinely feel this remains unclear. At home, the family sits around the kitchen table and the three of them celebrate Dan's 'birthday party'. He counts himself lucky to have such a wonderful family. Laura's day ends with her trying to fight off her grief for Kitty in the bathroom while Dan calls out for her to come to bed.

In New York, Clarissa, who is an editor, steps out onto the street. She wants to throw a party that evening for her friend Richard, who is going to be awarded an important literary prize that day for a novel, which is not easy to read, in which Clarissa is the clearly recognisable protagonist. She goes to a flower shop and takes an armful of flowers to visit Richard (Ed Harris), who is seriously ill with AIDS. Richard greets her by calling her 'Mrs Dalloway'. He is very unwell; due to the advanced stage of the disease, he hears voices (such as that of Virginia Woolf at the time of her first illness and then again shortly before her suicide). He lives in squalor in darkened rooms, is emaciated and can hardly struggle out of his armchair. Clarissa tries to cheer him up and urges him to eat and take his pills (just as Leonard Woolf urges Virginia to do so) but above all to come to the awards ceremony and her party. He reacts irritably to all this, saying: *'Oh, Mrs Dalloway, always giving parties. To cover the silence'*. Moreover, he feels like a failure because he hasn't been able to write 'about it all', as he had wanted to. *'We want everything, don't we'?* Remembering the way they kissed on the beach as students creates a tender atmosphere between them and they kiss. She leaves to go home and prepare the party. Sally (Allison Janney), her pragmatic, emancipated-seeming life partner, returns home from a shopping trip. She has brought a rather puny bouquet of flowers, which she throws in the bin when she sees how many gorgeous flowers Clarissa has already got herself. She mocks the efforts Clarissa is making for her party and is slightly offended because Clarissa's seating plan has placed her at a table with all of Clarissa's ex-boyfriends, so that she already feels like an 'ex' herself. But then she must go 'right out again'.

Clarissa puts a huge amount of pressure on herself in preparing for the party. She is baking, wearing an apron and rubber gloves and playing some Richard Strauss very loudly in the background, when her and Richard's old friend Louis Water (Jeff Daniels) comes by. She feels very put out but invites him in anyway, speaking and moving like a young girl. The pair of them also immediately start talking about their shared past while she cracks eggs into a bowl. Richard had left her because of Louis. Clarissa breaks down in tears, saying she is 'a bad hostess'. She realises that all the years her connection with Richard have been a strain on her and that she has not felt free. He in turn confesses that when he broke off his relationship with Richard, he felt free for the first time in years. He tells her that he has fallen in love with a student (he is a lecturer at a drama school). She is envious of him.

After Louis has left the house with a somewhat annoyed expression on his face, Clarissa's daughter Julia (Claire Danes) is seen rushing into the house, very lively and buoyant, taking the steps two at a time. She preempts her mother's accusations of having come too late to help and initially mocks her efforts in preparing the party and her entanglement in old friendships, until she notices that Clarissa has been crying. She immediately guesses that it is because of Richard, since she is apparently aware of her mother's neurotic attachment to him. The conversation takes a serious turn, and Clarissa falls into a kind of self-reflection: She thinks that Richard sometimes gives her a look that means to say her life is trivial and that she fills her life with *'daily stuff… schedules and parties and details'*. Julia makes an attempt at interpretation, saying, *'Mum, it only matters if you think it's true'*. Clarissa says that she only feels alive when she is with Richard and that, when she is not with him, everything else feels silly, except her daughter, of course. She even sees her partner, Sally, as false comfort. There then follows a very tender scene of mother and daughter on the bed, in which Clarissa speaks about the only moment of perfect happiness in her life: when she was very young, she went on holiday to a country house with Louis and Richard. She had slept with Richard and got up at dawn, stepping out onto the terrace. At that moment, when her whole life lay before her, she remembered thinking to herself that this was the beginning of happiness, and this was when it starts, thinking there would always be more. '[It] never occurred to me it wasn't the beginning. It was happiness. It was the moment'. Julia snuggles up to her as the doorbell rings. Clarissa detaches herself with an expression of unwillingness. She cannot indulge in the moment because of the stress of organising.

Clarissa goes back to Richard to dress him for the awards ceremony and party. Richard is upset because she arrives earlier than expected. He is aggressively clearing away everything from in front of the window, then opens it and sits on the windowsill. Clarissa is paralysed with fear. Richard asks her to tell him again about the scene of their first kiss on the beach. He quotes phrases from Virginia Woolf's farewell letter to her husband: *'You've been so good to me, Mrs Dalloway... I don't think two people could have been happier than we've been'*—and suddenly jumps out of the window right before her eyes.

At home, the three women, Clarissa, Sally and Julia, clear away the party set-up. The crab pan for Richard goes in the rubbish. The doorbell rings, and an old lady is standing on the doorstep: it is the aged Laura Brown, Richard's ('Richie's') mother. *'So that's the monster'*, Julia remarks in the background.

Laura Brown also played a significant role in Richard's novel, in which he killed her off (just as Virginia wanted the heroine in her novel to die, but has a poet who has been traumatised by war die instead). Clarissa and Laura hold a moving conversation, in which the subtle emotional facial expressions of both women are shown in close-up and shot-counter-shot. We learn that Laura Brown left her family after the birth of her second child and became a librarian in Canada and that her husband and daughter have long since died. Now Richard ('Richie') is also dead. She knows how bad it has all been: no one could ever forgive her, but she had no other choice ('It was death. I chose life'). She says that Clarissa must be happy because she wanted a child so much that she went ahead and had one without ever having met the father. Clarissa goes into the bedroom with tears in her eyes. Sally follows her and sits next to her on the bed. Clarissa takes her head in both hands and kisses her. Her face has brightened and taken on a tender look. Clarissa ends her day by turning off the light in her nightgown and going into her bedroom, which she shares with Sally.

Julia brings a cup of tea to Laura Brown in the room, and she let her stay in for the night. Before the closing credits, we see Virginia Woolf one more time, first lying in bed, then wading into the river and being engulfed by it.

Background

English director Stephen Daldry made a name for himself as a theatre director in London in the 1990s, receiving several major awards for his theatre productions. His first feature film *Billy Elliot* (2000) was multi-award winning. In 2002, Hollywood film studio Miramax commissioned him to adapt the novel *The Hours* (Cunningham 1998), for which American author Michael Cunningham had been awarded the Pulitzer Prize in 1999. 'The Hours' was Virginia Woolf's original working title for her novel *Mrs Dalloway*, which she began in 1923 and which was published in 1925. This, her second novel, plays a decisive role in Cunningham's novel as well as in the film adaptation. It could be said to be the linchpin around which the plot revolves. When I saw the film myself for the first time years ago, I immediately wanted to read both Virginia Woolf's and Cunningham's novel to get a better understanding of the film. Watching the film is consequently a complex palimpsest of interwoven interpersonal and intertextual elements: the viewer's relationship with the characters portrayed and reference to the characters in Cunningham's novel, who in turn have their point of reference in Virginia Woolf's novel, which itself naturally condenses the writer's life and ideas. Significantly, all three women are involved in literature: Virginia as an author, Laura as a reader and later a librarian and Clarissa as a publisher's editor, and a novel link them together. Their lives take place on two closely intertwined levels: reality and fiction. Virginia's sister Vanessa thus says to her young daughter: *'Your aunt is very lucky, Angelica. She has two lives. She has the life she's leading and also of the book she's writing. This makes her very fortunate indeed'.*

As well as these references, the film-makers have added more of their own, particularly in the editing techniques, which naturally 'manipulate' the viewer's perception and imbue the individual scenes with special significance by linking the women's brief gestures or remarks, and in the process also 'reality' and fiction.

The film not only addresses the many facets of femininity but also those of human existence in general. The whole contradictory palette of our inner worlds is shown in the three women, who could not be more different. From the fundamental question of our relationships with others, with our desire for freedom and self-determination on the one hand, and for attachment and security on the other, issues concerning sexual orientation, creativity and failure, fluctuating self-esteem and an ambivalent attitude towards motherhood, all the way to the 'ultimate questions' of the meaning of time (memory, the moment, the future) and transience, mental and physical illness, our self-responsibility, guilt and forgiveness and thus what the actual 'meaning of life' could be, our relationship towards loss and death.

The film poses all of these questions through the diversity of the women's fates, without answering any of them. Perhaps, they remain unanswered 'from eternity to eternity', as the subtitle implies in the German release of the film, so that each individual has to wrestle with them anew. This is entirely in the spirit of Virginia Woolf, who in her ideas and writing always leaves fundamental existential questions hanging.

The Staging of the Feminine

Like any selfhood, the women portrayed in the film are multifaceted, contradictory, unfathomable, ambivalent, ambiguous both in their sexual orientation and in their role as a mother—or their childlessness.

In the following, I would like to take up one aspect among all the themes, which I found particularly striking and which is also central to the novel *Mrs Dalloway*: the woman's role as a host. On the one hand, this leitmotif concerns the problem of social role attribution. However, it also seems to impinge on an 'innate' female desire, which becomes increasingly ambivalent as the wish for self-realisation develops. The parties taking place in the film are all very varied. In Virginia Woolf's novel *Mrs Dalloway*, which after all is the reference point for these women's stories in the film, Clarissa lives in a world of high society, which functions as a medium through which she can participate in social life, from which she is otherwise excluded. Meanwhile, in 1951, Laura Brown is reluctantly hosting a birthday party within her nuclear family. For twenty-first century Clarissa, on the other hand, a party is high on the agenda. She is hosting one for her long-time friend and old flame Richard to celebrate his literary award with many old friends and important figures from the literary scene. Laura Brown's resistance to the obligation of hosting a party is manifested in her failed first attempt at baking a cake. This is in stark contrast to the importance that the two Clarissas, almost eight decades apart, attribute to their parties.

This begs the question of what the underlying meaning, the purpose of hosting soirées, gatherings and parties has for women. In the first part of the film narrative, hosting is Virginia's sister Vanessa's privilege. Virginia herself, however, for whom hosting gatherings and taking part in them is linked to the very definition of life itself, has felt painfully excluded from them since her severe bout of mental illness.

Clarissa Dalloway in Woolf's novel, affronted by the men's criticism of her skills as a hostess, reflects on why she finds parties so important, concluding: 'What she liked was simply life' (Woolf 1925, p. 183). Later, she ruminates thus: 'But suppose Peter [an old friend] said to her, 'yes, yes, but your parties—what's the point of your societies?, then all she could say was ... They're an offering, ...' (ibid., p.184) 'And it was an offering; to combine, to create; but to whom?' (ibid., p. 185).

Women's need to receive people at home, to bring them together and have them converse with each other, to care for their well-being and host them (the famous salons were always run by women) does not seem to be a thing of the past. Even at the start of the twenty-first century, the party is high on the agenda for the emancipated Clarissa, right down to the potted crab for Richard. This genuinely female desire clearly has to do with motherliness, as does women's interest in home interiors and their dedication in maintaining them. It seems to be difficult for 'us women' to shed the time-honoured role of 'keeping the home fires burning', as if there were an unconscious message passed from one generation to the next, or an unconscious fantasy. Accordingly, the home interior could be understood as an extracorporeal uterus projected outwards, a space from which life is meant to come into being and be sustained. But as Clarissa realises in Woolf's novel, it is also a sacrificial offering: she offers up her own life for the sake of others so that they can feel comfortable at her party. However, the question remains: 'for whom'?

In the film, Clarissa seems to give into this compulsion to host for several reasons: On the one hand, she wants to do everything within her power to keep Richard alive. Beyond that, however, she still fulfils the woman's subservient role as an aide to genius, albeit in a very disguised form, staging herself as Richard's muse and sacrificing her own life as a result. Richard then confronts her with this, asking: *'What about your own life? … just wait til I die, and you'll have to think of yourself'*. However, she apparently not only feels the need to throw parties because of Richard's award ceremony. Like the Clarissa in Virginia Woolf's novel, as a hostess, she tries to 'connect, create', which in itself is the meaning of 'life' for her. She thus fulfils what Freud meant by the term 'libido' or the 'life instinct': namely, connecting in contrast to the disconnection and destruction of what he termed the 'death instinct'.

Laura refuses to make this sacrifice in 1951. In the sterile atmosphere of her terraced house and nuclear family, she cannot allow life and plenitude to flourish. The interior design of her lifeless 50s kitchen is both a cause and an expression of her depression, her 'interior space' with its corresponding paucity of social connection and meaning. It is as if her love for Richie, like that for the child she is carrying, is buried under her depression. She cannot 'connect' with her children. For the viewer, she represents the ambivalence towards her child, the 'dark side' that is there in every mother: the desire *not* to be there for others, *not* to have to 'sacrifice' a significant period of time in taking care of the children's (or the husband's) development so that she can grow and develop herself instead. Like any psychological symptom, her depression can therefore be seen as a message, a cry for help, except that she cannot find anyone to express it to.

Men see the female fixation on parties as trivial. In Woolf's novel, too, Clarissa Dalloway's compulsion to host gatherings is belittled and disparaged by her husband and her old friend Peter Walsh. However, she tries to counter this with the value she herself sees in it. In 2001, Clarissa Vaugham needs her daughter's interpretation to cushion the blow of Richard's low opinion: *'Mum, it only matters if you think it's true'*, says Julia. She is thereby restoring to her mother the interpretive authority that Richard has over her.

Further Considerations

Suffering and Self-Empowerment

This theme leads directly to the tension these three women experience between suffering, illness and depression on the one hand and self-empowerment in the sense of subjectification and self-confidence on the other hand, which includes the conflict between socially ascribed roles and the desire for self-determination. In Virginia's story, this conflict revolves around the bout of mental illness she has just overcome, during which she had tried to take her own life. Her husband Leonard has taken on the role of caring nurse and minder. He is thus an extension of the doctors who, as is now known, failed miserably in their treatment of her, first prescribing her an agonising period of isolation for several months and then rest in the country without a social life. In the highly emotional scene at the station when Leonard admonishes her for wanting to go to London, she tries to claim her right to have a say, to determine her existence and to interpret what is really going on inside her. The attack on the interpretive sovereignty of doctors is tantamount to insisting on universal human rights not only for the sick but also for women, which had become central to Virginia Woolf's political thinking (Lee 1999, p. 247; Fig. 26.1).

Laura Brown's story makes women's suffering under the yoke of their socially assigned roles particularly clear. She had good reason to set her story in the 1950s. After the devastation of the Second World War, the hard-won women's rights obtained in the 1920s were completely eroded due to the desire for an 'ideal' world. Laura is supposed to fulfil the role of housewife, since her husband has come home from the war and thus 'deserves' this (as she expresses to Kitty).

Fig. 26.1 'Mrs Dalloway said she would buy the flowers herself' (00:10:47)

The décor of the kitchen has a strikingly sterile and lifeless façade. It is a make-believe home, beneath which Laura's desire for vibrant self-determination and contact with her real feelings smoulders. She can only 'play' at being a housewife, loving wife and mother, as is masterfully portrayed by Julianne Moore. Her suffering is agonising. This way of life is a living death for her. She only feels truly alive and herself when reading a book. Her identification with the figure of Clarissa Dalloway is an act of subjectification, a fantasised creative self-image and also a medium for self-reflection. It is Dan's birthday, but Clarissa does not start her day by giving him flowers: he buys them for himself, as it were prophylactically, to preserve the image of the housewife's perfectly executed birthday party. Laura's contribution to this image in the form of a homemade birthday cake fails. She rejects the role of 'hostess' and at the same time suffers from her inability to give rise to any vitality by doing so.

When she kisses Kitty, she is very emotional and totally present. Her kiss, a blend of compassion and homoerotic desire, expresses that she is not living her life and that her personal development, including her possible sexual orientation, ground to a halt when she got married. She sees suicide as the only way of achieving self-empowerment, as Virginia Woolf did. But she then decides against it of her own free will. The viewer only learns at the end of the film that she leaves the family after the birth of their second child and is working 'in her element' in a library in Canada. She says she had *'no choice'*. However, since she left her young children behind, this act of self-determination is associated with irrevocable guilt (Fig. 26.2).

At the start of the new millennium, many things have changed for her as a woman: Clarissa lives with a woman, she is an editor and mother, and she seems to have everything that gives a woman confidence: a career, sexual self-determination, a child, a steady rela-

Fig. 26.2 *The Hours* (00:12:46)

tionship, financial independence and a beautiful flat in New York that is allowed to look creatively messy, in other words lived-in, with stacks of books and manuscripts scattered all over the place. Moreover, she is living at a time when women have a say in politics and society and are not confined to the role of housewife and mother, and they can even choose to have a child without a father (through a sperm bank).

Nevertheless, Clarissa, who her old friend Richard calls 'Mrs Dalloway', is not happy, or any better off: for reasons that are not immediately clear, her happiness is built on shaky ground. Like Clarissa Dalloway in the novel, she starts the day with the intention of 'buying the flowers herself'. The viewer has the impression that she is completely in control of her life. Her story is all about the party she wants to throw for Richard that evening and her role as hostess in it. However, it soon becomes clear that this self-imposed role stresses her out a great deal and binds her, as does her old attachment to Richard. He himself doesn't want a party. In this respect, she is very similar to the fictitious Mrs Dalloway. But for her, the party had a different function: excluded from the political and social life of the man's world, Mrs Dalloway invited this world into her home in order to participate in public life, at least in this way.

But what, in 2001, is Clarissa's motive for making such a great effort to throw a party, an effort that both her partner Sally and her daughter more or less make fun of, even though they lovingly and 'indulgently' help her? Is it true that she is trying to 'cover the silence', as Richard says (Fig. 26.3)?

In the course of this 1 day, Clarissa is confronted with several interpretations that give her clarity about herself and her dilemma. Richard gives her the first one: *'I think I'm only staying alive to satisfy you'*. She has been taking care of him for 17 years: *'What about your own life? What about Sally? Just wait till I die, and you'll have to think of yourself'*.

Fig. 26.3 'I'm having a party' (00:14:40)

He was right to call her 'Mrs Dalloway', whose marriage to (her husband) Richard in the novel made her 'invisible; unseen; unknown'. 'This being Mrs Richard Dalloway' means she is 'not even Clarissa any more' (Virginia Woolf, p. 11).

Other important interpretations come from Julia, her daughter, who confronts her mother with herself as would a psychotherapist: When Clarissa complains that Richard gives her a look that says how trivial her life is, Julia says: *'Mum, it only matters if you think it's true'*.

In fact, Clarissa only finds herself as a result of Richard's suicide. By kissing Sally, she reclaims responsibility for her own life.

The Prison of Relationships and the Longing for Freedom

Close ties can thus also mean death. For there is an existential conflict between the desire for freedom and for a relationship, and it affects both sexes. Virginia tells Vanessa that Leonard's ministrations on her behalf feel like 'imprisonment'. But the adult Richard, who has AIDS, is equally imprisoned by Clarissa's ministrations, just as Laura feels imprisoned by her husband's expectations of a 'happy home'.

Women, but also men, find freedom in many varied ways. Virginia and Richard's freedom is found in the creative poetic imagination. In contrast to real life, in poetic fiction, they are free to decide about their characters, can kill them off or decide not to. And yet, both of them see their own freely chosen suicide as *the* ultimate act of liberation. Moreover, by dying, both Virginia and Richard also want to relieve their partners of the burden of caring for them. The issue of suicide also concerns a fundamental human right and is highly topical in the modern debate on euthanasia.

Laura finds a niche in reading where she can grow herself. The open system of adolescence, in which a person only gradually finds themselves, above all through identification with people outside the family, was shut down far too early by her marriage. Even if she does not actually say so, she perceives the nuclear family as a prison (as death), which her actions make tangible in every sequence. She thus has a profound need to enter into other worlds through literature and to identify with the characters she finds there. Books thus give her scope for development. Her decision not to choose death but to leave the family is also an act of liberation, even though it places her in the lifelong prison of guilt.

Clarissa is trapped by her bond with Richard and is thereby missing out on her own life. Louis has 'never felt so liberated' as when he parted ways with Richard.

Clarissa identifies her only instance of perfect happiness as a moment that took place during her youth. She tells Julia she remembers getting up at dawn one morning after having slept with Richard (she was 18 at the time, he 19): *'There was such a sense of possibility! … And I remember thinking to myself: So this is the beginning of happiness. This is where it starts'!* The moment of absolute happiness seems to be the unique concurrence of being in a relationship and at the same time being free, which only very rarely happens in the real world. Maintaining a balance between commitment and freedom is probably the hardest task in people's relationships with one other.

Julia is so refreshing because she represents this happiness of youth in the film: the wide-open realm of possibility that older viewers can only wistfully look back on. Julia might be addressing this when she says to her mother, *'All your old friends are sad'*. As a viewer, whenever she came on the scene with all her power, liveliness, gift for empathy and unbiased view, I felt a little relief from the sadness left by the stories in the film. This film character and also the film ending differs greatly from the novel, as if the screenwriter (David Hare) had wanted to pay tribute to Hollywood with this happy ending.

The final scene in which she impulsively hugs the older Juliet is very touching and relieving: she is thereby releasing the old woman (and the viewer) from guilt and forgiving her. Juliet had believed that no-one was going to forgive her because she had done *'the worst thing a mother can do to her children'*. She only hesitantly returns the embrace, caught up as she is in the numbness of guilt. But her face shows the hint of a redemptive smile and tears come to her eyes as she affectionately says to Julia: *'Good night, sweetheart'*.

Concluding Remarks

Freedom also has a temporal dimension: liberation from the past. Louis has visited the holiday home of yesteryear, where he had spent a summer with Richard and Clarissa. Clarissa finds it 'courageous' to 'face the fact that we have lost those feelings forever'. Clarissa's refreshing daughter Julia, who still has her future with all its possibilities ahead of her, confronts her mother with the fact that she *was* once young, in other words that her youth and her youthful love for Richard are (or should be) behind her.

Clarissa also longs for freedom, without really realising it: freedom from her way of hosting, freedom from worrying about Richard, freedom for a present and a future that absolves her from the past.

When Louis shows up at Clarissa's house and she is busy baking, she hears one of Richard Strauss' 'Four Last Songs' playing very loudly in the background; this is the only external music quote in the film. The line from the song 'Beim Schlafengehen' ('When falling asleep'), based on a text by Hermann Hesse, which can be heard in the film, reads: 'And the unguarded soul/yearns to soar in freest flight/around the magic circle of the night/ profoundly and a thousandfold'.

In sleep and in dreams, the soul is 'unguarded' and finally free again and can 'live … a thousand times over' in its dreams. Sleep and dreams offer all the possibilities of life, as does poetry. In one scene, Leonard asks Virginia which characters will die in her novel, to which she replies: *'The poet will die, the visionary'*. Must the poets in this film, Virginia and Richard (and Septimus in Virginia Woolf's novel), find their final freedom in 'sleep's brother', death, because they 'live a thousandfold' in their visions, their dreams? The film's ending thus leaves the viewer grappling with an irresolvable paradox: We see Laura, deeply moved by Julia's embrace; then Virginia lying in bed (filmed from above, her face half lit, half in the dark as if the lighting is symbolic of this paradox); then Clarissa turning off the light, ready for her new life with Sally, free of Richard; and then Virginia again, walking into the river. As she does so, we hear her voice off:

'Dear Leonard, to look life in the face and to know it for what it is, at last to know it, to love it for what it is, and then to put it away. Leonard, always the years between us, always the years, always the love, always the hours'.

Translated by Annette Caroline Christmas.

Film Details

Original title	The Hours
Release year	2002
Country	USA
Book	David Hare
Direction	Stephen Douldry
Music	Philip Glass, Richard Strauß
Camera	Seamus McGarvey
Main actors	Nicole Kidman, Julianne Moore, Meryl Streep, Stephen Dillane, Miranda Richardson, Ed Harris
Availability	DVD

References

Cunningham M (1998) The hours. Farrar, Straus and Giroux/Macmillan, New York
Lee H (1999) Virginia Woolf. Vintage Books/Random House, New York
Woolf V (1925) Mrs Dalloway. Hogarth Press, London

Love with a Salty Taste: *Carol* (GB, US 2015) 27

Vivian Pramataroff-Hamburger

Introduction

Carol by Todd Haynes tells a poetic love story in all its complexity and in artistically framed shots. The film aesthetic is the first thing that captivates female viewers but also male ones. The viewer has the feeling they are the sole visitor at an exhibition of narrative images. This intimacy—and yet distance—between the imagery and the audience is maintained throughout the film.

Haynes' filmography is indeed extensive, but 'Far from Heaven' (2002) and 'I'm Not There' (2007) are particularly noteworthy. 'Far from Heaven' beautifully captures the facade of an ideal 1950s family, unravelling as the wife discovers her husband's homosexual activities. Meanwhile, 'I'm Not There' serves as a tribute to Bob Dylan, with Cate Blanchett delivering a remarkable portrayal of the young Bob. Haynes' ability to delve into diverse themes and eras is truly commendable.

Film Plot

New York, December 1952: The young woman Therese Belivet (Rooney Mara) and the older married woman Carol Aird (Cate Blanchett) meet at the department store where Therese is a sales assistant. Carol buys the model railway recommended by Therese for her 4-year-old daughter Rindy instead of a doll and accidentally leaves her gloves behind on the counter. Therese posts them to her, which prompts Carol to invite her to lunch. During

V. Pramataroff-Hamburger (✉)
Private Psychotherapeutic Practice, Munich, Germany
e-mail: vivian@pramataroff.de

V. Pramataroff-Hamburger, A. Hamburger (eds.), *From La Strada to The Hours*,
https://doi.org/10.1007/978-3-662-68789-5_27

the meal, Carol invites Therese to her house on the Sunday before Christmas. Therese agrees to go. At Carol's house, Therese witnesses an argument between Carol and her husband Harge (Kyle Chandler), whom she is in the process of divorcing: He wants to pick up Rindy earlier than agreed and also invites Carol to come with them and celebrate Christmas together with his parents. Carol refuses. When Therese arrives home sad, Carol calls her, apologises for the argument and asks if she can visit Therese the next evening. Therese is in the process of putting together a portfolio of pictures to apply for a job as a photographer. However, her boyfriend Richard Semco (Jake Lacy) has no interest in her professional plans. Instead, he wants Therese to marry him and spend the summer in Europe with him. Therese does not feel ready for this. Carol, on the other hand, encourages Therese in her wish to become a photographer. When she visits Therese, she gives her a new camera.

Carol is upset: her lawyer has told her that Harge has filed for sole custody of Rindy because she is not a suitable caregiver for their small child because she is homosexual. The 'morality clause' is justified by an affair Carol once had with her best friend Abby Gerhard (Sarah Paulson). Harge and his lawyer see this and similar relationships as evidence of a recurring pattern of behaviour.

Carol tells Therese about a road trip out west, which she has planned. She asks Therese if she would like to come along, and Therese does not hesitate in saying yes. During their road trip, they meet the travelling salesman Tommy Tucker. On New Year's Eve in Waterloo, Iowa, Carol and Therese kiss for the first time and spend their first, passionate night of love together. The next morning, Carol receives a telegram from Abby: Harge has hired a detective to track the women. Carol demands that the detective, who is Tommy Tucker, hand over the tape recording of the night she and Therese spent together. He tells her he has already sent the tape to Harge by post. She threatens him with a pistol, but it turns out not to be loaded. Carol is desperate and decides to fly back to New York, leaving Therese a farewell letter. In it, she tells her that they cannot have any more contact and that she will do everything to ensure that Therese is happy nevertheless.

Carol and Therese do not see each other for several months. In the meantime, a good friend and journalist has encouraged Therese to put together her portfolio of photographs—and she manages to get a job as a photographer at the *New York Times*. Carol goes to the lunch with Harge and his parents so that she can see Rindy. During lunch, it becomes clear that Carol is undergoing psychotherapy to treat her homosexuality. At the preliminary custody hearing, Carol implores Harge and the lawyers to decide in Rindy's best interests. She admits that the content of the tapes is true. In an emotional speech, Carol tells Harge he can have custody. However, she insists on regular visits with her daughter, with or without a guardian.

After the hearing, Carol writes Therese a letter asking to meet up. When they do, Carol says she has heard about Therese's professional success and mentions that she is going to work as a buyer for a furniture house and is moving into a flat on Madison Avenue that is big enough for two. She hopes that Therese will decide to live with her, but Therese declines the invitation. Rather hesitantly, Carol goes on to say she is meeting some associates in the Oak Room of the Plaza Hotel. With tears in her eyes, Carol whispers, *'I love you'*. Therese looks at Carol, deeply touched, unable to say anything.

The rendezvous is interrupted by an old acquaintance of Therese's. That same evening, Therese goes to a party where there are a lot of young people celebrating. A little later, she decides to meet Carol after all and leaves the party. She sees Carol in the Plaza among the other guests and takes a few steps towards her. Carol catches sight of her, too, and they look into each other's eyes. The last shot shows Therese gazing at Carol softly and tenderly. Carol's eyes light up, and a tender smile plays around her lips as Therese approaches.

Background

Patricia Highsmith was a trailblazing American writer known for her unique approach to crime novels. Unlike traditional whodunnits, Highsmith focused on exploring the intricate circumstances and motives behind why a seemingly ordinary person would commit a crime. Her keen interest in delving into the inner lives of her characters set her apart, emphasizing their psychology over moral judgments.

Highsmith's breakout moment arrived with her debut novel, 'Strangers on a Train' (1950), which was swiftly adapted into a film by the legendary Alfred Hitchcock in 1951. This catapulted the then 30-year-old Highsmith to overnight fame. Her literary legacy further extended with over 25 films based on her novels, including notable adaptations of 'The Talented Mr. Ripley' (1956) featuring renowned cast members. Highsmith's ability to dissect the human psyche and her masterful storytelling continue to captivate readers and audiences alike.

Carol is based on the novel *The Price of Salt* (1952), which was published under the pseudonym Claire Morgan; Highsmith did not agree to publish it under her real name until 1990. It is known that Highsmith, who was bisexual, did not want to scandalise the public with a novel about lesbian love. She herself believed that homosexuality was pathological and treatable, as did most scientists at the time. She was in psychoanalysis for years, which contributed greatly to the psychological development of her thrillers, but could not rid her of her erotic attraction towards women.

She wrote *The Price of Salt* after a real-life meeting with an elegant and beautiful woman, a customer in a department store where Highsmith was earning a living working as a saleswoman. Nothing happened other than an exchange of looks, but it was enough for Highsmith to start outlining the novel. It turned out she had been coming down with measles at the time, and in a feverish, all most trance-like state, sick and covered in a rash, she wrote the novel in just 2 weeks.

The title *The Price of Salt* can be understood in terms of Western European folklore. It refers to the well-known theme of the father asking his daughters how much they love him. When his favourite daughter unexpectedly says that she loves him like salt, he disowns her.

Highsmith does not explain the title of her novel. At one point, after the break-up with Carol, Therese wonders: 'How would the world come back to life? How would its salt come back'? (Highsmith 2004 [1952]). 'Salt' in this sense, as in the title, stands not only for taste but above all for something essential to life. For Therese, life without Carol seems to be life without any salt.

While the title of the novel refers primarily to the emotional and social price Therese and Carol are expected to pay for their love, there may also be a secondary level: It is also reminiscent of the biblical story of Lot's wife who is turned into a pillar of salt when she looks back at the burning city of Sodom, typically (if not accurately) understood to be a place of sexual transgression. From this perspective, the title is a coded reference to the risk of destruction that Carol and Therese face due to their affair (Sönser Breen 2018).

There were some initial obstacles to overcome in the filming: it turned out that the originally intended director John Crowly (*Brooklyn,* 2015) was unavailable, so Todd Haynes took over the direction of *Carol*. Haynes, born in Los Angeles in 1961, attended Brown University in Providence, Rhode Island. 'It was the East Coast, so it was a whole different world for me, especially the English department where I accidentally ended up, the only place to find film production courses, although you had to go through the theory. They called the programme semiotics. You forget—I am that old—that all these articles had just been written by Laura Mulvey. New French theory and feminist film criticism were new' (Haynes 2015).

Haynes was very pleased with the stellar cast, which included Cate Blanchett, who had won Oscars for both *Aviator* (US 2007) and *Blue Jasmine* (US 2013). They had already worked together on *I'm Not There*. Haynes says he remained more faithful to *Carol* Highsmith's novel than he usually does for films based on books. The result showed he was right to do so: *Carol* was nominated for six Oscars in 2016 (Best Actress in a Leading Role, Best Supporting Actress, Image Design, Costume Design, Best Adapted Screenplay, Musical Score) and however did not receive any.

How Is Femininity Staged in the Film?

What is the cost of love, and which form of love is in question? Is it Carol's love for her child or her love for Therese? Highsmith doesn't explicitly elucidate the title in her novel. Salt, being indispensable for life, symbolizes Carol's payment for the liberty to live on her own terms.

The film is called *Carol,* the title itself placing the emphasis on a female character or at any rate on a woman. The woman who used to be a girl, a child. According to Julia Kristeva, a woman inhabits various cosmic worlds, sometimes in parallel (Kristeva 1991).

Carol portrays various stages of womanhood. On the one hand, we witness the transitory stage of a young girl, still deeply connected to her mother. This bond is poignantly depicted in a scene before the mirror, where Carol lovingly brushes her daughter Rindy's hair, both of them counting each stroke. As the story unfolds, we discover that the child left a few hairs from the brush under Carol's pillow as a cherished keepsake—an intimate, shared memento that binds them together organically.

The character of the young girl, Rindy, plays a significant narrative role by becoming the focal point of a custody dispute between her parents. However, she is depicted more as a device than as an autonomous individual, resembling a momentarily attended-to doll in a nursery or the dolls found in Therese's store, capable to talk, cry and say 'mummy'—a phenomenon in vogue during the 1950s in the United States.

Therese, in a seemingly nonchalant comment, discloses that their inventory also includes dolls with a capacity for 'wetting themselves,' indirectly alluding to the representation of genitalia. This remark, delivered with an air of innocence, captures Carol's attention. On one hand, Therese is staged within the shop as a doll, complete with a somewhat whimsical Santa hat, and ensconced amidst an array of playthings. However, this childlike facade is subverted by her candid mention of anatomical details, thus positioning herself conspicuously as a mature, sexually aware woman (Fig. 27.1).

> Another pivotal phase in a woman's journey is her adolescence. At 19 years old, Therese is navigating the early stages of romantic and sexual exploration with her boyfriend Richard. While employed as a department store clerk, her aspirations lie in the realm of photography. Prior to encountering Carol, her photographic subjects primarily revolve around trees and birds, leaving her dissatisfied with her output. She grapples with a sense of uncertainty about her artistic direction and self-identity. As she candidly puts it, *'I barely know what to order for lunch'*, she tells Carol when they first meet.

While Therese may express uncertainty about certain aspects of her life, there is a clarity in what she adamantly rejects: the prospect of becoming a conventional housewife. She nonchalantly disengages from her relationship with her boyfriend and distances herself from his matrimonial plans, opting to honour her genuine emotions. It's through her new camera that Therese captures Carol, and from then on, we perceive Carol through Therese's

Fig. 27.1 'She cries and wets herself' (00:11:02)

lens. In the darkroom, as the images develop, we witness Carol's visage gradually coming into focus in the tray. **This enchanting process of photographic creation serves as a poignant symbol of the magical potency inherent in the formation of a profound love connection.**

The Re-found Daughter

Therese does not yet know how to define herself. From her first meeting with Carol to her separation, she is portrayed in the film as much younger than her chronological age; the clothes she wears are more childlike, her tam o'shanter and hairstyle are those of a little girl. Her eyes are always very wide, as if she wants to discover the world for the first time, like a child. She is reminiscent of Rindy with her fringe and her Kids robes. No wonder Carol falls in love with her while she is going through her divorce and about to lose her daughter. The comparison between Therese and Carol's daughter Rindy begins in the scene where they meet for the first time in the shop and Carol shows her a picture of Rindy. There is another comparison when Carol visits Therese's flat and sees a picture of Therese as a young girl Rindy's age.

Therese's transformation begins with her lived experience of love for Carol; another stage is when they separate, and she loses Carol. However, only when she succeeds at work in a prestigious magazine do we see a more mature Therese, with feminine hairstyle and elegant clothes. We see her grown up and beautiful, but we also miss her innocent, childlike charm.

The Woman

And finally, Carol arrives with her flourishing femininity, experience and sexuality. She is wearing a fur coat that makes her especially sensual and somewhat animalistic but at the same time rather morbid or dead, like the hair on Rindy's hairbrush. The coat swings around her, hugging and caressing her body. The fur gives her a hint of a predator—beautiful but untamed. The gold jewellery on her hands and the brooches on her chest convey a touch of divinity and magic. Carol's clothes (awarded an Oscar nomination for costume designer Sandy Powell) fit the curves of her body like a glove and seem tailored to her figure; admittedly, sometimes, we see buttons on the back of her dress, as if she herself is unable to undo them; the dress thus seems to restrict her movements like a corset. In many places, Carol is shown as if in a gilded cage. She lives in a stone house, like a fortress.

Carol is a chain smoker. There are many scenes in which a cigarette is being lit in an inhaling and exhaling of smoke, as if she had fire and smoke in her body. Carol is the queen who knows her strength and power. At one point, she shows this by pointing the pistol at the detective who is following her. She thus appropriates a male symbol—but it doesn't work. As a woman, she has and uses other weapons. Her awareness of her own power, which she can control, is her strongest weapon.

Carol seems distant and withdrawn even in the most dramatic circumstances. Sometimes, she grows stiff, like Lot's wife. On the one hand, Carol is a strong woman and adorned like an ancient goddess. She is ready to give up motherhood and live as a single woman (also like a goddess). Her eyes are like those of a wild cat, sometimes like two slits through which the pupils gleam; her nostrils flare when she is overwhelmed by emotion; and her mouth is red, wide and sensual. On the other hand, both through her restrained performance (affect control) and her cinematic staging, the character seems somewhat distant, as if she cannot abandon herself to her own sensuality. In this way, the film conveys the deep ambivalence that the author of the novel bore towards her own desire. Lesbian love is portrayed ambivalently; it implies a fear of transgression and the (supposedly) destructive consequences of this. The price Carol has to pay in the film for loving a woman is her connection with her child, not just with Rindy but also with a childlike perspective per se. From this perspective—which female viewers also take, and male viewers (in different way)—it could seem as if the splitting up of the parental couple consisting of mother and father engenders fear.

Through Therese's eyes, we see Carol as an Amazon hunter setting a trap with narrowed eyes. She leaves her leather gloves behind on the counter as if she were throwing Therese some bait. These gloves, as soft as silk, are worn by two hands, which are soft and tender as silk. Hands that can caress a child as well as a lover. They arouse in Therese the longing to be caressed—as a child and as a lover. Therese's backstory is not addressed in the film, although it is in the novel: Her mother abandoned her when her father died, and she grew up in a convent. This is how Highsmith explains her longing for the love of a mature woman. Haynes does not explain Therese's love for Carol. In contrast to Highsmith, he posits that it is self-evident. Therese asks Richard if he has ever been in love with a boy, which he answers in the negative. She goes on to ask if someone can fall in love independently of whether with a man or a woman. He answers: 'Of course, I mean have I heard of people like that? Sure...I don't know anyone like that. But I'll tell you this—there's always some reason for it. In the background'. 'So you don't think it could just happen to somebody, just—anybody'? ['No.']

Carol radiates distance, which the film conveys by filming the shots behind glass, and it is palpable in all her relationships. The nature of her relationship with her daughter remains unclear, despite her impassioned speech at the lawyer's office when she voluntarily renounces custody. She does not go to the family Christmas party even though Rindy asks her to. Even in the scenes with her old friend and ex-lover Abby, she has a formal and cool demeanour. Her relationship with Therese is somewhat strategic from the start—she seduces Therese, invites her home, but sends her away as soon as things get difficult with her husband. In the same way, Carol seduces Therese in the hotel but leaves her immediately after the detective is unmasked. Carol controls her emotions.

The effect *Carol* has on me is almost purely aesthetic. I enjoy the beautiful images of her, but they are still pictures behind glass, without any deeper content—empty. This emptiness remains constant almost until the last shot.

The erotic scenes are always an important measure of how strong an impact the film has. In *Carol*, they are shown with a fine sense of tenderness and also resoluteness. We learn something about the lawyer's take on Carol's homosexuality but follow the voyeuristic eye of the camera and enjoy the love scenes.

There is something on this in an interview (Haynes 2016):

Question: Cate Blanchett and Rooney Mara are perfect together. How did you find the chemistry between them?

Haynes: Chemistry is something no director or actor I think really knows how to create. I think chemistry is (…) in the imagination of the viewer. Our job is to give the clues and the conditions and maybe enough restraint and obstacles to desire so that you want them to be together.

Carol invites Therese on a 'Go West' trip. 'Go West, this is our destiny' is a slogan of the US manifest destiny doctrine at the end of the nineteenth century. 'Manifest destiny' was meant to justify the missionary appropriation of the entire continent by the United States with its (at least at that time) exemplary democracy and is still used in this sense today. However, the allusion to manifest destiny in the film refers to a second, modern use of the slogan 'Go West', namely, as a glorification of San Francisco as the centre of the gay liberation movement.

Further Considerations

The film leads us along its obscure pathways. Just when it makes us believe in love at first sight, it also reveals to us other, confusing clues: There is an interesting moment in the scene with Therese, Richard and a friend, right after Carol and Therese have met for the first time. They are all watching something on a small projector. We see a shot from Billy Wilder's *Sunset Boulevard* (1950) in the reflected image of the projector. Haynes explicitly engages with Billy Wilder's *Sunset Boulevard*, paying tribute to the film and its blend of melodrama and film noir. In *Sunset Boulevard*, ageing silent film diva Norma Desmond seduces a young, shy screenwriter. We see Therese and her friends sitting close together in the projection booth of a cinema, looking through the window at the big screen. The whole, almost claustrophobic setting tells us something about Hollywood and its image of women, on screen or off, when we think of Norma Desmond's most famous utterance criticising this normative image of women: 'I *am* big. It's the pictures that got small' (Sönser Breen 2018). The film sequence shows Norma and the young writer dancing in Norma Desmond's drawing room, surrounded by an orchestra but otherwise alone. Therese watches this scene with interest, as if she has an idea of what is coming, as if she can see into her future. It is a moment of suspense. Admittedly, in *Sunset Boulevard*, the boy dies, and the old woman goes mad.

Carol is not meant to be anti-homophobic, nor propaganda for the emancipation of women. Haynes puts it this way: 'I didn't want to make a political film, these are different times. It's a love story' (Haynes 2015).

Photographed in 16-mm, the film enshrines the authenticity of its time, the late 1940s and early 1950s. Austerely composed, he quotes famous photographers of the time: Ruth Orkin, Helen Levitt, Vivian Maier and Esther Bubley, but above all Saul Leiter, who became famous for his photographs taken behind glass and windows. Haynes says of him in the *Guardian* that he creates 'a chiming collision of reflected faces caught in glazing'. His work is impressionistic: 'Those extraordinary frames and the dark pastel colours slashed by a burst of light!' (Haynes 2015).

Indeed, one of the most striking features of the film is the photography of each frame (Fig. 27.2).

Apart from Saul Leiter, the film aesthetic resembles Edward Hopper's compositions with their glowing colours and nostalgic atmosphere. The film goes at a slow, calm pace, and its visuals and little gestures speak louder than the words. We watch the action behind glass and remain outside, as spectators in the cinema. **Sometimes the glass is visible, wet with rain or fogged, dirty; sometimes it reflects a clutter of objects or random, nameless things** (Fig. 27.3).

Even if we cannot see the separating glass, we feel it and sense that it keeps us apart from the era and the heroes. Just as Carol and Therese are trapped in their aquarium of desires and emotions, we feel unsure of what we really like in this space. At the same time, we dare not blink so we do not miss a scene.

Fig. 27.2 Carol behind glass (01:40:42)

Fig. 27.3 Therese behind glass (00:05:53)

The film's impact is mainly based on its aesthetics. As spectators on the other side of the glass, we stay distanced and cool until the end. The very first shot shows a highly filigree metal ornament that appears to be some kind of object d'art. The camera glides over its surface, first vertically, then horizontally, so that only later can we decipher what it is: a sewer grille on the streets of New York. This illusion is deliberate. For one thing, the audience is already prepared at the beginning that all that glitters is not gold. Then, the barriers naturally symbolically represent the barriers and obstacles that the protagonists will experience: the restrictions that society imposes on homosexual love, the clear boundary between the sexes.

The admiration we feel is for the aesthetics, each framing being a separately composed image. This could also be seen as over-aestheticization, breathtaking in its grace, but keeping our deep feelings cool and distant by condemning us to observe.

What cannot be expressed exerts pressure until it has found another form. 'A film can speak with such different voices—whether images or music—and this film has given all the voices a reason to speak. That's why you can appreciate the costumes so much, for example: You notice that they contribute something to the plot and you feel how everything interacts' (Haynes 2015).

Same-sex love and crime, Patricia Highsmith's other great theme, completely overlapped at the time of *Carol*. Haynes has us empathise with the conspiratorial secrecy of this love with great care and even yearning. In the wordless messages that Carol and Therese exchange, we discover the gentle subversion of social conventions. The film addresses this by looking back in time: Filmed at a time when the price for making such a decision is no longer as devastating as it was in the 50s, it shows the social and societal norms on homosexuality in the past from the perspective of a present in which public opinion on the subject has become more liberal, at least in the West.

The film conveys a poignant sense of melancholy, underscored by Cartel Burwell's mournful soundtrack. This encapsulates the 'price of salt': the desire to be an independent woman, free from reliance on a husband, even at the expense of forgoing maternal instincts, but still wearing the same restrictive clothes and the same heavy gold shackles. She says that the divorce is over, that things are working out and that she's moving into a new big flat, but these facts are merely stated and remain empty words. 'I love you', she says for the first time, but Haynes immediately intervenes and interrupts this declaration of love, as if he fears Carol might go soft: a friend of Therese's enters the room and interrupts the scene. Throughout the film, the audience remains outside as observers behind the barrier of the screen. The finale offers solace for the isolation that goes beyond the aesthetics of the photos, colours and reflections—the camera eye shows the Oak Room full of visitors, going back and forth between them, looking for and finding the heroines. The end of the film is the axis between two gazes in a room full of people. A happy ending?

Translated by Annette Cariline Christmas.

Film Details

Title	Carol
Release year	2015
Country	Great Britain, USA
Screenplay/idea	Phyllis Nagy, Patricia Highsmith
Director	Todd Haynes
Score	Cartel Burwell
Camera	Edward Lachmann
Principle actors	Cate Blanchett, Rooney Mara, Kyle Chandler
Availability	DVD, Blu-Ray

References

Haynes T (2015) Wenn du verliebt bist, fühlst du dich dauernd schuldig [When you're in love, you feel guilty all the time]. Der Spiegel magazine. https://www.spiegel.de/kultur/kino/carol-regisseur-haynes-wenn-du-verliebt-bist-fuehlt-du-dich-dauernd-schuldig-a-1068095.html. Accessed 2 Aug 2020

Haynes T (2016) It is almost like the amorous imagination and the criminal imagination have that same overproductive insanity—Fredfilmradio. http://www.fred.fm/enter/todd-haynes-carol-interview/. Accessed 31 Aug 2020

Highsmith P (2004 [1952]) The price of salt. Coward-McCann, W. W. Norton & Company (2004) US

Kristeva J (1991) Strangers to ourselves. Colombia University Press

Sönser Breen M (2018) The locations of politics: Highsmith's the price of salt, Haynes' Carol, and American post-war and contemporary cultural landscapes. Gramma: J Theory Criticism 25:9–29

The End of a Great Love? *Blue Valentine* (US 2010) 28

Ralf Zwiebel

Introduction

I presented Derek Cianfrance's film *Blue Valentine from* (2010) a few years ago in Kassel at the public event 'Film and Psychoanalysis' and discussed it with the audience. The films shown in this context were presented under the banner: *Love and its impositions*. The film is about the break-up of a young married couple, which painfully ends over the course of a single day. In several flashbacks, the viewer learns a condensed version of the love story. During the psychoanalytic commentary of the film at the time, I offered some reflections on the success and failure of couple relationships, a central issue for many people, which cinematography probes with aesthetic devices and psychoanalysis researched with its clinical method. At that time, couple dynamics were the focus of my interest. Now I will also take up this topic in the context of this book, but concentrate a little more on the role of the woman in this couple relationship.

Film Plot

Cindy (Michelle Williams) and Dean (Ryan Gosling) are a young married couple living in the New York area with their young daughter Frankie (Faith Wladyka). She is a nurse, and he is a house painter. The day of their separation begins with Frankie noticing Megan the dog is missing, which Cindy later finds dead by the roadside. The tension between the couple quickly becomes palpable to the viewer: Dean is still a boy at heart, without any

R. Zwiebel (✉)
Grebenstein, Germany

V. Pramataroff-Hamburger, A. Hamburger (eds.), *From La Strada to The Hours*,
https://doi.org/10.1007/978-3-662-68789-5_28

great ambitions, a playful dreamer but all the more loving a father for that. He later says that he has achieved his goal in life, namely, by being Cindy's husband and a father. Cindy, on the other hand, is clearly dissatisfied in her role and her relationship with a man she feels is more like an extra child than an adult man with a purpose in life. She had originally wanted to become a doctor, but her plans fell through due to her unplanned pregnancy and marriage to Dean. It could also be said that Cindy tends to represent the reality principle (e.g. dressing the child, tidying up, cooking dinner, taking their daughter to school, finding satisfaction in a job, career advancement, etc.) and Dean the pleasure principle (always joking, smoking and drinking beer, playing with his daughter, living for the moment, etc.). Their dog's death becomes a kind of trigger for the dramatic end of the relationship. After tearfully burying the dog, Dean persuades Cindy to spend a weekend at an adult-themed motel to try to put the spark back into their relationship. Cindy is rather unwilling to go along from the start. On the way there, the viewer learns the story of their relationship in various flashbacks (Fig. 28.1).

Dean was a removal packer when he met Cindy at a nursing home while she was visiting her grandmother there. He fell in love at first sight and did everything within his power to see Cindy again; however, she was still with Bobby. While they are arriving at the motel and their attempted rapprochement gradually proves both verbally and physically disastrous, a series of flashbacks tell the story of how they became close, the conquest, falling in love, their happy first lovemaking, Cindy becoming pregnant straight away, planning an abortion and not going through with it (Cindy is not sure whose child it is) and getting married. In the process, the viewer also gets to know a bit about the protagonists' life story and family background: in Cindy's case, her grandmother and mother's perseverance in

Fig. 28.1 The happiest moment (01:42:06)

unhappy relationships; in Dean's case, his parents separated and his mother who clearly left during his childhood and whom he never saw or heard from again. Early in the morning, Cindy is called out to work at her outpatient clinic. She leaves Dean sleeping.

When he wakes up and realises Cindy has gone, he gets drunk and drives to Cindy's workplace. Dean runs riot in a series of heated and violent confrontations, also involving the staff and the doctor. In a heartbreaking scene in Cindy's parents' kitchen, Cindy tells them she definitively intends to separate, that she can no longer stand living with Dean and that she no longer has any feelings for him. Dean leaves the house, his little daughter running after him, but Cindy calls her back. Dean vanishes into an unknown future.

Background

Derek Cianfrance is a relatively unknown director, now 46, who has made a number of films since 1998, probably the best known being *The Place beyond the Pines* (2013), which is likewise a complex relationship story. Cianfrance told the story of the film in an interview, saying it had taken more than 10 years to plan and make, but was also principally defined by an aspect of his personal background, namely, his childhood fear that his parents might separate. Relatively early on, the director also managed to get the two principal actors on board, Michelle Williams and Ryan Gosling. Clearly, the intense impact of the film is essentially also borne by these two American film stars. The design of the film also deserves special attention, and this is another aspect that Cianfrance addresses in the abovementioned interview:

> The scenes in the past were shot on Super 16 mm film, all with a handheld camera and a 25 mm lens. "We wanted to achieve an intuitive atmosphere that reflects the physicality and youth of our protagonists—a freedom that keeps all possibilities open. For the present tense, we used two digital Red cameras mounted on tripods and standing at a distance from the actors. We attached telephoto lenses for the oppressive-looking close-ups. The plan was to depict a claustrophobic world in which the characters feel literally trapped. We also wanted to express their desperation in the visual style." (DVD booklet)

I will come to some of these aspects later.

Film Psychoanalytic Approach

Psychoanalysts usually choose to discuss films that contain unanswered questions, perhaps even a mystery. This is what makes watching and discussing a film together fascinating and potentially fruitful. It is thus comparable to real life, which can never be completely understood or entirely grasped in its complexity. But can you get a hold on this mystery? (I am not asking how it can be resolved.) This reminds me of a psychoanalyst's approach when starting a session with a patient whom she may have known for a long time: she first tries to forget everything she has learned thus far in order to be attuned to the forthcoming, present, concrete situation, also essentially to the mystery of the human encounter in the moment. Thus, French psychoanalyst Laplanche also says that the best outcome of psychoanalysis is when the analysand comes into contact with the unknown (in other words, the unconscious) (Laplanche 2004). It is a form of surrender to the present moment, which, however, can easily be missed or obscured by overthinking and abstraction. Ideally, one oscillates between emotional engagement with the film images and their story on the one hand and reflective distancing on the other. This reflection requires a certain order or structuring, however without the pretention of capturing the entire film. I myself am interested in three contexts in this attempt at classification: the human problem situations depicted, their potential for change for the better or worse and the film as a mirror of the viewer's own inner world. This is also the way a psychoanalyst works: by exploring the analysand's problem situation, activating the potential for change and, as a participatory observer, by allowing one's own experience to come into play in the service of the analysand (Zwiebel 2019).

The Success and Failure of a Love Relationship

Viewers will immediately agree that this film lives up to its title, *Blue Valentine,* as it is a really sad, heartbreaking love and relationship story. It is emotionally moving because the characters' desperation is palpable and resonates for all of us, and we can perhaps also sense the hopelessness of their relationship. But where then is the mystery, since this kind of story is very familiar territory? Our aim is not to work out the possible analytical dimension of the relationship story itself but rather to take a second look at the film imagery and plot without projecting certain basic assumptions and theories onto the film from the outset. In doing so, I shall resist the temptation to understand and interpret the protagonists' development as if this were a psychoanalytical case history.

I'll begin by pointing out some of the formal aspects that struck me about the film: on the one hand, there is the unsteady, at times shaky and blurry camerawork, which can seem almost amateurish and unprofessional. Film experts will of course be reminded of the 1995 avant-guard filmmaking movement of the Dogma films, associated for example with the name Lars von Trier. But I personally feel that it perhaps is well suited to the film content: a young relationship in which there is a barely definable restlessness or disquiet from the outset, which increasingly moves towards a culmination. The amateurishness may also be appropriate: as human beings, are we even 'relationship experts' who are capable of sustaining untroubled and completely happy relationships? It would perhaps be reasonable to suggest that people are in fact 'laymen' when it comes to love and its vicissitudes, and that this does not change. Would it not be true to say that love relationships are rarely stable, solid, untroubled and equable? The recurrent blurring of the images also fits with this idea: one rarely gains clarity over the 'facts' in a relationship. The restlessness of the camera thus expresses something of the existential dimension of relational dynamics: even though happiness, stability and security are so longed for, there is still always a moment of restlessness and uncertainty, a constant challenge and strain in relationships.

More important to me than this small observation is the overall structure of the film. There are two temporal levels: the film takes place on a single day in the present tense when the relationship apparently breaks up for good and in the past probably over several months or a few years. This single day is repeatedly interrupted or broken up by flashbacks to the time the couple first met and the early development of their relationship. I kept asking myself what these insertions were really about: Are they the respective memories of the two protagonists? Or are they images derived from the omniscient film narrator who, as it were, is telling the love story from the outside? It is also interesting to ask exactly when these 'memory images' are interspersed and what message they actually contain. Perhaps, the memory or flashback is inserted when a particularly conflictual, troubled situation has arisen in the relationship. The first time this occurs is when Dean is waiting in the car outside his in-laws' house after he and Cindy have dropped off their little daughter; there is tension between him and Cindy and also his father-in-law, and while he is waiting outside, he seems to remember how he got the job where he was to meet Cindy. In this case, it clearly seems to be Dean's memory. The second flashback is of an unpleasant argument the couple had previously in the car on the way to the motel, and it is clearly Cindy's memory: She remembers the period shortly before she met Dean, when she was still with Bobby, whom she had just unexpectedly bumped into at the supermarket. A double hypothesis could be developed at this point, which would then have to be pursued further: The couple have these alternating memories when the painful separation situation takes place or comes to a head. The memory is perhaps fed by the wish for everything to be as it was at the beginning, if only they could start over again. The more things seem to be coming to an end, the greater the yearning to go back to the start. The more aware the couple becomes of the painful present, the more intense the escape into a seemingly happier past becomes. The alternation between Dean's and Cindy's memory images may perhaps (somewhat latently) express the central theme of the film: They are still a couple but at the same time already separated or still separated. It may come as no surprise that this brief micro-observation exposes the basic structure of human couple relationships: the individuals in them are together and yet separate. And this is in fact the real question, the real mystery of the film: How do people cope with this imposition, this apparently indissoluble contradiction of connectedness and separateness? The third flashback then fits in with this: while they are dancing together at the motel, a memory arises. Although it starts out depicting Cindy, it can perhaps be understood as their shared longing for the happiness they once had that now seems to have been lost. In the fourth reminiscence, another element is added: there is an attempt at physical intimacy, which fails. Dean is standing in front of the bathroom door in the hotel, wanting to get in. Cindy has locked it after their failed intimate sexual overtures. There is then a cut to episodes from the early days of the relationship, when they first became intimately close: the scene in the taxi, the first sexual contact, but also the pregnancy that immediately follows. Here, too, when the anxiety caused by the distance between them or the threat of separation reaches a certain agonising and painful intensity, the past is recalled. This itself reveals a kind of compromise and over-determinacy: a defence against the present pain of deepening separation, the wish to suspend time in the by holding on to the initial happiness, but perhaps also questioning what had gone wrong—where did the unhappiness which is now looming actually begin? Presumably, the couple themselves are struggling to understand what brought them together in the first place, what happiness meant at the time and why it was unsustainable. This would then be a 'psychoanalytical impulse', so to speak, namely, to remember the beginning of the relationship and to gain an insight into the reasons for their affection and their present problematic situation. But there can be no such insight, they are completely unable to use words to communicate about it. This seems to be an expression of their mutual speechlessness. It is also interesting that the longer the film lasts, the shorter the intervals between the present and the past situations become, perhaps as an expression of increasing anxiety, even despair, like a form of escape into a better past from the impending catastrophe of separation.

But perhaps this all seems rather like over-interpretation to the reader. One could also assume that these formal aspects are cinematic in nature and more related to the requirements of the film's narrative style. Are different conclusions reached if, for example, the starting point taken is a few core sentences of the film that stick with the viewer? The following are a few examples: At the hotel, Cindy says: *'I thought the whole point of coming here was to have a night without kids'*. Or when Dean asks his coworker at the removals firm if he believes in love at first sight and he says, *'If you get a little pussy, I think the mental-ness will get out your head'*. Or in the bus scene when Dean and Cindy met, talking about dying: Dean says he's *'not [going to] do it'*, whereas Cindy says she *'definitely'* will. Or in the scene with the ukulele: *'You always hurt the ones you love'*. Or Cindy in the hotel: *'You know, we rarely sit down and have an adult conversation'*, and a little later: *'I'd like to see you think about what you say instead of saying what you think all the time'*. Or Cindy questioning her grandmother: *'How do you trust your feelings when they just disappear like that'?* And finally, when Cindy's father reminds Dean that she wants to be a doctor 1 day, and Dean replies, *'I wish she'd be my doctor'*. A whole chain of thoughts and themes could be followed up after every individual sentence, each leading to different problem areas: the role of sexuality (when pussy calls), the problematic of growing up (Dean failing to do so, unwilling or unable to develop his potential), the meaning of transience and mortality (the conversation about refusing to die), the role of hurting and being hurt, of narcissistic self-centredness (*I wish she'd be my doctor*). However, in my view, this only underscores one of my central considerations: With all these conflicting and emotional aspects, the restlessness and anxiety of relationships is easy to understand—bearing in mind that all of this has to be managed in a relationship. Depending on the viewer's own experience and world view, the aspects that affect them the most then tend to be singled out. Let us consider, for example, the theme of transience, which in a way runs through the whole film: above all the transience of love, of course, but also of life in general. It begins with the death of the dog. The couple meet in an old people's home, a place of dying and death, and during their very first conversation the subject of dying comes up—and being a doctor itself means combating death. The interspersed memories, which I understood to be a struggle against the passing of time and fading love, fit the theme. But at the same time, love itself is used as the most effective remedy against transience—an irresolvable dilemma. Dean tries to cope with the pain of losing the dog by spending the night sleeping with Cindy. From this point of view, we could say that the film is about struggling against the stream of time and that love as a remedy is also caught up in the flow. The director's own words would seem to confirm this: He says he has always been fascinated by how the passage of time affects one's experience of the world and that these aspects of time play a leading role in *Blue Valentine* (Blue Valenine 2010, Senator Home Entertainment). At this point, I am reminded of the abovementioned quote from Cianfrance that the present and past scenes are shot with different cameras and also shown in different colours.

I have spoken about the mystery of the film. This film then deals with the question of the multi-layered conditions necessary for the success and failure of couple relationships. Thus far, I have cautiously approached the possible answer provided by the film, its 'unconscious message', as it were. The following is a further attempt at an answer based on the film imagery and storyline: When the director mentions the claustrophobic atmosphere of the film, he is doubtless above all alluding to Cindy's feeling of being trapped in a relationship. In terms of psychology, this 'trap' is due to a hopeless situation arising in which any inner movement towards or away from the other person is associated with unbearable anxieties and feelings of guilt. Every inner movement consequently leads to negative emotions, which result in emotional shutting down in the relationship. A couple in a 'relationship trap' can thus no longer achieve or tolerate circulation or pulsation between connectedness (closeness, unity, commonality, fusion, etc.) and separateness (distancing, difference, aloneness, etc.), with the associated inevitable feelings. Above all the margin that allows space for the freedom for the other and the self is lost. The resulting stagnation leads to intolerable feelings of disappointment, helplessness and hopelessness, which are often projectively defended against, or which give rise to hope that a third party will rescue them, or even ultimately end in violence. This complex movement can be roughly traced by means of the example of the film imagery: the loss of the dog represents a decisive trigger that reinforces the experience of the couple's separateness. (In grief, everyone is alone at first, and it is not unusual for severe losses, especially of children, to ultimately lead to the couple separating.) In the background, Cindy's impending career change plays another role. (In general, Cindy tends to emphasise their separateness, while Dean emphasises their connectedness). Dean responds to this troubling theme of separation by cajoling Cindy and even at times potentially violently forcing a connection by driving to the motel, thus revealing his desire to restore their former union. However, as this is not a shared desire, it reinforces the threat that the couple will split up. There is no longer any beneficial flow or pulsation of the tension between separateness and connectedness between them: Dean is upset by Cindy telling him about her chance meeting with Bobby, her former boyfriend, because it undermines his desire for connection. A glance at the protagonists' biography also reveals clues as to why this vital pulsation has failed. Dean has obviously experienced unhappy, perhaps even traumatic separations (his mother left when he was a boy, nothing is known about his father). Cindy, on the other hand, has traumatic fusion experiences (the role model of her silent mother, who puts up with a hateful husband). The family role models for Cindy and Dean are thus disastrous in both cases: Dean's parents have resolved their relationship trap with a break-up that was catastrophic for Dean; Cindy's parents have set themselves up to suffer in their relationship trap, the consequences of which are easily understandable in Cindy's case in her conflicted vacillation between staying and leaving.

But perhaps under this aspect of unity and difference, it all boils down to a repetitive pattern: the differences between the couple are attractive and arousing at the beginning of their relationship and are ultimately overplayed or bridged by biology (and eventually also through the consequences of the sexual encounter, pregnancy). The film traces the process of how initially unspoken, unconsidered but significant differences develop into a crippling taboo zone, since their marriage was forced due to having child, and it shows this at a critical point, taking place on a single day, when everything hangs in the balance and it is unclear—also for us as viewers—whether this will end in failure or an opportunity. The way the couple deal with their inevitable differences will then determine whether the relationship will become stronger or break up. But are these all satisfactory answers to the questions raised by the film, particularly from a psychoanalytical point of view? This question may also reflect the reality for many genuine couple relationships: do they really know why the relationship has become unbearable, what they are looking for in new love objects, why they undertake the agony of a break-up or can hardly bear it? Why do so many couples, like this couple in the film, fall into this briefly outlined relationship trap, from which there is only sometimes genuine release, but which much more often leads to resignation, hopelessness, perhaps even violence, addiction and illness? Perhaps, I will be able to examine these questions more deeply by now focusing on Cindy, especially since the separation starts with her and this volume is dedicated to the female perspective in films.

The Female Perspective

In accordance with my film-psychoanalytic working model, I have thus far presented some reflections on the problematic situation of the protagonists, which primarily concerns the failure of their relationship. I have barely yet touched upon the second point of view, the transformation of the protagonists. Whether the couple's separation is to be interpreted as a catastrophe (unhappy ending) or as liberation from a mutual relationship trap (happy ending) may also depend on the viewer's point of view. The third perspective—the film as a mirror of the viewer's own inner world—is implicit in all considerations. As an example, I refer to an earlier work on the films of Hitchcock (exemplified by *Windows on the Farm,* 1954, or *Vertigo,* 1958), in which a kind of relational dilemma can be discovered between 'abyss and trap', a not uncommon relational trap between fears of loss of the object and of the self (Zwiebel 2015). The viewpoint becomes even more personal when one starts thinking about one's own relationship choices.

First of all, I would like to emphasise again that my focus on Cindy is not about a clinical case study, but about grasping general or universal principles, which are more or less familiar to all film viewers. It is easy to forget that Cindy is an artificial figure who does not have an unconscious, an Oedipus complex or any childhood trauma, but that this film character is brought to life with the help of the psychic reality of the film author, the actress and above all the viewer. And, in contrast to film studies, sociological or philosophical perspectives, a psychoanalytic film interpretation means considering basic psychoanalytic assumptions, above all the unconscious (and not just repressed material), the Oedipus complex (in the sense of the formative role of childhood sexuality in the relationship with the mother and father) and central phenomena from the psychoanalytic context (above all transference and resistance). If I were to single out a central point of view in this respect, namely, that love relationships are primarily about decisions that often turn out to be life decisions, then psychoanalytically speaking, two aspects play a decisive role: the question of object choice, which is inevitably determined by childhood factors of a pre-oedipal and oedipal nature (i.e. the early patterns of the relationship between the mother, father and child), and the question of disappointed expectations that ultimately lead to the separation of the couple. When approaching these two questions in the film, it is certainly important to consider whether this question of female object choice is asked by a male or female viewer. From a female perspective, past actions and Cindy's decision to have the child and the present-day separation will surely be seen as an act of emancipation or self-determination: a woman stands by her 'strength' and the reality principle and separates from a 'weak', childish-regressive man. Taking a closer look at the dynamics, one comes across an aspect that has been rather neglected in the discussion thus far, namely, the physical and sexual side, which is also central to the success and failure of couple relationships in psychoanalytical thinking. This is often a black spot in the whole dynamic, since one's own sexual desire is often still unknown or unresolved, conflictual and also unfulfilled. Could examining the film plot elucidate such an important point more clearly?

There are the two scenes in the middle of the film that I feel are central to the questions I have raised about object choice and disappointed expectations: Cindy and Dean have arrived at the hotel; they have already drunk a great deal of alcohol and are trying to have a conversation. The main question is why Dean does not make more of himself, why he is not fulfilling his potential and why he does not look for a more demanding job? He cannot understand these questions, because he does not know what Cindy means by 'potential', since he feels he has already achieved everything by becoming Cindy's husband and

Frankie's father. Dean thinks she's talking 'gibberish', while Cindy finds Dean's attitude ridiculous. They then switch from the verbal level to the physical level: before long they end up on the floor in a kind of scuffle, which may have started out as an attempt at playfulness but soon turns bitterly serious. During this, the camera moves so close that the details of the scene can no longer be made out. It is a sexually aggressive scene in which Dean expresses the desire for a baby, Cindy finally gives herself to him passively, but this disgusts Dean because he sees her behaviour as an invitation to rape: 'Don't give me this shit, this fuckin' like you can have my body bullshit', he says, 'I don't want that shit'. Cindy hides in the bathroom, and Dean angrily bangs on the door while Cindy sits on the toilet in despair. The physical rapprochement and understanding have thus also failed. This is when Cindy has her flashback or recollection of her first sexual encounter, the moment she finds out she is pregnant, and telling Dean that he is obviously not the father, the conversation at the clinic before the abortion when which her sexual history is shared (her first sexual contact at 13, 20 or 25 sexual partners so far), the scene during the abortion which she herself calls off, and the caring companionship of Dean who stands by her, saying: 'Let's do it. Let's be a family'.

Since the protagonists do not comment on any of these actions, it is left to the viewer to guess their conscious and unconscious motives. Rarely have I come across such a high level of ambiguity as in all these scenes, nor such a high tolerance for ambiguity and lack of clarity demanded of the viewer. And there is a great temptation to gloss over not knowing and not understanding by making assumptions and interpretations. In order to resist this temptation, you have to watch the film several times and grapple with the crucial scenes. For Cindy, there are two scenes in the film that concern major life decisions: one of object choice, when she decides to keep the child and stay with Dean, and another when her disenchantment leads to a separation.

The significant moments of Cindy's decision about her relationship decision are shown in this first key scene of her object choice: thus far, Cindy's relationships had been short-lived and non-committal, perhaps also as a compensatory escape from an unhealthy home life with her parents. Her encounter with Dean is probably no different at first. She is shocked when she finds out she is pregnant, which she did not want to be. She has no close contact with the presumed father Bobby, so she turns to Dean, whom she barely knows. She doesn't want to tell him about the pregnancy at first, and then he practically forces her to by threatening to jump into the Hudson River. However, she also tells him openly that he is probably not the father. In the counselling talk about the pregnancy, we learn about her sexual history but nothing about her inner conflict. This only becomes clear in the actual abortion scene: in the middle of the operation, she sits up and gets the doctor to stop the procedure. Dean is waiting for her outside. He smiles and hugs her, offering to become a family with her. She looks at him questioningly, in perplexed wonder, saying: 'You don't have to do this, you know, it's not your fault'. But they both declare their love, effectively deciding for a long-term relationship together.

So, these are the decisions that Cindy made at the time: *in favour* of the child, *in favour* of the relationship with Dean, *against* the non-commitment of her prior relationships. This form of object choice must have something to do with her inner, predominantly unconscious images of her parents and herself. To put it very cautiously, it could be assumed that idealised images of a mother and father are mobilised in this critical situation, awakening her hitherto repressed desires: namely, to become a better mother herself, to realise her womanhood by having the child and to look for a better father, whom to her surprise she believes she has found in Dean. So, these are complicated childhood transferences, which the film naturally cannot tell us more about in any greater detail. All this perhaps also against the background of the American idealisation of family. Incidentally, this also shows the limits of film psychoanalysis: since we cannot enter into a conversation with Cindy to talk about her wishes, dreams and fears, all these reflections say more about us as viewers than about a fictional film character. But since we as viewers can so easily identify with the film's protagonists, we experience the potentially illusory nature of the object choice, namely, the deep desire to have a better family than her own. The decision to keep the child is the only one that seems to be self-determined. The other decisions are co-determined by Dean's behaviour, whom she fantasises to be an ideal father, since, unlike her real father, he is willing to accept her unconditionally. This significant decision perhaps lies in finally making an autonomous decision about her own body as a woman. The abortion scene is thus a key moment. A man is exercising control over her body, which she no longer tolerates, since she wants self-determination over her own body. By deciding to have the child, she is opting for a different, more committed relationship with her body and her sexual desire and rejecting her promiscuous behaviour. This is confirmed in the brief encounter with Bobby, who asks whether she has been faithful to her husband, which she affirms. But what then is the deception or illusion of compatibility right from the start that indicates the root of the later separation? It seems that Cindy's decision skips over too many other unresolved issues—about leaving her parental home, the fulfilment of her professional goals, perhaps also her unrecognised sexual longings—which then partially surface during the separation scene. In their conversation, Cindy accuses Dean of his lack of masculine activity, and she attacks his passivity. In the sexually aggressive scuffle, it becomes very unclear what either of them wants: They seem to want to abandon themselves to physicality, but their bodies can no longer provide a clear orientation, perhaps in part because they are drunk. The viewer senses that there are a lot of unresolved issues in this encounter overshadowed by alcohol. Cindy can apparently only see Dean's desire for another child as a desperate attempt to save their relationship. It seems as if the clarity of the decision to keep the child and continue the relationship, perhaps also transfigured in memory, is gradually being pushed to the surface by the many unresolved and ignored issues and now find its terrible and sad conclusion in this terribly dark scene.

And now find its terrible and sad conclusion in this terribly dark scene. Cindy's disillusionment is clearly due to the fact that the conflict of divergent father and mother images has become intolerable for her: she is still looking for the ideal father and does not want to be confined to the role of mother by a regressive man. Her ultimate escape to her problematic parental home at the end of the film leaves the viewer feeling uneasy (Fig. 28.2).

Fig. 28.2 The desperate end? (01:38:15)

Final Considerations

After this, my second attempt at addressing this film, I am left with feelings of great sadness. I now see the fictional characters in the film as a mirror image of many real-life couples who so often end up with relationship malaise that they themselves ultimately cannot understand and find very difficult to resolve. In this, too, the questions of the primary object choice and the fate of disillusionment always remain central. And I see the character of Cindy as a relatively typical representation of a young woman who struggles for her female self-determination but remains trapped in an uncertain situation. From this perspective, a partial liberation from living conditions based on largely unavailable factors such as family background, early internalised relationship patterns, the development of psychosexuality and the social environment appears seems to be an eternal, never-ending Sisyphean task. But as the incomparable Alfred Hitchcock once said: It's only a movie. The consolation in these words is that, as viewers, cinematic art offers us scope that is sometimes lost to us in real life. If the film spectator can adopt some of this scope in his real life, can he not then consider himself, in the words of Camus, 'a happy man' in the face of all adversity?

Translated by Annete Caroline Christmas.

Film Details

Title	Blue Valentine
Release year	2010
Country	USA
Screenplay/Idea	Derek Cianfrance, Cami Delavigne, Joey Curtis
Director	Derek Cianfrance
Musical score	Grizzly Bear
Camera	Andrij Parekh
Principle actors	Ryan Gosling, Michelle Williams, Faith Wladyka
Availability	DVD, Blu-Ray

References

Cianfrance D (2010) Interview with the director in the booklet to the film. DVO-Große Kinomomente

Laplanche J (2004) From the enigmatic message of the other to the unconscious alterity the temptation of biology: Freud's theories of sexuality translated by Donald Nicholson-smith. New York: The unconscious in translation, 2015, XII, 140 pp

Zwiebel R (2015) Über einige Ängste des Analytikers aus filmpsychoanalytischer Sicht [On some of the analyst's fears from a film psychoanalytic perspective]. Psyche 69:936–961

Zwiebel R (2019) Die innere Couch. Psychoanalytisches Denken in Klinik und Kultur [The inner couch. Psychoanalytic thinking in clinic and culture]. Psychosocial, Giessen

Said with Flowers: *Bread and Tulips* (*Pane e tulipani*, I, CH 2000)

29

Dagmar Leupold

Introduction

At first glance—and perhaps also at second glance—*Pane e tulipani* is a typical Italian romantic comedy, in other words a healthy mix of zest for life and slapstick: *Opera buffa*. Only a closer look reveals the film's underlying seriousness and socially and politically explosive nature. This only becomes clear a little at a time, as cracks appear in the blithely smooth exterior. This is a bit like geological processes, in which the complexity of the underlying structure can only be appreciated in cross-section: It is no coincidence that the turning points and crises in the protagonists' life are set at the turn of the millennium, amidst the unrest that goes with it. The carefully crafted system of references, primarily a flower metaphor throughout, show the importance of the symbolic dimension of the film, which is by no means limited to the burlesque antics of a woman's search for meaning, but rather invests the individual plot elements and props with leitmotifs, deploying them in counterpoint. The female search for meaning, in contrast to the male 'quest', is not set in motion by a sense of resolve or vocation but by mishaps and failures. It is determined more by dreams than by deeds and prefers drifting and dawdling to purposeful striving. This is why the protagonist has a tendency to passively resist any kind of instrumental questioning—about housework, marriage and motherhood. In this film, *saying it with flowers* does not mean diplomatically and hypocritically avoiding speaking about sensitive issues but bluntly confessing one's own feelings—feelings that are at odds with the demands of a conventional, largely preordained (petit) bourgeois way of life and the concomitant suppression of the self-assertion of women.

D. Leupold (✉)
Munich, Germany

V. Pramataroff-Hamburger, A. Hamburger (eds.), *From La Strada to The Hours*,
https://doi.org/10.1007/978-3-662-68789-5_29

Film Plot

Rosalba (Licia Maglietta), a scatterbrained woman in her mid-40s, a housewife and the wife of a plumber from Pescara with his own business, takes a bus trip to Paestum with her husband and teenage sons. Obligingly, they take photos of each other in front of the Temple of Minerva and listen to the tour guide's tedious explanations. At the rest stop, Rosalba goes to the toilet. She clumsily knocks one of her earrings into the toilet and takes a while fishing it out. When she finally goes back outside again, she sees the bus pulling out of the carpark. She decides to hitchhike home, despite agreeing with her husband Mimmo (Antonio Catania), who is raging at her on the phone, to wait at the rest stop. She changes plans again when the second car offers her a lift to Venice. Once there, she spends the first night in a shabby boarding house that is going to close the next day. In the 'Marco Polo' trattoria, which is still open late, she meets the Icelandic waiter Fernando Girasole, who meets her with exquisite politeness and, once she has told him her plight, offers her temporary accommodation in his own flat for the second night. The following day, Rosalba misses the train she was supposed to take and dawdles through a Venice that is nothing like the city in the glossy tourist brochures. Again, by accident, she comes across a flower shop looking for temporary staff. The owner, an eccentric anarchist called Fermo (Felice Andreasi) who loves flowers but not the customers, has broken his arm. He hires her. Rosalba stays with Fernando and, due to another mishap—a burst water pipe—makes friends with his neighbour Grazia (Marina Massironi), the owner of a massage parlour with a penchant for esotericism. In search of a full-length mirror (!) in Fernando's flat after officially moving in, Rosalba opens an old cupboard and finds an accordion next to the mirror in the door. She used to play the instrument in her youth, but it had no place in her life as a wife and housewife. Playing the accordion, the resonating body par excellence of seduction and erotic closeness, the sound of Paris, Tango and amour henceforth becomes the soundtrack of newly awakened and rekindled longing, of feelings of friendship and love. When Mimmo realises that his wife will not be coming back to Pescara, even his mistress being unable to console him for the slight, he hires an out of work plumber who admits to a passion for detective novels as an amateur sleuth: His remit is to find Rosalba in Venice and bring her back. Costantino (Giuseppe Battiston) looks the part in his professional garb of a typical mackintosh, briefcase and sunglasses, and with an accent, however as a *figlio di mammà* (mummy's boy), he is not really up to the task. He moves into a crummy hotel boat and, after a few days without any success, puts up posters all over town with a picture of Rosalba and his telephone number. Rosalba contacts him; they arrange to meet, and when they do, she realises that her husband has set Costantino after her, so she takes the opportunity of a phone call from his mother to escape. He follows her and sees her disappear into Fernando's house just as Grazia appears, who assumes he is the expected new client, Vittorio. He does not disabuse her, and the subsequent massage becomes a magical moment: Grazia and Costantino (alias Vittorio) fall madly in love. Rosalba has taken a liking to her new improvised life by now—and to the mysterious Fernando Girasole, who leaves her a letter every morning on the lovingly laid breakfast table.

When Mimmo's mistress shows up in Venice, tracks her down at the flower shop and begs her to return to the family because of the younger son's drug addiction, Rosalba gives in and returns to Pescara and thus to her old routine: washing, cooking and shopping.

Fernando, sitting alone in front of a bouquet of wilting tulips, decides not to leave his happiness to chance any longer. Together with the by now happy couple Grazia and Costantino, he drives to Pescara in Fermo's van—the florist also misses his beloved 'temp'—and the showdown takes place in the car park of a supermarket, a nice corrective to the masculinely connoted high-noon settings of desert sand and smoking pistols habitually used for such situations. Rosalba, on the other hand, is armed with plastic bags. Her younger son is there and by no means a drug addict: he just smokes a little pot due to his longing to escape his cramped and stuffy living conditions. In his presence, the couple confess their feelings towards each other. Rosalba returns to Venice with Fernando.

Tulipani

The film, as noted at the beginning, works with a flower metaphor throughout, beginning with the names of the protagonists Rosalba and Fernando Girasole: Her name contains a rose and the dawn*(alba)*, in other words fresh blooming and the promise of the morning, while his surname is a sunflower: *girasole*. This has already played an important role in an early shot, namely, when Rosalba digs out a souvenir she bought in Paestum from her backpack, a ceramic plate with a glowing sun shaped like a flower. It is broken in the middle. And in a dream setting, the woman who first offered her a lift at the rest stop appears, the antithesis of the conformist Rosalba, who makes polite and helpless conversation, an eloquent advocate of female autonomy and liberated sexuality. She responded to Rosalba's account of her travels with: 'Copenhagen? That's when I had my second abortion at 21!' In the dream she gives the surprised woman a bunch of tulips and asks to be instructed in the art of motherhood, since it turns out she now has a son. The cupboard door opens and out comes Rosalba's younger son in a yellow wig (sunflower!), who admits that he has accepted the new mother on a trial basis. This is the clear, dreamlike, figurative marking of one of the ruptures mentioned at the beginning; motherhood is not a destiny at all, but a choice. In another dream, a bunch of sunflowers plays a central role. Rosalba comes across her husband and sons playing cards. The game is called 'Scopa', which actually means broom, although as a verb *scopare is* a vulgar expression for sexual intercourse. A short conversation ensues, in which Rosalba expresses her amazement that it could be played in threes. Here, too, the audience is required to read between the lines for the subtler meaning: A mistress, whom Rosalba knows about, is an integral part of Mimmo's chauvinistic male concept of marriage. And, in the dream, Rosalba no longer plays along with this. Everyone gets up and leaves the room, and she is left alone with a bouquet *(mazzo)* of sunflowers, which the younger son places on the table. *Mazzo* in Italian means both ostrich and bunch in the sense of bunch of keys. This symbolically reinforces the key role of the sunflower. The Italian word *girasole* contains a reference to the sun as a directional guide: the flower turns *(gira)* towards the sun, and it directs itself towards the light. This is also important for photography, another central motif in the film, as exposure. In an early scene, we see Rosalba in front of a mirror in the shabby boarding house room, taking a selfie, capturing her happy smiling face in the mirror (Fig. 29.1).

It is a common topos that the search for identity, self-knowledge and self-questioning should be associated with photography, light and illumination. In this case, it avoids becoming clichéd because the different moods associated with such a search are symbolically conveyed, namely, through the flower(s). The sunflower combines light and blossoming. Rosalba's 'self-exposure' is as crucial for her further development as photosynthesis is for plants. At Fermo the florist's, Rosalba makes bouquets for wedding couples and other wonderful occasions; however, she is actually composing and articulating an emotional palette by blending the colours and scents of the flowers. She also brings flowers into their shared home every day. They serve as atmospheric registers in that they are sometimes exotic, for example, the parrot flower, and sometimes native daisies. The original title of the film, *Pane e tulipani*, symbolises the protagonist's development through the way the words coincidentally sound alike: Bread, *pane,* stands for the domestic, the everyday, the withered, which almost magically blossoms into something else, something wonderful, with the addition of the prefix: *tulipani*. Because, as Fermo explains to his temporary assistant during one of their teatimes in the back room of the shop, tulips do not come from the Netherlands at all, but from Persia: **'There are abundant tulips in the Thousand and One Nights'.** Fernando's account of their first meeting is also like a fairytale. When Rosalba asks him about his striking accent and somewhat antiquated Italian, he says he is an Icelander. The lie is so blatant that the deterministic question of origin becomes irrelevant. Arrivals are far more important in this context.

Fig. 29.1 Rosalba with a mirror (00:17:35)

Pane

Fernando Girasole is by no means a *nom de guerre*, but rather one of tenderness. This tenderness is also evident in the artfully and lovingly arranged plate of cold cuts he serves her at the restaurant the beginning, since the cook is ill. And then varied again and again in the breakfast arrangement, his handling of the cipher *bread* is complementary to Rosalba's language of flowers. *Pane* stands for daily bread and the daily grind; in Fernando's symbolism, in contrast, it stands for devotion, care and dedication: the way to the heart is through the stomach. The extremely artistic preparation of the meal also contains a resistant moment of self-assertion. In the midst of the shabby surroundings of a run-down trattoria, Fernando holds a supper, marrying culinary delights and language, the tongue's movements on the palate in pleasure and in speech. For his comments on what he is serving are as carefully composed as the dishes themselves. In sacred, liturgical contexts, bread is associated with wine, a priest performs transubstantiation. In contrast, in preparing the food Fernando is taking on a role with strong female connotations and the complementary addition to the bread are the tulips, Rosalba's 'emotional currency', not the wine. The sacred becomes secularised, and the hierarchical love of God becomes emancipated as an equal love relationship between a man and a woman, both of whom begin to free themselves from the codified and assigned role models (Fig. 29.2).

Fernando turns to people like the sunflower to the sun. The side of him not facing the light is dark: He had stabbed a good friend who was cheating on him with his own wife in the heart, killing him, as we learn in a key scene with Rosalba towards the end of the film.

Killing the rival and thus declaring the woman a sovereign possession is a classically male behaviour pattern. Fernando has a rope and noose ready in the next room, as if he has

Fig. 29.2 Dance (01:24:27)

to kill the person he had once been. Two attempts at hanging himself are interrupted and prevented by Rosalba's unexpected arrival. Through his encounter with her, his 'feminine' aspects are revitalised, as it were, his tender care and attentive communication. His gentle language, his elegant way of expressing himself are not characteristic features of power but indicators of his ability to relate intimately and respectfully with his interlocutor.

Mirrors and Likenesses

The rope disappears under the bed, but a little later, the accordion appears. Such a mirror-image or dialectical construction is, along with the flower and bread metaphors, constitutive of the film's structure: The plot elements are driven in parallel; Rosalba, wanted by the detective Costantino at the behest of her husband, engages in her own detective work and tracks down Fernando, who is rumoured to have a son. At the same time, the search for Rosalba is a transposition of the topos of *cherchez la femme*, and Costantino will indeed find a wife (of his own). Fernando is also looking for a woman, although not on the offensive or actively, but waiting. In this sense, he is also rather feminine. When Rosalba returns to the flat very late one evening after watching romantic films with her newfound friend Grazia and apologises, he replies: **'I would be lying if I said I had not noticed your absence'**. A scene that takes place in Rosalba's family's flat in Pescara can be seen as a mirror image of this. In it, Rosalba's absence is not registered as an emotional emptiness, but as a loss of work, illustrated by mountains of dirty laundry, empty pantry shelves and towers of dirty dishes.

Meanwhile, Rosalba is out investigating; one morning she secretly follows Fernando, who actually does pick up a little boy and takes him to school. In the following scene, the carousel of characters continues to spin, opera-buffa style: Grazia, freshly in love with the detective-plumber Costantino—who she believes is called Vittorio—wants to tell Rosalba about her happiness, who in turn is just as excited by the discovery of Fernando's presumed secret paternity. Before they can tell each other their respective news, the doorbell rings and in come a little boy and a young woman. They have misplaced their front door key and want to pick up the spare, which is kept at Fernando's house. Rosalba asks the child his name: Eliseo, answers the boy, the sunflower. Here, on the one hand, Italian and Greek correspond, and on the other, two generations are mirror images of one another. The story of betrayal and infidelity of the child's father told by Adele, the young woman, is mistakenly connected by her listeners with Fernando, who in turn has discovered picture of Rosalba posted all over the city and, moreover, has noticed that she has been spying on him. Everything becomes clear in the subsequent meeting of the pair, and the lost trust is restored: Rosalba tells the full story of her desertion, and Fernando confesses to the murder of his best friend, whom he caught in flagrante delicto in the marriage bed and talks about his wayward son who abandoned his daughter-in-law, Adele. So, he is Eliseo's grandfather and wants to make up to his grandson what he failed to do for his son. Before he went to prison, he had been a singer and performed in his own group. The language of music is both their mother tongue. They communicate in it, and it lay buried in each of them. The accordion contains the word *chord,* the harmony comprising different tones and, in Italian, also agreement: *essere d'accordo*. Music is Rosalba's and Fernando's means of bonding and expression, their common concert pitch. And it is thus only logical that Rosalba accompanies the singing Fernando on the accordion in the final scene.

Cherchez la femme

Turbulence and confusion galore—what are they for? Dramaturgically, they function as supporting elements for the tension, leading to the climax of 'laying the cards on the table' just described and an openness towards the fairytale finale. Psychologically and poetically speaking, on the other hand, one must read the burlesque entanglements as a meandering path in a search for truthfulness and identity that is hampered and torpedoed by habitual pretence and conventional role patterns. This search for a self-determined life and, on an aesthetic level, for appropriate narrative and visual devices can only succeed and be effective if both the characters and the cinematic-artistic realisation rid themselves of the ballast of adaptations, routines and thoughtless acceptance of (self-)images. For all its situation comedy and playful exaggeration, this is the deeply serious theme underlying the film. The fairy tale musical finale described above does not ultimately answer the question as to whether the final image is to be seen as dreamlike or actual reality. But even if it were 'only' dreamed, the final wish fulfilment would still come about due to an imaginative force that overcomes the normative of the factual.

Rosalba is neither a fighter nor a victim. She does not set any goals but abolishes the predetermined ones, particularly those expected of women in terms of life aspirations. To put this in modern parlance: She deletes the auto-complete function and changes the delivery setting. She becomes a conscientious objector, going on strike as a mother, wife and housewife by gently and persistently withdrawing, after a very brief interlude back in Pescara. The motif of *cherchez la femme*, already mentioned in relation to the male protagonists, is of course most applicable to Rosalba herself: She is searching for the woman she really is. And leaves behind the one who lived according to a false script. On two occasions, she goes through Fernando's flat looking for mirrors that enable her to see *all of* herself. On one occasion, she climbs a pile of books to do so—the other path to self-knowledge. Rosalba sabotages the expectations placed on her without campaigning. She sleepwalks into her emancipation process, which is not intellectual, nor analytical. Thus, in her aimless wandering and to her amazement—which, unlike in Paestum, no longer needs to be legitimised like a museum piece—and in her relish of music-making, a subversive-anarchic energy is revealed that provides the power for the great effort, which lies at the glowing heart of the film: love. Fernando answers Rosalba's son's question about why he has come to Pescara to see his mother: *Perché la amo*—because I love her. This could be seen as romantic. Better still, it is bold.

Translated by Annete Caroline Christmas.

Film Details

Original title	Pane e tulipani (Bread and tulips)
Release year	2000
Country	Italy, Switzerland
Screenplay/idea	Doriana Leondeff, Silvio Soldini
Director	Silvio Soldini
Musical score	Giovanni Venosta
Camera	Luca Bigazzi
Principal actors	Licia Maglietta, Bruno Ganz, Giuseppe Battiston
Availability	DVD, Blu-Ray

9783662687888